# PRAISE FOR *LAST ACT*

"In this affectionate and often moving book, Craig Shirley has given us a remarkable account of Ronald Reagan's 'long goodbye,' chronicling the final years of an American original who bent history in the service of freedom. This is an invaluable book about an invaluable man."

—JON MEACHAM, PULITZER PRIZE–WINNING
AUTHOR OF *AMERICAN LION*

"Ronald Reagan may have had a 'Last Act' in this life, but his principles are timeless. Craig Shirley reveals new information about Reagan's last days on earth in a deeply moving book that will bring tears to your eyes, strengthen your political resolve and inspire you to build on his legacy."

—CAL THOMAS, SYNDICATED COLUMNIST

"As we consider the next Reagan, here is the last Reagan, whose legacy must serve as a roadmap for the next American comeback."

—MONICA CROWLEY, PH.D.,
FOX NEWS POLITICAL AND FOREIGN AFFAIRS ANALYST
*WASHINGTON TIMES* EDITOR AND COLUMNIST

"Craig Shirley is a walking encyclopedia on all things Ronald Reagan. His latest, *Last Act*, delves into Reagan's post-presidential life with verve and insight, breaking plenty of new ground. The story of Reagan's battling the curse of Alzheimer's disease is utterly riveting. Highly recommended!"

—DOUG BRINKLEY, EDITOR OF *THE REAGAN DIARIES*

"With this book, Craig Shirley cements his place as the premier Reagan biographer. As revealing as his earlier volumes on Reagan were, this one is especially fascinating, chock full of new revelations and captivating observations about the former president's twilight years."

—DR. LARRY J. SABATO, FOUNDER AND DIRECTOR OF
THE CENTER FOR POLITICS AT THE UNIVERSITY OF
VIRGINIA; AUTHOR OF *THE KENNEDY HALF CENTURY*

"Craig Shirley's *Last Act* is a worthy successor to his earlier, fine accounts of Ronald Reagan's life and times. The book offers striking insights into Reagan the man—and also into America the country he so loved."

—WILLIAM KRISTOL, EDITOR, *THE WEEKLY STANDARD*

"Through never-before revealed interviews and expert analysis, *Last Act* by Craig Shirley pulls back the curtain on the life, last days, and legacy of Ronald Reagan—an exceptional president who believed in American exceptionalism above all else. Important. Essential. Bravo."

—JANE HAMPTON COOK, AUTHOR OF *AMERICAN PHOENIX*

"In the past, Craig Shirley meticulously documented Reagan's pre-presidential years; now, he meticulously documents Reagan's post-presidential years. His enlightening concept is punctuated by his usual exhaustive research and diligence in interviewing so many of the people who knew Ronald Reagan. And beyond the research is simply a touching story of a great man's final days. *Last Act* is a look at Ronald Reagan that is well worth your time."

—DR. PAUL KENGOR, PROFESSOR OF POLITICAL
SCIENCE AT GROVE CITY COLLEGE

"Ronald Reagan's story is so rich and resonant—so profoundly American—that it can only be told, in its full range and complexity, by a biographer of extraordinary dedication to subject and craft. LBJ had Robert Caro; and Ronald Reagan has Craig Shirley. In *Last Act*, Shirley brings us the final years of a twentieth-century icon, issuing a challenge not just to other Reagan biographers but to the discipline of biography itself."

—JAMES ROSEN, FOX NEWS CHIEF WASHINGTON
CORRESPONDENT AND AUTHOR OF *THE CHENEY TAPES*

# PRAISE FOR *DECEMBER 1941*

"I love historical nonfiction. I read it everywhere, in the bathroom, wherever I am. But typically it's written from sort of a distant perspective. You went through newspapers and magazines, and all the accounts of time. It gives an immediacy that I think it's difficult to find in these types of things."

—JON STEWART, *THE DAILY SHOW*

"I'm confident it'll be a bestseller."

—Don Imus

"Masterful new book . . . Shirley not only transports us back to that tumultuous time, but reminds this generation that denial about an enemies intentions can have grave consequences."

—Cal Thomas, syndicated columnist

"Folks, if you want a good read this Christmas season check it out."

—Steve Doocy, FOX News

"The book also reveals . . . blockbuster historical moment[s]. Shirley . . . takes a new tack in his book about Pearl Harbor. Instead of just writing how it all went down, his book attempts to give readers a feel for how the country felt 70 years ago. He accomplishes that by providing anecdotal information from nearly 2,000 newspapers and magazines."

—US News & World Report

# PRAISE FOR
# *RENDEZVOUS WITH DESTINY*

"An unbelievable book . . . I was part of the Reagan Revolution and I didn't know 80 percent of this stuff! . . . It's worth reading, and reading right now."

—Mark Levin, bestselling author of *Liberty and Tyranny*

"This exhilarating history . . . arrives, serendipitously, at a moment when conservatives are much in need of an inspiriting examination of their finest hour."

—George F. Will, from the foreword

"There have been hundreds of books written about Ronald Reagan and this is the question that always irritates an author, why do we need another one? Well, we don't have to get very far in Craig Shirley's new book about Reagan to know that, yes, there is still a lot we don't know about Reagan and how he came to the White House. . . . It is a fascinating book!"

—Bob Schieffer, CBS

"Shirley puts to rest one of the great political mysteries: who stole Carter's debate briefing books? . . . Shirley also reveals that the Kennedy family had a long memory on Election Day. . . . when it came time for the election, virtually all of them voted for Ronald Reagan."

—NEWSMAX

# PRAISE FOR *REAGAN'S REVOLUTION*

"All in all, Shirley's work has much to commend it. His book should be read by anyone interested in Reagan, the rise of conservatism in the Republican Party, or American politics in the mid-1970s."

—ANDREW E. BUSCH, *CLAREMONT REVIEW OF BOOKS*

"An indispensable resource for anybody who wants to understand just how Mr. Reagan lost and why his defeat set the stage for victory four years later, upending history's supposed dialectic."

—QUIN HILLYER, *WALL STREET JOURNAL*

" . . . a vividly written tale of this largely forgotten campaign."

—MATTHEW DALLEK, *WASHINGTON POST, BOOK WORLD*

"One of the season's most exciting political books . . . "

—MICHAEL POTEMRA, *THE NATIONAL REVIEW, SHELF LIFE*

# Last Act

# OTHER BOOKS BY CRAIG SHIRLEY

*Reagan's Revolution: The Untold Story of the
Campaign That Started It All*

*Rendezvous with Destiny: Ronald Reagan and
the Campaign That Changed America*

*December 1941: 31 Days That Changed
America and Saved the World*

# *Last Act*

## THE FINAL YEARS AND EMERGING LEGACY OF

# RONALD REAGAN

## CRAIG SHIRLEY

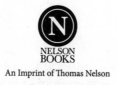

NELSON
BOOKS

An Imprint of Thomas Nelson

Published in Nashville, Tennessee, by Nelson Books, an imprint of Thomas Nelson. Nelson Books and Thomas Nelson are registered trademarks of HarperCollins Christian Publishing, Inc.

Thomas Nelson titles may be purchased in bulk for educational, business, fund-raising, or sales promotional use. For information, please e-mail SpecialMarkets@ThomasNelson.com.

Scripture references marked KJV are taken from the King James Version.

Scripture references marked ASV are taken from the American Standard Version.

### Library of Congress Cataloging-in-Publication Data

Shirley, Craig.
Last act : the final years and emerging legacy of Ronald Reagan / Craig Shirley.
    pages cm
  Summary: "His name in American politics is more cited than any other president. Both the Republican and Democratic parties are radically different today, mainly as a result of Ronald Reagan and the force of his ideas. No twentieth century president shaped the American political landscape so profoundly. Craig Shirley's Last Act is the important final chapter in the life of Reagan that no one has thus far covered. It's the kind of book that widens our understanding of American history and of the presidency and the men who occupied it. To tell Reagan's story, Craig has secured the complete, exclusive, and enthusiastic support of the Reagan Foundation and Library and spent considerable time there reviewing sealed files and confidential information. Cast in a grand and compelling narrative style, Last Act contains interesting and heretofore untold anecdotes about Reagan, Mrs. Reagan, their pleasure at retirement, the onslaught of the awful Alzheimer's and how he and Mrs. Reagan dealt with the diagnosis, the slow demise, the extensive plans for a state funeral, the outpouring from the nation, which stunned the political establishment, the Reagan legacy, and how his shadow looms more and more over the Republican Party, Washington, the culture of America, and the world"-- Provided by publisher.
  ISBN 978-1-59555-534-2 (hardback)
  1. Reagan, Ronald. 2. Reagan, Ronald--Influence. 3. Reagan, Ronald--Anecdotes.
  4. Presidents--United States--Biography. 5. Presidents--Retirement--United States.
  6. Republican Party (U.S. : 1854- ) 7. Political culture--United States. 8. United States--Politics and government--1989- I. Title.
  E877.2.S55 2015
  973.927092--dc23
  [B]
                            2015002184

*Printed in the United States of America*
**15 16 17 18 19 RRD 6 5 4 3 2 1**

# DEDICATION

*Writing is a joy.*

*And in writing history, each day is a new chance to learn new things. Gloria Steinem once said that writing was the only thing that when she did it, she didn't feel like she should be doing something else. I utterly agree with that sentiment. Even so, authors tend to be their own worst critics, falling too easily in love with their work, and thus they need forthright and honest advice and support.*

*That comes from my mother, Barbara Shirley Eckert; our friend, Diana Banister; and our children, Matthew, Andrew, Taylor, and Mitchell Shirley.*

*And also from friends like Borko Komnenovic, Fred Barnes, Michael McShane, John Morris, Newt Gingrich, Marilyn Fisher, John Heubusch, Joe Scarborough, Mark Levin, Stewart McLaurin, and Laura Ingraham.*

*As always, though, above all, from Zorine, my wife and my best friend, comes my greatest sustenance. "She is clothed with strength and dignity; she can laugh at the days to come. She speaks with wisdom . . ." as Proverbs 31:25–26 tells us about a wife of noble character.*

*Zorine—and others—in their own way gave me encouragement and inspiration, and I am in their debt, as I am in God's debt.*

*Without Him and them, I am nothing.*

# CONTENTS

# FOREWORD

## *Ronald Reagan, the People's Choice*

R onald Reagan was an extraordinary man and a transformational president. He traveled a unique path to the White House, with fruitful careers in broadcasting, film, and television before he entered politics. Because he'd done well at so many things, Reagan rarely defined himself as a politician, even after two productive terms as governor of California and two as president of the United States. He saw himself as the people's president and prized the bond he'd forged with ordinary Americans.

This bond is at the core of *Last Act*, Craig Shirley's fascinating account of the Reagan post-presidency. It is Shirley's contention—which he supports with considerable evidence—that a majority of the American people identified with Reagan and appreciated what he had accomplished even as he was denigrated by much of the media and academic establishment.

Shirley, an admirer of Reagan, is the author of two excellent books on Reagan's campaigns for the presidency in 1976 and 1980. He is an unabashed conservative who doesn't hesitate to take conservatives to task when they deserve it. Neither did Reagan. Shirley recounts a hilarious anecdote about Reagan's reaction to a harangue by Jerry Falwell that I will not spoil for the reader by relating in this foreword.

Many modern presidents enjoy long, happy lives after they leave the White House. Reagan's post-presidency, however, was sadly overshadowed by the dark scourge of Alzheimer's disease. Reagan reacted to the grim news of this diagnosis by sharing it with his fellow Americans. He wrote a remarkable letter to the American people that explained what was happening to him and offered a flash of his famous optimism. "I now begin the journey that will lead me into the sunset of my life," he wrote. "I know that for America there will always be a bright dawn ahead."

Reagan wrote that letter on November 5, 1994. He lived another nine and a half years, lovingly cared for by his adoring wife, Nancy Reagan, who told me that the experience of her husband's Alzheimer's had taught her "a crash course in patience." Shirley notes that these years were "dreadfully hard" on Mrs. Reagan. "Aides and family came and went, but for her, she lived with the disease 24 hours a day, 7 days a week, and 365 days a year," writes Shirley.

Reagan died on June 5, 2004, touching off a week of national mourning. He was celebrated in a state funeral in Washington, DC, and buried on June 11 at the Ronald Reagan Presidential Library in Simi Valley, California.

Much of this book focuses on these ceremonies, about which Shirley provides interesting new details, and on the subsequent memorialization of Reagan. For the American public, Reagan's passing released pent-up feelings of affection and gratitude. Some of his political critics, however, reacted by trying to diminish a president who had so often confounded them, trivializing Reagan's achievements and exaggerating his shortcomings. Even the phrase used so often to describe Reagan—"the Great Communicator"—became a put-down that emphasized his rhetorical skills at the expense of his policies.

Shirley takes blunt issue with the critics in his own words and those of others who valued Reagan. Many of Reagan's defenders were, of course, conservative, but this list also includes former Soviet officials who had seen Reagan in action at four summit meetings with Mikhail Gorbachev and came to respect the American president. The revisionist historian John Patrick Diggins also took sharp issue with his fellow liberal academics for undervaluing Reagan, whom Diggins believes is one of the nation's greatest presidents.

Reading this book triggered personal memories. After Reagan died I made final changes—with much help from editors—in an obituary I'd written for the *Washington Post,* for which I'd worked twenty-six years. Then I became one of several commentators who assessed Reagan's life for ABC News. On the day of the burial, Peter Jennings generously released me from contractual obligations so I could attend the ceremony, to which Mrs. Reagan had graciously invited my wife and me. I'll never forget it. It was a moving event that ended with the playing of "Taps" as the sun sank behind the ridge of hills that extend beyond the Reagan Library to the Pacific Ocean. Ronald Reagan— actor and president—would have loved the drama.

*Last Act* captures the mood and spirit of these ceremonies— and much more. Shirley writes also about the emerging legacy of Reagan abroad and at home, a legacy that grows larger by the day. Former White House speechwriter Peggy Noonan has observed that post-Reagan presidents often dwell on their prospective legacies. Reagan didn't. As Shirley observes, Reagan rarely talked about his legacy and when he did he gave the American people the credit for what he'd accomplished. That was pure Reagan. When I once asked him what his legacy would be, he said in so many words that if he did the right thing his legacy would take care of itself.

It has. Truth will come to light, in Shakespeare's phrase. Shirley notes that even academics who once rated Reagan as at best a mediocre president now give him improved marks. In one ranking of U.S.

presidents, Reagan has advanced from twenty-eighth to fourteenth. He does even better abroad. A ranking of U.S. presidents by forty-seven British academics, for instance, puts Reagan eighth on the all-time list.

When the American people do the rankings, Reagan is at or near the top of the heap. In the last Gallup poll of his presidency, Reagan had a public approval rating of 63 percent, the highest for any president leaving office since Franklin D. Roosevelt died early in his fourth term. The *New York Times*–CBS poll had him at 68 percent.

These ratings soared even higher in the years after Reagan's death as Americans became nostalgic for his presidency. Gallup annually asks Americans whom they think is the best president. Reagan routinely ranks among the top three, sometimes first, sharing the preference of the people with two martyred presidents, Abraham Lincoln and John F. Kennedy. Historians may dispute these judgments, but the opinion of the people should not be taken lightly.

Indeed, Reagan remains popular because he reached ordinary Americans of my generation in a way no other president did, save Kennedy. So it's no accident, as Shirley observes in this estimable book, that Reagan often quoted JFK over the objections of liberals and conservatives alike. In fact, Shirley tells us that Reagan once received a letter from JFK's son, John Kennedy, Jr., urging Reagan to keep quoting him.

Reagan did. He was always in touch with the people.

LOU CANNON
AUTHOR, *PRESIDENT REAGAN:
THE ROLE OF A LIFETIME*

# PREFACE

## *A Tide in the Affairs of Men*

*"He sits around telling stories, and they're all fond
of him, but they don't take him too seriously."*

T he day Ronald Reagan died, Ardeshir Zahedi, the noted Iranian
diplomat, wrote to Nancy Reagan and said, "Our great Persian
poet Saadi says that a man who leaves behind a good name shall never
die for he shall have eternal life in the memories of generation after
generation of humanity. President Reagan was such a man."[1]

Mr. Zahedi was prophetic, as the second week of June 2004—
the seven days of the Reagan funeral—proved to be a titanic struggle
between those who wanted to enlarge the legacy of Ronald Reagan and
those who wanted to diminish his place in history. For Reagan, some
things never changed.

As with his entire life and even in death, the vast majority of the
elites had little regard for Reagan. The vast majority of the citizenry
thought otherwise. New York City closed its government for the
deaths of Franklin Roosevelt, John F. Kennedy, Martin Luther King,
Jr., Robert Kennedy, and Lyndon Johnson. The New York City government, however, did not close for the passing of Ronald Reagan.

Instead, the day Reagan died, a play called *Assassins* was being performed on Broadway, which featured an actor playing John Hinckley firing a gun at a cardboard cutout of Ronald Reagan.[2]

Celebrated atheist, commentator, and dyspeptic scold Christopher Hitchens called the week of the Reagan funeral "pseudo-monarchical, hagiographic trash." In the face of the realities of the Cold War, nuclear annihilation, and the dire economy of 1980, liberal analyst and *Nation* editor David Corn said of Reagan, "It seemed at times that he was untethered from reality." Gay activist Larry Kramer called Reagan a "gigantic sinner."[3]

As for Reagan's place in history, FDR and JFK biographer Arthur M. Schlesinger, Jr., said, "He's like a nice, old uncle, who comes in, and all the kids are glad to see him. He sits around telling stories, and they're all fond of him, but they don't take him too seriously." Historian Stephen Ambrose said Reagan was simply the beneficiary of "very good luck."[4] And yet another essayist of history, Doug Brinkley, who edited the Reagan diaries, came away impressed with the agility of the man's mind. So, too, did an underrated historian, John Patrick Diggins, a liberal whose book *Ronald Reagan: Fate, Freedom, and the Making of History* praised Reagan as one of America's four greatest presidents because like Washington, Lincoln, and FDR, he also freed and saved many, many people. Diggins believed, like Thomas Carlyle, that the "history of the world is but the biography of great men."[5]

The populist Reagan's sometime nemesis, the *Wall Street Journal*, noted the day before he left office in 1989 how much had been accomplished in eight years.

Not the least of Mr. Reagan's accomplishments is how much the nation has forgotten. He took office in the very shadow of a hostage crisis, remember? Remember gasoline lines? Remember double-digit inflation and interest rates twice today's? Remember Watergate? Remember Vietnam? As Ronald Reagan hands over the reins tomorrow . . . he leaves quite a different America. It cannot be all luck, and it is not likely to vanish as the outgoing President leaves center stage.[6]

For many opponents, facts weren't enough. Hollywood doyen Bette Midler claimed Reagan had emptied America's insane asylums when in fact it was the courts at the behest of the ACLU.[7]

Democratic pollster and Bill Clinton confidant Stanley Greenberg contended during the week of the Reagan funeral that the Gipper's long-lasting impact on the country would be ephemeral, unlike FDR and JFK. Reagan "'is a historical figure whose relevance to today's politics is quite limited. Reagan,' he said, 'remains a revered figure among Republicans, but a more controversial leader among non-Republicans.'"[8]

The week of the Gipper's death, syndicated liberal cartoonist Ted Rall would show an absence of tact and an absence of a soul when he said, "I'm sure he's turning crispy brown right about now."[9] A former conservative, Kevin Phillips, wrote in his book *The Politics of Rich and Poor*, "The 1980s were the triumph of upper America—an ostentatious celebration of wealth, the political ascendancy of the richest third of the population and a glorification of capitalism, free markets and finance."[10]

The word *greed* was thrown about by many pundits and Phillips was no exception. The Clintons called the 1980s the "decade of greed,"[11] but the prosperity of the 1990s, which had its underpinnings in Reaganomics, was not. During the week of his funeral, the *Washington Times* reported, "A best-selling author, says of him: 'Killer, coward, con man—Ronald Reagan, goodbye and good riddance.'" Also, a "gay activist" penned that Reagan would "spend eternity in hell."[12]

Walter Williams, author of *Reaganism and the Death of Representative Democracy*, told *U.S. News & World Report*, "He didn't know what was going on under him."[13] In 1980, "radical chic conductor Leonard Bernstein said Reagan's election would unleash the forces of fascism in America."[14]

Few men in public life suffered the enmity of the elites more than Reagan, even as statues of him continue to dot the world, in the rotunda of the U.S. Capitol; in Simi Valley and Sacramento, California; in London; in Budapest; in Warsaw; in Dixon and Eureka, Illinois. Possibly, Reagan's reverence for a quote attributed to Cicero that "the arrogance of officialdom should be tempered and controlled" had something to do with their contempt for him.[15] Or as Reagan aide Mike Deaver once told another Reagan aide, Peter Hannaford, "These guys have never been with us."[16]

The story of Ronald Reagan and the story of his passing and the week of his funeral is really the story of two vastly different Americas. This in and of itself was ironic as Reagan despised class and cultural warfare. He said, "Since when do we in America accept this alien and discredited theory of social and class warfare? Since when do we in America endorse the politics of envy and division?"[17]

When he left office, he was regarded as successful and highly popular—68 percent approval according to a *New York Times* poll—but that wasn't enough for his detractors. The last Gallup poll taken on the elites' beloved FDR was in 1943, two years before his death. It pegged him at 66 percent approval.[18]

*Last Act* is also about the sixteen years of Reagan's life following his two terms as president. Reagan was never going to just sit in a rocking chair. He'd been vital and active his whole life and for years afterward—even after the Alzheimer's he remained active for years. But the battle over the Reagan legacy and the meaning of Reagan came to a head the week he died, and it remains a matter of debate to this day.

This new volume is the story of his post–White House life and death. It also is a story of people trying to understand him, misshape him, rewrite him, venerate him, and destroy him.

The week of the Reagan funeral, makeshift shrines of flowers and such sprung up at Eureka College and in Dixon, Illinois, at the presidential library in Simi Valley, at the Reagan Ranch Center in Santa Barbara, at the Reagan home in Bel Air, and in towns and villages across the nation. Memorials appeared, too, in Prague and Budapest and in cities and villages across the former "Captive Nations" of the Baltics, as well as in the former Warsaw Pact countries. Few, if any, were visible on the campus of Harvard or in the tony Georgetown section of Washington, nor in the Upper West Side of Manhattan or in Cambridge, Massachusetts.

A decade after his passing, polemicists and plagiarists posing as historians still write prevarications about who he was, what he represented, and what he accomplished. A slim book called *Tear Down This Myth* was penned by liberal Will Bunch, whose premise was the Reagan presidency was all hype and no substance. The book featured a glowing dust-jacket endorsement by a minor left wing political activist who had already put in a long career at a left wing pressure group denouncing and attacking conservatism.

Another book by a liberal Ivy League historian claims Reagan was "reactionary," which flies in the face of most every issue he spoke out on or took a position on.[19] *Gambling with History* by Laurence Barrett and *The Triumph of Politics* by David Stockman were like most books about Reagan—snarky and myopic. When Stockman finally left the Reagan administration as a shell of himself, the disgraced former aide modestly wrote, "The president had accepted but never understood the revolution I had brought to him on the eve of his election."[20]

The fight to preserve the facts of history is never ending.

The calumnies heaped on Reagan over the course of his political career and into his retirement were nothing short of extraordinary. Nothing was left untouched. During the assassination attempt in March 1981, a college newspaper said John Hinckley should have had better aim. A radio commentator said Hinckley should have used a heavier caliber gun. When Reagan died, "the crowd whooped and cheered" at the offices of the leftism group ANSWER.[21]

Three years into his Alzheimer's, the *Onion* ran a story under the headline "Doctors Say Reagan's Dementia Increasingly Hilarious." "The fact that this particular patient was once the leader of the free world, only reinforces the intense comedic impact of seeing him put both feet into the same leg of his trousers and then, attempting to stand up, pitch violently forward into the waiting arms of Secret Service personnel."[22]

Just months before his Alzheimer's was announced, the Italian high-fashion company Benetton purchased print ads in magazines all over the world depicting the Gipper with AIDS lesions all over his face. It was "accompanied by a fake obituary . . ."[23]

Inside his own party and even after winning a landslide two years earlier, in 1980, Reagan had his doubters. An RNC aide and Bush booster taped a piece of paper to the door of her office, which said, "Sign Up Here for the Bush 1984 Campaign." This was after the off-year elections of 1982 when the GOP fared poorly and Reagan and the poor economy were blamed. As far as anybody was concerned, Reagan was going to run for re-nomination and reelection in 1984, much to the chagrin of the Bush Brigades at the Republican National Committee.

Two weeks after his funeral, the *New York Times* published a column by a doctor in which he hemmed and hawed "well, maybe" but then "come to think of it, no" Reagan did not suffer from dementia or the early stages of Alzheimer's during the presidency. Deep into the column Dr. Lawrence Altman in fact noted of Reagan "his recall was sharp" and admitted that Reagan's mental acuity was never an issue after observing him and interviewing staff and colleagues. But that did not stop the *Times* from running a very misleading headline, "A Recollection of Early Questions About Reagan's Health." To Altman's credit, his piece backed off his earlier beliefs about Reagan's mental health.[24]

Reagan's sleep habits were heavily and derisively reported, but the national media largely ignored that "Reagan chaired 355 meetings of the NSC [White House National Security Council] or its smaller and more secretive component, the National Security Planning Group," as Marty and Annelise Anderson wrote in their important volume, *Reagan's Secret War.*[25] Instead, "The president's afternoon naps and frequent trips to his California ranch reinforced this out-to-lunch image. A 1982 *Miami News* cartoon depicts Reagan sitting up in bed to take a phone call, with a bubble that reads: 'World War III? Six hours ago? No Kidding? Well, gee, thanks for calling . . .' "[26]

With a year left in the Gipper's administration, *Washington Post* columnist Charles Krauthammer wrote that the Jim and Tammy Faye Bakker scandal signaled "the end of the Age of Reagan" and his time in Washington was marked by "more disgraces than can fit in a nursery rhyme." And, "Now that the Wizard's Teflon magic has worn off . . ." and "There is no doubt that Reagan has reached the nadir of his political effectiveness,"[27] and there was even more slamming of Reagan by Krauthammer, the former liberal speechwriter for Walter Mondale.

Liberal reporters also got him wrong. Susan Page of *USA Today* wrote that "Reagan said the GOP should be a 'big tent' that tolerated opposing views . . ."[28] In fact, not only did Reagan never utter that phrase (Lee Atwater coined it), his speeches and his life were about anything but a political party that was many things to all people rather than one thing to all people.

Reagan always was aware of the beating he was taking in the national media. In 1990, he wrote a private note to Cal Thomas, joking the "*L.A. Times* is not exactly in my corner. Oops!"[29]

The battle was officially enjoined years earlier about the Reagan legacy, but it took on even greater intensity the week of his funeral in a pitched battle between the defenders of Reagan and the skeptics of his legacy. Tom Toles, the left wing political animator for the *Washington Post*, drew a sketch making fun of Reagan on various paper currencies, each denoting a federal deficit. Like his predecessor Herbert Block, Toles was often too mean and too caught up in his own odium to be funny when it came to Reagan.

After the week of the Reagan funeral, critics wrote postmortems about the television coverage, attacking some hosts for being too gentle on Reagan. Brian Williams was lashed heavily by the Left for simply saying the Gipper's life was "about as well lived as any in the history of the Republic."[30]

There were also plenty of articles about the nonsense that Reagan and Tip O'Neill were great friends, but nothing could be further from the truth. Reagan respected O'Neill but never trusted him, especially after 1982 and being bamboozled over the TEFRA bill. O'Neill did not respect Reagan and said so freely, openly, and often, including in his autobiography *Man of the House*. There were also plenty of deeply flawed articles that week comparing Reagan and President George W. Bush. There were a few similarities, yes, but there were also great differences.

The intelligentsia, if asked, would contend that Barack Obama's inaugural drew more television viewers than did Ronald Reagan's but in fact Reagan in 1981 had 42 million viewers while Obama in 2009 had 38 million, according to Nielsen Media Research. And, in the nearly thirty-year interval, the country had grown by almost 100 million people. Still, both events pale before Bill Clinton's televised apology to Monica Lewinsky and his admission of infidelity, which drew more than 67 million sensationalized viewers.[31]

The Nobel Committee presented its peace award to Mikhail Gorbachev, for essentially having the wisdom to give up, but not to Ronald Reagan, nor to Margaret Thatcher, nor to Pope John Paul II—whose actions freed millions imprisoned behind the Iron Curtain. Even years after the fall of the Berlin Wall, liberal historians were still giving Gorbachev more credit than Reagan for the collapse of the communist state. And they still are.

In 1992, former president Reagan was giving a speech to the National Association of Broadcasters in Las Vegas, where he was the recipient of a crystal-styled award. A crazed left wing environmental activist, named Rick Springer, snuck on stage and smashed the ornamental glass at the elderly man's feet, shattering it, and tiny pieces went dangerously flying everywhere. After Springer was hauled away by the Secret Service, Reagan calmly picked up the glass pieces of the award and then returned to the podium and finished his remarks. NBC's *Today* show brought the assaulter onto their show, where he was treated respectfully by Bryant Gumbel, a frequent Reagan critic.

Ira Allen was a reporter for UPI (United Press International) in the 1980s and, during a lecture he attended at the University of Maryland in 1984, hotly denied that Reagan had been seriously injured in the assassination attempt three years earlier, even as Reagan had lost half the blood in his body with a punctured lung and a detonator bullet burned in his chest, less than one inch from his heart.

Even in his demise, the establishment often reviled him, though the people by and large embraced him.

As in most cases, Reagan had the answer himself. His old friend and chronicler Lou Cannon recalled Reagan telling an NBC reporter, "Would you laugh if I told you that I think, maybe, they see themselves and that I'm one of them? I've never been able to detach myself or think that I, somehow, am apart from them."[32]

Giant cultural and political fissures were laid bare in America the week of the Reagan funeral. The mainstream media, at the beginning of the week, generally continued the pounding of Reagan and what he stood for as they had since his rise in the mid-1960s. The great unwashed thought otherwise and as the week progressed, more and more Americans turned out, called up, wrote in, and came forward to support the legacy of a president many had grown to love. Most establishment Republicans knew they'd been beaten by this populist outsider reformer and either said little or more wisely cheered—some only softly—his legacy. Curiously, most elected Democrats, when they spoke out, were favorable to Reagan because they had seen up close and personal the rise of the Reagan Democrat and knew the Gipper had established a cultural and psychological bond with such individuals years before.

Of course, the mainstream media reported heavily that African American leaders opposed him even though he left office with a 40 percent approval rating among blacks,[33] as high as it had been in memory for a Republican since and even before the New Deal.

The city-state of Washington and indeed most urbanites had difficulty understanding Reagan. Cynicism was fashionable for the sophisticates and because so many of their friends and neighbors worked in government or were dependent upon government, they reacted with hostility toward Reagan's criticism of government.

Political philosopher and writer Angelo Codevilla wrote in his book *The Ruling Class* of the Country Party and the City Party. It took little imagination to see which party Reagan belonged to and to what party his critics belonged. "He stood against communism, he believed in small government," said an engineer, Bill Richardson of Kentucky, a member of the Country Party.[34]

Before he went to Washington, most especially while he was in Washington, and after he left Washington, the dominant culture loathed Ronald Reagan, had always loathed Reagan, would always loathe Reagan and spent many an hour trying to tear him down. Simply understood, Ronald Reagan had made a lifetime of challenging conventional wisdom. Even in the hours after his death, they attacked and criticized him, even taking time to lambaste his movie career, which had ended exactly forty years earlier in 1964.

A writer for the *Washington Post*, Stephen Hunter, devoted a long piece to trashing much of the Gipper's movie career. "As an actor,

Ronald Reagan just don't get no respect. Almost nobody will argue that he was good at it," Hunter disingenuously wrote, " . . . the New Biographical Dictionary of Film, calls him, less charitably . . . a loser in pictures." Pretty much the only features Hunter liked about Reagan the actor were his good looks, his eyes, and his hair or that "he also seemed . . . to lack subtext."[35] But again the American people thought otherwise. In Hollywood, Reagan received so much fan mail, he eventually employed his mother Nelle to answer much of it.[36] He also was often in the top five among the studio's box office attractions.

During his years in Hollywood, he generally received good reviews for his work, which was constantly evolving and improving. There had been real flashes of talent but, in a system that turned out eight hundred movies a year,[37] the emphasis was not always on quality. Reagan sometimes quipped that some movies "didn't have to be made well, they had to be made by Thursday."[38]

It was only after his politics evolved from FDR liberal to populist conservative that people on the Left started to criticize his acting career. When he was stumping for Roosevelt and Harry Truman and Helen Gahagan Douglas, that was one thing, but his move to the Right shifted the focus of critics. They seemingly could not help but to view Reagan through the taint of a left wing prism. Reagan had been very popular among his fellow actors in Hollywood—until his conservatism began to emerge—and then many discovered how much they disliked his acting skills. To wit, Tinseltown royalty Jane Fonda was a hardwired Reagan hater, bashing the Gipper from the 1960s right up to and even after his death. "Ronald Reagan was a lousy actor and he'll make a lousy president,"[39] Fonda acidly said the day after he was elected president in 1980.

The day after Reagan's death, the *Post* devoted the entire component of their notorious Style section to an often superficial, smarmy, and shallow look at the fortieth president of the United States and Nancy Reagan, repeatedly channeling the Reagans through glitz, glamour, and Hollywood and for the most part not treating him seriously. Even another story about the marriage of the Reagans was about Nancy's care and feeding of his "image" and that she was some sort of Lady Macbeth character, manipulating him from behind the throne of power. It also repeated unfounded and nasty rumors about Nancy Reagan and that he may have proposed to another woman in between Jane Wyman and Nancy Davis.[40] Many a Washington outsider over the years had come to despise the snarky Style section, including the men around Jimmy Carter.

In defense of the *Post*, they were not alone, although their front section political reporters treated Reagan more fairly than their columnists, featurists, and editorialists. The *Post* was at the head table of the media-establishment complex, but nearly all members of the kommentariat were devoted to opposing Reagan over the years, from Wall Street to K Street to America's Fleet Streets. The media also noted, however, that Reagan was never really all that hot to trot for the culture of Washington. And it was true.

In the hours after Reagan's passing, the most praise many insiders could muster was he was a nice guy who told funny jokes. This was pervasive in the cable and network coverage during the following days as well. He was not entirely and not always under siege during his years away from Washington beginning in 1989. There was the occasional intellectually accurate and historically correct portrayal of Reagan the man, Reagan the political leader, and Reagan the world leader. Often though, they got things both large and small about Reagan wrong.

The elite media had miscalculated Reagan. Even in death. Only after a giant blowback by the American citizenry did some come around, by the end of the week of the official period of mourning for Ronald Wilson Reagan, and even then often only grudgingly.

To be sure, there have been the almost obligatory mentions of failings, misdeeds, and controversies—above all, the Iran-Contra scandal and Reagan's initial denial of wrongdoing. There have also been reminders of the inattention to the spreading AIDS epidemic, the widening economic inequalities that accompanied the go-go boom of the 1980s, and, of course, the soaring budget deficit and a near tripling of the national debt.[41]

Not reported was the work Ronald and Nancy Reagan did for the Pediatric AIDS Foundation, including taping fund-raising appeals. Along the way, they became friends with the actor Paul Glaser and his wife Elizabeth, who'd contracted AIDS through a blood transfusion. She died in December 1994, just one month after Reagan had announced his Alzheimer's and yet among the first people Glaser heard from were the Reagans.[42] Nonetheless, years later, a columnist for the *Post* called Reagan "infamous" for not taking up the issues of AIDS earlier in his presidency.[43] *Webster's Dictionary* defines *infamous* as "having a reputation of the worst kind."[44] The news magazines and weekend TV shows, after monitoring a full week of outpouring from the American people, struck an often different tone than did the newspapers and columnists and commentators during those seven days.

Over the weekend of June 12, after the funeral, every public affairs show on cable and network television was devoted to the legacy and memory of Ronald Wilson Reagan, and a more substantive understanding took hold with many guests and hosts. From Cal Thomas's *After Hours*, which featured a deep discussion with former Reagan policy aide Marty Anderson, to CNN's *The Novak Zone*, which had no guests, just columnist Bob Novak hosting, reminiscing about Reagan, interspersed with footage of the life and times of the Gipper, there was also serious consideration. Outside of Lou Cannon and a few other veteran beat reporters, Novak had known and covered Reagan nearly longer than anyone else in American journalism. As a conservative columnist, Novak was allowed to offer his opinion of Reagan over the years and frequently was favorable—though not always.

On another news show, *Fox News Watch*, the topic was: "Media coverage of the Reagan funeral. How can journalists strike a balance between appropriate and excessive coverage of a major national event?"[45] Also, many explored the impact the Reagan funeral had on the presidential campaign. And the discussion began in earnest about Reagan's place in history. When Warren G. Harding had unexpectedly died in office, there had been a respectful outpouring of favorable commentary and observations, but within a year, historians began to tear his legacy apart and, as Lewis Gould, a political party historian, reminded his readers, "historian Paula Fass delivered this stinging verdict . . . 'The presidency of Warren G. Harding began in mediocrity and ended in corruption.'"[46]

The counter-counteroffensive against the counteroffensive against the offensive had begun. Lewis Lapham of *Harper's* said that Reagan not only probably did not write his own memoirs, "He probably didn't read it."[47]

Other papers and columns began to appear almost immediately, disputing the plaudits and praises of the last week for Reagan and his legacy. Katie Couric had said some kind things about the marriage of Ronald and Nancy Reagan, words that resulted in her receiving some criticism. The network talking heads could not win for losing. At the beginning of the week, they'd been too harsh, viewers thought, and many citizens had called to complain. By the end of the week, having heard from and seen the outpouring, they had pulled back and now were in trouble with the professional critics. Even Dan Rather got knocked a bit because he described the origins of the 21-gun salutation and read from the Navy Hymn. Bernie Shaw, who'd retired from the anchorman gig, had been personally invited by Nancy Reagan to the

National Cathedral, and he bravely had no hesitation about describing the funeral and the week as "American majestic."[48]

After he left office, Reagan's place in history was clarified by several things, including the contrast with his successors—George H. W. Bush was perceived as a good man who did not understand the presidency or power and Bill Clinton whose legacy was as a "Good Time Charlie" was more interested in the trappings of power and the love of the crowd than any great revolutionary ideas. He left the White House popular but also scarred by scandals. The jury in the spring of 2004 was still out on George W. Bush. He'd started in a deep hole, and the Florida recount in 2000 and that unprecedented and nation-splitting path to power, despite losing the election by half a million votes, caused the intelligentsia to gag. Then September 11, 2001, changed everything for the younger Bush—but only for a time. Barack Obama seems to understand power only too well, but only as a means to deliberately divide Americans. He is easily the most polarizing president since Richard Nixon.

The second altering event was Reagan's classy and dignified manner in which he told the American people of his Alzheimer's—manly, calm, courageous—with no whiff of victimhood.

The third was the release of the books *In His Own Hand* in 2001 and *Reagan: A Life in Letters* in 2003, both collections of his letters edited by Marty and Annelise Anderson and Kiron Skinner. The publication of these tomes was fortuitous as Reagan's legacy was in real danger of drifting into irrelevance. His opponents on the Left in academia and the media and the GOP establishment were only too delighted to consign him there, but these books showed an erudite, wise, well-read, witty, and solicitous man, nothing like the caricature his opponents had tried to portray him as over the years.

Fourth and most important were the facts of his world-altering presidency. For all the talk of him being divisive, in two national elections, Reagan received 1,014 electoral votes to the 62 electoral votes for Jimmy Carter and Walter Mondale. For all the talk about deficits during his presidency, it shrunk as a percentage of GDP from 6.3 percent to 3.2 percent by 1988, according to the *Wall Street Journal*.[49]

Pick up nearly any high school textbook in America today and most books of history and they are filled with agenda-driven misstatements of facts if not downright prevarications about Reagan or just downright misunderstandings of the man. Too often, writers bend history to their own liking rather than bending themselves to satisfy the facts.

Larry Kudlow, a top official in the Reagan administration and one of the few supply-siders to come out of Wall Street, grasped this better than most. "Reagan would say something and people would say, here's what he really meant, but what he really meant was what he said."[50] Kudlow was part of a small group of conservatives in 1991 who had enjoyed a private lunch with the former president at the City Club in New York. Ed Meese was there, as was Caspar Weinberger and conservative writer John Fund. It was at a time when some on the Right were having growing concerns about President Bush but Reagan made clear he was sticking with Bush, supported his reelection, and that was that. Kudlow also recalled happily that Reagan had always hated the International Monetary Fund. Kudlow was impressed with Reagan's loyalty to Bush *and* judgment about the IMF.[51]

As is too often the case, American history is reduced to a shorthand interpretation or construction, rooted not in fact, but based upon a fallacy. George Washington in fact lost more battles than he won during the Revolution. It is taught that America's entry into World War II began with the Japanese attack on Pearl Harbor, when in fact Roosevelt studiously avoided declaring war on Germany and Italy and only did so after Hitler and Mussolini had declared war on the United States on December 11, 1941. Even after the attack on December 7,

1941, there was no will for getting involved in another European war, though there was 100 percent will for going to war with the Empire of Japan.

As George Santayana once said, "History is a pack of lies about events that never happened told by people who weren't there."[52]

The history of Ronald Reagan is too important to be left to people who weren't there who wrote about things that never happened.

# CHAPTER 1

# MORTAL COIL

*"Even though the day must ultimately come,*
*it will be hard to say goodbye."*

For years Jim Hooley had been dreading the phone call, even though he knew it was inevitable that Ronald Reagan, the man to whom he'd devoted much of his life, was going to die.

Soon.

Days were now down to hours and maybe even minutes.

It was early June 2004 and the private word from California about President Reagan's condition was getting steadily worse. No one who had been diagnosed with Alzheimer's ever got better. People frequently recovered from surgeries and cancers and broken bones. But no one ever got better who was diagnosed with the horrible disease—about which so little was understood—that ravages and ultimately does fatal damage to the brain and the body.

Hooley and other key Reaganites had already had one false alarm just a week earlier, getting an urgent phone call from the president's chief of staff, Joanne Drake, telling him Reagan's time was nigh and he'd better get on the next plane. Reagan, according to sources, had been unconscious for a week.

But then the ninety-three-year-old Gipper rallied, as if pushing back against death, as he'd pushed back his whole life: against Eureka College administrators who wanted to fire professors during the Great Depression; against Hollywood moguls who refused to share residual profits with actors and actresses; against political opponents, both Republican and Democratic; against the entrenched Washington bureaucracy; against dictators who ran Evil Empires.

Just a few days earlier, on Memorial Day weekend, Robert Higdon received a call from Nancy Reagan. "I just wanted to call and tell you, you need to get ready." He pulled the car over to the side of the road to give Nancy his undivided attention. "As in?" he gravely replied. "The doctor's just here and he said we need to get ready . . . I think by the end of the week," she said.[1] Higdon was a family friend who'd been asked to help raise money to get the presidential library off the ground many years earlier.

One week later—on June 4—Drake called Hooley again and said, "Things are looking close."[2]

Those involved in the planning of the Reagan funeral—Fred Ryan, Joanne Drake, Higdon, Rick Ahearn, Hooley—had been on call for years. As a longtime advance man for Reagan, Hooley—and many others—had to make sure the rites came off without a hitch. There were thousands of moving parts involved. Ryan, Drake, and Higdon had been personally close to the Reagans for many years and knew how many friends and associates and admirers and detractors and critics and enemies they'd picked up over the years.

The logistics for the movement of a president were difficult enough, but for the funeral of a president they were mind numbing. Imagine every ego in Washington jammed into a small animal cage, each armed with a sharp knife, an American Express card, and battery acid.

Reagan had always believed he was the master of his own fate but also, as a man of God, believed in divine destiny. Reagan used the phrase "Man with God"[3] because he believed he, like all people, was made in the image of his Creator. But he also embraced Immanuel Kant's rational being because God wanted man to be a rational being. He was going to go when God called him but not one minute sooner.

The disease was named after Alois Alzheimer, the Bavarian German scientist who'd first undertaken the use of high-performance microscopes to study brain tissue nearly a century earlier while searching for the causes of dementia. According to *How We Die*, "The fundamental pathology of Alzheimer's disease is the progressive degeneration and loss of vast numbers of nerve cells in those portions of the brain's cortex that are associated with the so-called higher functions, such as memory, learning and judgment."[4]

Twenty-one years earlier—in the fall of 1983—President Reagan designated November as "National Alzheimer's Disease Month."[5] This was just as nationwide attention was slowly beginning to awaken and become more familiar with the affliction. He himself went through the seven stages as defined by the Alzheimer's Association, from Step One "no impairment" to Step Seven "very severe decline."[6] Still, the fact that it took ten years was a testament to his physical endurance and capacity. Lou Cannon noted that Reagan was very proud of the weight room that he'd installed in the White House after the shooting and that did much to help him recover, "but, there's a price that he paid. If he hadn't been a healthy man, he probably wouldn't have lived all those years."[7] Many Alzheimer's patients—such as his old friend Jeane Kirkpatrick—went very quickly, in a matter of months or a few years.

For months, Hooley had had a suitcase packed and waiting by the door for the phone call, so he would be ready to head out to Andrews Air Force Base and go west to perform one more task for his beloved old boss. Still, no one could accurately forecast how long Reagan would live. "It could be weeks, it could be months," said one individual with knowledge but unidentified to the Associated Press.[8] That same day, however, the wire service had already moved several stories on Reagan's sudden decline but again without attribution and few details.

Also on June 5, President George W. Bush—"43"—was in Europe and while there met with the ailing Pope John Paul II, who gave Bush an earful about the U.S. invasion of Iraq, which the Vatican had opposed. Thousands were protesting Bush as he moved around the continent. "There is a lot of hatred of Bush in France, real hatred," said an aide to French president Jacques Chirac.[9] Protesters burned American flags and carried Palestinian flags and signs denouncing Bush as a terrorist. Simultaneously, anti-Bush protests were underway in Lafayette Park, just across Pennsylvania Avenue from the White House.

The mood of the American people was guarded and somewhat demoralized. The terrible events of September 11, 2001, still hung over the country as the War on Terror continued unabated. Some felt that Bush had made a mistake in praising Islam too effusively and too often, as it muddled the picture as to who the enemy was.

On the other hand, the French had routinely denounced American presidents with the only exception being JFK and that was in part because his wife Jackie was of French descent and she spoke the language fluently. Dwight Eisenhower got rough treatment from the French even though he'd led the D-day invasion that liberated their country from the Nazis and the Nazi accomplices in the Pétain Vichy government exactly sixty years earlier. While a former president lay dying and the current president was in Europe, the news of the world continued.

In secret at a hotel in New Jersey, Department of Justice officials gathered together the families of the victims of September 11, 2001, and played the recordings of the phone calls made from the planes to loved ones.[10] This was the first time they'd been played for the survivors. More than a hundred attended the sad and horrible reliving and retelling of the new day of infamy.

O. J. Simpson sat down for an interview with the Associated Press and told the wire reporter he was no longer in the hunt for the real killers because of the pressures of being a single parent.[11]

The lineup of the Washington insider Sunday shows was announced, and the usual suspects of insiders were expected to talk about the usual insider stuff, including fireworks at the CIA. The shows were routinely ignored by Middle America and Reagan had never paid them much mind, only mentioning them in passing in his diary, which spanned eight years in the White House.

The *Peoria Journal Star* was reporting that Governor Rod Blagojevich wanted to close the Pontiac prison because the inmate population had diminished.[12]

In Washington, Vice President Richard Cheney was being questioned by investigators looking into the illegal leak of the name of a CIA operative to columnist Bob Novak. The investigation was centering on Karl Rove, Bush's political aide and I. Lewis "Scooter" Libby of Cheney's staff.

Later, Cheney flew to Chicago for a fund-raising event for Jack Ryan,[13] a handsome and successful banker who'd once been married to actress Jeri Ryan. They divorced in 1999. His Democratic opponent took the high road publicly saying the divorce was private and the records were private. Behind the scenes, however, his supporters were agitating hard for release of the records. Finally, in a bizarre decision worthy of the long history of corrupt judges in Chicago, it was ruled that the private agreement was somehow in the public interest, and the private agreement by two private individuals was unsealed and splayed all over the media.

In their divorce, Jeri Ryan had charged that her husband wanted to have sex with her in odd, public places but one was hard pressed to understand how this helped the electoral process or their young son.

Ryan, trailing badly in the polls and humiliated, withdrew from the race, clearing the way for the election of his opponent, Barack Hussein Obama. Meanwhile, Obama's academic and medical records remained sealed and unquestioned by the ruling elites. Bush was facing a tough reelection, but the good news was the economy had added nearly 250,000 jobs in the month of May alone.[14] Appearing at a recent book symposium, Al Gore's former campaign manager, Donna Brazile, trashed Reagan harshly, saying he had initiated "the politics of telling poor people they are worthless."[15]

The National Spelling Bee was taking place in Washington with David Tidmarsh, an eighth grader from South Bend, Indiana, correctly spelling *autochthonous*. It meant "indigenous." For his fine efforts, winning out of nine million competitors, David won seventeen thousand dollars in prize money and other awards.[16]

South Bend was the home of Notre Dame and the setting for the movie *Knute Rockne, All American*, in which a young actor portrayed star Fighting Irish fullback George Gipp. On his deathbed, he asked his coach, Rockne, "Sometime, when the team is up against it . . . the breaks are beating the boys . . . tell them to go out there with all they got . . . win just one for the Gipper."[17]

Now Reagan, at the last, was "up against it."

In the last three weeks and in the last stages of his own battle with Alzheimer's, Reagan's eyes had been closed. During ten years, the once inquisitive mind had been slowly shutting down one system after another, as the terrible disease did with all its victims. First, short-term memory; second, long-term memory; then, voluntary motor functions; and finally, as the brain dwindles, goes with it the involuntary heart and lungs and other organ functions.

The disease peeled away the essence of the person as one peels an onion. Layer by layer. Patti Davis, Reagan's pretty if also controversial daughter said it was like "plateauing."[18] Later, Higdon received yet another call from Nancy. "The doctors are here, and I think you need to get everything ready."[19]

Reagan, for his whole life, had been proud to share the "humble roots"[20] of every other American and yet Reagan was also proud that he was singularly unique. As Leader of the Free World, Reagan was the irrepressible American Exceptionalist. He'd once been an inimitable and successful man and president and world trailblazer who, at the end, would die, just like every other man since the time of Adam.

No one, not even occupants of the Oval Office, escaped death.

Reagan had bounded out of the White House and Washington in January 1989 on a wave of good will, the affection of many of his countrymen, and an astonishing record of accomplishment. The country he'd inherited eight years earlier was broken and demoralized. The best days seemed in the past. A country that under Franklin Roosevelt had defeated the evil of Berlin and Tokyo—which in turn under Harry Truman rebuilt a war-torn European continent, created the United Nations, and asked nothing from those countries except some land on which to bury her dead—was a thing of the past.

A nation that became second to none in war and peace, hurled rockets into the depths of the solar system, clothed and fed the poor of the world, provided superb free education to all children, denied opportunity to none, had the strength to admit wrongness and the integrity to throw crooked politicians out of office, had been brought low by unpopular foreign adventures, internal discord, centralized corruption, ill-mannered progressivism, the soullessness and depravity of the Flower Children and anti-war movements, and the radical chic of the 1960s. The traditions of reliance on faith and family had been pulled down, but ironically, as one political philosophy argued for more concentrations of power in the nation's capital, it simply led to more dismay and skepticism about Washington, especially with leaders who were "lost in power," as Bill Buckley said.

In 1980, America was losing a Cold War, the American economy was in tatters, and the American spirit was all but snuffed out. Cynicism was the celebrated disposition and Jacobinism their warming fire.

Eight years later, that country was winning the Cold War, while a humiliated and discredited Moscow was on its knees, suing for peace. Reagan believed that America operated on a higher moral plane than any other country in history, and he approached the presidency in that fashion. Like all Americans, he rejected monarchy, he rejected empire, he rejected High Toryism and neo-conservatism, and he approached the job with reverence and humility and a fundamental belief in the individual. He knew that if the American defense was to be raised, he first had to raise the American economy, and to do that he had to raise America's morale and spirituality. In his overlooked 1980 election eve address, he spoke of his goal to "revitalize the values of family, work, and neighborhood."[21]

The crippling double-digit inflation and interest rates that had decimated the economy and Americans' savings in the 1970s had been eradicated. When he left office, inflation was almost nonexistent and interest rates were at a supportable level. Gasoline was less than a dollar a gallon. Unemployment in January 1989 was 5.4 percent,[22] which some economists said was impossible. The debt was falling rapidly. The vitality of the economy had been restored, but only after Reagan had restored the citizenry's belief in itself.

Polls across the board showed broad approval for Reagan and not just from his base, but historic highs from young voters and from African Americans. Americans finally thought their country was on the right track. He'd left his party with a coherent governing philosophy, his country freer, and the world safer. The U.S. economy, between 1975 and 2000, expanded 128 percent,[23] most of it coming in the Reagan years and in the Reagan-inspired years when the Republicans wrested control of Congress in 1994, led by a young Reaganite, Newt Gingrich.

John O'Sullivan, editor of the *National Review*, said that the "fact of America" would survive, but Ronald Reagan had restored the "idea of America."[24] Reagan himself stuck his chest out a bit and said toward the end of his presidency, "The way I see it, there were two great triumphs, two things that I'm proudest of. One is the economic recovery, in which the people of America created—and filled—19 million new jobs. The other is the recovery of our morale. America is respected again in the world and looked to for leadership."[25] For romantic Americans their shining country was shining again. For Reagan, he left office more popular than when he was sworn in—unlike Carter, Ford, Nixon, Johnson, and Truman. Only Ike could make the same claim.

It hadn't been easy. There had been political brawls and prowling bears and terrorist plots and scandals and exploding shuttles and cancers and shuttered factories and assassination attempts and more. And yet Reagan confronted even more difficult problems than many of his predecessors. Even the *Washington Post* said on the last day of his presidency,

> Ronald Reagan has absolutely confounded prediction . . . Today, at the age of 77, he relinquishes the office so many people thought he never could get, being, it was said eight years ago, too old, too ideological, too conservative, too poorly informed, too politically marginal—in short, too out of it. But there he is, going out in a rare end-of-the-term surge of good feeling, his critics—on key issues, we are emphatically among them—still at a loss as to how to assess and finally even understand this man.[26]

His critics at the *Post* were forced to concede that Reagan's presidency had been "consequential."[27] The country was united and had become part of that "community of shared values"[28] of which he'd spoken at the Republican National Convention in Detroit in 1980, when he accepted the party's nomination, after trying and failing to gain it twice before. As Robert Higdon recalled, "Things were good in the world, and it was time to go away."[29] But he wasn't going quietly.

In late 1988, he'd given a series of speeches drafted by favored wordsmith Clark Judge, taking on the "Iron Triangle" of the media, K Street, and Capitol Hill.[30] His days were filled with meetings, appointments, letters, and receptions. And endless resolutions sent to him by Congress, declaring February 1989 as "America Loves Its Kids Month"[31] and "Fire Safety at Home Day"[32] and "National Burn Awareness Week."[33] He exchanged pleasant letters with Barry Goldwater, who after eight years opened one letter by saying, "Dear Mr. President: It's still hard for me to call you that."[34] Reagan replied and said, "As you can imagine, I'm looking at January 20 with mixed emotions. There is, of course, anticipation about getting back to California and the ranch, but then some regret because of things we didn't get done here."[35]

Nearing the end of his presidency, he delivered remarks in New York honoring Jack Kemp. "And come January, when I saddle up and ride into the sunset it will be with the knowledge that we've done great things. We kept faith with a promise as old as this land we love and as big as the sky. A brilliant vision of America as a shining city on a hill . . . America's greatest chapter is still to be written, for the best is yet to come."[36]

Tucked in his presidential papers was the farewell address of George Washington, which Reagan wanted to study in anticipation of the day he would deliver his own farewell remarks to the American people. They also left with sixteen scrapbooks of their eight years of leading history.[37]

Ironically, some conservatives were dismissive of Reagan and his eight years as president. Paul Weyrich, a leading New Right operative, called the Reagan Revolution "an illusion." But speaking for other conservatives, Mitch Daniels, a veteran of the Reagan White House, said he and others on the Right were "morose" about the Gipper leaving

Washington.[38] They were also dubious that the scion of New England Mayflower society, George H. W. Bush, would run with the conservative baton Reagan had handed off to him.

But that was all behind him now. He told audiences that when he got back to the ranch, his plan was to "lean back, kick up my feet, and take a long nap. Now, come to think of it, things won't be all that different after all."[39]

Most everybody liked Jim Hooley. Hooley had the manly Irishness that Reagan was fond of, but the low-key efficiency that Mrs. Reagan appreciated. He was never in the newspapers, never caught off base, but enjoyed a good laugh, friends, a good cigar, and a glass of whiskey as much as the next guy. Hooley had been married once briefly—it didn't take—and had devoted much of himself to Ronald and Nancy Reagan.

As an advance man, he'd often been in charge of Reagan's movements from the 1980 campaign through much of the presidency and now, Reagan's last journey. Hooley's horoscope on June 4, 2004, had advised, "do not take shortcuts with your work," while also hinting about a "sting of unpleasantness."[40] He was known for his thoroughness with his work but this week it would be accompanied by the sting of an unpleasantness of managing much of the service for a man whom he not only deeply admired, but even loved.

Hooley's status was somewhat remarkable as he'd been at the center for a long time and yet had few knife scars to show for it. Even James "Jim" Baker and Ed Meese had scars from their years of service in Washington to Reagan. There wasn't an administration going back to Washington's time—some involving duels, foreign intrigue, and prison for more than a few—in which people did not emerge bloodied and battered and worse for wear. The fog of alcohol was often a miasma for the high and mighty of Washington politics as was the comfort of a stranger in a strange bed.

Hooley looked like a cop straight out of Central Casting and in fact had once been a Capitol Hill police officer. He'd also—not surprisingly—once been a bartender at the Black Rooster until he finally graduated from American University in Washington. "I was basically screwing around."[41]

Like Reagan, Hooley had also once been a Democrat, volunteering for Hubert Humphrey's 1972 presidential quest. But by 1976, he was performing small tasks for the Reagan campaign. When he'd go home to upstate New York, near the Hudson Valley, his family and parents would rib him good. "So you're going to work for this 69-year-old ex-actor because you think he's going to be president? That's what we put you through college for?"[42]

In 1978, his often but not always reliable friend Rick Ahearn called and told Hooley to come down to Alabama and help him get Guy Hunt, an Amway salesman, elected governor. Ahearn said Hunt was a great guy and easy to work with, both of which Hooley found out were not true when he dropped everything and went to Alabama— and discovered Ahearn had skipped the state, leaving Hooley there for "almost nine months in the middle of 16 dry counties."[43] It was enough to drive any man to drink.

But Hunt was a Reagan supporter and Lyn Nofziger, longtime Reagan political consigliere, asked Hooley to stay in Alabama because they would need Hunt's help in 1980 in a state where Ambassador George Bush and former Texas governor John Connally were attempting to make inroads. Hooley reluctantly stayed and in so doing had made large deposits to the Reagan Favor Bank from which to draw, especially since he handled a major Reagan event in the state, filling the Birmingham Coliseum on a Friday night, which, by the way, seated seventy-five thousand people. Hooley hired every Kelly Girl in the state and then had them phone every Boy Scout troop, every Girl Scout troop, every American Legion post, every Masonic Hall, every Grange Hall, every country club, offering them "free tickets" to go see Ronald Reagan.[44]

The Reagan people were impressed, and the next day Dave Fischer, a Reagan staffer, invited Hooley to Reagan's suite for coffee and a photo with the governor. When Reagan chatted Hooley up and gave him a knowing wink, the young man was hooked and on board for good for the Gipper.[45]

Later, Charlie Black, Reagan's political director, rescued Hooley from Alabama and brought him aboard the national campaign. He was the first advance man on the payroll of the 1980 campaign, and by Labor Day he was handling the advance for many of the Gipper's big events, including the official kickoff of the fall campaign at Liberty State Park in New Jersey, with the Statue of Liberty in the background and hundreds of Slavic Americans in the foreground. The event was executed flawlessly, the "visuals" were terrific, and it all came down as a big feather in Hooley's cap. And the band of Hooley and Ahearn was back together.

As of the last days of the Reagan administration, Hooley had been head of the advance office in the White House, now planning and supervising the president's transition back to California. Hooley left briefly in 1981 and 1982, taking other jobs in the administration but was back with Reagan for good by the end of the second year.

On January 20, 1989, as the moments of the Reagan administration drifted away, he was one of the last few members of the Reagan Revolution. Everybody else was off payroll and had turned in their passes. Hooley arrived at the White House early to have a Bloody Mary and make one last silent toast to President Ronald Reagan.

There was a lot of tension between the incoming Bush Brigades and the outgoing Reaganites, but Hooley brushed it off. The White House was deathly quiet except for the phone calls coming in to Duberstein's office that morning. A radio talk show host had gotten ahold of the direct line to the chief of staff and urged his listeners to call him.[46]

In the last several weeks, there had been a number of good-bye parties and receptions and send-offs. No one was overlooked, not the permanent staff, not the personal staff, not the East Wing or West Wing staff. All were remembered by the Reagans—and all would remember the Reagans.

The night before his last day as president, Reagan's entry in his diary was, "Tomorrow I stop being President."[47]

The Resolute desk was cleared of Reagan's personal effects; so, too, were the pictures of Nancy and family members on the credenza behind the desk. Reagan, his personal aide Jim Kuhn, military advisor Colin Powell, Chief of Staff Ken Duberstein, Marlin Fitzwater, and Reagan's secretary Kathy Osborne all gathered in the Oval Office one last time. Also present was White House photographer Pete Souza, who would memorialize the historic event. It was just after 10:00 a.m.[48]

Powell had one final duty to perform. "Mr. President, this is my last briefing for you. I can tell you that the world is quiet today."[49]

Reagan simply said, "That was nice of you, General. That was a nice thing to say."[50]

Powell then reminded Reagan that as soon as Bush was sworn in, he had to surrender the card with the nuclear codes to his military aide. As Reagan moved to the door, he turned and looked at the room that had defined him and that he had defined for the past eight years and then silently left. Hooley noted, "One of the things I really admired about him was I always thought that Reagan was not only very secure in himself, but he was there to do something, not to be somebody. Unlike Nixon or others, he didn't have to have the job."[51]

It suddenly dawned on Hooley that Reagan was not unhappy to leave the presidency. "And that moment . . . made me realize that . . . he's moving on. I think he loved every minute of the job. But I don't think he wanted to stay. I don't think he had any remorse. He was done."[52]

Jim Kuhn recalled that the very last phone call Reagan took in the White House was from his old friend and aide Lyn Nofziger, which Kuhn found "fitting." "Lynwood"—Reagan's pet nickname for Nofziger—had been there at the beginning, even before the beginning in 1965, just as people who were more confident in Reagan's political skills than Reagan was himself were urging him to run for governor of California.[53] Nofziger was once described as the Sancho Panza to Reagan's Don Quixote but in fact, Lyn was a bona fide war hero, and Reagan almost never tilted at windmills.

It was odd to see Reagan standing behind the Resolute desk, its surface bare, talking on the phone using his left hand, his right jammed in his pocket. The Remington statuettes of cowboys had also been removed from the matching small cabinets in which they'd sat for eight years. In 1981, White House carpenters had to add a shim to the base of the desk because the six-foot-one-inch Reagan's knees and thighs banged against the bottom of the well of the Resolute.

Even to the last, and past Reagan's time of office, Hooley was involved in many things. Three weeks earlier, Duberstein called Hooley and asked him to write a memo detailing the handoff of power from the former president to the new president. The plan that evolved had the Reagans depart via Marine One (whose call sign became "Nighthawk Two" for ex-presidents and other private citizens who used the VP's helicopter) from the east side of the Capitol, after being walked down the steps by President Bush and First Lady Barbara Bush.

Bush didn't get the symbolism of the event, so Duberstein and Hooley explained things to the incoming president, who was afraid not only of offending sensibilities but of somehow insulting Reagan. They explained it would be a symbolic handing off, from Reagan to Bush. After Bush was sworn in on the west side of the Capitol, the four would walk down the steps of the east side. At the bottom, they'd bid their good-byes, the Reagans would walk to the helicopter, and there Reagan would turn and snap off a final salute, now to his commander in chief.

Reagan also began another tradition of leaving a handwritten letter in the top drawer of the Resolute desk in the Oval Office for Bush. Later, Bush left one for Bill Clinton, and so forth. Reagan also left a jokey note in the private quarters of the White House for the new president. Under the heading of "Don't Let the Turkeys Get You Down," the note read "George, I treasure the memories we share and wish you all the very best. You'll be in my prayers. God bless you and Barbara. I'll miss our Thursday lunches."[54]

Bush, in turn, gave Reagan his chair from the Oval Office and the last flag to fly over the White House on January 20, 1989.

On that clear, bright, and cold day, the departure ceremony came off without a hitch, and Reagan asked the chopper pilot to take him and Mrs. Reagan and their small traveling party, which included Hooley, over the White House one last time. "Look, honey, there's our little bungalow," he teased his wife. Also on board were Secret Service agents, Kathy Osborne, Duberstein, and Kuhn. Hooley had discretely boarded the helicopter but not before catching a glimpse of Jim Baker watching the Reagans depart, tears streaming down his face.[55]

At Andrews Air Force Base, the Reagan White House staff and campaign staff and friends gathered to bid the Reagans a final adieu. Military bands played, there was a 21-gun salute, Reagan reviewed the troops for the last time, cannons fired, and the National Anthem was performed. Hooley had been in charge of the traveling party, but Rick Ahearn had been in charge of the departure ceremonies. As Hooley climbed on board the plane, he turned around to see Karen Roberts, Shelby Scarbrough, and hundreds of others in tears, watching the man to whom they had devoted so much leaving them, never again to be the Leader of the Free World.[56] He was, once again, private citizen Ronald Reagan. And yet, it was the very title he glorified more than any other—to him, the phrase "private citizen" was the most important of all in America. Fred Ryan said that Reagan "loved the idea of being a private citizen."[57] Reagan, Lou Cannon said, "didn't have any problems with his term being over."[58]

On board the presidential plane "Special Air Mission"[59] at Andrews—only Air Force One now to the newly minted President Bush—Reagan went back to the staff section as he often did and told Hooley, "Well, let's set our watches." He then asked what was for lunch, which everybody knew was his favorite: meatloaf and macaroni and cheese. The plane had some kids and families, including Duberstein's, on board and journalist Lou Cannon, but relatively few staffers, and Hooley thought ruefully that there were some people from the campaigns who should have been invited aboard to fill the empty seats. Later, the inevitable champagne and cake were brought out and promptly consumed. Throughout, Mrs. Reagan was mostly quiet, and Hooley was surprised to find that, for himself, the trip conjured up few emotions of any sort, maybe because there were so many unfamiliar faces on board. Even so, "the old man" was "up front so . . ." that always made any trip special.[60]

They landed in Los Angeles to a comparatively restrained ceremony and a crowd of around seven hundred. Some waved "Welcome Home" and "Happy Trails Again" signs, but just so no one would think that political opponents had deserted the field, someone also waved a placard that read "The King and Queen Return."[61]

A band from USC played, and Hooley again was in charge of the motorcade to take the Reagans to their new home in Bel Air, 668 St. Cloud. It was 666 when they bought it but Reagan asked it to be changed because the number was the "mark of the beast"—the devil— in the Bible.[62] Waiting at the airport was Joanne Drake, who had already assumed her duties at the new Reagan offices. Also on hand were Mayor Tom Bradley and actor Robert Stack, a Reagan friend who had done the voice-over for some of the 1980 campaign commercials.

On the plane ride home, Nancy had been weepy and Reagan was "relaxed and subdued." He was looking forward to getting home, saying their life there they had loved "very much. California isn't a place in my mind; it's a way of life."[63]

Upon landing, he told the crowd, "It has been a bittersweet several hours . . . There were many wonderful associates that we have been working with the last eight years that we had to say good-bye to. It was hard to say good-bye." But when asked, he ticked off a list of things he had not accomplished while president, including "outlawing of abortion."[64]

On the trip back to Washington, Hooley and company had the big jet nearly to themselves, and Jim invited a small group of remaining Reaganites to join him, consume some cocktails, and commandeer a table at which they kicked around old times. All told, the plane had maybe twelve people winging their way back to Washington, drinking and laughing and remembering fondly the enormous and momentous eight years of the Reagan presidency. A group of advance men had gone ahead to California to smooth the way but now they, too, like Hooley, were unemployed, and the plane became essentially a flying halfway house for jobless, not entirely sober, Reaganites.

There would be no job for Hooley in the Bush administration nor would there be for almost all the Reagan team. "I was out. In fact, it was four cold years because . . . the Bush advance people didn't like the Reagan advance people." The advance people used to joke they weren't the geniuses of American politics and government. As one Reagan advance man was known to say, they were "every cleft palate and club foot in America."[65]

Hooley knocked around after that, trying to set up his own business, going to work for other Washington firms, but wasn't really happy and so, several years later, jumped at the chance to organize the advance for the opening of the Reagan Library, which was a gigantic task as it involved four former presidents—Reagan, Jimmy Carter, Gerald Ford, and Richard Nixon—President Bush and Mrs. Bush, and all the former First Ladies, plus children of presidents, former Reagan cabinet officials, and hundreds of high-maintenance attendees. It was the first time in history five presidents were gathered together in one location.

Mike Deaver had hired Hooley to handle the advance but gave him no manual for the handling of demanding and high-maintenance ex-presidents. In a way, the Reagan staff had been spoiled working for the Gipper but Nixon, Ford, and Carter could be much more difficult; throw in the former First Ladies for good measure and it was enough to give any advance man nightmares.

Richard Nixon showed little interest when his wife grew faint in the sun and had to lie down on a cot in the Library for a moment as Mike Deaver comforted her. "Tell Nancy I wanted to be here for her," Mrs. Nixon moaned to Hooley and Deaver, as if she were about to expire. At the time, they took her plight seriously but later after she recovered, they had a laugh about it, especially since President Nixon kept talking to the men there about college football while completely ignoring his wife's plight. Nixon was also indifferent to his wife as she struggled to get to the other side of the limousine and open her own door while getting into the car himself and shutting the door. The closest door.

Anticipating he was "gonna get clobbered" with all the demands, Hooley recruited an extra amount of volunteers to help him out. Charlton Heston and Lee Greenwood were scheduled to perform. Jets flew over, Universal Studios helped in the production, including producing instant trees on Hooley's request, and it turned out to be a lovely and successful event as far as the media and the spectators were concerned.[66]

Later, Hooley grinned to himself listening to Ford drawl in that distinctive Michigan voice of his, "We are very, very late," because Ford always used the phrase "very, very."[67] He also knew Ford was in a hurry to get home because he had a tee time to make.

Carter was grinning but it seemed as if he was really just gritting his teeth, mockingly telling his wife, Rosalynn, that there were more and more pictures to take. "We haven't done enough photos. We haven't taken enough pictures," he said repeatedly and sarcastically to his wife.[68]

Despite all the backroom hijinks and clashing personalities, and playing to type, the opening of the Reagan Library was a successful event as far as the world was concerned as four former presidents and President George Bush all appeared simultaneously before the audience. It was a rare moment in American history.

For his competence, his ability to get things done, his ability to organize and play well with others, Ryan and Deaver selected Hooley to handle many of the important logistics of the state funeral, which he started planning in the last year of the Reagan presidency. Hooley would report to Drake and Fred Ryan. They were both battle-hardened veterans of the Reagan White House and the Reagan post-presidency, including supervising the building and opening of the Reagan Library in Simi Valley, California, and the Reagan Foundation and its charitable works.

Hooley hadn't fawned over the candidate—later the president—the way some others did. Still, he and the president joshed each other, told jokes to each other, and, because of their closeness over many years, Hooley did the best Reagan impression of anyone in the administration.

Hooley was one of the few now in charge of Reagan's last journey. The one, as Ronald Reagan wrote, "that will lead me into the sunset of my life,"[69] in his parting letter to the American people on November 5, 1994, in which he told his fellow countrymen of his Alzheimer's. It was less than ten years earlier that he'd written that historic and poignant and brave and tear-jerking letter. And it was just a few years before that he was finishing his last months in office, campaigning hard for his successor, George H. W. Bush. Reagan knew if Bush lost, it would be seen as a rejection of his eight years. The last vice president to succeed his own president via election was Martin Van Buren in 1836, which was "OK" with Andrew Jackson.

Reagan was also okay in January 1989, just exhausted after eight years in the belly of the beast, fighting the Soviets, fighting the bureaucrats, fighting House Speaker Tip O'Neill, and fighting slothful, entrenched anti-intellectualism. He was tired, mentally and physically, but after a few days back in his beloved California, he was raring to go again. After all, the last sentence of his diary on January 20, 1989, had said, with his typical optimism, "Then home & the start of our new life."[70] Reagan was seventy-seven years old.

The country in 2004 was in the heat of a pitched presidential campaign between the incumbent, George W. Bush, who claimed the Reagan mantle—even if he governed in a drastically different way— and Senator John Kerry of Massachusetts, who rejected the Reagan mantle outright.

A minor kerfuffle was just beginning to break into the national consciousness—and become a major scandal—involving the blown cover of Valerie Plame, a CIA operative, by White House officials. Plame's husband had angered administration officials by disputing claims about terrorist incentives. Bush told reporters in the Rose Garden, "I want to know the truth, and I'm willing to cooperate myself."[71] The FBI was starting to look into the matter, and Bush assured investigating officials that he and his staff would cooperate fully. In short, the accusation was that the White House exposed the cover of a CIA operative because they were mad at her husband, but it would be silly to compare Washington to a bad soap opera.

Weapons of mass destruction had yet to be found in Iraq, a year and a half since the incursion and since Bush had ordered a very un-Reagan-like invasion. The news was filled with stories of Iraq, of Afghanistan, and of the explosive growth of government, of government spying operations, and of the new world brought to the American people by the Big Government Republicans. The head of the CIA, George Tenet, was being bombarded with questions and second guesses and accusations over the faulty information about Saddam Hussein's regime. The TSA, the new scourge of that portion of the traveling public that cherished their privacy and their private parts, announced it was making plans to screen checked bags at Union Station,[72] the charming train depot in Washington that some mistakenly identified as Second Empire but in fact was in the Beaux-Arts style of architecture. The Bush administration also announced it was spending billions on facial recognition technology for every person coming into and leaving America.[73] Oil on the world market had just moved to about forty dollars per barrel.[74]

Secretary of Defense Donald Rumsfeld told CNN that al-Qaida was "active in Iraq." He also alleged that the fanatical organization was "recruiting volunteers from various parts of the world for carrying out terrorist acts in Iraq."[75]

Of the newer architecture in Washington, all were pleased but some quietly questioned the design of the new World War II memorial on the Washington Mall. It was beautiful, stark, heroic, but to a few, it had echoes of Roman architecture and to others, even more darkly, of Albert Speer, the master architect of the Third Reich.[76] Rome and Berlin had been the capitals of two of the four major enemies of humanity in World War II. But each day tributes to veterans and to the fallen appeared at the immense out-of-doors amphitheater. Flowers, teddy bears, forty-eight-star flags, and other memorabilia were left to honor the Greatest Generation.

During World War II, Reagan had tried for combat duty three times and three times he was turned away because of his lousy eyesight. It was so poor, at "7/200 bilateral," that "a tank could advance within seven feet of him before he could identify it as Japanese."[77] But he'd served honorably in the army as a captain, as a part of the movie industry devoted to making training and morale films for the military.

Reagan had always brooded about not being able to make it into combat. His friend Eddie Albert came back from the Pacific, where he'd seen plenty of combat as a daring navy pilot. Reagan and Albert had starred together in the screwball comedies *Brother Rat* and the sequel, *Brother Rat and a Baby*. Both were cadets at the Virginia Military Institute. Upon his return from the Pacific, Albert had given Reagan a Japanese "*netsuke*, tugged off the uniform." Reagan blanched and shrunk away, sorry that he had not faced live ammo like other men of his generation.[78]

Probably few Americans had thought much about Reagan over the past several years but when they did it was for the most part warmly and affectionately. He was the last successful president since Eisenhower and the most popular since JFK. The country had trudged through troughs of bad or mediocre presidents and soared to great heights with great presidents. The country, from George H. W. Bush to Bill Clinton to George W. Bush, was enduring yet another drought of greatness.

Reagan was mentioned often in a political or governing context but for average Americans—as in wondering what Reagan was doing that day—they had turned their attention to other matters, which would have pleased the Gipper, who often said, "We don't ask the people to trust us; we say trust yourselves."[79] Like his fellow Americans, Reagan also prized his privacy and the future.

Oh, he'd shown up occasionally over the years in the newspapers at a birthday party for himself, or to make a surprise appearance at his Library in Simi Valley, or be seen walking in the park near his post-presidential office in Century City.

The office in Century City was warmly appointed, with Western-themed paintings including a Charles Reiffle over the desk, the chair he'd had as governor, pictures of Nancy, pictures of himself with dignitaries, including one of himself with Dwight Eisenhower, which Mike Deaver said had been in every office Reagan ever had. Remington sculptures adorned the office and photos of all the children as well.

In a glass dome was a .22 caliber bullet with the inscription "This is it!" It was the bullet pulled from his chest and that nearly killed him in March 1981.[80]

Right after leaving the presidency, Reagan went to Europe where he was knighted by Queen Elizabeth; attended a dinner in his honor at 10 Downing Street, hosted by Prime Minister Margaret Thatcher; went to Paris and was feted at the Eiffel Tower by Jacques Chirac. The French inducted Reagan into the Academy of Moral and Political Sciences, which was a great honor. He then went to Rome to see his old comrade Pope John Paul II. Finally, in the pouring rain in front of thirty thousand Polish shipyard workers, Reagan gave a barn burner of a speech after being introduced by another old comrade, Lech Wałęsa. The thirty thousand men and women then serenaded Reagan with a favorite song, "May You Live a Hundred Years."[81] He also paid his respects at the Warsaw ghetto and spoke to the Polish Parliament.[82]

Reagan called an inning for an all-star game in Anaheim, he went whitewater rafting, he went fishing in Alaska, he went to the re-dedication of the Eisenhower Library, and, for the first few weeks out of the presidency, he was startled to hear on the television, "Today, the president . . ." and then "wonder what he had done."[83] He also spoke at the Nixon Library. He spoke out against the 22nd Amendment, he spoke in favor of the line item veto, spoke out against gerrymandering, and spoke in favor of some limited gun control, putting him at odds with President Bush. But that was his only public disagreement with Bush.

And for the first time in years, his car stopped for red lights.

Startled commuters would turn their heads idly and see arguably the most famous man in the world waving and smiling at them!

He met with college students, former aides, and heads of state; wrote letters; wrote two books, including his well-received autobiography; went golfing; went for a blimp ride; went to the ranch—all in all, a dizzying whirlwind of activity.

Away from the glare, he and Mrs. Reagan went to visit his parents' gravesites.[84] He would stop for photos and always seemed to enjoy it when children asked to shake his hand. There were quiet rumors and occasional sightings but, as years passed, that was all. Around 1997, he stopped going to the office on a daily basis.

In Washington, plans were underway for the 2004 GOP convention, to be held in New York City for the first time ever. Because of the attack of a handful of insane Islamic terrorists, it was also the first time in the nation's history that thousands of civilians had been killed on the American mainland. The World Trade Center had been their target, as had the Pentagon and either the U.S. Capitol or the White House. George Bush had come to office promising a gentle foreign policy but events had forced his hand into something no one could have imagined before September 11, 2001.

The world and the world of America changed radically and forever. In the process, Bush's policies changed the organizing philosophy of the Republican Party from Reagan's "Freedom" to Bush's "Security."

The Security State led to—and was the result of—a worldwide war against terrorism.

The beleaguered head of the CIA, George Tenet, announced his resignation but most believed he'd been pushed. America was at war in two countries and with all the second-guessing going on, many fingers and long knives were pointed at Tenet. He was described as "psychologically worn down." To his ultimate misfortune, he would be forever linked to the words *slam dunk*[85] when describing for Bush the

chances of finding nuclear and biological weapons in Iraq. The phrase
and the intelligence blunder also forever scarred the Bush administration. Afghanistan and Iraq were aflame with war, and skirmishes
were breaking out elsewhere and there was no resolution, some of it
due to miscalculations by U.S. diplomats, military personnel, and
politicians.

Kerry and Bush went back and forth in their own seesaw battle
over size of forces and duration but, like the war, there was no end
in sight to this pitched political battle. In an effort to woo Catholic
voters, Bush journeyed to Vatican City to meet the pope but his campaign's polling showed him lagging with American Catholics, who
sided more with Kerry on many issues than with the president. Reagan
never had any problems with the Catholic vote, especially since he was
the first president to send an ambassador to the Vatican. Because of
the expected closeness of the election, every voting bloc took on an out-
sized importance, especially the veteran vote. Kerry was a decorated
war hero and Vietnam vet, whereas Bush had not seen combat while
in the Alabama Air National Guard where he served.

Democrats were champing at the bit to beat Bush. They just didn't
like him, didn't like his people, and certainly didn't like his policies,
even though he was the most pro-government president since Richard
Nixon. The cream of the Left met at the Campaign for America's
Future conference and there Hillary Clinton, the Xena Warrior
Princess of the Left, told the assembled liberals, "Do you remember I
once mentioned the vast right wing conspiracy? Some doubted me."[86]

It was at this confab where the matter of the nomenclature "liberal"
was deliberated. Once, it had been a prized and cherished idiom. No
longer. It came to symbolize nerdy out-of-touch bureaucrats ("faceless
bureaucrats"[87] as Reagan used to deride them) and frazzled, obnoxious
out-of-touch college professors. One prominent liberal said of his own
tribe, "The stench of their failure is simply inescapable."[88] Liberalism
had become a tired cliché. Better to shuck the whole thing and go

back to the descriptive "progressive" that had once before defined the American Left during the time of Woodrow Wilson until it had become sullied—and the Left opted for the term "liberal."

Nuclear fuel rods went missing at two New England reactors and the Nuclear Regulatory Commission asked the management of the other nuclear reactors in America to check their inventory but said they doubted the missing rods fell into the hands of terrorists.[89]

The NBA Finals were in full swing and the Stanley Cup Finals were underway. It was June and many still remembered when basketball and hockey were played in the winter. The boys of spring were fully engaged in the national pastime and in the growing game of lacrosse, and national awards resembling football's Heisman Trophy were awarded to the top male and female college players in the country. The award was sponsored by a middlebrow Washington social club.

A 5k race was taking place in Washington to support breast cancer research, and as such, the runners were decked out in pink. Studies showed the nation's capital had the highest rate of mortality for women due to breast cancer, but no one knew why.[90]

A national conference was taking place to determine how companies could control health care costs but one attendee revealed the futility. "You can't talk to a CEO without hearing them complain about the rate of increase in their health care cost."[91]

The biggest movies in June 2004 were *Harry Potter and the Prisoner of Azkaban*, *Troy*, *The Day After Tomorrow*, and *Mean Girls*, starring an up-and-coming clean-cut actress, Lindsay Lohan, whom many thought had a bright future in wholesome family movies.

Rain was forecast for much of the East Coast and cooler weather was said to be on the way for much of the mid-Atlantic and New England, though thunderstorms were also a part of the long-range projection. Meanwhile, the temperature in Los Angeles for the first week of June was typically monotonous—highs in the seventies and lows in the sixties.[92]

Unlike many around the fortieth president, Hooley never got dragged into the spotlight nor did he drag the spotlight onto himself. He was content to do his job and let others be the judge of his work. Jim was a "Reaganite's Reaganite."

After the assassination attempt, his fellow Reagan advance man Rick Ahearn became an accidental personage as he'd been standing right behind the president as John Hinckley fired six shots. Ahearn was full-sized and husky with horn-rimmed glasses. The photos of Reagan—looking to his left, reacting to the shots, depicted Ahearn right behind him—forever to become a part of presidential history.

Ahearn had been working for then-Ambassador Bush in 1979 during the lead-up to the 1980 campaign but after some disagreements and clashes Ahearn left Bush, and his friend Hooley brought him aboard the Reagan campaign. Both were as Irish as Paddy's pig. As singular as Hooley was, he was also much like most in the trusted inner Reagan circle.

Good men seek other good men, and history cannot contemplate the presidency of George Washington without considering Alexander Hamilton or Benjamin Franklin. Lincoln cannot be mulled over without taking into account John Hay or William Seward or Ulysses S. Grant. FDR cannot be seriously entertained as a president without including George C. Marshall or Cordell Hull or Henry Stimson. But all these leaders also had aides and assistants who were not written large in history and yet were still important in their own right.

So it was with Reagan. He sought public-spirited people much like him. Ethical, honest, successful, humorous, modest and patriotic. Men such as Baker and Meese but also George Shultz and Caspar Weinberger and Richard Allen and Richard Schweiker. He wasn't always successful but he tried hard to find men and women of high integrity.

One advisor and close confidant was Stu Spencer, who first got to know Reagan well in 1966, when he handled his first campaign for governor. They'd had their ups and downs but the bond and trust also ran deep, especially by and after 1980.

Spencer traveled often with Reagan on political trips, including one to Lynchburg for a meeting with Reverend Jerry Falwell. The men gathered and Falwell did all the talking; Reagan did all the listening. Falwell told Reagan he needed to emphasize social issues and other such matters, to the exclusion of all others. As they departed and got into the limousine, Spencer said to Reagan, "Are you giving any serious thought to . . ." all that? Reagan deadpanned, "Do you think I'm crazy?"[93]

Alzheimer's ravages not only its victims but also the families of victims. There is nothing to look forward to except decline, and the same was true for Nancy Davis Reagan. Nancy and Ronnie were mad for each other and had been for more than fifty years. Stu Spencer recalled many years earlier—long before the presidency—going on a political trip with Reagan and meeting him at the Los Angeles train station. Mrs. Reagan was not going and the two embraced there in the terminal saying good-bye, as the passengers and redcaps and newspaper boys and secretaries and businessmen came and went—as if the two were all alone—the only two people in the world. Spencer had never witnessed such remarkable love, such singular devotion.

For years and increasingly, Nancy Reagan had been living alone as Ronnie sank deeper and deeper into the darkness of his Alzheimer's. As he slowly faded, she tried to will him back, as if she was giving a part of her life to him to bring him back. The toll showed in her tiny physique and her mood. "She is physically frail."[94] It did not take much for her eyes to well up at the thought of the decline of her husband. By

1999, she had told Brian Lamb of C-SPAN that she and Reagan could no longer carry on conversations.[95]

It was exactly what he'd wanted to spare "Mommy" from as he'd written in his letter to the nation a little less than ten years earlier. Her spirituality never flagged but her morale drooped, and she ate infrequently. Friends who had not seen her for a time were aghast at how fragile and thin she'd become because she was spending all her time helping and worrying about Ronnie—but not about herself.

The Bush White House and the president's entourage in France were closely monitoring the developing situation in California, and a wire service reported a source as saying, "the time is getting close." Bush aides had been informed by Reagan aides that his "health had changed significantly in the past several days."[96]

The gossip mill was slowly spreading among knowledgeable people and some in the media. Former Reagan aide Mitch Daniels said, "Even though the day must ultimately come, it will be hard to say goodbye. Few Americans have done more for their country than Ronald Reagan."[97]

By the end of the day, June 4, Hooley got the long-feared phone call telling him to get to California as quickly as possible. Robert Higdon also got a call from Joanne Drake, telling him the same.[98]

Two days before, Nancy had broken down in the garage, clinging to Patti. Sobbing into her daughter's arm, she said, "Nothing is ever going to be okay without him."[99]

The death watch had begun.

# CHAPTER 2

# THE DEATH OF THE HIRED MAN

*"We've lost him."*

Fred Ryan was one of the original members of the California mafia around the Reagan White House. He was low-key, despite his towering height of six feet four inches. For years, people in national politics had known of Mike Deaver, Lyn Nofziger, Marty Anderson, Ed Meese, and the other Californians around the Gipper, but not as much about Ryan. He'd been in the presidential scheduling office and later in the White House Office of Private Sector Initiatives. Because of his work and his height, he was much respected and impossible to miss among those who knew him.

Regardless of his blond California surfer appearance and laid-back manner, for his entire life Ryan had put the "O" in overachiever. He was president of his college fraternity at USC, a standout high school football player, a nationally ranked karate competitor, and member of his college ski team. He graduated with honors from USC and again with honors from USC's law school. Later, he became the chairman of the Reagan Library, chairman of the White House Historical

Association, founder of *Politico*, and president and COO of Allbritton Communications.

Ryan had been there at the beginning and would be there at the end, a witness to and participant in the history of Ronald Reagan.

In 1987, as the Reagans were preparing for their move back to the Golden State, Ryan was tapped to become chief of staff for the post-presidential years. These were expected to be eventful years because the Reagans had always been busy and showed no signs of slowing. There would be the new office and staff to assemble and put in place. Reagan's and Mrs. Reagan's schedules would include not only social engagements but also plenty of policy speeches for the former president and charitable work for both. Plus, they had a hankering to travel, just as many former presidents had done, like Teddy Roosevelt. "In 1989, he visited London, Paris, New York, and Washington, and in 1990, he went to San Francisco, Seattle, Berlin, Warsaw, Leningrad, Moscow, Rome, New York, Dixon, Illinois and Cambridge, England," recalled John Barletta, his riding companion and longtime Secret Service agent.[1]

The rap on Reagan early on was that he was lazy, but it was a myth that had largely been dispelled during his presidency. He'd nodded off several times during boring cabinet meetings as president, but knowledgeable aides knew he preferred motion. During his tenure as governor, it came up as an issue from time to time but as staff and others knew, Reagan did not like to idle at the office. Upon moving back, Reagan also wanted to get some golf in and liked to attend Sunday services at the Bel Air Presbyterian Church. In church, he always sat on the aisle because, as daughter Patti said, her father was "claustrophobic."[2] He also preferred the aisle seat on airplanes.

As of January 1989, the plan was for Reagan to go to his new office in Century City for meetings, business, photographs, and such but if nothing was pressing, he wasn't going to stick around. At their new house in Bel Air, there was a gym in the basement where Reagan would work out. They had traded down from the 55,000-square-foot White House to the 7,000-square-foot home, but if truth be known, he preferred the rustic Rancho del Cielo, only 1,800 square feet, outside of Santa Barbara. Reagan had owned several ranches before finding this "ranch in the sky" in 1974.

There was a lot of time at the ranch—about one week per month—built into the post-presidential schedule. In his Farewell Address to the nation in January 1989, Reagan made clear that "the sweet part" of going home to California was freedom on his ranch.[3] He drew energy from Rancho del Cielo, and he needed to go there often. There would also be a lot involved in the planning and building of Reagan's presidential library but like many things in his life, there were fireworks too.

In 1991, Ryan got caught in the cross fire between some conservatives like Lyn Nofziger over the departure of Ed Meese, Bill Clark, and Martin Anderson from the Library board. It was falsely assumed they'd been ousted by moderates there, and that somehow Ryan was the architect of the in-house coup; but in fact, all three men were on the original board, and service on the board was limited. The men's terms had simply expired, and Ryan was blameless, but this did not stop some from grumbling against him over the matter.[4]

Back in the fall of 1988, Ryan had gone to Los Angeles to search for office space. He didn't tell anyone he was looking for space on behalf of Ronald Reagan, and one building struck his fancy. When he spoke to the owner, Marvin Davis, Ryan was tartly informed the newly built ultra-modern Fox Plaza was booked. Yet when Davis later found out that Ryan worked for Reagan and was looking for a business suite for the Reagans, the top floor somehow became available immediately, even though filming of the movie *Die Hard* was just wrapping up.

"They still had all the props up. There were literally spent gun shells on the ground, fake broken windows, all kinds of stuff." Ryan returned to Washington to tell the Reagans he'd found a great suite in Century City that had a terrific view of both the Pacific Ocean and the hills, plus it was near their home in Bel Air. The Reagans were pleased, though the Secret Service was less so. "You've just picked a building where a movie was made about how terrorists can blow it up," an agent noted to Ryan.[5]

There was also a touch of poignancy to the leasing of the office as it was near the location where Reagan's film career had begun many years earlier. Reagan often liked to go to the top of the building and look out on the Pacific to watch the morning sun burn off the fog and reveal the Channel Islands in the distance, recalled Ryan.[6] Reagan also kept a pair of binoculars in his office, and with these he could see his house in Bel Air, said Joanne Drake, who later succeeded Ryan to become Reagan's final chief of staff.[7]

According to a pretty young aide, Peggy Grande, who'd begun as an intern and worked her way up to executive assistant to the former president, he received "buckets and buckets" of invitations and letters immediately upon his return to the Golden State. It was a standing order that all letters were to be answered, and promptly.[8] Another aide with his hands full was Mark Weinberg, who was in charge of the post-presidential media relations. Reagan was inundated with interview requests from writers, electronic media, and book authors. Weinberg was an eight-year veteran of the Reagan White House, and because of his yeoman-like work, Ken Duberstein had asked him to go with the Reagans to California, which he gladly did.[9]

Reagan was supposed to take off two weeks after January 20, 1989, but after a few days, he got bored and showed up unexpectedly at his new workplace, as Ryan and others were in dungarees unloading boxes, hanging pictures, and the like. When they found out the Gipper was heading in, the staff hastily pulled together a makeshift office for him and after he settled in, they went back to work.

A couple of hours later, Reagan came out and handed Ryan a sheet of paper, telling him to set up meetings with the people listed. Ryan scanned it and saw no familiar names. "Can I just ask who these people are?" Ryan asked Reagan. "Well, they've been calling," said Reagan nonchalantly. It turned out that the phone lines had been installed incorrectly and while the receptionist sat at her desk, her phone not ringing, the calls were going through right to Reagan, who naturally answered them.

"The phone rings and he picks it up. 'Hello. Yes, I'm calling for Ronald Reagan. This is Ronald Reagan. What would you like? I'd like to come and see you. OK.' He's writing these things down. He hangs up. The phone rings again. It's somebody else. 'I'd like to speak to Ronald Reagan,' because everyone who called, they want to speak to Ronald Reagan," Ryan mirthfully recalled. Those calling just for the heck of it were average John and Jane Q. Citizens, only to find themselves on the line with the former president of the United States![10]

But true to his word, each was invited in for a treasured meeting with Reagan. One guy told Ryan he wanted to bring his neighbor, but Ryan sternly said, "Look buddy, lightning struck once here. You're not going to get a second chance."[11]

The rule agreed to by Ryan and the Reagans was that anyone who worked in the White House or on the campaigns or in Sacramento or had some professional association with the Gipper would be invited to come to Century City for a photo with President Reagan.[12] Even after the Alzheimer's, he was still going into the office for photographs and meetings. In 1996, Lt. John Shirley—a decorated firefighter from Syracuse, New York—got to meet Reagan again, after first meeting him at a CPAC conference in the 1980s.

When not at the ranch entertaining the likes of Margaret Thatcher and Mikhail Gorbachev, Reagan was sometimes seen at the local California Pizza Kitchen, or Christmas shopping at a mall near his office in Century City. In the first years out of office, the Reagans often went to Chasen's restaurant and sat in the booth where he'd once proposed to her. But he did not consider his time back in California as taking his leave from life. "I don't use the word 'retirement.' I think there are a lot of things yet to be done."¹³ Reagan was planning on writing his memoirs and producing a tome of his speeches. He'd even been approached by some studios about taking up acting again but on this he quietly demurred.

During Gorbachev's visit, Reagan had given the former Soviet premier a cowboy hat that the Russian promptly put on backward. Not wanting to embarrass Gorbachev, Reagan said nothing and the two were photographed, Reagan the confident cowboy and Gorbachev the Moscow city slicker. Later in his new blue jeep, given to him by Nancy, he gave the nervous Russian a tour of the ranch, driving over extremely rough dirt roads, some of them barely passable. They met several times, both men long out of office, and Ryan said a genuine affection had grown between the two. They joshed with each other and argued over economics, but it was clear the banter was all in fun.¹⁴

The Reagans got crosswise with the media over their new house in Bel Air, paid for with a loan by some wealthy friends at a cost of 2.5 million dollars. It was later repaid in full by the Reagans. Also, Reagan went to Japan for a couple of short speeches for which he was paid an enormous amount of money, 2 million dollars, and had to eat some crow over that as well, even though he needed the money. The government provided for some staff and offices and franking privileges, but there were more costs associated with being an ex-president than most anticipated. Reagan had never been a wealthy man—though he was fortunate not to have experienced what Jimmy Carter did upon his return to Georgia in 1981. The Georgian found his carefully constructed blind trust a mess, and he was deeply in debt.

In fact, Reagan was aware of appearances, saying just after leaving Washington, "No . . . there's a kind of a lingering feeling that would look a little bit like trying to cash in on this job that I've had."¹⁵ He spoke around LA occasionally, both funny and fascinating. In 1991, he was addressing the local Junior Chamber of Commerce and departed from his prepared remarks to quip, "When [Saddam Hussein] was born, they didn't give his mother a medical bill—they fined her for dumping toxic waste."[16]

They were anything but recluses although he and Nancy never attended another presidential inaugural after 1989.

Saturday, June 5, began as an uneventful day for the rest of the world, other than for the families of five American troops who were killed in Baghdad. President George W. Bush was in Rome for a meeting with the pope and Prime Minister Silvio Berlusconi before heading to Normandy for the sixtieth anniversary of the D-day invasion. The practice of speaking at Normandy on June 6 had begun with Ronald Reagan on the fortieth anniversary. Bill Clinton spoke on the fiftieth and now Bush would speak. The ranks of the American and British and Canadian veterans who landed ashore as part of the greatest invasion in history, or parachuted in, or flew missions, like Army Air Corps Lt. Dick Snyder, were thinning quickly. Snyder was the exception even though his P-47 had been shot down flying close air support for the invasion, and he spent eleven months in a German POW camp as a result.

The highlight for Bush in Europe was the speech at Normandy with a backdrop of 9,387 marble stone Christian crosses—and Star of David cenotaphs—where American GIs were buried.

Twenty years earlier in 1984, Reagan had started the tradition of celebrating the day when America saved Europe from Nazism. It became a presidential routine, one of many initiated by Reagan. Pointe Du Hoc had become famous for liberation after Reagan spoke, when before it had just been infamous for the tyranny of the German occupation at that very location.

It was all curious, though, because the man who'd led the Normandy invasion, General Dwight David Eisenhower, did not attend the tenth anniversary of the invasion—even though in 1954 he was president of the United States—yet Ike instead only issued a statement marking the occasion.

President Eisenhower visited Normandy in 1964 for the twentieth anniversary, but this was three plus years after his presidency and
again he gave no speech while there. He was accompanied by Walter
Cronkite and a camera crew from CBS for a documentary entitled
*D-day Plus 20 Years*. Cronkite had covered the D-day invasion as a
young reporter for United Press. Lyndon Johnson was president in
1964 but he did not visit Normandy, although he did send a delegation
headed by General Omar Bradley.[17] In June 1974, Richard Nixon was
fighting a losing battle, preoccupied with his political survival. The last
thing on his mind was the anniversary of D-day.

Huge anti-war protesters greeted Bush in Italy, and the government
deployed more than ten thousand police officers to quell the violence.
Pope John Paul II implored Bush to end the hostilities in Iraq. The
awful hangover of Abu Ghraib, where Iraqi prisoners had been abused
by U.S. troops, still hung over the national debate and the war itself.

In 1987, President Reagan had sent an unequivocal letter to the
Senate—rejecting the advice of Douglas Feith, his own deputy assistant defense secretary for negotiations—stating his belief and his
policy that U.S. troops in combat settings must act at all times as
gentlemen and officers.[18] American soldiers were not to make war or
otherwise abuse or chastise civilians and other noncombatants, the
fortieth president said.

Reagan subscribed to the longstanding rules of the U.S. military
and the Geneva Conventions, both of which made clear that soldiers
should behave correctly and civilly toward the population of invaded
countries. Reagan was acting on the advice of his defense secretary
Caspar Weinberger. But seventeen years later, there was widespread
and sharp criticism of U.S. troops in Afghanistan and Iraq about how
some were treating the local civilian populations, in contravention of
Reagan's previous orders.

Senator John Kerry, the soon-to-be Democratic presidential nominee, unveiled his own plan for national health insurance and Barry Bonds hit his 673rd home run.[19] Everybody was figuring him as a lead pipe cinch for Cooperstown on the first ballot, despite the fact that many fans didn't like him or his attitude and his antics when he ran the bases. The sportswriters did, at least in public.

In Granby, Colorado, a local auto mechanic was angered about proposed changes in zoning ordinances by the town government so he proposed to change the landscape more to his liking by taking an armored bulldozer and essentially leveling the entire town as the police repeatedly fired at and bombed the bulldozer, but to no effect.

Bush sent the nomination of former Missouri senator John Danforth to the Congress for their advice and consent as the U.S. ambassador to the United Nations. Some Democrats squawked about a handful of votes that the moderate Republican had cast against the liberal orthodoxy but Danforth was a man of the Midwest: unshakable, stoic, impossible to anger or intimidate. He was also deeply devout, and in addition to being an attorney and a former U.S. senator, he was also an ordained Episcopalian minister. Danforth was an heir to the Ralston Purina Company, maker of fine products including dog food, but he was anything but a professional inheritor or wastrel.

Danforth was so well thought of, the Clinton administration appointed him to lead a blue ribbon commission to investigate the tragedy at Waco, when the FBI and the BATF stormed a compound comprised of Branch Davidians, a religious sect, and dozens died, including women and children, at the hands of government agents. Some liberals despised him, however, as he'd been the chief sponsor of the nomination of Clarence Thomas to the Supreme Court. He'd been briefly considered as a running mate for Bush in 2000 before they settled on Dick Cheney, who was a well-thought-of quiet man, formerly of Congress.

The government was debating a new form of identification for American citizens to cross the borders into Mexico and Canada that emitted a radio frequency. The world had changed since September 11, 2001, and a security state, aided by contractors and their lobbyists' hunger for federal largess, was quickly taking root in what was once the freest country in the world. The concepts of privacy and personal dignity and unfettered freedom of movement were devolving into antiquated concepts, as was the old expression, "It's a free country!" An unusual coalition of those elites who favored a collectivist state with more economic regulation over the citizenry was merging with a corporate America culture that pursued a bottom line in spite of any risks to the Constitution.

For all the dismissive concepts by the establishment against left wing and right wing populists, concerned about the agendas of such groups as the Trilateral Commission and the Council on Foreign Relations, their fears seemed to be well founded.

Word was slowly leaking out, rumors spreading, that Ronald Reagan's last breath was close. After ten years of suffering, of never good news but always bad news, the Gipper's time was approaching. Some suspected leaks by the Bush White House staffers while others believed that some Reagan family members were talking in the background to reporters about Reagan's worsening condition.[20] ABC News reported, "And just in the last week, his health took a turn for the worst . . ."[21] Joanne Drake was desperately attempting to keep control of the story. She'd been through this the year before when CNN inadvertently posted Reagan's obituary on its website, and it caused a momentary din.[22]

The family had been summoned to his bedside at 668 St. Cloud Road in Bel Air. Both his children from his second marriage to Nancy, Ronald Prescott and Patti, had arrived early that morning, summoned when it was believed that the time was near. Ron had been in Hawaii but rushed back to his home in Seattle, packed some clothes, and headed for LA.

Reagan was now nearer to death. The family and close friends and aides had kept a tight lid on things but inevitably rumors began to leak out that Reagan was *fading, going*. Though he was physically strong nearly to the end, routinely only Mrs. Reagan and a live-in nurse now saw the failing Reagan. A source close to the situation told a reporter, "Don't be surprised. Time is getting close."[23]

Reagan had been staying for several years in what had been his den, but now converted to his bedroom although it was spare. "His room" was "a hospital bed, an armchair, a small television set for whichever nurse was on duty, and a table full of medical paraphernalia," recalled Patti.[24]

Joanne Drake was forced to deal with more and more media inquiries about Reagan's condition. Bluntly she said, "He's 93 years old. He's had Alzheimer's disease for 10 years. There are plenty of rumors. When there is something significant to report I will do so." Drake had more than a plate full of matters to deal with from the Reagans to the staff to the presidential library, the planning for the funeral, and a thousand other things. In the past day, more than three hundred calls had come into her office because of the spreading rumors.[25]

Mrs. Reagan took just one phone call from a reporter, her old friend Mike Wallace of CBS. They had known each other since she was a student at Smith College, sixty years earlier. "Is it conceivable that it could happen this weekend?" Wallace asked Nancy. "This is it," she disconsolately replied.[26]

She periodically spoke to two other old friends, Stu Spencer and Mike Deaver, in the days leading up to her husband's final moments. She also spoke with her confidant, Fred Ryan, and to former Canadian prime minister Brian Mulroney. "Brian, I think the end is near," she told him. "It's a great loss for the United States and for the world," he reportedly told Mrs. Reagan.[27] She also spoke regularly with Joanne and with Robert Higdon.

Nancy had been Ronnie's support system and now at the end she needed her own as well. She found it in Patti, with whom she'd battled for years, and who was now her mother's rock, her port in the storm. They tried to busy themselves with tea and small meals but no one was very hungry—just hungry for memories and the imagined one last conversation with him.

The day before, Patti and Mike Reagan and Mike's children had gathered around their father's bed in the room that had once been his office, as they were told of the eventuality. But it hadn't come as thought and both departed. Patti went home and spent a sleepless night looking at the moon, tossing over their turbulent life together. She returned early the next morning to find the frail man still alive, still fighting. She hoped her brother Ron could be there before the end. Fortunately, he arrived in time to comfort his mother and sister and say good-bye to his father one last time.[28] It was all taking place in the small den that had been his bedroom for years, in which Nancy had dinner each evening with her husband.[29]

The human heart beats approximately 72 times per minute, which translates to more than 100,000 times per day, more than 37 million times per year and, depending on the lifespan, roughly about 2.5 billion beats over a lifetime. Now Reagan's heart was nearing its finish.

As Patti recounted in *The Long Goodbye,*

> My brother is . . . sitting beside the hospital bed; his eyes are soft and sad. His hand is resting on our father's back—a back grown thin, the bones sharp and narrow as twigs . . . My father's breathing is even more ragged, and his closed eyes are rimmed in shadow . . . As the morning goes on and sun burns through the fog, his breathing grows more threadbare. At several moments we think this is it. We tighten the

circle around him, touch him lightly, tell him we love him. He inhales sharply; he makes a snoring sound and we laugh through our tears . . . there is nothing else we can do . . . Just before one o'clock we know that this really is it. His breathing is telling us—so shallow it sounds like it can't even be reaching his lungs. His face is angled toward my mother's. He opens his eyes—both eyes—wide. They are focused and blue. They haven't been blue like that in more than a year but they are now. My father looks straight at my mother, holds onto the sight of her face for a moment or two, and then gently closes his eyes and stops breathing. The room is quiet except for soft weeping; my mother whispers, "That's the greatest gift you could have given me."[30]

At 1:09 p.m. Pacific daylight time, 4:09 p.m. on the East Coast,[31] the fortieth president of the United States—Dutch, the Gipper, Ronnie, Ron, "The Teflon President," "The Great Communicator," Ronnie Ray-Gun, Leader of the Free World, Conqueror of Worlds, Beloved, Hated, Destroyer of Evil Empires—Ronald Wilson Reagan was dead.

At his passing, Reagan was surrounded by Ron, Patti, and Nancy. Dr. Shaack was also there as was the day nurse, Laura.[32] Michael unfortunately arrived after his father passed.[33]

Reagan's death came almost to the day of the sixtieth anniversary of the greatest invasion in history, one that liberated a continent and millions of people. Fox News was the first television network to report the passing of the Gipper at just a few minutes past 4:09 p.m. in the east, having first "teased" the story by saying on air that bad news was forthcoming from California about Reagan.

All four children including Maureen, who'd predeceased her father, often had rocky relations with their parents over the years, but much of that anger and hostility had dissipated at least as far as the public was concerned; however, privately Michael sometimes fumed over his stepmother and the people around her. He issued his own statement on the passing of his father, saying that he "changed America and the world for the better."[34]

Drake called Hooley, and choking back tears simply said, "Jim, he's gone."[35] They'd left nothing to chance, and the first page of "The Book" said she was to call "Duke (Blackwood), Gary Foster, Fred Ryan, Mike Wagner, Jim Hooley, Mike Deaver and Rick Ahearn."[36] "The Book" was the plan that had been developed over the years for the implementation of Reagan's funeral. Bemused by the planning for his own bereavement, Reagan liked to josh Ryan over the whole matter.

Nancy called Fred and through her tears told him, "We've lost him." Ryan told her he would leave Washington immediately for the West Coast and then discovered he was crying too.[37]

The fact that Ronald Reagan had made it nearly ten years after announcing his own Alzheimer's, and at his age of ninety-three—a life that included a lot of rough and tumble living, that featured surgeries and being bucked off horses, and broken bones, and cancers, and a near-fatal shooting—was a testament to his physique, his stamina, his genes, and his outlook.

He'd always been a superior athlete and a particularly outstanding swimmer. In 1932, he was offered a chance to try out for the U.S. Olympic swim team but declined, as he needed to make money for school.[38] He loved all sports except tennis and jogging. Bill Buckley recounted how years earlier at their first meeting where Reagan was to introduce the writer to a packed hall in Los Angles, the sound system had been turned off and no one was available to get it working. Reagan spotted a third-story window and managed to climb out on the ledge, break the window, climb in, and turn on the public address system, all the while in a suit and tie and never mussing his hair.[39]

Even after his Alzheimer's was revealed, Reagan still went golfing, swimming, and horseback riding frequently, and to the office for several years, said Joanne Drake. Even in his advancing years, "he was still the same kind, humble, funny guy . . . his natural personality was a very calm demeanor. The only time I ever saw him get angry was when he couldn't think of a word," Drake said. He kept going to the office, Drake said, in part because the doctors said routine was important. "The last thing we wanted was for him to be sitting home, doing nothing. That frustrated him and it frustrated Mrs. Reagan."

Reagan kept active, going to the office and going to the Library until 1999. And Drake said he was still going golfing, still going to lunch as of 1998 and 1999.[40] The state of California took the opportunity to unveil a Reagan license plate, and sales were brisk.

Reagan had been in near complete seclusion since his ninetieth birthday in 2001, however, when a touching photo was released of him and Nancy in matching red sweaters with a cake, kissing. His hair, cut shorter than what people remembered, had whitened greatly but other than that he still looked to all like the Gipper they'd remembered, albeit older. He was "too ill," however, to attend a birthday celebration for him attended by seven hundred people at the Library. And as it turned out, it was the last photo to be released of Reagan. In 2001, the Century City office was closed and Drake "downsized" the staff and offices, moving to Westwood.[41] When they cleaned out his desk, inside they found an ancient letter from his mother, Nelle, to her son with the advice, "if you learn to love reading, you will never be alone."[42]

A military honor guard moved immediately to protect the remains of President Ronald Reagan, and a quickly growing media contingent gathered outside the Reagan home despite the fact they'd been asked to keep a respectable distance from the fence surrounding the property. Mrs. Reagan issued a short and correct statement, but that was the public Mrs. Reagan. In private, it was another matter. Ryan said,

"She was just totally overcome."[43] Her husband of more than half a century was gone.

"My family and I would like the world to know that President Reagan has passed away after ten years of Alzheimer's disease at 93,"[44] Nancy Reagan said in her initial statement. The official cause of death was pneumonia. As the Reagan sons departed, they both civilly nodded to the media. Mike left in his Jeep and was heard to politely say to some reporters, "Thank you."[45] Within a short period of time, a police presence showed up as a swelling crowd gathered outside the Reagan home and then a trickle of flowers began to arrive, to be left on the side of the street, the sidewalk, and the fence.

Nancy Reagan was not just losing her husband. It was a life and a life partnership. "The central Reagan command meets in bed at night," said Teddy White.[46] They were best friends and soul mates, and his letters to her over the years left no doubt as to the depth of their mutual love. It was not unusual for his letters to open, "Darling Mommy Poo"[47] and "To My Roommate."[48]

Unlike the Kennedys, the Nixons, and the Clintons, the Reagans did not have separate bedrooms in the White House. It was once said that if Reagan had wanted to be the best shoe salesman in the world, she would have made sure he was. It was just that he wanted to be a national and international leader and he never would have without her. In more than fifty years of marriage, there had never been one tiny rumor about them or the state of their marriage. Except for the shallow Kitty Kelley, even the foulest Reagan haters knew better than to ever go there. Reagan wrote a handful of letters to friends who'd commiserated with him and Nancy about the "total dishonesty" manufactured by Kelley in a widely discredited book about Nancy Reagan.[49]

Their love had been one of the great stories of the American presidency. She'd devoted years to helping him rise, and now, over the last ten years, was helping him toward the inevitable fall. Bob Colacello, a personal friend who'd written an intimate portrayal of the two, said, "I think until quite recently, he still had some sense of who she was and that she was there for him."[50] Even as Reagan succumbed over the years, she was still his partner, still looking out for him, still protecting him. "She was called ruthless," claimed one wire story. But she wasn't afraid to protect him. Once she stormed to trusted aide and close friend Mike Deaver, "What have you done to my husband?"[51]

Unfortunately for Nancy Reagan, the role of family disciplinarian fell to her because as Reagan himself said, "I should have been sterner than I was." The children agreed. Maureen said he was a "soft touch" and Ron said his father was a "better friend than a father."[52] So Nancy had to often be the heavy and get on the Reagan children's cases about school, life, responsibility, relationships, and behavior, especially with his travel schedule for General Electric and, later, national politics. He wrote in his diaries about Ron hanging up on him and arguing with Nancy and how mad he was at his son for doing so.[53]

When it came to governing, however, he could be tough, such as the time when as governor he personally mediated a strike by Los Angeles bus drivers against the city. Or the time, also as governor, when thousands of student protesters descended on the state capitol, angry over cuts in education spending. Rather than hiding out in his office, Reagan went out to meet with them and tersely explain his policies.

The very first story moved by the Associated Press was a short list of books about Ronald Reagan including those by Lou Cannon, Nancy Reagan, Mike Deaver, and others. The very second story moved by the AP came from NBC.com, written by Tom Curry, and was a very harsh review of Reagan's life that used tired catchphrases such as "glib," "doctrinaire," and that his "adversaries" said he was "uninformed—a mere actor."[54]

Curry also tracked down Ralph Reed, former deputy to Pat Robertson at the Christian Coalition, who offered a very harsh view of the just deceased Reagan. Reed "viewed the Reagan presidency with chagrin. 'His eight years in office did little to transform a political culture that had become insensitive to religious values and uncaring about innocent human life,'" said Reed. The slight, former assistant and business partner of Jack Abramoff elaborated and said conservatives "woke up the morning after Reagan's two terms to discover that many maladies still afflicted our nation and many pathologies had grown worse." Reed was the only person interviewed for the story.[55]

The rest of the NBC story followed Reed's lead, superficially focusing on the failings of Reagan's father ("alcoholic . . . ne'er-do-well"), the failing of Reagan as an actor ("the foil to leading men . . ."), and the failings of Reagan's presidency. "Bitburg, S&L mishaps . . . Reagan made some costly miscalculations. In the last two years of his presidency Reagan was hobbled . . . by . . . the Iran-Contra fiasco . . ."[56]

The story never mentioned the restoration of the American spirit, the revival of the national economy, the crushing defeat of Soviet communism, or the fortieth president's many other accomplishments.

Having failed to defeat him in life, the NBC story was typical of much of the national media this day and in the coming days—they would attempt to defeat him in death and bury his legacy once and for all.

And yet, the early praise of Reagan that was offered by some of his international adversaries and political opponents was more fulsome than it was from some so-called friends and certainly the national media or the universities. The former deputy foreign minister of the Soviet Union Alexander Bessmertnykh shot down the myth that Reagan was a creation of his staff or his 4 x 6 notes. "He would throw those notes away and start talking to us in that direct way . . ." Bessmertnykh elaborated that "he admired the president and thought that he was a very good negotiator and that he had ideals . . ."[57]

Within minutes of confirming the passing of Reagan, all three networks broke away from their regular programming for the announcement. At 7:00 p.m., National Public Radio went with special Reagan coverage, hosted by Linda Wertheimer, a liberal, and wife of longtime liberal and Reagan critic Fred Wertheimer. The broadcast began, "A former actor and broadcaster . . ." Indeed, the first several minutes on NPR focused exclusively on Reagan's movie and television career. By the time Wertheimer and her cohost, Neal Conan, got to reporting on the 1980 campaign, they completely messed up the real story of the famous Nashua debate while glossing over the meaning and historical importance of the 1980 election.

A derisive reference was also made to the "so-called Reagan Revolution," and even his athletic skills as a football player at Eureka were questioned in the news report on the taxpayer-funded radio network. Further, NPR implied that Nancy Reagan's father had opened up political doors for his new son-in-law but this was yet another misnomer. Even in reporting on Reagan's announcement of his own Alzheimer's, the story reported that he'd done so "in a shaky handwritten letter."[58] One word had been crossed out but other than that, in fact, it was a pretty firm and clear script for a man eighty-three years of age.

Fred Ryan had been there almost ten years earlier when Reagan was told of his deadly affliction. It was a Saturday, just before the 1994 elections, and they were at the Reagans' home in Bel Air. Reagan had gone to the Mayo Clinic every year for many years to get complete physical and psychological testing that consisted of remembering sequences of numbers, colors, and other tests for acuity and memory. He'd passed each year with flying colors until the spring of 1994 when doctors noted he was slipping, "seeing memory loss that was more than age-appropriate."[59]

Later that fall, the decision was made to tell Reagan himself. It was a Saturday afternoon in November. They were in the brightly decorated library of the house in Bel Air. The afternoon sun was streaking through the glass windows. Nancy Reagan already knew; she had been told the night before by Dr. Oliver "Ollie" Beahrs, Reagan's doctor at Mayo. "Very upset," she called Ryan and told him she needed him to be at the house the next day when Reagan was told.[60]

Mrs. Reagan was weeping as the doctor matter of factly told Reagan of the diagnosis. Ryan recalled that Reagan took it in stride, never showed any emotion, and understood what he was facing. Almost immediately he went to a small round table and pulled out a piece of paper and a pen. Ryan asked the president what he was doing, and he replied, "Well, I guess we've got to tell some people about this."[61] With that, he composed the letter read and heard round the world, announcing his affliction.

Nov. 5, 1994

My Fellow Americans,

I have recently been told that I am one of the millions of Americans who will be afflicted with Alzheimer's Disease.

Upon learning this news, Nancy and I had to decide whether as private citizens we would keep this a private matter or whether we would make this news known in a public way.

In the past Nancy suffered from breast cancer and I had my cancer surgeries. We found through our open disclosures we were able to raise public awareness. We were happy that as a result many more people underwent testing. They were treated in early stages and able to return to normal, healthy lives.

So now, we feel it is important to share it with you. In opening our hearts, we hope this might promote greater awareness of this condition. Perhaps it will encourage a clearer understanding of the individuals and families who are affected by it.

At the moment I feel just fine. I intend to live the remainder of the years God gives me on this earth doing the things I have always done. I will continue to share life's journey with my beloved Nancy and my family. I plan to enjoy the great outdoors and stay in touch with my friends and supporters.

Unfortunately, as Alzheimer's Disease progresses, the family often bears a heavy burden. I only wish there was some way I could spare Nancy from this painful experience. When the time comes I am confident that with your help she will face it with faith and courage.

In closing let me thank you, the American people, for giving me the great honor of allowing me to serve as your President. When the Lord calls me home, whenever that may be, I will leave with the greatest love for this country of ours and eternal optimism for its future.

I now begin the journey that will lead me into the sunset of my life. I know that for America there will always be a bright dawn ahead.

Thank you, my friends. May God always bless you.

Sincerely,

Ronald Reagan[62]

Reagan must have sensed the historic nature of the letter, as he dated it and he almost never dated his handwritten communications.

"They had dreams of what they wanted to do," said Ryan, but that was all gone. Reagan showed Fred the letter and said, "I guess we should get this typed up," but after Ryan looked at it, he thought, "It's in the president's own hand. That's the best possible indication of his thinking . . ."[63] Ryan departed for the office to release the supposed "shaky" letter to the world. The Reagans then left for the ranch.

Mrs. Reagan called the four children and told them about their father's affliction, and Ryan, arriving home, noted that during the Notre Dame–USC football game, the Gipper's diagnosis was announced live on national television.[64] That the game pitted the school where he depicted George Gipp and a school from his beloved California only deepened the poignancy. Later, he made calls to the board members of the Library and close associates and friends to let them know.

The only times Reagan ever discussed his Alzheimer's was in

private with Ryan and a couple of others, but only in the context of
what his decline would do to him. After Reagan's remarkable letter, his
doctors issued a statement explaining how the Reagans went to Mayo
each year for testing. It continued,

> Over the past twelve months we began to notice from President
> Reagan's test results symptoms indicating the possibility of early
> stage Alzheimer's disease. Additional testing and an extensive obser-
> vation over the past few weeks have led us to conclude that President
> Reagan is entering the early stages of this disease. Although his
> health is otherwise good, it is expected that as the years go on it will
> begin to deteriorate. Unfortunately, at this time there is no cure for
> Alzheimer's disease and no effective treatment exists that arrests
> its progression. We applaud President Reagan for the courage he
> has demonstrated by sharing this personal information with the
> American people.[65]

Five doctors signed the statement, including Beahrs and General
John Hutton, MD, of the Uniformed Services. Hutton frankly told a
reporter several years later that Reagan was "in the throes of continual
neurological degradation."[66]

Nancy Reagan always thought there was a correlation between
his fall from a horse in 1991 when he hit his head and the onset of
Alzheimer's. Everybody around him said for the first several years out
of office he was fine, his memory was fine, and it may be that she had
a point.

In 2013, *Neurology* magazine published an article saying there
was potentially a causal relationship between head trauma and
Alzheimer's.[67]

Sergeant Murphy was the last horse he ever rode.[68]

Margaret Thatcher on June 5, 2004, understood better than most the
complete significance of Reagan's time on earth—and not just that

he was a nice man who told funny jokes. "He will be missed not only by those who knew him and not only by the nation that he served so proudly and loved so deeply, but also by millions of men and women who live in freedom today because of the policies he pursued," the Iron Lady said of the Great Lion.[69]

Jack Kemp had once elegantly called Reagan the "last great lion of the twentieth century," evocative of Churchill, FDR, MacArthur, de Gaulle, and Eisenhower.

The Great Lion Reagan was now dead.

The details surrounding Reagan's death were simple and reserved in an effort to protect his and Mrs. Reagan's privacy.

Behind the scenes, tacky and tasteless questions were asked but none in the open as most reporters chose to respect the wishes of Mrs. Reagan and few details were reported.

The weather in Los Angeles was hot—ninety-four degrees—and mostly clear.[70]

Tributes began to pour forth. The Reverend Billy Graham said in a statement, "The love between Ronald and Nancy Reagan was an example to the nation."[71] A kind but ill-timed letter dated June 5—the day of Reagan's passing—from Graham to Nancy had arrived and said he was aware of Reagan's failing health.[72] Nancy Reagan had originally wanted Graham to preside over the funeral of her husband but Graham's health was poor, so she turned to John Danforth, former Republican senator and ordained Episcopalian priest, several years earlier.

Senator Jesse Helms released a two-page statement praising his old friend.[73] President George W. Bush said, "A great American life has come to an end."[74] Bush had learned of Reagan's passing after Fred Ryan had called his chief of staff Andy Card.[75] Ryan was also tasked with calling former president George H. W. Bush, Jim Baker, Ed Meese, and other close friends and associates.[76]

Bush stepped before the media in Paris late in the evening and read a heartfelt and profound statement.

On behalf of our whole nation, Laura and I offered her and the Reagan family our prayers and our condolences . . . He leaves behind a nation he restored and a world he helped save . . . Now, in laying our leader to rest, we say thank you. He always told us that for America, the best was yet to come. We comfort ourselves in the knowledge that this is true for him too. His work is done. And now a shining city awaits him. May God bless Ronald Reagan.[77]

Bush was visibly moved as evidenced by the tears that welled up in his eyes. And then he ordered the flags at the White House lowered to half-staff.

Simultaneously, governors around the nation ordered flags flown at half-staff, as did ballparks, racetracks, and other facilities.

It was only the beginning.

In Kennebunkport, former president George H. W. Bush and Barbara Bush went outside to meet the press, as well, and express their condolences. There Bush revealed he'd spoken to Nancy Reagan just hours before Reagan's time on earth was over. "She made clear to us that his death was imminent." Expanding, the Bushes were gracious and unfailingly kind in their comments. He said, "Barbara and I mourn the loss of a great president and for us a great friend." Mrs. Bush said, "I don't think I've ever known anyone who was so innately polite. Ronald Reagan was a gentleman."[78] She also kindly said of Nancy, "We love her and we're missing her husband already."[79]

Tastelessly, a reporter asked Bush if he'd seen any sign of "mental deterioration during his tenure in the White House," but Bush contemptuously brushed it away, saying he'd never seen anything of the sort. The AP story also mistakenly reported that Reagan had never served in the military[80] when in fact he had, first in the reserves and later as an active duty captain during World War II, though he did not see action.

The relationship between Bush and Reagan had been complicated to say the least. Bush, ever the gentleman, often spoke of their friendship but in fact, there was more of a slowly growing mutual respect, like neighbors who discovered something impressive about each other but still did not socialize. ABC noted, "There was some talk after Ronald Reagan left office that there was bad blood or some hurt feelings."[81]

For one thing, Reagan and the Bushes were simply from different social classes. Though Nancy Davis Reagan was from the Bushes' economic class, she and Barbara Bush eyed each other warily in spite of both attending—though Nancy graduated in the spring of 1943 and Barbara entered in the fall of 1943 but did not graduate—Smith College. It was noted "over the past quarter-century the relationship between the families has been strained for periods by political ambition, social resentment and a lack of chemistry between two formidable first ladies."[82]

Plus they had battled mightily for the 1980 nomination, Reagan the conservative and Bush the moderate, and bad blood, which never completely resolved itself, had developed between their staffs, even as the two men got comfortable as running mates and later became friends as president and vice president.

In Reagan's principal hometowns of Dixon and Tampico, citizens who knew Dutch in the old days shared with reporters and others their recollections of the handsome young lifeguard who grew up to be president. His college, Eureka, had been somewhat ambivalent about how to treat Reagan over the years as a large contingent of the faculty was politically liberal but by 1980 had unabashedly embraced its most famous alumnus. "In January 1974, graduates of tiny Eureka College pulled out their pens to complete a routine questionnaire from the alumni office. 'Present employment: governor of Calif,' scribbled 1932 graduate Ronald Reagan."[83]

Reagan wrote that it was because of Eureka College that he'd gotten involved in national politics because getting involved was expected of students there.[84] In the Ronald Reagan Peace Garden at the school, flowers and jars of jelly beans began to pile up at the base of a handsome bust of Dutch Reagan.

Dixon had no internal conflicts or liberal opponents. His boyhood home was a museum and designated federal historic location, and next to the house was a life-sized statue of Reagan. Dixon citizens were already laying flowers at the base of the statue. On the other side of the small and charming if also spare house was a tiny museum and gift shop run by a handful of energetic and devoted women. At the First Christian Church, Disciples of Christ, where Reagan and his mother, Nelle, attended, the Reverend Lynn Bond was presiding, telling the congregation, "The son of a shoe salesman becomes president of the United States. It truly is an American story."[85] Reagan had been born in Tampico, thirty miles away. At the time of his birth in 1911, Tampico had a larger population than it did at the time of his death ninety-three years later.

At 7:00 p.m., ABC went up with a special episode on the life of Ronald Reagan, hosted by Peter Jennings. Reagan's remains were still at his home in Bel Air but would shortly be moved to a funeral home in Santa Monica. The local police began to seal off the roads around the Reagan home and the Gates, Kingsley & Gates Moeller Murphy funeral home.[86]

The plan was for the former president to repose at the Reagan Library in Simi Valley and then make his last trip to Washington to lie in state in the Capitol Rotunda, undergo a funeral at the National Cathedral, and then finally head back to Simi Valley for interment. The entire event would cover the course of almost a week. Two tombs had been constructed at the Library. One was for Ronald Reagan. The second was for Nancy Reagan. But to get the laws changed for someone to be buried at the Library they had to send the director, Ralph Bledsoe, some years earlier to "be licensed" and " . . . get certified . . . because you can't just go bury somebody, even in your own yard,"[87] Ryan said.

Jennings was cool and detached in his reporting. Rarely betraying any personal feelings one way or the other, despite his own liberal leanings, he was at times reflective and even wistful. "As we said, President Reagan, who ushered in [a] conservative era to the United States in a way that gave the country back its self-confidence in many ways, no matter what people thought of the president's record."[88]

Old Reaganites such as Ed Meese were spread far and wide. Meese was at the mysterious and ultra-private men's club Bohemian Grove, but a message was gotten through. Meese hustled out quickly, consumed with wistful thoughts about his old friend and boss and their many years together.[89]

An ABC News reporter, Judy Muller, was reporting live from the funeral home and was astonished at how many people began to show up just to catch a glimpse of the vehicle bringing the body of Ronald Reagan there. One woman, crying, told Muller, while carrying a small American flag, she wanted "just to be near him. I loved him. I thought he was a great man . . . this disease is so devastating."[90]

ABC, along with the other networks, was making hasty preparations to report on the life and times and America's long good-bye to Reagan. In a sense, the good-bye had begun in late 1994 when his Alzheimer's was announced.

Two of the first to appear with Jennings were Sam Donaldson, with whom Reagan had often crossed swords over the years, and Lou Cannon, who first began covering Reagan in 1965 in the stirrings of his first run for governor. Later, he covered Reagan's terms as governor, his runs for the White House in 1976 and 1980 for the *Washington Post*, and then wrote five very fine books about the object of his reportage over a nearly fifty-year period. Cannon was regarded by 2004 as the best and fairest and most knowledgeable of all the Reagan biographers. Cannon believed, he told Jennings, that Reagan's "greatest asset was that he was underestimated." Cunningly, Reagan knew it. In fact, said Cannon, "He did everything to make people underestimate him."[91]

Donaldson was in character, somewhat complimentary, somewhat superficial in his analysis, though he did give Reagan credit for actions that "hastened the ends of the Soviet Union without a war." Jennings chimed in that Reagan had brought Moscow "to its knees."[92]

Cannon, like Thatcher, had a better grasp on the man than most, calling him "deceptively complex. And this 'aw, shucks' style of his . . . concealed a very, very smart political brain." Later in the broadcast Jennings used the phrase "The Great Communicator."[93] It would be an appellation heard often in the coming days.

ABC had a video obituary of Reagan ready to go. Narrated by Donaldson, it made much of the assassination attempt and how it bound him closer to the American people, saying it showed "grace and courage of a true, self-assured Hollywood hero, it became a defining moment . . ."[94] CBS also aired a special on his death that was for the most part surprisingly kind.

One of the better early insights of the attempt on Reagan's life came unexpectedly from former aide David Gergen, viewed with suspicion by conservatives and Reaganites. "When Reagan came into office, the affection was there that Eisenhower had but there was no sense of personal courage. The shooting changed that. People saw Reagan with all the handlers and the PR masters and everything like that stripped away, they saw him as he truly was . . . his true character and I think they felt that there was a man with true grit."[95]

The short documentary on ABC reviewed the Reagan presidency and was fairly favorable if also blunt about the growth of government, Afghanistan, Star Wars, the summit meetings with Mikhail Gorbachev, and the Nicaraguan Contras. Of course, the Iran-Contra scandal was also heavily dwelt upon. Like many other videos and pronouncements, the ABC documentary lodged a heavy number of asides at Reagan as a performer, even as president, even though Reagan always understood.

Reagan knew that, as Shakespeare once wrote, "The play's the thing."[96] After his presidency, he wrote in his autobiography, *An*

*American Life,* "I've sometimes wondered how you could be president and not be an actor?"[97] Reagan always understood that stagecraft was as important in many ways as statecraft.

The past ten years had been dreadfully hard on Nancy Reagan. Aides and family came and went, but for her, she lived with the disease 24 hours a day, 7 days a week, and 365 days a year. She was never away from it and rarely from him. Even when she'd go out occasionally for lunch with "the girls" it would be at a restaurant nearby their home in Bel Air, just in case. Overnight trips were very, very rare for Nancy Reagan, especially since 1999 when he "plateaued"[98] down another step.

Nancy went to Maureen's funeral without him in August 2001, where she sat with Jane Wyman and the two held hands. She journeyed to Norfolk for the christening of the USS *Ronald Reagan* in 2001 and its commissioning in 2003. But other than a speech at the GOP convention in San Diego in 1996 and receiving the Congressional Gold Medal in Washington in 2002 that was about it—besides a speech she'd given a few weeks earlier urging increased stem cell research.

There, she bravely if forlornly spoke of the Alzheimer's that was taking her husband away from her. "He doesn't go for walks or he doesn't swim anymore. It is probably the worst disease you can ever have because you lose contact and you're not able to share, in our case, you're not able to share all those wonderful memories that we have. I mean, we had a . . . wonderful life."[99]

Following the order by Bush to lower the American flags at the White House, the president then ordered all flags at all federal buildings and overseas embassies to be lowered; most assumed they would be at half-staff for a lengthy period. Behind the scenes, officials and military personnel were all assuming their duty stations for the week of the Reagan funeral. President Bush and Laura Bush also placed a phone call to Nancy Reagan to personally express their condolences.

By early evening, cable and the networks were filled with reporters and Reagan experts and not-so-experts speaking of the life and times of Ronald Reagan, many of them not very competently. The rough outline of several themes was emerging in these interviews, including that Reagan was good on camera ("Reagan knew that the camera was his friend"),[100] which wasn't very instructive or insightful and possibly a little backhanded, as if to say he was inauthentic. With many, it was chalked up to his time in Hollywood, which was also heavily deliberated.

One of the early guests used by CNN was David Stockman, the banished former budget director. A young congressman from Michigan, Stockman had been flying high, wide, and handsome during the 1980 campaign as a stand-in for John Anderson and later Jimmy Carter in mock debates with Reagan, and as a reward for his performances was appointed head of the Office of Management and Budget at the tender age of thirty-four. But he flew too close to the sun and his wings melted when he spoke too frankly and too often to the national media. He was reduced to a ghost of supply-side past, rattling his chains in the halls of Washington desperately trying to get someone's attention.

He'd been banished from Reagan World years earlier and worked hard in his appearance on CNN to try to get welcomed back in, praising Reagan's preparation for his press conferences effusively as viewers were shown pictures of the black hearse bearing the body of Ronald Reagan in a flag-covered coffin moving toward the funeral home. Then CNN went to a commercial break.[101]

Stockman had written in a widely panned *roman à clef*: "If the SEC [Securities and Exchange Commission] had jurisdiction over the White House, we might have all had time for a course in remedial economics at Allenwood penitentiary."[102] Try as he might, he would never be welcomed back into the band.

Years earlier, Reagan couldn't resist jerking Stockman's chain when the young man had to testify before Congress. "We won't leave you out there alone, Dave. We'll all come to the hanging," the Gipper said, laughing.[103]

When CNN returned to their Reagan coverage they aired a short documentary somewhat like that on ABC, though the CNN video paid more due to the Gipper's theatrical career, including *Knute Rockne, All American*, and, of course, *Bedtime for Bonzo*. A clip of the movie aired with Reagan conversing with the chimpanzee. "Well, Bonzo, I never did thank you for saving my life this morning, did I?"[104]

Throughout his life, Reagan had been painfully and acutely aware that some of the movies he'd made were real dogs. Indeed, Reagan hated his last movie, *The Killers*, his only portrayal of a bad guy.

The Tinseltown to which Reagan was introduced in the late 1930s really was a factory town. The Great Depression–era American public had an unquenchable thirst for the movies, and at the time Americans went to the theater on average twice a week and, all told, nearly fifty million people—well over one-third of the population—happily forked over nickels and dimes to see their favorite actors and actresses, including Ronald Reagan. By 1941 he had an active and large fan club numbering in the thousands.[105]

He wasn't a great actor (although he steadily improved) but he was competent and reliable—he oozed sincerity and likeability—he was the boy next door without the earthy sex appeal of Clark Gable or the cavalier bon vivant Cary Grant. He was the boy every parent would be happy to have date their daughters or befriend their sons, even if some thought he was just too good to be true. Even when signing up with Warner Bros., studio executives did not try to change his name like so many other leading men, including Grant.

Reagan had a devilish side, but he kept it mostly in check. He and his brother, Neil, got in scrapes as kids, including setting off fireworks from a moving car as teenagers in Dixon that landed him in the local police precinct where his father had to pick him up. He could enjoy a drink, but knew when to say when. After a SAG meeting, Reagan went out for cocktails with Dana Andrews and Robert Taylor, two good friends. They drank the first round but when it came time for a second, Reagan balked and gave both his friends grief for ordering more. Both Andrews and Taylor ended up alcoholics (although Andrews did eventually stop drinking in 1972). Reagan could enjoy playing the field and dated many starlets before and after his first marriage, but he really liked being married. He liked the clubs and the nightlife and the celebrity culture, but he also enjoyed intimate dinners talking about politics and world affairs.

He let on to columnist Bob Novak years later how many women he'd been friendly with in between marriages and Novak was astonished, saying he'd never seen this side of Reagan before.[106]

Reagan was a rootin' tootin' supporter of FDR and the New Deal (his father Jack had gotten a New Deal job during the Depression) and had been part of "Hollywood for Truman" in 1948; even as late as 1950 he had campaigned for the "Pink Lady" Helen Gahagan Douglas and against Richard Nixon when they battled for the U.S. Senate seat in California. It didn't hurt that Reagan and Douglas's husband, Melvyn Douglas, were friends, despite Douglas's avowed support for collectivism. He expressed admiration for Adlai Stevenson, said Doug Brinkley.[107] Reagan had many friends who were liberals and many enemies who were conservatives.

There was probably never a time in the 1930s or '40s in which he said to someone that he was going to one day be president of the United States, but politics were becoming more and more important to Reagan. His movie career was on the wane as "good guy" roles became less and less and film noir roles for leading men increased. In 1950, he made only one movie, the forgettable *Louisa*, and even worse it featured Reagan in a comedic role, not his strongest suit. Humorous banter he could do with the best but as a straight man for ninety minutes was something else.

Westerns had always been popular, but in the late '40s Reagan was being passed over by other male actors who were flawed in the style of the era, such as Humphrey Bogart, Randolph Scott, and Montgomery Clift. And by his friend John Wayne, who defined the imperfect Western hero for all time in the American cinema. Still, Reagan made several westerns post–World War II, including *Cattle Queen of Montana* with Barbara Stanwyck and *Stallion Road* with Alexis Smith.

But it had been a long, slow decline from the heady pre-war days of *Kings Row* when Reagan won plaudits from all. Nearly all. The movie reviewer for the *New York Times*, Bosley Crowther, trashed Reagan's performance and the movie.[108] Over the next fifty-plus years, Reagan often got the "treatment" from the old Grey Lady.

He was a success at many careers but not all. At a particularly low point in his life, he headlined a review show in Las Vegas as kind of a song and dance man, but he wasn't very good. After two weeks the Last Frontier resort cancelled the floor show. "He was never invited back by the Frontier or any hotel," said Harvey Diederich, the PR man for the resort.[109]

Later that night CNN brought on Jeff Greenfield, longtime liberal, to discuss the Gipper; but unlike others and like Cannon, he demonstrated more sophistication in explaining and understanding the deceased man, including the self-deprecating humor that Reagan had used to great effect throughout much of his political career. "In politics, humor is like nitroglycerin. Powerful but dangerous. In the wrong hands, attempts at humor have ended political careers. In the hands of a master like Ronald Reagan, there is no better tune," said Greenfield. Ted Turner's cable system then astonishingly turned to former liberal congresswoman Pat Schroeder for her take on Reagan, who blurted out, "I wish he had more substance."[110]

By this point, there was some cross talk involving Greenfield, Cannon, Mike Deaver, and Paul Wolfowitz (who'd worked in the State Department under the Reagan presidency) with Paula Zahn trying to act as traffic cop. Zahn cut away to a CNN correspondent, Thelma Gutierrez, at the Reagan Library in Simi Valley who reported on the growing number of flowers and cards left along the wall and sidewalk, at the foot of the hill, and the long road that led up to the top where the huge presidential museum and record-storing structure resided on twenty-nine acres. It was nearly a quarter of a million square feet and cost initially sixty million dollars to build. "You make me proud to be an American," read one of the cards. The Reagan Library was closed on June 5. On average, it saw four hundred visitors each day, but that was about to change.[111]

Officers from the Military District of Washington were already winging their way to California to begin the implementation of the plan that had been created and edited and revised and tweaked over the past number of years. Some called it "The Book."

The Book was quite literally a playbook for the Reagan procession including places, times, distances, names, phone numbers, etc. It had been assembled with the precision of a Swiss watch and the timing all mapped out. "They'll confer with Mrs. Reagan tomorrow because the president's funeral will be of enormous importance to the nation and to the world and for the country, of course, particularly."[112]

For their planning, they'd studied past state funerals and drew some inspiration and insight from each, especially those of Lincoln, FDR, and Kennedy, all of which were marked by an astonishing amount of outpouring from the American people.

What was interesting and overlooked, however, was these three men had all died in office—two by assassination and the other, the commander in chief, near the victory of a great world war—and thus it was understandable how great was the emotional outpouring for these men.

Reagan, on the other hand, had been out of office for more than fifteen years and yet he still had a tight grip on America's imagination.

The planning had begun in 1981 and progressed throughout the years. Fred Ryan assumed the responsibilities late in the second term when he agreed to go back to California to run the Century City office. Each time he sat down with the Reagans to discuss the funeral arrangements, Reagan resisted. Ryan pressed him on choices of honorary pallbearers and speakers but he "outlived almost every one of the people he wanted to be an honorary pallbearer. He outlived a lot of people who were going to be speakers. It was a constant revision because he lived so long," Ryan recalled.[113]

Bush's press secretary Scott McClellan announced that Bush would keep to his schedule, including speaking at Normandy on the next day. Rain had begun the fall in the hot and humid city of Washington but it did nothing to cool things. It simply evaporated into the atmosphere, thus did not diminish the sticky and clammy feeling everybody had.

Over the next few days the city, the political world, and America would see Reagan men and women they hadn't seen in quite a while, in some cases years. The networks and the cable stations were already gearing up for extensive coverage of the Reagan funeral and would need guests and commentators and polemicists on the life and times of Reagan. After all, Lou Cannon could not be everywhere.

Most of Reagan's old friends—like Caspar Weinberger—knew what had been going on out of the public view in Bel Air and what Reagan and Nancy had been going through. Weinberger said frankly, "I think it's a release from what had only been pretty much agony the last few years, unable to recognize anyone or do anything that he loved most doing."[114]

Weinberger told the story of an important meeting between Reagan and Canadian prime minister Brian Mulroney for which they were both given enormous black briefing books. Reagan looked at his and pushed it aside and Mulroney did likewise and they spent the meeting telling each other Irish jokes and "at the end of that . . . Mulroney was ready to agree to almost anything that President Reagan wanted."[115]

By the afternoon of June 5, the street outside the Reagans' concealed house on St. Cloud was jammed with media and satellite trucks. The growing "whap, whap, whap" of helicopters overhead was beginning to drown out the television correspondents. A media riot was quickly growing, and the LA police were trying to maintain order, finally herding the throng off the street and onto the sidewalks so vehicles could get to and leave the Reagan home. In deference to the moment, some were being polite and hushed.

Shortly, a lone and empty hearse escorted by one motorcycle cop arrived at the Reagan home to take him to the Gates, Kingsley & Gates Moeller Murphy funeral home.

His casket was supposed to be moved from the house to the funeral home somewhere between 4:30 and 5:00 p.m. (PDT).[116] From the funeral home, a procession would move to Simi Valley—where the Reagan Library had opened in 1991—and place the casket in the vestibule where citizens could pay their respects. From there, Reagan would make one last trip to Washington to lie in state in the U.S. Capitol, on the same catafalque used for Abraham Lincoln and JFK. Lincoln had been the first president afforded this honor in the Capitol in April 1865. The last was LBJ in 1973.

A service would be held at the National Cathedral and then back to the Library—his last trip back to California—for an afternoon interment ceremony on Friday, where he would be buried facing West.

His last White House chief of staff, Ken Duberstein, was with Reagan when he chose the location for his burial during the groundbreaking event for his presidential library. Fred Ryan said that at Reagan's request, bagpipes would play "Amazing Grace" at the conclusion of his committal service at the Library.[117]

No fewer than four former presidents and the current president, George W. Bush, were expected to attend the services in Washington for the fallen member of the most exclusive club in the history of the world. Hundreds of world leaders and thousands of power brokers were also expected at the U.S. Capitol and the National Cathedral, but so, too, were hundreds of thousands of what he'd called the "quiet, everyday heroes of America."[118]

The casket finally left for the funeral home at 5:15 p.m., with a full police motorcycle escort and now a half dozen helicopters overhead.[119] Also, some Secret Service agents accompanied Reagan's body. Abraham Lincoln's remains were rumored to have been stolen in the years after his death and held for ransom and the Service was sure this would not happen to their beloved protectee. From the day they met him until the day he passed away, the men and women who guarded Reagan did so with devotion and affection. They were sworn to take a bullet for the president and in March 1981, Agent Tim McCarthy did just that, but all knew there were some presidents who the agents were more enthusiastic about putting their lives on the line for than others. Stories about the mutual affection between the Reagans and the agents had been going around for years.

Joanne Drake, dressed in black with the wind gently mussing her hair, stepped before the throng of media, read a short statement, and then calmly and coolly explained how the week of the Reagan memorial services would play out. It was a typically gorgeous California day.

Behind the scenes thousands of men and women were already at work preparing for this day. Skilled in organization, travel, security, traffic control, theology, printing, advance work, media relations, crowd control, and on and on, for which few were paid, all pitched in because of their devotion to the Gipper. Everything was being done with a maximum amount of professionalism and courtesy and solemnity and a minimal amount of friction. Invitations to the various ceremonies were being handled by phone, by the distribution of tickets, and by fax machine.

As it would be a state funeral, the military had a central role, as did the State Department, but Mrs. Reagan's personal invitation list was being handled in a suite of offices at the Mayflower Hotel in Washington. Hundreds of volunteers were actively engaged, though as noted, they were "grayer, broader and two decades older . . ."[120] Rick Ahearn was in charge of the Washington events, and Jim Hooley was in charge of the California events.

It was debated whether or not when Reagan's remains traveled on a military plane if that plane would be designated "Air Force One." (Reagan's remains were indeed moved out and back on the big plane, but designated as SAM "Special Air Mission" 28000.)[121]

As a state funeral, everything came under the jurisdiction of the Military District of Washington, including the invitation lists to the various memorial services in California and Simi Valley. The Reagan funeral was going to be huge, along the lines of a presidential inaugural, and would involve thousands of local police and firefighters and federal security. More than three thousand military personnel alone would be involved and thousands of VIPs, both foreign and domestic. On the side, plans were going forth for unofficial gatherings of many Reaganites, especially in Washington. One featured a gathering of some former Reagan speechwriters while another was a dinner for the 1976 Reagan campaign staff. Mrs. Reagan had always said of Ronnie's five campaigns (neither of them ever included the 1968 presidential campaign), 1976 was the more exciting and the staff from that effort utterly agreed.

As with all such large Washington events, a social cast was evident and some were already finagling and squawking behind the scenes to make sure they were invited to the "right" events for the week. Some things never change in Washington.

John King on CNN speculated that the upcoming week would be mournful but also "a celebration of his [Reagan's] optimism, a celebration of his spirit." In his yearbook at Dixon High School, Reagan had said his motto was, "Life is just one grand sweet song, so start the music." The week ahead would attempt to follow at least part of that maxim.[122]

For most Reaganites, the memories of the revolution filled them with wistful joy, a smile through tears.

"It hadn't been that long ago, had it?" Was it really sixteen years ago that they were all together, all brought together by this man, this vision, these goals? For some, it had been even longer. California. Sacramento. The roller coaster of 1976, the wilderness, the uphill climb of 1980, day one of 1981, doing battle with the liberals in the national media, who gave no quarter to this man they hated and whose followers they reviled. He didn't care and they didn't care.

Those who knew him in Sacramento were engaged in a bit of revisionism about what had gone on for eight years but they also chose to put the best light on those days. "There are very few people left in Sacramento from that period, but those that are never say anything against Reagan personally," recalled Kevin Starr, the "state librarian emeritus."[123]

Memories fly though the mind, rushing back. Images of things that did not seem so consequential then but now in retrospect became important history. This campaign, that speech; this legislation, that convention. They were all just doing their jobs then, happily, merrily, a band of brothers and sisters in common cause. It wasn't about a love of power but a love of camaraderie and a belief in the individual.

They fought among themselves but to a greater good—how to achieve a more perfect union. Few were there for the money and nearly all were there for the joy. There was something joyful about working for Reagan that outsiders would never understand; refused to understand; possibly could never understand. These Reaganites didn't care as it made it all the more special that they got it and the Washington elites did not.

Fellini said one must live his or her life spherically, and Reagan did, and his followers tried to. The time as soldiers and captains and generals in Reagan's Revolution was merely one part of their lives, but it was a very important part of their lives, one they would cherish and never forget. As they now streamed back to Washington, all were burdened with the sadness of the inevitable but also deeply, deeply proud they'd had a chance to be a part of history, to witness great things being done by a great man who believed in a great country.

As with the assassination of Abraham Lincoln, the bombing of Pearl Harbor, the death of FDR, and the assassination of JFK, each American citizen and especially every Reagan man and Reagan woman—everyone who had ever worked for Reagan or knew him in Sacramento or Washington or Century City or at the ranch or at Simi Valley or worked on the campaigns or knew him in Hollywood or Eureka or Dixon—remembered exactly where they were and what they were doing when they learned of the passing of Ronald Reagan.

# CHAPTER 3

# TO BURY REAGAN

*"He wasn't elusive and he wasn't inscrutable."*

A man born in 1911 could expect to live just over fifty years, according to the actuarial tables. Reagan had beaten the odds by forty-three years.[1] He had lived longer than any president, surpassing John Adams, and would often joke that his longevity was "a source of great annoyance"[2] to his political opponents. By all rights Reagan should have passed away around 1961, given his generation. Born in the same year as Reagan, Dodgers manager Walter Alston, playwright Tennessee Williams, singer LaVerne Andrews, and comedic actress Lucille Ball had all passed away years earlier. In the span of his ninety-three years, he covered "43 percent of the time from the inauguration of George Washington to today," wrote columnist Michael Barone.[3]

That Reagan lived so long, accomplished so much, and stirred up much debate was clear to many but equally confusing to others. Most of the citizenry "got" Reagan. The elites did not.

On the first full day after Reagan's passing, both ABC and NBC led their broadcasts with the news of his death, while CBS did not and chose to lead with Bush's speech at Normandy.[4] Many vets had returned to Normandy sixty years later to remember, in remembrance, and to recall—possibly for the last time.

The preparations at the Reagan Library were not just related to the ceremonial. Some were tedious, others logistically difficult, and the details were numerous. Some involved the reality of the post–September 11 world. "Duke Blackwood to contact terrorist agencies to schedule meeting to determine terrorist threat," read a line item in the funeral manual. Then handwritten was the addition, "schedule meeting to determine threat assessment."[5]

The nation's newspapers were now filled with reports on the death of Ronald Reagan. On Sunday, June 6, it was all everybody was talking about. Every front page in the country boldly and bluntly carried the headline "Reagan Dies" or "Ronald Reagan Dead" or "Ronald Reagan dead at 93."[6] In the old days, such newspapers were referred to as "five star editions," usually reserved for the beginning of wars and the end of presidents.

The day before, former president, former naval officer, and former Annapolis graduate Jimmy Carter was in Groton, Connecticut, to christen a new submarine bearing his name.[7] The charming photo of the smiling former First Lady Rosalynn Carter breaking the requisite bottle of champagne across the prow of the boat should have been on the front page of every paper in America. Instead, the Sunday papers were filled with photos of the president and Nancy Reagan.

"From all corners of the planet, the eulogies streamed in—a barrage of quotations and orations for the president known as the Great Communicator, the man whose enemies and friends agreed he changed the world."[8] The lead editorial of the *Chicago Tribune* was headlined simply, "Ronald Reagan, Revolutionary." After reviewing the high and low points of his presidency, it closed by saying, "He will be remembered as one of this nation's most influential and successful presidents. If you want to see Ronald Reagan's legacy, just look around."[9]

On the other hand, *Washington Post* columnist Harold Meyerson wrote that Reagan had "destroyed" the "moderate wing" of the GOP and made it a Southern party, ignoring the fact that Reagan had carried most of the states of the Northeast in 1980 and all of them in 1984. "Ronald Reagan changed America . . . not for the better." He said only that Reagan "helped wind down the Cold War abroad" but "he absolutely revived class war here."[10]

A clear pattern was emerging after Reagan's death. The liberal elite of the national media and academia were skeptical of his stewardship of the presidency, as well as of Reagan as a man, and said so loudly. On the other hand, the citizenry who "got" Reagan were nearly all complimentary. "He was a good president. He did our country great. He was a better president than Bush," said one mourning American citizen.[11]

As the word spread across the nation, attendees at Yankee Stadium were asked over the public address system to observe a moment of silence and then they joined in and sang "God Bless America," as recorded by the Gipper's old friend Kate Smith.[12] Across town at the Belmont racetrack, the unruly bettors were asked to do likewise and they did.[13]

There'd been some early discussion about where the week of grieving should begin. One option suggested was Reagan's Presbyterian church in Bel Air, but it was eventually decided that the Reagan Library was the only appropriate location. There was also some initial consideration given to moving Reagan by train, like Lincoln and FDR and RFK and using Roosevelt's famous "Ferdinand Magellan," which was used in Ohio during the 1984 campaign, but that idea, too, was shelved.[14]

Jim Hooley, after speaking with Joanne Drake the previous day, got a call from Fred Ryan and that began the process of beginning to implement their carefully constructed plans.[15] The plan was extremely organized, even having calls scripted for each staff member, such as Drake calling one group of people; Melissa Giller, who was in charge of media relations for the Library, contacting national reporters, the wire services, and the networks; and assigned duties for senior staffers such as Kirby Hanson.

Drake was to go immediately to Mrs. Reagan's home to call "family, friends and honorary pallbearers." Duke Blackwood, the director of the Library, had numerous duties to carry out. Even Mrs. Reagan had calls to make to her friends Merv Griffin and "Mrs. Wick," wife of Charlie Wick, both of whom had been lifetime friends of the Reagans. Footnotes showed the entire plan had been updated as recently as May 25, 2004.[16]

The entrance to the Library on Presidential Drive was closed for the day and precise instructions were given to the guard. "Guard is ONLY to say that the Library is closed for access." Handwritten on the document was "security needs to watch hillside." The plan also said to make sure to place trash bins near the media outside the Library, which demonstrated experience.[17] Anyone who ever worked with the national media knew that whatever environmental sensibilities they avowed on television and in print, they practiced none of those concerns when on a stake out.

Just the day before, Ryan, Hooley, General Galen Jackman, and others had met at Andrews Air Force Base in Maryland where, by prearrangement, a military jet would take them to California. The plan said the "East Coast team gets on flight" at 2:00 p.m.[18] but there was some confusion and the plane carrying Ryan, Hooley, General Jackman, who was head of the Military District of Washington, was hours late in departing, which helped no one's mood.[19] Meanwhile, memos were faxed by Library staff to local florists with clear instructions and rules for making deliveries.

The plan left nothing to chance. It addressed the obvious details related to people and speeches and schedules but also tended to other finite details such as the emplacement of American flags on Presidential Drive, "meeting with docents . . . to give out work assignments for line detail." Bands and color guards and parking assignments, refreshments, and the care and feeding of dignitaries, and a thousand other things.[20] Nothing, it seemed, was overlooked. It was impressive also because everything seemed to be covered in great detail but with a politeness and dignity that was emphasized throughout.

When Hooley arrived in California, he proceeded immediately to the chapel at the funeral home and waiting upon his arrival were some thirty volunteers, mostly former advance men and women, most of them crying. Someone—maybe it was Andrew Littlefair—said, "Jim, tell us what you need." Also there to pitch in to help was Ashley Parker Snider, daughter of actor and Reagan pal Fess Parker.[21]

In the next room was the body of Ronald Reagan, discretely under a sheet as the undertaker prepared him for his final resting place. There was a Secret Service agent sitting patiently in a chair next to Reagan's remains.[22] Even as they prepared for their last week working for the Gipper, both Hooley and Littlefair shed tears, overcome with the reality of the moment. They were not alone in expressing their grief, a grief that was not part of any script.

That very day and twenty-six years earlier, Ronald Reagan, Leader of the Free World, had stood on a windswept bluff overlooking the English Channel, directing the eyes of the world to the heroes of D-day and the liberation of a continent forty years prior. Now his remains were on another coast, but this time looking out over the Pacific Ocean, almost six thousand miles away from Normandy, the eyes of the world now affixed on him. Nancy Reagan always said he liked heights and indeed, he'd reached the pinnacle of world power and fittingly he would be buried at the top of a prominence.

He always liked heights, according to Patti, because it gave him a "feeling of openness." Sometimes he'd take his daughter to a nearby hill to fly kites. He told her, "I'm not crazy about riding on flat land . . . you can always see what's ahead. There are never any surprises."[23]

Scientists had discovered around the time of WWII something that many sailors had already suspected—that there was a distinct difference between the Atlantic Ocean and the Pacific. The Pacific was indeed bluer, while the Atlantic was indeed greener. Generally, the Atlantic was also colder and saltier than the Pacific.

In a moving but often overlooked speech, President Kennedy once observed that people were of the sea and "we are tied to the ocean. And when we go back to the sea . . . we are going back from whence we came. It is an interesting biological fact that all of us have in our veins the exact same percentage of salt in our blood that exists in the ocean, and, therefore, we have salt in our blood, in our sweat, in our tears."[24]

Reagan was never the sailor that JFK was but he was an excellent swimmer. And like Kennedy, he loved the ocean. Now the former lifeguard's passing was engendering millions of salty cries from Americans and millions around the world, just as the death of JFK had in late November 1963.

Patti recalled her father teaching her how to body surf and Ron recalled racing his father in many pools. She told herself that sometimes as a public man she overlooked "the song beneath the myth."[25]

Both Reagan and Kennedy in their youth had saved others from drowning. Reagan had never been much of a Kennedy basher; at least his heart was not into heavily criticizing the family. The same could be said for the Kennedys when it came to Reagan. Maybe it was their shared Gaelic heritage. They had much in common, and those who knew both men say they would have liked each other. They had winning smiles and winsome ways, liked people, and were terrific public speakers and superior athletes. Reagan as president had been the star attraction at a fund-raiser for the JFK Library in 1985 where he delivered remarks that brought tears to the eyes of those present, including Jackie Kennedy Onassis.

While Reagan was often criticized by liberals and conservatives alike for quoting John Kennedy, he once received a letter from son John Kennedy, Jr., praising Reagan's use of his father's words and urging him to keep on quoting President Kennedy.[26] In 1980, nearly all the extended Kennedy family had voted for Reagan rather than Jimmy Carter.[27]

It was also twenty-three years earlier on June 5, 1981, that Reagan had presented the Congressional Gold Medal posthumously to Robert Francis Kennedy, who was also a victim of an assassination, like his brother John Kennedy had been and like Reagan had almost been. As Reagan once said, "History is . . . a record of human will."[28]

One of the first people to call Nancy Reagan and offer his condolences over the death of her husband was Ted Kennedy.[29]

At various times over the past ten years, all the members of the Reagan family had opened up about his affliction. Son Mike told people in 1999 that his father hadn't spoken his name in two years. Two years earlier, in 1997, he told UPI that his father still recognized him—"I think he knows me more from the hugs than anything else."[30] Ron said his father "hadn't recognized him for five years." Maureen noted that even with the advancing Alzheimer's, he was doing what he could to make it easier for his family, adding, "He's very lovable."[31]

Patti once taught a class entitled, "Recovering from Dysfunctional Families." The family was strained at times, and that is an understatement. After all, Patti had once posed for *Playboy*. Maureen, at age twenty-six, was hurt to read a biography of her father making reference to Ron and Patti but not to her or Mike. Mike was shipped off to boarding school and once complained that his father did not recognize him standing in line. A college roommate of Patti's, Wendy Weber, said that the kids were close to their parents as children "but as adults, it was different." The disease brought them all together again, bumpy as it may have been. Patti said, "I had a choice. Am I going to try to look at it in a loving, forgiving way, or am I going to be a punk?"[32]

Earlier, the Reagans' old friend Mike Deaver spoke of how he saw Reagan fumble over a joke to a group of businessmen—the one about the pile of horse manure and the pony and the little boy that he'd heard Reagan tell a thousand times—and wondered to himself what was wrong with Reagan.[33]

In January 2001, Reagan fell at his home and cracked a hip. He was rushed to the hospital to undergo surgery and afterward a statement was issued that he was "fully alert, in good humor and in stable condition."[34] He asked for and received a lot of ice cream. Nancy was with him the whole time, except when he was in the operating room, and even then she tried to stay by his side. "But otherwise, I was there."[35]

Afterward, though, he was almost never seen in public and only infrequently a photo was released. He would go for quiet walks and for lunches, and timid school children, encouraged by their parents, would go up and introduce themselves to the former president of the United States.

Mothers and nannies occasionally spotted him, with only his nurse Diane Capps, in Roxbury Park in Beverly Hills, as he watched the children play. When greeted, he would say hello. "Reagan didn't speak much to the adults. It was our children he was interested in." He'd say hello brightly to the children and one mother who saw him said wistfully, "It was the most Reagan thing left of Ronald Reagan in those days."[36]

He gave the children autographs and cheered on their soccer games and once even kicked the ball into the goal. He'd also throw errant balls back, earning a "Thank you, Mr. President!" from the kids.[37]

For some time, his clothing included a jacket and tie but as the disease progressed he would be seen in baggy, comfortable pants and an oversized baseball cap. As more time passed, he was seen at the park less frequently and when he was seen, he had pretty much stopped speaking. A mother saw him one last time. "He was very gray and very thin." She wanly told her children "that not remembering meeting the president was not nearly as sad as not remembering being president."[38]

It was all Nancy Reagan could do to choke back the tears each time she spoke in public of "Ronnie." "I have found that even though the person I love and have loved for forty-four years is slipping away, my love for him grows," she said mournfully.[39] It had been noted even before he went into seclusion that "slowly, perceptibly, he was undergoing a wrenching change."[40] He still was broad-shouldered and handsome, even for a man in his eighties, but at the Nixon funeral in the spring of 1994, some people whispered, "Something's not right with Ron." On her husband's eighty-ninth birthday, Nancy appeared by phone on Larry King's show and he asked her, "How is Nancy doing?" and not missing a beat, she answered in the third person, "Nancy is hanging in there, I guess." She also told King of how her husband had lost his world-famous sweet tooth and was eating very lightly.[41]

Lou Cannon wondered if he should have known or whether he should have been told of Reagan's condition. But his illness was becoming more apparent: "The public received its first inkling of his decline on February 6, 1993, when Reagan repeated a toast to . . . Thatcher verbatim during the celebration of his eighty-second birthday at the presidential library. Guests pretended not to notice, but the number of public events on Reagan's schedule was soon reduced."[42]

Maureen Reagan—"Mermie"—had seen all the consternation and heard all the bluster and false statements spoken about her father, including from the pages of the book *Dutch*, a widely panned Reagan biography authored by Edmund Morris. In writing the book, Morris had channeled Lewis Carroll. ("Who in the world am I? Ah, that's the great puzzle?"[43]) After years of work, Morris had pronounced Reagan a mystery and someone he could not "get" or understand, which, as any of the men and women around Reagan knew, was utter nonsense.

Maureen "got" her father more than most. In the early 1960s, she was in Washington earning her way as a secretary when she wrote a letter to her father telling him he ought to run for governor of California before most had given any thought to her father running for office. Reagan replied, "Well, if we're talking about what I could do, Mermie, I could be president," as recounted by Cannon.[44] Mermie and her father were often on the same wavelength.

Reagan wasn't an open book but he wasn't Lamont Cranston either. He had his need for privacy—sometimes deeply private—and he could lose himself in a Louis L'Amour novel or on a horseback ride or writing. But so many of the men and women who had spent so much time with Reagan traveling, working, eating, joking, campaigning, governing, arguing, pushing, pulling, laughing, and crying, hardly recognized the Reagan portrayed in the Morris book and many were infuriated at the false image, how Morris strangely "channeled himself" into the narrative. Some were angered by the factual mistakes, such as how many children Gerald Ford had or what day Reagan announced for president in November 1975.

Morris also recounted a cruel rumor that claimed an Alzheimer's-ravaged Reagan raked the same leaves over and over out of the pool while discrete Secret Service agents kept replenishing them.[45] A very close aide disputed this.[46] John Podhoretz said the book was "a work of lunacy." For his lunacy, Random House paid Morris three million dollars.[47]

While a myth emerged that the Reagans courted Morris to write the book, the truth was Morris had pitched Reagan on the biography idea, "describe[ing] parallels between the Gipper and T.R. [Theodore Roosevelt]." News accounts said Reagan was "beguiled."[48] But apparently not for long.

Both Lyn Nofziger and Peter Hannaford, two longtime intimate aides to Reagan, knew what the problem was with Morris. Simply put, Morris got on Reagan's nerves and he clammed up. That was how Reagan dealt with people who bugged him. He wouldn't talk.[49] When

Reagan didn't like somebody, he wasn't rude or off-putting. Plenty of Reagan men over the years said they saw this with the Gipper as how he dealt with people who irritated him.

From Nancy Reagan to the staff at the Reagan Library and Foundation to the hundreds who had worked in the Reagan administration to the thousands who knew him and worked with him over the years, all were angered and disappointed with the Morris book. The *National Review* devoted its cover and several stories to ripping the book. Years of planning and access granted and hopes had been invested in *Dutch*. Reagan was a guy who, shirtless and in his sixties, was getting up on the roof of his ranch house to repair it and was working with Dennis LeBlanc, who was years younger than the Gipper. This was a man who was so open and charming that he disarmed nearly all, but who could be tough and resilient, as old friend and advisor Stu Spencer knew.

What was also strange was how Morris injected himself into *Dutch* and how he bounced between first and third person narratives and how he awkwardly disputed that Reagan was in the ballpark about the true meaning of the word *Chernobyl*, which in some interpretations of the Ukrainian Bible meant the name of the "star" in Revelation 8:10–11.

"That sounded too good to be true," whimpered Morris when Reagan referred to it as Armageddon, but Morris became even more truculent when he discovered that Reagan was essentially right since many saw similarities between a nuclear disaster and the biblical description of the blazing star "Wormwood" falling on earth.[50]

Morris also abused Mrs. Reagan horridly in the narrative. "Mrs. Reagan . . . is otherwise treated shabbily as a rich Republican with a blinkered view of life . . . ," said *National Review*. Morris also created fictional characters including "Paul Rae a . . . homosexual writer (and early AIDS victim) who regards him [Reagan] as the vacant repository of narrow small-town virtues," wrote John O'Sullivan.[51]

It was only when it was too late and Reagan had passed away that Morris grasped the significance of the man, telling Dan Rather,

> Well, I feel that a large part of the earth has crumbled away. There was something epic about Reagan and his sheer historic size. For example, where is Soviet communism? Where is the Berlin Wall? Where is national malaise? Where is our contempt for and our embarrassment about the American military? It's what we no longer see in the world that testifies to the way he changed things.[52]

All felt this was what the Morris book failed to capture.

Morris had been given unprecedented access to Reagan in the final two years of the presidency and even more so in the post-presidential years. Morris concluded that Reagan was unfathomable and then pronounced—in so many words—that the fortieth president was a lightweight and an "airhead."[53] The book was a failure as a work of history and commercially it struck many as downright weird while containing obvious errors of fact and judgment.

Morris never understood Reagan, but that was only part of the problem. The choice of Morris was a mistake in many ways. He was never going to write a balanced or favorable biography that would place him at risk of receiving the disapproval of liberal academia. Second, he was born and raised in a British culture and simply could not fathom American populism or American conservatism. Third, being an academic, he looked down his nose at Reagan as some sort of hayseed. The concept of upward mobility was foreign to both the British culture and the ivory tower elites.

*Dutch* was excluded from the Reagan Library gift shop and Morris was nearly nonexistent in the media commentary during the week of the funeral. Meanwhile, the Reagan Library vowed to never put a toe in the water again of designating a Reagan historian, preferring, ironically "to let a hundred flowers bloom," as communist leader Mao proclaimed.

Maureen said of her father before her own death, "He wasn't elusive and he wasn't inscrutable," but that was with people he liked, had just met, or at least tolerated. "He was a kind, caring, fun person," she said defensively.[54] In the years after his diagnosis, they often did puzzles together and she told people how much he delighted in her red nail polish.[55]

There was a special relationship between Reagan and his eldest daughter, as there was with Patti. Maureen had made mistakes and gotten into scrapes but she was also smart and some said a better public speaker than her father. Maybe, but he did love her and protect her, same as he did with Patti. In 1982, Maureen decided to embark on a political career of her own by running for the U.S. Senate in California, when the incumbent, Republican senator S. I. "Sam" Hayakawa was "retiring" mostly because his approval ratings had fallen faster than a starlet's career. The GOP primary contest was a mess involving Pete Wilson, Barry Goldwater, Jr., and others.

It had leaked out of the White House that Reagan wasn't all that pleased she was taking the plunge, but he never expressed his concerns in his diaries. The White House's political director at the time was Ed Rollins, who was sent out on a scouting trip to see what Maureen's chances were. Rollins spoke to a reporter who then betrayed the "off the record" agreement and there was Rollins in black and white jumping all over Maureen and her lousy campaign.[56] He was in many ways the protégé of Lyn Nofziger. Both were bald, sported chin spinach, and were combustible, droll, conservative, and sometimes reckless in what they said publicly and privately.

Rollins knew he was in trouble and, when he went back to the White House, Jim Baker told him Reagan wanted to see him because the president was "going to really ream your a—." Sheepishly, Rollins crawled into the Oval Office and there was Reagan. Rollins apologized profusely, knowing Maureen had given her father a hard time over the newspaper article. Reagan said grimly, "Ed, let's make a pact: you don't say anything about any of the candidates; I won't say anything about any of the candidates."[57]

Reagan sometimes jokingly referred to a "strange meeting"[58] involving a young actress, Nancy Davis, who'd inadvertently ended up on a list of suspected communists in Hollywood in 1949 that had been published in the *Hollywood Reporter*. Frightened, she asked director Mervyn LeRoy, in whose movie *East Side, West Side* she was starring, for advice, and he suggested she reach out to the president of the Screen Actors Guild, Ronald Reagan.[59] They shared a dinner so memorable that years later she could still recall what she ate and what she wore. Steak and a black dress.[60]

They later took in a show, enjoying the performer Sophie Tucker. Tucker, ironically, was a Russian, known for her risqué songs and her ribald humor in a one-woman show. She was known as the "Last of the Red Hot Mamas."[61] In case the evening didn't go well, they both told the other they had "early calls." They both later confessed they'd each made up the little white lie.[62]

Nancy Davis did not get home until 2:00 a.m., and in a way their first date lasted fifty-five years. They went on that one date and, though for a time continued to see other people, they really never stopped dating for the rest of their lives. They married in 1952 and a commentator said on the day Reagan passed away, "Their love story has always been a part of the presidential story."[63] In the one movie they starred in together, *Hellcats of the Navy*, in 1957, Reagan said to his wife, "How do you know so much about the moon?" and she replied, "I know a lot about it. I spend all my time looking at it when you're away."[64]

Of his marriage to Nancy, Reagan said, "Clark Gable had a line once. 'There is nothing more wonderful for a man than to approach his own doorstep knowing that someone on the other side of the door is listening for the sound of his footsteps.'"[65]

In 1953, just after their marriage and as Reagan was hanging on by an economic thread—doing Chesterfield cigarette newspaper ads and

Van Heusen shirt magazine ads—over the hill like the cavalry came the General Electric Company with an offer just in the nick of time that he could not refuse. It was an offer that would again alter the trajectory of his life. He was invited to host—and occasionally star in—the *General Electric Theater* broadcast that aired each Sunday at 9:00 p.m. eastern standard time on CBS television and radio for $150,000 per year.[66]

General Electric was a company that was as American as apple pie. "Progress is our most important product"[67] was the corporate slogan, and it fit right into the 1950s of an optimistic, confident, and forward-looking country. People were familiar with GE's many appliances such as washers and dryers and ranges and dishwashers, but at the crest of the second half of the twentieth century, the giant corporation was unveiling many new products, and they needed a spokesman who was equally apple pie American and who would be welcomed into American homes like the boy next door.

Reagan was the perfect choice. He'd never been associated with any Hollywood scandals. In all his movies he was the good guy—or at worst a good-natured rascal or a sidekick good guy. *GE Theater* debuted in February 1953 and ran until May 1962. All told, 209 episodes were broadcast. Reagan was a natural, not only because he was a household name, was clean-cut, and represented stability, but also because he'd had some practice appearing previously in the *Lux Video Theatre* and the *Ford Television Theatre*.

The show ran until 1962 when Reagan was fired by GE in part for criticizing the Tennessee Valley Authority, known more commonly as TVA, a Great Depression creation that sold taxpayer subsidized electricity to its customers. General Electric was also a large provider of equipment to the TVA. General Electric was conservative by nature, conservative in its culture, and conservative in its politics, even distributing copies of *National Review*[68] to its employees. But business was business. At the time, GE had a fifty-million-dollars-per-year customer in TVA.[69]

Years later, Mike Reagan said his father had been fired from GE because of pressure from the Kennedy administration.[70] Others specifically fingered Robert Kennedy, guardian of the family's reputation. But no one really knows for sure. What also went unanswered was why all Reagan's men (and women) thought for years that their man often got the roughest treatment from CBS as opposed to the other two networks, in spite of Reagan's happy relationship with the "Tiffany Network" for the decade of the 1950s.

For ten years, GE Theater was a top-rated show and millions tuned in to see the adaptation of plays, movies, and novels for the glowing box in living rooms and bars across the nation. This was quality programming, and while movie stars at the time often turned up their noses at "the little screen," guests who appeared on the long-running hit show included Fred Astaire, Claudette Colbert, Ronald Colman, Greer Garson, Judy Garland, and even Reagan's ex, Jane Wyman. GE Theater was nominated for many Emmy awards over the years and attracted top writers, including Kurt Vonnegut.

Part of Reagan's contract stipulated that he travel a certain amount of time to GE's plants around the country, and at the time there were hundreds in places like Syracuse, New York; Louisville, Kentucky; Rome, Georgia; and Evendale, Ohio. The contract also allowed Reagan to avoid commercial air travel as he was terrified of flying at the time. He'd had two bad experiences and that was enough for him. So he traveled long distance by train.

In those ten years, Reagan went to 135 GE factories around the country and toured the plants and spoke to the workers. It was in these factories and their lunchrooms that he developed into an exceptional public speaker. But it wasn't just the GE factory workers and management to whom he spoke. Reagan would also address civic and social organizations, sometimes putting in as many as twenty-five appearances a day! Reagan would occasionally complain about his schedule. "I won't! No mortal man can endure this schedule!" "But," said Edward Langley, a former GE publicity man who worked with Reagan on his tours, "he did it."[71]

In the evenings, Reagan was also often called upon to sup with local businessmen and to "say a few words." Never a boozer, Reagan would pretend to drink martinis while all the while downing glasses of heavily watered-down Rhine wine. Langley estimated that Reagan "made 9,000 extemporaneous speeches." He also recalled Reagan speaking "fondly of Roosevelt" in those days.[72]

"No one has been that saturated—marinated—in middle America, not even William Jennings Bryan," said Langley.[73] In the course of his years on the road for GE, Reagan transformed himself from an entertainer into a political force.

CBS was scrambling to go live with their news of Reagan's passing, just like the other networks and cable systems. Dan Rather was anchoring and was straightforward in announcing the death of a president but went almost immediately to the Gipper's celluloid career, airing clips from various movies. The network did manage to insert a humorous clip of Reagan as governor, however, making sport of several sign-waving hippies. "The last bunch . . . were carrying signs that said, 'Make Love, Not War.' The only trouble was they didn't look like they were capable of doing either."[74]

They naturally went into Iran-Contra early and deeply. They blithely noted that Reagan had escaped the scandal by "riding horseback and doing chores on his ranch, he kept his all-American image intact . . ." But CBS also aired early on a very telling and insightful quote from the Gipper, midway through his presidency. "Let history say of us, 'These were golden years when the American Revolution was reborn, when freedom gained new life, and America reached for her best.'" To his credit, Rather did say Reagan was the president "who devoted his presidency to winning the Cold War."[75]

The logistics involved for the week were astonishing. They involved the movement of Reagan's remains but also the movements of Mrs. Reagan, the family, the dignitaries, the VIPs, and the crowds. Media coverage, meals, housing, and transportation and a thousand other important items needed to be considered and executed. State funerals typically took up to seven days.

What had not been fully anticipated by the planners was the gravity of the outpouring from the American people. A trickle of appreciation would shortly crest into a tidal wave and wash across the nation.

Tributes were coming in faster from the grassroots than from the privileged. Many citizens remembered some kindness of Reagan's or the time he visited their town. From Indiana, the Associated Press headline that moved on the state wire proclaimed, "Reagan Remembered as Giant Whose Policies Resounded Strongly Here."[76] His speech at Notre Dame in 1981—the first trip he made beyond the nation's capital after the assassination attempt—was extraordinarily well received at the school where he'd filmed *Knute Rockne, All American* in 1940.

He'd told the graduates, "A university like this is a storehouse of knowledge because the freshmen bring so much in and the seniors take so little away."[77] After the gales of laughter subsided, Reagan got down to a heartfelt address on life and living to the graduating class of 1981. During his presidency, he journeyed back to Indiana a number of times, including in 1988, to unveil at Notre Dame a new Knute Rockne postage stamp.[78]

One member of the First Christian Church in Dixon, where Reagan attended services, Wanita Trader, said, "He was our hero, he was our hometown boy made good."[79]

In Pittsburgh, Thomas Delahanty, a very special retired policeman who nearly died when he, Reagan, and several others had been shot by John Hinckley in March 1981, spoke for the first time publicly about the assassination attempt and the day when he also stopped a bullet intended for the president. "He was a great man and had a strong faith in God and his country."[80] While recovering at George Washington hospital, Reagan noted that he, press secretary Jim Brady, Delahanty, and Secret Service agent Tim McCarthy were all of a particular lineage. "What did this guy have against the Irish?" Reagan quipped.[81] Reagan also cracked that they should have a reunion and bring their bedpans.

The *Chicago Tribune* had two big stories on the front page on Sunday, June 6. His local roots were played up greatly. One story by Jon Margolis, a highly respected and longstanding political journalist, made the case that Reaganism inside the party was stronger in 2004 than it was while Reagan was in office. "It energizes a host of scholars, writers and political organizers . . ."[82] Still, the praise from the writing class was slow and spare in coming.

Reagan was an accomplished writer (he'd often thought of himself as essentially a writer and creative storyteller)[83]—a fact he vividly demonstrated for years with his five-minute radio broadcasts. He once entertainingly wrote, "A farmer of any kind is in a business that makes a crap table or roulette wheel look like a guaranteed annual income."[84]

He in turn attracted equally talented writers. Peter Hannaford, Ken Khachigian, Tony Dolan, Mari Maseng, Peggy Noonan, Landon Parvin, Clark Judge, and others. Hooley and others drawn to Reagan represented the small-town Irish side of Reagan. Devoted, hardworking, loyal, and mischievous. And because Reagan thought young and thought about the young, he in turn attracted young Americans who also thought about the future: Mark Tapscott and Jim Pinkerton and Michele Davis and Robbie Aiken and others, all young. Reagan attracted thousands of youthful conservatives to his cause.

While governor, he was meeting with a group of young Californians, including hippies and anti-war protestors. One of them stormed to Reagan, "Governor, it's impossible for you to understand us, to understand our generation." To which Reagan smartly replied, "Well, I know more about being young than you do about being old."[85]

The Missouri Republicans honored Reagan with a moment of silence at their state convention. They'd already named their headquarters in Jefferson City after him.[86] The chairman of the Alabama GOP, Marty Connors, offered some of the most interesting and insightful observations on Reagan. "Ronald Reagan taught us how to win—taught us how to articulate our conservative thinking. He taught us to have confidence in ourselves, not just as Republicans, but as Americans." But even better, Connors said, "My 12-year-old daughter has no idea what an air raid drill is, and the reason she doesn't know this is because she doesn't have to practice dying in a nuclear disaster. She is ignorant of air raids and that's Ronald Reagan's fault."[87]

Newt Gingrich, first a Rockefeller Republican who later evolved into a Reagan conservative, would become an important foot soldier and leader in the Reagan Revolution. Having ascended to the speakership, he articulated what the fortieth president had gone through. "President Ronald Reagan proved that an American, raised in difficult family circumstances, in a small town, with no personal money, not only could succeed but could rise to lead the cause of freedom and declare victory over the tyranny of the former Soviet Union."[88]

Few of the men around Reagan had been approached by the national media as of yet, and only Ed Meese showed up initially on an obscure cable system, CTV, to talk about his old boss. An effusive quote by Bob Dole was buried in the papers. Some news outlets began reporting "man on the street" comments about Reagan, most of which were praiseworthy in an unsophisticated and sweet sort of way. There was also more criticism, though, which was highlighted. Said one, "But when you evaluated what he did during his presidency, he was all talk."[89]

Leading the charge for the establishment media, *New York Daily News* then went even further saying that under Reagan, "Poverty increased, jobs vanished and more homeless began appearing as Reagan gutted more than 50 years of social programs. Thousands died before

Reagan acknowledged there was an AIDS crisis." The piece, by liberals Tom DeFrank and Maggie Haberman, was formulaic and hostile, had a deep unprofessional bias, and contained serious factual errors, including the charge that Reagan tried to "dismantle the liberal legacy of Franklin Delano Roosevelt" when he did no such thing.[90] Even the limited praise from the liberal media, such as from the *St. Louis Post-Dispatch*, was faint when it compared Eisenhower and Reagan. "Both were two-term Republican presidents; both were older men whose credentials drew snickers from the elites."[91]

Few Reagan defenders were included in the harsh piece.

Paul Laxalt, former governor of and senator from Nevada, was devastated by the news of the president's death. "I feel lower than a snake's belly . . . it hurts," he told reporters.[92] Laxalt and Reagan had been warm friends since the 1960s, when both were governors of their bordering states. They went riding together, camping together, and campaigning together. Laxalt was the chairman of the 1976 Reagan campaign when everybody else in the party was supporting Gerald Ford. He was the chairman in 1980 when everybody secretly thought Reagan would go down to a crashing defeat to President Carter. He'd placed Reagan's name in nomination in Kansas City in 1976 and Detroit in 1980. He truly was one of the original Reaganites and one of the most important. But he hadn't seen his friend in years, urged not to by Nancy, who wanted Paul to remember Ronnie the way he'd been.[93]

Of all his friends over the years, Laxalt may have been the closest. In private, he called Reagan "Ron" and Reagan called the senator "Paul." Nevada and California shared hundreds of miles of border and many issues involving water, timber, parks, and tourism. Through it all they worked together, two sunny and irrepressibly happy men from humble beginnings. Laxalt called the Gipper a "citizen-politician,"[94] something Reagan had always called himself. Nancy Reagan utterly adored Laxalt and actually fought for him to go on the ticket in 1980 with her husband.

Former president Gerald Ford also made a statement later that day. "Betty and I are deeply saddened by the passing of our longtime friend President Reagan. Ronald Reagan was an excellent leader of our nation during challenging times at home and abroad. We extend our deepest condolences and prayers to Nancy and his family."[95] Every part of Ford's statement was utterly accurate except the part about being "longtime" friends.

On Sunday evening, a group of Washingtonians held a candlelight vigil for Reagan in Lafayette Park, which sits across the street from the White House. Grover Norquist, who'd worked on the 1980 campaign, spoke to the group that included conservative activist Kay Daly, who came to the gathering with her one-year-old child.[96]

After initially remaining silent, a few Democrats were now coming forward with statements of condolence. Some expressions were warmer than Establishment Republicans and certainly warmer than most of the media. "On foreign policy he will be honored as the president who won the Cold War," said Ted Kennedy. The Democratic governor of Michigan Jennifer Granholm was also effusive. So, too, was Senator Tom Daschle of South Dakota.[97] Former president Bill Clinton called him "a true American original." The soon-to-be nominee of the Democratic Party, John Kerry of Massachusetts, was fulsome, as was Senator Harry Reid of Nevada. As the Clinton Library had yet to be completed, officials in Little Rock announced that a "Reagan bereavement display" would be erected downtown. Skip Rutherford, head of the Clinton Library, said, "It was customary for other presidential libraries to take note of the passing of a former president."[98]

The Washington State Democrats, who were holding their convention, paused for a moment of silence to honor Reagan. "A collective gasp was heard" from the crowd when Reagan's death was announced. The chairman of the Democrats in the Evergreen State, Paul Berendt, paid Reagan a compliment of sorts, saying that he'd helped reenergize the liberals in the state because of the opposition to Reagan's conservative policies.[99]

An interesting dichotomy was emerging on the Left. Elected Democrats, having faced voters, knew how many of their own supporters felt about Reagan, so they were cautious and even complimentary toward the Gipper. But reporters, who'd never faced anything other than an angry editor or bartender, could be more cavalier about Reagan.

John Cochran of ABC recounted how he'd been stationed in Europe during the Reagan presidency and how they would accost him and say, "How could you elect a stupid cowboy actor?"[100] Of Reagan, CNN's Candy Crowley had her own take, and it was a good one. "He made conservative cool again."[101] But again, the elite media's praise for Reagan was often faint.

Another old Reagan friend, former Pennsylvania senator Dick Schweiker, said, "Here's a guy that lost the presidency and yet he found time to write personal notes to my children . . ."[102] In 1976, Schweiker had risked the wrath of Republicans everywhere when he made the decision to go on the ticket with Reagan, even as they trailed Gerald Ford in the delegate count. While Reagan-Schweiker did not prevail in Kansas City, they came close enough that it could be said they had won the daring gamble. That and Reagan's off-the-cuff and off-the-chart comments on the last night of the convention in Kansas City.

Dick and Claire Schweiker had performed so well in the weeks leading up to the convention and had become so close to the Reagans that a few hoped that Reagan would choose the Pennsylvanian again in 1980. He would choose then-ambassador George Bush, whom the Reagans were, at best, ambivalent about at the time. Schweiker did join the cabinet, though, as secretary of HHS. The Schweikers were scheduled to share a private dinner with the Reagans the night the president was shot in March 1981.[103] George and Barbara Bush were never invited to the Reagans' private quarters during the eight years spent in the White House.[104]

Iran-Contra was popping up often in stories and commentaries on the passing of Reagan. The investigation had lasted well past his presidency, when he was forced to testify before a grand jury in a performance that some thought halting and disjointed. But in the final report, Reagan was completely cleared by the special prosecutor Lawrence Walsh.

Sourly, Danny Glover, the popular movie actor, said, "We all know Reagan's legacy, from the Iran-Contra affair to the funding of the Nicaraguan military in which over 200,000 people died."[105] Bill Plante was on the air at CBS continuing his hard-nosed criticism of Reagan. He had been on a liberal warpath for years and claimed Reagan had spent "so much there was . . . no money left."[106] The AP wire service also kept up a steady drumbeat of criticism. "He was a notably hands-off president. He kept aides at bay . . . He left almost everything . . . to underlings." As usual, the myth that Reagan was "detached" was often thrown in for good measure. Even after so many years, the story also dug up the goofy rumors about Reagan dying his hair![107]

If possible, Bill Schneider at CNN was even more ruthless. "Ronald Reagan frightened people. They were concerned that he was a dangerous man who said often very radical things, too extreme, too right wing, too old."[108] Later in his monologue, he did warm up a bit about Reagan but even so, there were plenty of double entendres. He then reverted back to more Reagan bashing, saying, "In 1982, his economic program had never worked."[109] Also at CNN, Bruce Morton acidly said, "To a country haunted by Vietnam, he offered easy wins, Grenada." And then he poured it on. "It didn't always work, of course.

Marines died in Lebanon. And the president who cared deeply about the hostages there traded arms for them."[110]

Haynes Johnson of the *Washington Post* appeared on NPR to derisively call Reagan "the first celebrity actor," and he also disputed the notion that Reagan could be considered a great president.[111] The lead epitaphic on the front page of the *Washington Post* opened, "A movie actor . . ."[112] Yet another *Post* story, this one by David Hoffman, scoffed at his role in defeating the Soviet Empire, saying the "events are larger than Reagan . . ."[113] A headline in the *Post* simply called Reagan "A Master Political Performer."[114]

Yet another Associated Press story roughly reviewed his years as governor. The AP argued that his term of office was simplistic, stumblebum, marked by sloganeering and jingoistic pronouncements, although there was also some grudging praise for some of his actions.[115] The first sentence of the *New York Times* obituary called him "a former film star" and proceeded to call him America's "oldest" president. Iran-Contra naturally was prominently mentioned again, and the story pitched the idea that the victory over communism was simply "Reagan's good fortune that . . . the Soviet Union was undergoing profound change, eventually to collapse . . ."[116]

The self-aware Reagan was always aware of the media and what he could do and what they thought of him. During his presidency, the press was constantly hounding him about misstatements. When White House press secretary Marlin Fitzwater asked Reagan about challenging some of the accusations, Reagan said, "No, Marlin, don't even waste your time. First of all, they won't believe you. Secondly, the American people, they don't need it because they know me."[117]

Stories about Reagan's passing and observations about him would not be complete without an elitist college professor calling Reagan a racist, and sure enough, Professor William Stewart played to type. He claimed that Reagan and George Wallace were essentially the same and that

Reagan "introduced the new face of the GOP, one that seemed more 'legitimate' than the racist characteristics associated with ... Wallace."[118]

The usual refrain about "guns and butter" was brought up again and again. Also resurrected were myths about the gap between the rich and the poor being created in the 1980s. Many on the Left in America were trapped in a Keynesian past, unable to break out of their anti-intellectual ghetto and see the world anew. They were incapable (or unwilling) to believe in an ever-growing pie. Instead, they remained in a static world in which the population grew and resources remained constant, a world that would be forced to deal with less and less. Reagan offered his own New Deal in 1980, plainly telling Americans they did not have to go on sharing in scarcity.[119]

Nearly twenty million new jobs later,[120] along with the eradication of "stagflation" and high interest rates, the expansion of the private economy grew at a rate six times faster than the growth of the government (thus diminishing the influence of Washington over the private sector). Yet the professional critics on the Left and in the establishment still were not happy with Reagan. But they never would be. All of a sudden, Keynesians who never cared a whit about deficit spending were now wringing their hands like J. P. Morgan. They lamented that the growth in defense spending had led to this hole in the budget. Again, they saw little benefit in the holes blown through corrupt walls dividing cities or corrupt ideologies imprisoning millions as a meritorious return on the investment.

Some saw the assassination attempt and the firing of the air traffic controllers as the two most important events of the eight years of the Reagan presidency. The attempt on Reagan's life probably did create a bond between him and the American people in a way that few understood. The strength and robustness of the way he dealt with the illegally striking controllers union PATCO, which was one of the few unions to endorse him in 1980, did send a message to his political opponents and international adversaries. George Will, who had begun his writing career as a Reagan skeptic but later was often a Reagan admirer, said of how he dealt with the strike, "But this was a moment that people noticed . . . that he was decisive."[121]

From the time he arrived in Washington until the day he left, the national media gave him and Mrs. Reagan a rough ride. Herblock, who some regarded as a mediocre political cartoonist (but he had the favor of the powers that be at the *Washington Post*), must have awoken each day with the notion of tormenting the Reagans with some new cheap shot, including one infamous cartoon in which he mocked Reagan for his deafness. Even Herblock had to grudgingly apologize for that one. Most political aficionados thought the *Post* should have had the superior Mike Peters or Pat Oliphant, both of whom were sharper wits and better artists.

When the attacks and disinformation got too much, grassroots conservatives could and did fight back. CBS had created a horrific mini-series called *The Reagans* in which Reagan was depicted as an out-of-touch and doddering old fool, while Mrs. Reagan a kind of Dragon Lady. The series did not use a single reliable individual, such as biographer Lou Cannon, and did not bring on key Reagan aides as consultants. As the word spread, conservatives across the land rose up in revolt. The executives at CBS were astonished and taken aback. The network broadcast was cancelled and was only aired on an insignificant Viacom-owned cable system with an insignificant audience.[122]

Hollywood remained nearly silent about Reagan's passing, except for those who went public in order to trash him. The man who had done so much for so many—including devising the "royalty" system that allowed actors and actresses to collect money from the studios each time their old TV shows and movies were rebroadcast, saving hundreds of actors from destitution—was otherwise mostly ignored. Reagan's successor as president of the Screen Actors Guild, Melissa

Gilbert, did, however, issue a statement of appreciation for his work impacting "the compensation and working conditions for the nation's screen actors."[123] American television viewers remembered Gilbert best for her role in the 1970s show *Little House on the Prairie.*

Inside the GOP, the Reagan legacy had been debated for years. The outsiders to Washington and the GOP, who embraced federalism and individuality—American conservatism—said Reaganism was an ideology for the ages; a healthy skepticism of centralized authority or, even worse, a police state, yet without the anarchy of the absence of government. Maximum "freedom consistent with law and order," as Reagan said in 1964.[124]

The insiders, often dismissed as "country club Republicans" by the conservatives, were just as convinced that skepticism about government was unhealthy for the country and that the GOP should not be so chary about Washington or government's ability or desire to move or entice the citizenry in a more watered-down collectivist direction. But "at the time of Reagan's retirement, his very name suggested a populist brand of conservative politics that still inspires the Republican Party."[125]

Some liberal editorialists knocked Reagan for cutting government too much, while others knocked Reagan for promising to have cut government more than he did. Others bashed him for suggesting that some homeless were on the streets "by choice." Despite the booming economy he left behind, some economists like Alan Greenspan were dubious of his economic policies that had been productive.[126] Greenspan had once been a member of the Reagan economic team.

On the Left, it depended on who you talked to and when as to their opinions about Reagan. Democratic politicians who did not represent safe seats or states knew it was best to not criticize the deceased Reagan too harshly or unfairly. The more liberal officials from liberal districts tended to be harsher, and the leftist tenured academics who reported or were responsible to no one (other than their own consciences) reviled him with impunity in his lifetime. Across the nation, some of the seats of higher learning lowered their rhetoric when it came to the Gipper. But not all. "His policies infuriated the left and . . . his simple verities made him the butt of jokes."[127]

The Associated Press veered from straight-up news reporting into opinion and editorials. "Reagan's presidency overlaid the spend-thrift 1980s, tagged by some as the 'Greed Decade.' It was a time of conspicuous consumption, hostile takeovers, new billionaires. And for all the glowing talk of Reagan's folksy appeal and infectious optimism, it was a time of growing division between rich and poor."[128] The wire service also said Reagan's was a "career built on image making and public relations."[129]

George Will responded, saying, "Washington had not been hospi-table to conservatives, to put it mildly, since—well, since one of Ronald Reagan's heroes, Calvin Coolidge left. And there was a sense that the media elites and the intelligentsia were in control in Washington, and would look upon any conservative as a temporary interloper."[130] That applied to the tiresome elites, but at the other end, Taryn Solcoff of Boston said, "He shaped the way I saw the world." She was thirty-three years old.[131]

ABC was waxing the competition in content and substance. In addi-tion to Will, Cannon, and others knowledgeable about Reagan, they also featured the esteemed historian Michael Beschloss to add his perspectives. Beschloss was approbatory of Reagan and his presi-dency. CNN later produced their own important historian, Douglas Brinkley, who'd been selected personally by Mrs. Reagan to edit her husband's secret presidential diaries. Reagan was one of the very few chief executives to keep such documents and had they been known during Iran-Contra, they most definitely would have been subpoenaed and the world would have learned that Reagan thought Connecticut Republican senator Lowell Weicker was a "pompous, no good, fathead." Or that he thought Oliver North was "lying" when it came to what Reagan knew about arms for hostages.[132]

In 1994, Nancy Reagan and Paul Laxalt took the unprecedented step of endorsing North's primary opponent, Jim Miller, a veteran of the Reagan years. It wasn't because Mrs. Reagan was deeply enamored with Miller; rather, it was because she—and many other Reaganites—couldn't abide by North trying to drag Reagan into the Iran-Contra mess to try to save his own hide.[133] At times, Nancy Reagan not only got mad, she also got even. North won the Virginia GOP nomination but was badly damaged and was one of the few Republicans to lose in the Republican commonwealth in the Republican year of 1994.

As of June 2004, the existence of the Reagan diaries was still a secret.

Margaret Thatcher was one of the first to come with a formal public statement on Reagan's passing among the former and current world leaders, but within hours these, too, began to flood newsrooms. The current prime minister, Tony Blair, also issued a kind testimonial. Élysée Palace put out a magnanimous statement on behalf of President Jacques Chirac. The French leader "pays homage to the memory of a great statesman who will leave a deep mark in history because of the strength of his convictions and his commitment to democracy."[134]

Brian Mulroney of Canada was kind, saying, "an absolutely marvelous human being and a great and historic leader" about his deceased friend. The president of Germany—not West Germany or East Germany but just Germany—said that Reagan's speech calling on Gorbachev to tear down the Berlin Wall would "remain unforgettable."[135]

Yelena Bonner, wife of Soviet dissident and Nobel Prize winner Andrei Sakharov, said, "To have achieved so much against so many odds and with such humor and humanity made Ronald Reagan a truly great American hero . . ."[136] A large contingent of foreign dignitaries was expected to attend the Reagan funeral, possibly the largest since JFK's in November 1963.

Former Soviet dissident Vladimir Bukovsky bluntly said, "His phrase 'evil empire' became a household word in Russia. Russians like a straightforward person, be he enemy or friend. They despise a wishy-washy person."[137]

Thatcher later said Reagan was "one of my closest political and dearest personal friends."[138]

Speculation abounded about who would and would not attend the Reagan funeral, such as heads of state and the famously recalcitrant Jimmy Carter, who had to be practically begged to attend the opening of the Reagan Library, even though Reagan had attended his and made extremely gracious remarks in Atlanta. It was believed by all that Thatcher, seventy-eight years old, would not attend, as she was ailing and had already taped a video tribute to Reagan to air at the funeral services in the National Cathedral. However, for the past ten years, whenever and wherever she traveled, she took a valise in which she always carried a black dress, the right shoes, and other appropriate memorial accoutrements, just in case she was on the road and her dear friend Ron passed away, as she explained to another friend, Gay Gaines, during a visit to the Gaineses' home in Palm Beach.[139]

The elders of the National Cathedral were themselves being difficult as they wanted most of the tickets for the Reagan service. Fred Ryan was in no mood to negotiate so he simply told them they were moving the services to another Washington church unless the Cathedral acquiesced. They did.[140]

The networks, having made the announcement of Reagan's death and gotten beyond the live interviews with some who knew Reagan well (and some who did not), began to move into reporting and footage reviewing his life. The Beirut bombing was kicked around ("Today was my most difficult moment"[141]), which included the horrendous death of 299 marines and French soldiers. Also, the airplane crash and death of hundreds of military personnel on their way back to the United States for Christmas was reviewed.

From Europe, another military man and Reagan aide, Colin Powell, issued a statement about the passing of a president. "I was proud to be a soldier during his presidency as he restored the morale and fighting prowess of our Armed Forces."

It was also clarified that President Bush wanted all American flags at all government installations to be lowered for thirty days, beginning on Sunday, June 6.[142]

At the foot of the hill leading up to the Reagan Presidential Library in Simi Valley, dozens and then hundreds and eventually thousands of American citizens gathered throughout the afternoon and into the early evening. Flowers—first a trickle and later a flood—began to pile up at the entrance. Local florists ran out. American flags began to appear, too, and condolence cards—someone even placed there a jar of jelly beans, Reagan's long-favored candy. The radio of a parked car began playing "Amazing Grace," and several pedestrians wandered up and began singing in unison.

The library contained more than fifty million documents from the presidency, and later, the Air Force One jet 27000 on which Reagan had travelled "211 missions, 631,640 miles."[143] The Library went through considerable expense to build the magnificent pavilion and bring in the retired plane, piece by piece, and rebuild it. Richard Nixon, Gerald Ford, and Jimmy Carter had also used it, and contrary to myth this was not the plane that transported the body of JFK back to Washington on November 22, 1963. That was the previous Boeing VC-137C SAM 26000. The logistics and cost involved were staggering, but were lessened by a ten-million-dollar donation from Texas oilman T. Boone Pickens.[144]

There was also a large chunk of a wall that once divided freedom from slavery. Reagan had told a communist dictator to tear it down by trumpeting his horn of freedom, just as trumpets had once called down the walls of Jericho.

The affairs of state went on, undeterred by death. The Bush administration was engaged in a heated argument about whether international and national laws against torture applied to their government. The Defense Department produced a lengthy memo saying that the Bush administration should be deterred from the use of torture against enemy prisoners.[145]

The United States had at least one blemish on its record in the treatment of prisoners during the Civil War, but never in the history of the country had torture been state policy. Nine more American soldiers were pronounced dead in Iraq.[146]

A documentary—based on a book by a left wing author and produced by two friends of Bill Clinton about the Clinton impeachment and Senate trial—saw its debut postponed "out of respect," the organizers said, for the passing of Reagan.[147]

Both Nancy Reagan and Thatcher had their own wistful memories. Nancy was philosophical, reflecting on happier days but how, in the end, "you pay for everything." Visiting sometime after the announcement of the Alzheimer's, Thatcher said, "You don't say, 'Do you remember?' You talk about things. You look at the beautiful grounds . . . I know he has good days and bad days."[148]

Dr. Bernadine Healy, who'd worked in the Reagan White House, described in *U.S. News* what the disease did, exactly.

Alzheimer's knows no mercy . . . it relentlessly nibbles at the neural networks of the brain, first attacking the memory pathways, then spreading like an oily wave to engulf the higher cerebral centers. An organ known for its commanding might diminishes to a shrunken shadow of itself, choked with waxy protein clumps . . . millions of its neurons disappear . . .[149]

Several years later, Dr. Healy died of brain cancer.

Reagan's suffering was over and that in and of itself was a blessing. With the release of his suffering came the release of the awful pain his family and friends had gone through for the last several years. His passing, though painful, was also a blessing for all, especially Reagan.

"And whatever else history may say about me when I'm gone, I hope it will record that I appealed to your best hopes, not your worst fears, to your confidence rather than your doubts."[150]

He'd said that at the last Republican convention he ever addressed, in Houston in 1992.

# CHAPTER 4

# ROUGH REQUIEM

*"It took six hours for a bus."*

In July 1975, I concluded my remarks in the Reception Room of the U.S. Senate with these words: "Very soon, all too soon, your government will need not just extraordinary men—but men of greatness. Find them in your souls. Find them in your hearts. Find them within the breadth and depth of your homeland." Five years later, I was overjoyed when just such a man came to the White House. May the soft earth be a cushion in his present rest.[1]

So proclaimed the great intellectual writer and Soviet dissident, Aleksandr Solzhenitsyn, upon hearing of the death of Ronald Reagan.

There had been a deep and mutual respect between the two men. Reagan quoted and cited Solzhenitsyn often. So deeply significant was their relationship that Solzhenitsyn may have been the single most important reason why Reagan chose to take on Gerald Ford in the 1976 primaries, something up until July 1975 he'd been reluctant to do.

In late winter 1974, the Kremlin kicked the Nobel Prize–winning nonconformist out of the Soviet Union. He'd been imprisoned in Soviet gulags for eight years because he'd criticized Marshal Joseph Stalin in private letters. Solzhenitsyn had for a time become a cause for the trendy and the avant-garde in America, and he came to the United States where he was welcomed officially in Washington by Senator Jesse Helms (who was most definitely not celebrated by the elites) and Senator Joe Biden of Delaware (who was most certainly celebrated by the elites) at the U.S. Capitol in a crowded ceremony.

But President Gerald Ford snubbed Solzhenitsyn at the recommendation of Secretary of State Henry Kissinger. Kissinger's policy of détente—like the Helsinki Accords, which ceded the Warsaw Pact countries to the Soviets—seemed like so much more bowing and scraping before the Kremlin for many conservatives, including Reagan. They had put up with it from Nixon but they sure weren't going to tolerate it from Ford.

Yet rather than manfully say why Ford would not meet with the Russian dissident, the White House offered up one lame excuse after another. Ford had to meet with the Strawberry Queen of West Virginia and he had to attend a birthday party for his daughter Susan, were two of the lamest. George Will devastatingly wrote, "It is pathetically obvious that Secretary of State Henry Kissinger is not very interested in Solzhenitsyn's plight."[2]

The eyes of the world community and the national media were on Ford and Solzhenitsyn, and Ford's fraidycat performance grated on many Americans, especially Reagan, who wrote his own nationally syndicated column blasting the president for the cold-shouldering of Solzhenitsyn. It also marked the time when Reagan moved from his Hamlet-like "Maybe I'll run" against Ford to a Jack Dempsey-like "Let me at the son of a gun!" attitude. He also did a radio commentary on the topic, just as blistering as his column.[3]

How isolated were Ford and Kissinger from reality? Solzhenitsyn gave speeches to the AFL-CIO in Washington and New York, introduced by George Meany in the nation's capital and his deputy Lane Kirkland in New York. Thousands of commie-hating union men and women stood and applauded the old Russian of forbidden letters. The American labor movement and the American working man despised the Soviet Union and collectivism (though not collective bargaining) in 1975, but the big business Republicans of the era could never see who was really their friend and who was willing to sell someone—anyone—the rope to hang the Republicans with. Meany had once ordered union members to refuse to load ships with grain headed for Russia under a deal Ford had made with Leonid Brezhnev.

The American left eventually moved away from Solzhenitsyn as they discovered he believed in a moral God, believed in Christ, and believed in moral absolutes. His cache with the Left further dissolved as they moved away from the anti-communism of Harry Truman, John Kennedy, and Hubert Humphrey and toward the accommodationist positions of George McGovern.

Reagan could be a little touchy about who was at the front lines with him and who was bringing up the rear. After all, it wasn't Reagan who once said he'd crawl on his hands and knees to Hanoi for peace.[4] It was the American left that had championed North Vietnam and Moscow and the American right that had opposed communism.

At the 1992 GOP convention in Houston, Reagan was recounting the just-completed Democratic convention and how the opposition party had opposed him on so many anti-communist initiatives but were still trying to take the credit. "We" did this and "we" did that. "Just who exactly do they mean by 'We?'"[5] he thundered to the cheering crowd of thousands about the other party that had just nominated an accused draft dodger for president of the United States.

Reagan, of course, lost to Gerald Ford at the Kansas City convention in 1976 by a nose and an eyelash (and some hanky-panky in some state delegations), and yet it was Reagan who benefited more from the primary battles and the GOP gathering alongside the Missouri River than did the president. And when Ford lost narrowly to Jimmy Carter in the fall, the evidence was irrefutable that Reagan had a national following and could mount another attempt for the 1980 nomination—not that it would be easy. But 1976 led to 1980 and 1980 led to a changed America and a changed world. Without Solzhenitsyn and his snubbing by Ford in 1975, Reagan might never have run for president.

To Solzhenitsyn, there was never any doubt about the East versus the West. He always credited Reagan with the victory over communism. So, too, did another knowledgeable observer, Dame Baroness Margaret Thatcher, peerage of the House of Lords and to the rest of the world the "Iron Lady." "Ronald Reagan had a higher claim than any other leader to have won the Cold War for liberty and he did it without a shot being fired," said Thatcher at the news of her friend's passing.[6] Before the week was over, she would have a lot more to say about her old ally.

Like "The Great Communicator," Thatcher's nickname had been used derisively by her enemies, thinking it would earn ridicule but, like Reagan's, her unofficial title also became enduring and, for their enemies, intimidating.

The Reagan family, led by Mrs. Reagan, attended a private family service in the lobby of the Library early Monday morning. The lobby wasn't enormous, about the size of "half . . . a basketball court."[7] Nancy looked gaunt and frail but also very much in control of herself and events. During the private ceremony, she knelt at the flag-draped coffin and turned her left cheek and gently placed it on him. Her gold wedding band was readily apparent.

The family service was brief, about fifteen minutes. Patti Davis was very emotional. She loved her father dearly, even through their often rocky relationship over the years. She and her mother clasped their hands together and both could be seen teary. The Reagans' former reverend at the Bel Air Presbyterian Church Michael Wenning conducted the service and gently consoled the family. A band had performed "Hail to the Chief" upon the arrival.

Nancy Reagan had begun the day in private at the Gates, Kingsley & Gates Moeller Murphy funeral home in Santa Monica with her husband's remains. The funeral home was Spanish Tudor and had a comfortable "old shoe" feel to it.

She had a quiet and solitary moment there with her husband and then was joined by Patti and Ron. Michael was not with them but later stood silent and alone at his father's bier. Reagan had been prepared for burial, and there was a private family service at The Little Chapel of the Dawn at Gates, Kingsley & Gates Moeller Murphy. Some of the staff also shared a few private moments with Reagan.

Andrew Littlefair, along with the other Reagan advance team members, had met the evening before at the funeral home to go over assignments. The next day, on the unannounced trip from the funeral home to the Reagan Library, they were flabbergasted to see the spontaneous outpouring of citizens all along the route, which snaked about forty miles. "Along one stretch of freeway, the motorcade passed beneath a huge American flag that local firefighters had hung from the ladders of two fire engines."[8]

Nancy Reagan emerged just after 9:30 a.m. She followed a military procession and the coffin and briefly looked at a small, newly assembled memorial of flowers, teddy bears, and pictures of Ronnie. She waved to the applauding crowd and then got into her limousine for the forty-mile trip to Simi Valley. Along the way, Nancy saw handmade signs applauding the Gipper and citizens with their hands across their hearts as a show of their admiration and appreciation. Part of the trip took them over Ronald Reagan Freeway.

Also attending the private rites at the Library were son Ron; son Michael and his wife, Colleen, and their children Cameron and Ashley; and Reagan's honorary pallbearers. Maureen Reagan's widower,

Dennis Revell, was also in attendance. Nancy Reagan clung for stability on the arm of Major General Galen B. Jackman, the commanding officer of the Military District of Washington.[9] His arm and strong, calm presence would be there for her for the entire week.

Nancy Reagan went first. Her emotions got the better of her several times and Patti reached for her mother. Nancy replied, "Thank you, Patti," to which her daughter softly replied, "He's here."[10] A half hour later, she emerged from the Library and departed with Ron and Patti in a limousine.

Already, thousands of cars from California, Arizona, and other states and tens of thousands of people were lining the Ronald Reagan Freeway. Hand-painted signs were spotted praising the Gipper and Nancy Reagan and at least twice fire engines were seen on bridges with an American flag on display. Nancy was dressed simply in a black dress and one strand of pearls. She was also wearing oversized glasses, which in an earlier time she never would have allowed anybody to see.

Hundreds of security workers walked the grounds of the Library in search of any terrorist device and Duke Blackwood met with representatives of the local sheriff's office, the Secret Service, the Simi Valley police, and the FBI. Foundation senior staffer Kirby Hanson also had her hands full with a number of tasks, including the printing of one thousand programs that would not be nearly enough. There was the daily meeting of all the principals involved, from Blackwood and Hanson to Jim Hooley and Andrew Littlefair. Blackwood also had "to determine which staff (noncritical) can go home (hotel) to sleep and what time they should report back . . ." according to The Book.[11]

The Reagan team took care of their own. At the Library, the restaurant was open for free to any staffer or volunteer working full time on the funeral. There were also legal hurdles to clear to allow Reagan Library staff to volunteer for the week with the approval of the "Library's General Counsel."[12]

The building then opened up to allow private citizens to begin to come and pay their last respects, many of them weeping. As they entered, they passed a ten-foot-high statue of Reagan in western garb. The name of the statue was *After the Ride*.[13] Speaking for many private citizens, Joe Dunnigan said, "I walked by the mortal remains of a man who changed the face of the earth."[14]

At a rate of two thousand individuals per hour, Americans went to bid a final good-bye to Ronald Reagan.[15] The entrance to the Reagan Library was silent, the only sounds heard were the shuffling of feet and muffled sobs. Behind the velvet cordon, some dropped to their knees if even only for a moment.

Because of the size of the crowds, shuttle buses were running from the parking lot of Moorpark Community College nearby. A thoughtful, anonymous individual sent thousands of bottles of water to the school for the citizen mourners because of the three-hour wait in the heat to get on a bus. Still, no one complained, no one littered the parking lot. All were hushed and those who spoke did so in low tones. One man standing in line in shorts and a T-shirt described himself as a "Christian surfer." It was, after all, California. Mourners were told to turn off their cell phones and the taking of photos was forbidden. No food could be taken in. As they entered, they stepped on blue carpeting. At the foot of the casket on the floor were two white roses.[16]

A military honor guard stood watch over the casket.

The networks broadcast much of it utilizing a "pool" in which they all used one camera system, in this case Fox Broadcasting. The viewing was supposed to end at 6:00 p.m. on Monday evening but because so many Americans had turned out to see their president off one last time, the decision was made to extend the visitations to 10:00 p.m. All night and all day, the buses went up and down the small mountain, up and down. "The mourners who walked solemnly past Reagan's casket Monday, blowing kisses and wiping away tears, were a mural of American life—hobbled old war veterans, suburban moms and ministers, students and software consultants. Reagan . . . had touched them all."[17]

The number of people who trekked up the hill in a little over one day was the same as the population of a good-sized city. And thousands of others were turned away because of time constraints.

The national media watched in astonishment, still wondering what the citizenry saw in Reagan, an understanding that had eluded them for years. They may have had a better grasp of him if they'd bothered to listen. In 1952, giving the commencement address at William Woods College, he told the graduates, "I, in my own mind, have always thought of America as a place in the divine scheme of things that was set aside as a promised land."[18]

As of 10:00 p.m., roads all around the Reagan Library in Simi Valley were jammed in every direction and police and other law enforcement were turning people away. Before it was all over, 118,000 mourners passed by the bier of Ronald Reagan in thirty-six hours, according to the advance men on the ground who were keeping a meticulous count, Hooley and Littlefair along with Blackwood and the Library itself.[19] The planners had expected 60,000.[20]

Nancy Reagan had gone home to rest and get ready for the Washington portion of the funeral, which would be a very intense and emotional time. She watched the television coverage of the outpouring at Simi Valley and was incredulous at how many people were coming and coming and coming.

Even those who did not agree with him came to show their esteem for the Gipper. By the late afternoon of Tuesday, June 7, the wait to get on a shuttle bus was as long as six hours. But there was no wait for John Kerry. He'd been in Los Angeles to see his daughter while his campaign was on hold, but then journeyed to Simi Valley and was whisked ahead of the tens of thousands waiting to pay his last respects in the "rotunda" of the Library.[21] The Roman Catholic candidate stood alone in front of the coffin for a moment, gently touching the flag, and did the sign of the cross. He then bowed and departed the room.

Kerry spoke with reporters afterward, contrasting his greater respect for Reagan with his lesser respect for Bush. (In fact, Kerry had ripped Reagan eagerly and often during the 1980s.)

He told of a time when in 1985 he carried a cease-fire proposal from Daniel Ortega, head of the communist regime in Nicaragua, personally to Reagan in the White House. Reagan rejected the proposal out of hand. Kerry slipped in a jab saying he'd met with Reagan more often than he had with President Bush.[22]

Sprinkled among the hoi polloi were the rich and famous, such as actor Efrem Zimbalist Jr. and his daughter Stephanie Zimbalist, who waited patiently and unobtrusively.[23] Also attending was actress Morgan Fairchild, representing the Screen Actors Guild according to Littlefair. Littlefair said the celebrities who came to pay their respects, including Governor Arnold Schwarzenegger and his wife Maria Shriver, generally behaved themselves.[24] Some of the Hollywood men like producer A. C. Lyles kissed the Reagan men. "Very Hollywood," muttered one hardened political operative.[25]

One man told of having voted for Reagan four times for governor and for president, and how in 1976 he had to fix Reagan's phone lines at their home in Pacific Palisades. There he found Reagan outside with a shotgun, shooting at squirrels "that were making a racket." The young man didn't have to worry though. "Don't worry, it's not for you, it's only buckshot."[26]

A little boy, Bryce West, stood in line with his mother, Terri, and forlornly said he'd been going to the Library since he was three years old.[27]

The plans for the Reagan funeral were becoming clearer publicly. The three-hundred-page script had been drafted, written, and polished over the years with a lot of early input from Mrs. Reagan, which she personally reviewed annually.[28] In Washington, the casket would be placed on a caisson drawn by a single, riderless horse at Sixteenth Street and

Pennsylvania Avenue and proceed past the White House and up to the U.S. Capitol, where Vice President Richard Cheney would lead the congressional delegation in a memorial. Cheney had worked for Ford in the White House but if you scratched the surface, just underneath was the heart of a western Reaganite.

The stirrups of the horse would hold Reagan's riding boots backward. It was an ancient ritual dating back to Genghis Khan, with some myths holding that it was so a commander could view his troops one more time and another, so he could see the troops he would lead in the afterlife. According to the U.S. military, it simply meant that the officer would never ride again.

All was going forward under the jurisdiction of the Military District of Washington, also known as the "Old Guard." Reagan's casket would be carried up the west formal steps and not the east, but not in deference to his 1981 inaugural that took place for the first time in history on the west façade of the Capitol. Going back to the first outdoor inaugural featuring another populist, Andrew Jackson, in 1829, all presidents had been sworn in on the east side. It hadn't been Reagan's idea, though, to change to the west side, contrary to myth. The decision to move the inaugural ceremony from the east to the west had been conceived by a congressional committee chaired by Senator Mark Hatfield of Oregon for one simple reason: to save money.[29] This time Reagan would enter the Capitol from the west because the east side was closed due to the construction of a new visitor's center.

Reagan would then lie in state in the Rotunda, only the twenty-eighth individual to do so, beginning with Henry Clay in 1852. Lincoln was, of course, the first president to lie in state in the U.S. Capitol, even though the building wasn't completely finished in 1865. Only presidents and former presidents were automatically granted state funerals, but they could also designate state funerals for others. Presidents after Lincoln who were honored in the Rotunda included Garfield, McKinley, Harding, Taft, Hoover, Kennedy, and

Johnson.[30] But not Nixon, who had a state funeral in California, and not FDR, whose private funeral was at his favorite place in the entire world—Hyde Park. Many presidents, in fact, chose not to have state funerals.

Americans who had lain in state in the Rotunda included General Douglas MacArthur; General John J. Pershing; the Unknown Soldiers of WWI, WWII, and Korea; J. Edgar Hoover; and a handful of senators and congressmen, along with a few private citizens.[31] Some erroneous reports said the Reagan memorial would be based on the LBJ funeral. Meanwhile the Rotunda and the Capitol had been closed to tourists since Monday.

As of 2004, Carter and Bush Sr. had their funeral plans on file with the Military District of Washington but Clinton in character had not yet filed his funeral plans.[32]

The Bush and Kerry campaigns had announced a twenty-four-hour cease-fire to be observed on the day of the Reagan funeral. All political advertising would be pulled down for the day of national mourning. "There are moments where partisan differences must be put aside for the better of the nation. Friday is one of those moments," said Kerry's spokeswoman Stephanie Cutter.[33] But this did not stop Kerry from trying to politicize Reagan's death, saying Bush was a "divider," unlike Reagan, who was a "master at amicable disagreement."[34]

Though the Bush and Kerry campaigns officially—if not un-officially—suspended their campaigns, the impeachment of Governor John Rowland of Connecticut for a myriad of crimes would not be postponed for Reagan.

To everyone's surprise, it was also announced that Margaret Thatcher would attend the Reagan funeral, despite her poor health resulting from a series of strokes a couple of years earlier. She'd already taped a ten-minute eulogy for Reagan some months before because her doctors told her she could not travel. "She is absolutely determined that nothing will stop her from traveling to Washington for the funeral," said her aide Mark Worthington.[35]

The Capitol police estimated that tens of thousands of people would come to the Capitol to pay their respects to Reagan one last time. More than 170 foreign dignitaries were expected to attend the funeral,[36] all the living members of the Reagan cabinets and campaigns, and four former presidents and first ladies. The current president of the United States, George W. Bush, would give the eulogy but his father, former president George H. W. Bush—Reagan's second in command for eight years—would also speak.

A squadron of F-15s would streak over Constitution Avenue in the familiar "V Formation," with one plane missing, to represent that of the fallen.[37] Washington had not seen a state funeral in three decades, since Lyndon Johnson's death, and security would be much tighter this time around. In 1973, there was little security but while his funeral was well attended by dignitaries, few private citizens attended, and the sidewalks were mostly empty when Johnson's hearse moved through the streets of Washington.

Of course, September 11, 2001, had changed everything in America. During the week of the Reagan funeral, a strong police and military presence could be felt and seen everywhere, including bomb sniffing dogs, radiation detectors, gas masks, and heavily armed soldiers and thousands of law enforcement officials.

The *New York Times* snarkily said, "Many of the rites for the last production of the man who was the best-known practitioner of presidential stagecraft . . ."[38]

Only hours after his death, at the foot of the Reagan Library, at the statue of him in Dixon, at his birthplace in Tampico, at Eureka, and on his star along the Hollywood Walk of Fame, there began to grow makeshift shrines with flowers, candles, framed photos, jelly beans, signed cards, and personal effects piling up. The statue in Dixon was also draped in black and purple bunting.

Despite the fact that Ronald Reagan had only been dead for two days, a hotly contested debate was already ensuing over his legacy and place in history and would accelerate over the coming week. It was a continuation of a lifetime debate.

Several years earlier the Nobel Committee had snubbed him, choosing instead the vanquished communist Mikhail Gorbachev but not Reagan, who had actually won the Cold War. (Unlike Solzhenitsyn, Reagan was never a *cause célèbre* among the elites and the Nobel Committee moved sharply to the Left over the twenty-year period.)

Academics and others of their ilk from the campuses that manufactured Reagan odium and contempt of conservatism on a daily basis also worked overtime in making their case that the Cold War ended with Gorbachev's happy cooperation and not that America defeated a savage and evil empire. Moral questions such as the millions exterminated under Lenin, Stalin, and other Soviet leaders were swept aside as beside the point. In the worldview of the academy, there was no such thing as good or evil, only collectivism, society, and the power of the state over the individual. They argued for a collectivist state in America and shockingly always placed themselves at the top of the heap. Some American leftists actually mourned the demise of Moscow, preferring its triumph over America rather than the other way around.

Others, who had been little more than bootlicks, shills, lackeys, and "useful idiots" for the Soviets, saw the handwriting on the wall and tried to claim they, too, had opposed communism (wink, wink) all the time.

The American people thought differently. "He stamped out communism," said Slavic American Milan Kondic. A woman from Ethiopia left a poem at the Reagan Library in Simi Valley. She said, "He means a lot to me."[39] And though he did not receive the Nobel, there were many in America who wanted to see his image on the ten-dollar bill, replacing Alexander Hamilton, or a concurrent ten-cent piece so that Americans could choose their favorite, FDR or Reagan.

A "Reagan Legacy Project" had been the brainchild of Grover

Norquist, longtime combatant in the conservative wars and longtime Reaganite. The goal of the legacy project was to name one thing in every county in America—all 3,144 counties, parishes, and independent cities—after the Gipper. Roads, schools, bridges, and what have you.[40]

Also, a Nimitz-class aircraft carrier had been commissioned in 2001, the USS *Ronald Reagan*, and in Illinois the "Reagan Trail" had been dedicated by Maureen Reagan some years earlier. It was a ninety-plus mile journey that made its way through Eureka and Dixon and Tampico and Galesburg and Monmouth, all towns Reagan had lived in as a child and a young man.

The *New York Times* continued their pounding, saying Reagan "was not a strategic thinker . . . he thought in terms of anecdotes, not analysis. His knowledge of international developments was considered thin, and those who met with him said his participation in discussions was usually limited to what his staff had provided him on the 3-by-5 cards." The *Times* trotted out liberal historians like C. Vann Woodward and Tom Cronin. "Professor Cronin" told the publication that Reagan "was not willing to be a leader."[41]

One better-known historian, Paul Johnson, was given a slight chance to defend the Gipper but the paper then rebutted him. "But to many other historians and political scientists, Mr. Reagan's accomplishments will not secure his place among great American presidents." Noticeably, the paper did not rebut the harsh assessment of liberal historians who trashed Reagan. Near the close of its long and mostly harsh obituary, the paper stuck one last parting shot against Reagan, saying he was "not a man given to introspection . . ."[42]

One of the brightest and most interesting intellectuals of the day saw Reagan differently than the *New York Times*. Jeane Kirkpatrick had burst onto the national scene as Reagan's first ambassador to the United Nations. There, she out-dueled her communist counterparts often, and the American liberal establishment—of whence she'd once come—hated her for it. She'd begun life as a garden-variety leftist before moving to a Hubert Humphrey–style anti-communist liberal and then as a neocon, but by 2004 she'd shed the last vestiges of statist leanings and had flowered into a full-fledged Reaganite. "Ronald Reagan believed, as I see it, that the individual is the creative principal in history and in society and economics . . . and in foreign affairs."[43] Reagan could not have said it better himself, seeing always the individual as the world's protagonist.

The Alzheimer's Association of America issued a long and tender statement on Reagan's passing while making note that it was one of only three organizations recommended for contributions by the Reagans to commemorate the president's passing. Their website was publicized to facilitate donations to the Alzheimer Association's Ronald and Nancy Reagan Research Institute.[44]

Later in the week, they also took out a full-page ad in the *New York Times* that featured a touching photo of the Reagans walking on a rural road, hand in hand, as the Gipper held a stick in his right hand with a small dog trying to fetch it. "As our nation mourns the passing of President Ronald Reagan, we remember and honor all that he and Mrs. Reagan have done to give hope, strength and courage to millions in the fight against Alzheimer's disease. Yet, even in our sadness we find hope."[45]

"Ronnie's long journey has finally taken him to a distant place where I can no longer reach him,"[46] said Nancy Reagan. "Because of this, I'm determined to do whatever I can to save other families from this pain."[47] She said this one month before he passed away.

When he found out he had Alzheimer's, he thought not of himself but of the love of his life. "I only wish there was some way I could spare Nancy from this painful experience,"[48] he said in his letter to the nation in the fall of 1994.

To the end, like an O. Henry story of romance and mutual

sacrifice, they thought of the other before they thought of themselves. Presidential historians agree that Nancy Reagan was as strong an influence on her husband as Eleanor Roosevelt was on hers. She was also a shrewd judge of character, knew a lot about medicine because both her father and brother had been medical doctors, and had graduated from the academically challenging Smith College. Her critics dismissed her as a clothes horse and unsophisticated, but more than one adversary came away the worse for wear in a contest of wits with Nancy Reagan.

She was both the immovable object and the irresistible force. She was proud to be Mrs. Ronald Reagan, even in their drooping financial days, and made no bones about it. And when necessary she was smart as a whip and tough as nails, and with him it was sometimes tough love. But also there was a lot of tenderness.

She once wistfully wrote of her idea of romance together in the canoe *Tru Luv* on the little pond he'd built at the ranch, him with a ukulele. "I'm old-fashioned, I know, but I thought it would be so romantic . . ." Reagan replied, "I don't have a ukulele," and without missing a beat, Nancy said, "That's ok, you can hum."[49]

Or maybe he could have brought his harmonica. Little did anyone know, but according to Joanne Drake, Reagan played the harmonica in private. He wasn't great but good enough to amuse himself. He kept one in the top drawer of his desk and would occasionally pull it out and toot on it by himself, thinking, and musing things over.[50] A couple of days before he was to leave the White House in January 1989, the Marine Corps Band presented Reagan with a new, gold-plated harmonica.

In a way, playing a harmonica made perfect sense for Reagan. Poor boys in America whose parents could not afford expensive instruments or music lessons could afford a shiny and inexpensive harmonica found at the local variety store. Tom Sawyer had a harmonica, and there was once even a "Tom Sawyer" brand of the mouth organ. The instrument was evocative of a poverty-stricken and even sometimes lonely little boy.

It was about this time as a child that Reagan for the first time saw his name in a newspaper. On August 3, 1928, the Dixon paper noted that the young lifeguard at Lowell Park, Ronald Reagan, had saved at that point twenty-five lives. In the seven summers he worked there, the tall and handsome young man was paid fifteen dollars per week that eventually became twenty dollars per week, most of which he saved for college.[51] All told, he rescued seventy-seven people and each was carefully notched on a wood log at the Park by Dutch Reagan.[52]

It was easy to imagine the adult Reagan as president, the younger Reagan as a Hollywood movie star, and the boy Reagan in rural Illinois. He always seemed to fit his surroundings and there was connectivity to each. It was hard to imagine Eisenhower in Gettysburg but easy to see him in Kansas. It was hard to imagine Jefferson in Washington but easy to imagine him at Monticello. The minister at the First Christian Church in Dixon, where Dutch Reagan had been baptized and later taught Sunday school, said, "What's remarkable is the extent to which it was carried in his life—that the things that made him president were begun right here in Dixon." To no one's surprise, the accounts of those who attended his Sunday school lessons were all favorable, including that of ninety-one-year-old Dixon resident Ken Detweiler.[53]

To fill airtime, some TV commentators began playing the speculation game, playing doctor, even if they'd never played a doctor on television. At ABC, Barbara Walters—with little evidence—injected herself into the story and said, "And when people began to think that he had Alzheimer's, it was because he was repeating many of those same jokes, it was the first sign, perhaps that some of us got."[54]

Walters then reviewed only the bad and superficial recollections of the eight years the Reagans were in Washington including one disconsolate aide who tried to commit suicide (and fortunately failed) and another who'd served time in prison. She also told the viewing audience she'd been to the Reagan home in Bel Air and the ranch in Santa Barbara. It went on. She even speculated on the relative closeness of the Reagans to their children.[55] Tragedy and celebrity were Walters's specialties, mixed with a healthy self-regard.

Elizabeth Vargas, also of ABC, made a gratuitous comment about Republicans opposing stem cell research and how that put Nancy Reagan "at odds" with them on the matter.[56]

Fortunately, the cross talk moved on to gentler ground, focusing on a book Mrs. Reagan had recently published of Reagan's letters to her. Their release was to a greater purpose. As Reagan began to fade from the national debate in the latter part of the 1990s, the revisionism was already starting about him and his presidency. To help counter the fallacious image of Reagan as a hardhearted character, the decision was made to go ahead with the slim and elegant book. Proceeds went to the Alzheimer's Foundation and the Reagan Library.[57]

"For so long, he was not taken seriously. Nobody knew that he ever did anything like this. They said he didn't read. He always read. He never went any place without a book," Nancy said. In an interview with George Stephanopoulos completed earlier, Mrs. Reagan revealed a startling fact: "He didn't like the phone at all." Reagan, the lifetime citizen politician, did not like to use the telephone but he was a prodigious writer of letters. Her personal favorite was actually a letter the supposedly indifferent father had written to his daughter Patti when she was a mere twenty-one months old.[58]

"Pretty soon the moon and the stars and this breeze got together and filled me with a longing so great that it seemed I'd die of pain if I couldn't reach out and touch your mommy," Reagan wrote his daughter. "I'm counting on you to take care of mommy and keep her safe for me because there wouldn't be any moon or stars in the skies without her. The breeze would whisper no secrets and the warmth would go out of the sun."[59] In one of her varied careers later in life, Patti taught a class, "Recovering from Dysfunctional Families."[60]

At various times, all the children were headaches to their parents. Reagan once confided in his diary, "Insanity is hereditary—you catch it from your kids."[61] He also wrote frankly at times about all four. Mrs. Reagan said as much in her book, *My Turn*. Mike Reagan for years had floated between two worlds, that of his adoptive mother Jane Wyman and of his adoptive father and his wife Nancy. He wrote a book, the title summing it all up: *On the Outside Looking In.*[62]

He complained, according to news reports, that his father missed his wedding. And "according to Michael, the standard holiday invitation from Ronald and Nancy Reagan was, 'come at 5 and be gone by 7.'"[63] Patti had been a rebellious California flower child, Ron "Skipper" had his issues over the years (including estrangement from his parents), and all said and did and wrote things that would have made any sane person climb the walls. On the one hand, many parents in America could have said, "Yeah? Take a look at my kids." On the other hand, all the Reagan children also had fond memories of their parents and told people as much.

Some philosophers said that the worst times brought out the best in people, and Patti Davis was a case in point. She was nothing if not utterly helpful to her mother, stayed in the background, and took her father's passing as hard or harder than her brothers, comporting herself with style and class. Like most fathers, Reagan celebrated his sons but doted on his daughters. Patti had evidently inherited some of her father's writing abilities, too, and in this and a love of animals they shared, among other passions. "As my father leaves, slips away into the shadows of Alzheimer's, a mysterious and cruel disease, his hand still reaches for another hand to hold. His grip is still surprisingly strong, and I will always believe that he knows when it's my mother's hand he's holding."[64]

For all their battles over the years, Reagan had also taught his daughter about fireflies and angels and talking to God and forgiveness.

Pat Buchanan, an acerbic conservative columnist and commentator, had his own take on Reagan in the days after his death. "For Ronald Reagan, the world of legend and myth is a real world. He visits it regularly, and he's a happy man there."[65]

Reagan's pet name for Nancy was "Mommy" but only after his own mother had died in 1962. Nelle Wilson Reagan may herself have died from complications associated with Alzheimer's.[66]

The actual cause of Reagan's death was listed on his death certificate as "pneumonia," but in fact this was only brought upon by the onset of Alzheimer's that was cited in the Certification of Vital Record as "contributing to death." Also cited was his place of birth, his age, his Social Security number, "surviving spouse," his residence, and the signature of the mortician, Robert M. Boetticher. Under the heading, "Usual Occupation" was listed, "President of the United States."[67]

The presidency was not his first goal as a child and young man. He thought about being a cartoonist. He thought about a career in the army as a cavalry officer. He interviewed for—but didn't get—a job at Montgomery Ward in Dixon. He finally became a radio announcer but was fired from WOC. Then hard networking and fate gave him a screen test and eventually a contract with Warner Bros. Studios in Hollywood. Had the war not come along and put a large dent in his career, Reagan might have happily stayed an actor, which he loved doing. He was good and dependable said the directors and studio heads, he was popular said the audience, but he was a journeyman as a thespian said the critics, although he was especially good in "light comedy."[68]

According to Ryan, there was no autopsy.[69] "There was a rule: No extraordinary resuscitation measures."[70]

The body of knowledge about the dreaded affliction was growing, but not so much as to find a cure or even an adequate explanation for what caused it. But Reagan's passing began a public discussion about Alzheimer's, which at the time afflicted as many as 4.5 million Americans.[71] Scientists projected there would be an exponential growth of diagnosed Americans as they came to understand the disease more and more.

They did not know what caused it but, in examinations of brain tissue of deceased victims, saw clues in the buildup of "amyloid plaques and neurofibrillary tangles."[72] There was no cure; the cause could be genetic or environmental. Doctors and research scientists simply did not know.

Ryan remembered the first time he saw that Reagan was not right. It was the spring of 1994 when they were in New York City, and Reagan had reflected an anxiety, almost a fear, about the hotel room simply because it was unfamiliar.[73]

The Reagans had been more open than most first couples about the state of their health. As Ryan pointed out, Reagan could have hidden behind his Secret Service for years, but chose not to do so.[74]

Most presidents, up to Dwight Eisenhower and then continuing again with JFK and thereafter, concealed the president's and the First Lady's health and behaviors. From Washington to Truman, the health of the president was routinely hidden from the press and the people. Jefferson suffered from migraines, Lincoln battled deep depression, Grover Cleveland had surgery for cancer of the jaw (and had a rubber prosthetic implanted), and Wilson suffered an incapacitating stroke in the last years of his presidency. While FDR's confinement to a wheelchair was more commonly known than is now believed, it is also estimated that no more than two or three photos were ever taken of him in his contrivance. The White House press, the staff, and the Secret Service were all in on the cover-up. If some new photographer took a thought-to-be-embarrassing photo of Roosevelt, he'd get the once-over from the boys of the press and the Secret Service would confiscate his negatives and destroy them.

The first president to reveal to the American people his health in real time was Eisenhower. His very first day in office he met with his personal physician, Dr. Howard Snyder, also a career army man and general. The new president made the decision right there and then that there would be no FDR-like concealment. Any health problems would be told to the American people in real time. And so they were. The American people knew of the heart attack and the stroke and the ileitis as Eisenhower suffered from each and other maladies during his presidency. Almost nothing was concealed except for his frequent flatulence.[75]

History has in some instances been unfair and inaccurate to Snyder, such as when he was falsely accused by liberal author Evan Thomas of misdiagnosing Ike's heart attack, though later it was shown Snyder probably saved Eisenhower's life. In fact he was a superb physician, a personal friend, and the person who convinced Ike to give up his four-packs-a-day cigarette habit and take up painting to calm his nerves.[76]

In 1961, JFK reverted back to the concealment policies of FDR and Wilson, thus the public had no inkling of his Addison's disease or his drug dependencies, his ulcers, his colitis, or the fact that he wore a back brace and a lift in one shoe because one of his legs was shorter. RFK had once famously quipped that "if a mosquito bit Jack Kennedy, the mosquito would die."[77]

LBJ vulgarly displayed his appendix scar for the American public, but they did not know of his other problems including the drinking and ongoing battle to quit cigarette smoking. Nixon? Forget it. The drinking and the pills and the paranoid rants were all concealed from the voters. Ford never had any real health problems (except for his bad football knees that caused him to fall down sometimes and that caused unfair speculation), but Betty Ford publicly revealed her breast cancer surgery during his presidency. Her drug and alcohol problems came out after they left the White House, so no one knew at the time she used to slip away in the afternoon and go drink by herself in the back of PW's Saloon on Nineteenth Street, the Secret Service posted to protect her privacy. Jimmy Carter was more open, such as telling the Americans about his persistent hemorrhoids.

The Reagans took a page from Eisenhower and decided to let the American people know from the beginning of the state of their health. Reagan's age at the time of his election—sixty-nine, turning seventy just one month after the 1981 inaugural—was a major issue at the time, even as he was what gerontologists called "young-old." Some of the characteristics of these healthy Americans included "greater social contact," "better health and vision," and "fewer significant life events."[78] Reagan was very social his whole life, and while he had atrocious vision, his health was always excellent. Though advanced in years, they did not exhibit the individualities of other oldsters.

Reagan did not look old but only older—except for the veins on his hands—and certainly did not act old, not with the horseback riding and the constant clearing of brush (a method of conserving ground water and to prevent wildfires that few Easterners understood), and the axes and chainsaws and swimming and other strenuous activities. The dark, luxurious hair also helped, but it was more than appearances. Sheila Tate, Mrs. Reagan's press secretary, told of how it took him several weeks of convalescing at the White House after the shooting, but being startled one day to see the president "bounding down the hall. And Nancy Reagan, ever the protector, held out her hands . . . and said 'slow down, slow down.' And he came pounding up and he joked, 'I can't help it, it's my boyish exuberance.'"[79] He was hard of hearing in his left ear, and he had his appendix removed in the 1940s. But his physique and his indomitable belief in his physical capabilities carried him through all.

At his birth, Reagan was a gigantic ten pounds, and his mother had such a strenuous time delivering him she was advised by her doctor not to have any more children.[80] When Reagan was a child, his mother had the influenza at a time before antibiotics, and he related how his family doctor told him to give her moldy cheese, which may have cured her of the infection.[81]

Even when Reagan was shot, there was only a confused, but understandable, initial attempt by the White House to conceal just how close he'd come to death. Although for whatever reasons the national media also chose to downplay the seriousness of his injuries. Maybe because when he arrived at the hospital he got out on his own steam, hitched up his trousers as he always did, and walked in and then collapsed, but out of sight of spectators. He had lost half the blood in his body, had nearly gone into shock, and then had his chest cut in half to find a bullet that was one inch away from his heart. The doctors at George Washington were amazed at the musculature of Reagan when they began cutting his skin. Tip O'Neill once accidently brushed up against Reagan and said his arm "was like iron."[82]

He also fought colon cancer and skin cancer during his presidency. Nancy Reagan had several brushes with dangerous health problems including breast cancer. Because she was always concerned about him, she did not always take care of herself, which contributed to her health issues. She used to wanly joke that he could fall asleep easily, but she would sit up for hours munching on an apple, fretting and thinking and worrying.

Even in the post-presidency, the private Reagans continued to inform the American people of their health. In 1989, the seventy-nine-year-old Reagan had been in Mexico horseback riding—jumping, galloping—at Bill Wilson's ranch when he was thrown by the rangy horse he was astride. He hit his head and later went to the Mayo Clinic to have fluid drained from his brain. Quite literally, holes were drilled into his head to drain the excess fluid.

He showed his plucky side, even then. The doctors at the clinic had to shave the hair from the right side of Reagan's head. Arriving back in California, he doffed his baseball cap to let the world see his half-shaved head and the big grin on his face. Mrs. Reagan could be seen behind him in the photograph, a troubled look on her face as she reached to put the cap back on, but for Reagan it was one big joke. He loved telling jokes—Irish jokes, the farmer's daughter jokes—but he also loved making fun of himself. He once said the jokes you tell on yourself are the best kind, and he often used his age or tall tales of his laziness to poke fun at himself and endear himself to his audiences.

While in the hospital Boris Yeltsin came to visit him.[83]

When it came to the diagnosis of his incipient Alzheimer's, there was no humor—only honesty. Nancy Reagan said of when they learned of Ronnie's affliction,

> That day we had talked it over and we both thought that we should make this, he should make this public. We always had done that. With his two cancers, my cancer. Because we felt that it helped people, which it did. He had had colon cancer, prostate cancer. I had had breast cancer. And it did help. And we felt the same would happen here. And we went into the library and he sat down at the table and just wrote.[84]

At the time, the only real way to be sure if someone had the dreaded disease was through an autopsy.

Over the years, she kidded about her proximity and influence but also spoke bluntly. During the presidency she joked, "This morning I had planned to clear up the U.S.-Soviet differences on intermediate-range missiles but then I decided to clear out Ronnie's sock drawer instead."[85] But in her book *My Turn: The Memoirs of Nancy Reagan*, she remarked, "For eight years I was sleeping with the president, and if that doesn't give you special access, I don't know what does! So yes, I gave Ronnie my best advice—whenever he asked for it, and sometimes when he didn't."[86]

In her book of letters from Reagan, she said, in past tense, "We've had an extraordinary life . . . but the other side of the coin is that it makes it harder. There are so many memories that I can no longer share, which makes it very difficult. When it comes right down to it, you're in it alone. Each day is different, and you get up, put one foot in front of the other, and go—and love; just love."[87]

She was also frank about the years of ordeal and understatedly said, "Well, it's not a wonderful time."[88] All through the ordeal she was remarkably candid and also strong. In public when asked about her husband's condition she would often just shrug her shoulders and say, "He's okay," or "It's okay." She was eloquent if also angry at times. "You know that it's a progressive disease and that there's no place to go but down, no light at the end of the tunnel. You get tired and frustrated, because you have no control and you feel helpless."[89]

Joanne Drake understood. She told reporters that while all were mourning, there was also a certain amount of relief that Reagan was no longer in pain. "While it is an extremely sad time for Mrs. Reagan, there is definitely a sense of relief that he is no longer suffering and that he has gone to a better place."[90]

Drake was doing her best to hold it together, but even this strong and competent and fiercely loyal woman was sometimes seen fighting back tears. She was the consummate professional, who everybody said was the first person to call in a crisis because she'd know what to do, but for her it was also very personal. "Working for President Reagan was an honor, one I wish every American could experience. He was an extraordinary man."[91]

Over the years, she'd become close to the family, especially Nancy Reagan. "It's going to be a hard six days ahead of them. As you can understand, the family is in deep mourning over the loss of a husband, a father, a grandfather and their hero . . ." She was asked by reporters about her twenty years with Reagan but, true to form, Drake kept the attention off her and on the family and the moment and the solemnity.

Only briefly did she let on that the whole ordeal had been personally tough. Of his passing, Drake said gently, "It was a very, very private moment."[92]

Other aides were coming forward now to tell their stories and recount memories about Reagan. Frank Donatelli was an original Reaganite, going back to his years as a "YAFer"—the Young Americans for Freedom—and organizing the very first Conservative Political Action Conference in 1973 along with Jim Roberts, a fellow young conservative activist, at which the featured speaker was outgoing California chief executive Ronald Reagan.

Donatelli later worked on an independent campaign in 1976 supporting Reagan and in 1980 and '84 as a top aide on the Reagan campaigns and, in between and after, a top aide in the Reagan White House. Over the years, Frank had seen everything in the revolution.

Late in the life of the Reagan administration, he was accompanying Reagan on Marine One out to Andrews Air Force Base. Reagan was looking out the window idly, Donatelli thought. He asked, "Mr. President, what do you see down there?" Reagan replied, "Look at that . . . look at those homes. They're beautiful homes and they're owned by working people. I've got to show Gorbachev how much freedom works in America and how American working men and women can make a better life for themselves. There's no reason why they can't do that in his country also."[93]

Sometime thereafter, Reagan did just that.

He did not want to defeat the Soviet people; he wanted to defeat the Soviet system. Reagan, like a canny old fox, knew the way to beat an idea was with a better idea.

Bob Novak went on CNN to say that the Gipper was "an intellectual. He read the economic texts of Bastiat, Steel, and Compton in Britain." Even more so, Novak said, "I don't believe there was anybody who controlled him or had his ear."[94]

The Reagan Library was actively encouraging aides, staffers, and friends to tell their stories to the national media, knowing it would be an important part of the historical record. Most kept the focus off themselves and on the man they had once called Mr. Reagan, Governor, and Mr. President. Pete Souza, the affable and friendly White House photographer, wrote a long piece for the *Chicago Tribune* on his travels with Ronnie. Souza had been a silent witness to history, recording the good times, the bad times, and the tragic times. He told of the breakdown at Reykjavik, and how Reagan stuck to his guns on the Strategic Defense Initiative. Souza said Reagan had no ground rules for photos except to please not photograph him when he was putting in his hearing aids.[95]

Some aides in the Bush White House moved quickly to politicize the death of Ronald Reagan. "From the shores of Normandy to President Bush's campaign offices outside Washington, Mr. Bush and his political advisers embraced the legacy of Ronald Reagan on Sunday, suggesting that even in death, Mr. Reagan had one more campaign in him—this one at the side of Mr. Bush . . ." Bush's chosen chairman of the Republican National Committee, Ed Gillespie, was leading the Bush band, beating the drums on how similar Reagan and Bush supposedly were. "The parallels are there. I don't know how you miss them."

Somehow, the media discerned that both Bush and Reagan had a "swagger."[96] But the first time a comparison was made, the Bush aides squawked because the networks, rather than broadcasting Bush's speech at Normandy, devoted most of the time to airing old footage of Reagan at Normandy and talked about Reagan. It was the same with the nation's newspapers. Reagan's passing dominated the front pages while coverage of Bush was relegated to deep inside the "A" section.

Tackily, some Bush aides were speculating to the media if Nancy Reagan would campaign for Bush and dug up quotes by John Kerry attacking Reagan. Kerry's aides responded in kind by circulating quotes from the elder Bush, stumping in the 1980 GOP primaries, attacking Reagan. A lot of news stories just hours after Reagan's death were devoted to how it could all be politicized, demonstrating how little the GOP consultant classes had learned. In 1980, when the Desert One mission to rescue more than fifty American hostages being held in Iran failed and eight American servicemen died, Reagan could have rightly leveled President Jimmy Carter, but instead, he softly said, "It is a time for us as a nation and a people to stand united."[97]

Some other Bush aides and GOP consultants worried that the contrast between Reagan and Bush would redound badly to Bush if they put too much emphasis on the comparisons. Bush was no "Great Communicator" and conservative writer Tucker Carlson once quipped that watching Bush give a speech was like "watching a drunk man cross an icy street."[98] The coverage Bush did receive—especially in the European press—was hostile and angry. The Europeans were steaming mad about the invasion of Iraq and though Bush in his speech did not mention the country, he tried to draw an allegory between the liberation of Europe and the invasion of Iraq.

Meanwhile Senator John Kerry simply cancelled all his public events the week of the Reagan funeral. He did keep a previously scheduled commitment to give a commencement speech at Bedford High School in Michigan where he again praised Reagan lavishly and called him a "modern giant." He told the students, "Because of the way he led, he taught us that there was a difference between strong beliefs and bitter partisanship. He was our oldest president . . . but he made America young again."[99]

Bush later announced he, too, would cancel his week of events and those of his surrogates but not before "Bernard B. Kerik, the former New York City police commissioner" attacked "Mr. Kerry for raising questions about the antiterrorism law known as the USA Patriot Act."[100]

Mrs. Reagan had gotten involved in Alzheimer's research in part because of the son of old friend Charlie Wick. Filmmaker Douglas

Wick had a daughter who had developed juvenile diabetes and in turn had started to work on diabetes research. Doug's parents, Charlie Wick and his wife, Mary Jane, had been practically family to the Reagans dating back to the late 1950s. From that point to the present, the Wicks and the Reagans spent every Christmas together. It made perfect sense that Wick would be a Reagan pallbearer.

Just weeks before Reagan passed away Nancy made a very rare trip to the Juvenile Diabetes Research Foundation and gave a touching speech there about her husband's struggles against his own illness. She received an award, which was presented by Michael J. Fox. Her work on behalf of Alzheimer's research to promote education and understanding was widespread and deep and impactful.

All hailed her efforts and all the snarky comments about Nancy Reagan and fashion and high society and other unflattering things had almost stopped entirely. When she spoke publicly, it was a passionate plea for more research on diseases or to deflect questions about her husband's condition. Only sometimes did she talk through her own self-imposed zone of privacy. Two years earlier, she'd told Mike Wallace of CBS, "the golden years are when you sit back, hopefully, and exchange memories, and that's the worst part about this disease, there's nobody to exchange memories with, and we had a lot of memories."[101]

Through her grief she said, "I'd love to talk to him about it and there were times when I had to catch myself because I'd reach out and start to say, 'Honey, remember when?'"[102]

Only families in such situations really understand how horribly tragic Alzheimer's is and not only what it does to its victims, but also what it does to the victim's family. The ten-year battle was a loss that was pre-ordained. With cancer, or strokes, or other maladies, there was hope, even just a glimmer. With Alzheimer's, there was never any hope of a recovery. The news was always bad and always got worse. Mrs. Reagan took on the brunt of the family's obligation, not because the children didn't want to help—they did—but because she would not have it any other way. When someone suggested a vacation for herself, she scoffed. She was going to take care of Ronnie her way.

Reagan's White House doctor, John E. Hutton, came forward to tell his frank tale. It had been two years since he'd last seen the Gipper, the care passing to round-the-clock nurses who specialized in Alzheimer's and senior care. On a Sunday afternoon in 2002, Hutton went to the Reagan home and saw his patient sitting on the back patio with a view of Los Angeles. "Mr. Reagan displayed his usual friendliness and affability, but his mental deterioration was apparent. 'I knew he did not know me.'"[103]

He did not know how Reagan finally died, but speculated that it may have been due to "food inhaled into his lungs" that led to "aspiration pneumonia." This, Dr. Hutton said, was how many Alzheimer's patients passed away. "Two weeks ago, he was kind of status quo," he said based on a phone conversation with Mrs. Reagan.[104]

Although he only had been Reagan's doctor since the end of the presidency, he was one of the few people Mrs. Reagan would allow to see the president; he sometimes would stay for a week, helping Reagan and Mrs. Reagan by doing little things such as helping him in and out of chairs and once catching him in a hallway. "Mr. President, I will never let you fall," he told the failing man.[105] Still, he said Reagan seemed unconcerned.

In 2001, when Reagan fell and broke his hip, Hutton said everyone was amazed how easily Reagan went through the process, talking to the doctors, urging them to see other patients more in need. "Whatever challenge he met, he just took it in stride." Hutton was a retired army brigadier general. After the hip surgery, the first thing Reagan ate was some vanilla ice cream, which made perfect sense since everybody knew what a voracious sweet tooth he had.[106]

Along with Charlie Wick, Joanne Drake announced the other Reagan pallbearers including Frederick ("Fred") J. Ryan, who was chairman of the board of directors for the Reagan Foundation, longtime friend Mike Deaver, entertainer Merv Griffin, and Dr. Hutton.

It was also announced that the Reagan coffin would remain closed for the week. In fact, there would be no open coffin at any of the memorial services. Dignity was the watchword.

The world had seen and would forever see the terrible assassination of John Kennedy in Dallas, thanks to Abraham Zapruder and later the Internet. One can only imagine how much pain and suffering, wasted time, effort, and money would have been spared without the existence of the Zapruder film. How much pain would the Kennedy family have been spared from, from not only the imagery of his death but also from the conspiracy theories espoused by nutcases. Those and other crazies got lots of publicity and generated lots of profit off the pain and suffering of the American people, and as a by-product never allowed the Kennedy family to bury their beloved Jack and move on.

In the end, the Zapruder film only created questions and produced no answers and spawned a culture of cynics and a cloud of doubt that spilled over on Vietnam, Richard Nixon, and the nation as a whole. Few believed that Lee Harvey Oswald acted alone even in the face of overwhelming evidence. And the nation and the Kennedy family had to live with all this for the rest of their lives.

Kennedy family historian Arthur Schlesinger Jr. had written that the family wrestled for a few moments with an open casket, but when they saw what the mortician had not been able to do, they quickly decided to have a closed casket for JFK.[107]

Going back even farther, during the Lincoln funeral procession, a photograph of his body had been surreptitiously taken while on display in New York. The photograph was in direct contravention of the directives of the Lincoln funeral planners. And, from time to time over the years, rumors swept the nation that Lincoln's corpse had been "kidnapped" and was being held for ransom. Indeed, on one occasion it was attempted. His remains also were interred and disinterred on several occasions. It was humiliating.

Near the turn of the century, city fathers in Springfield decided to reinter Lincoln once and for all, under tons of concrete, and thus put to rest the rumors forever. So poor Lincoln was disinterred yet again, and all his former friends and aides including John Hay and his last living son, Robert, were summoned to Springfield to inspect the corpse and pronounce it to be Lincoln. When the coffin was opened, there was Abe, looking just as he had the day he died. Only his black suit was deteriorating. They then realized that to survive the two-week train trip across the country, with multiple stops along the way, Lincoln had been heavily embalmed. He was covered with little sprinkles of red, white, and blue cloth and this, too, they could not discern until it dawned on the men there that this was the deteriorating remains of the American flag that had covered his remains.

All this and more was on the minds of the Reagan family and their intimate friends like Ryan, who had been a part of the funeral plans for years.

Earlier that morning, Reagan's coffin was sealed at the funeral home. The fortieth president of the United States would never again be seen by the American people.

## CHAPTER 5

# A RANCH IN THE SKY

*"In Washington, Reagan would count the days*
*before an upcoming trip to his ranch . . ."*

When Thomas Jefferson left the presidency in March 1809, he went home to Monticello, and in the seventeen years before his death on July 4, 1826, "The Sage of Monticello" never returned to Washington. Not that he didn't have plenty of invitations but he'd always despised the city and preferred to walk among his gardens, spend time with his children and grandchildren, entertain guests, and supervise the building of the University of Virginia, which he considered a more important accomplishment than serving as the third president of the United States. "I am supremely happy in being withdrawn from these turmoils," he said of his retirement from politics.[1]

After his presidency Ronald Reagan felt much the same as Jefferson, and he avoided Washington and he, too, would supervise the building of a place of education, his presidential library just down the road in Simi Valley, between Santa Barbara and Los Angeles. The library was to house millions of presidential documents and personal effects, including thousands of letters written over the course of his lifetime, a treasure trove of history covering the monumental times and life of Reagan and the men and women around the fortieth president.

The first letter Reagan wrote after leaving office was to Richard Nixon. "Dear Dick: Your letter caught up with us here in California. In fact I'm in our new office from which I can see the blue Pacific."[2] A year later he wrote Nixon another letter, this time complaining about the IRS, who had moved into Reagan's offices for six months as they audited Reagan because some designers had donated some of their dresses to Nancy.[3]

Jefferson also had financial problems.

Jefferson, it was said, had achieved philosophical balance and spiritual harmony by the age of sixty-six, when he returned home to his beloved "Little Mountain." Reagan, eleven years older than Jefferson at his own retreat from the "turmoils," had arrived at that point also, content to look forward and not dwell on his time in office. His very last entry into a presidential diary was, "then home & the start of our new life."[4]

The ranch was also spiritual for Reagan and he repeated Psalm 121:1–2: "I will lift up mine eyes unto the hills, from whence cometh my help. My help cometh from the LORD, which made heaven and earth."[5]

Stu Spencer, a frequent golf and luncheon companion of Reagan's in the post-presidential years, said the president almost never spoke about his time in office and never about his legacy.[6] He enjoyed talking about politics, who was up, who was down, baseball, the ranch, his days in Hollywood, and other things, but not his presidency.

When there at his ranch Reagan dressed down. Way down. He clutched "casual" until it could no longer scream. Mostly, he wore old dungarees and frayed shirts that sometimes Nancy would try to toss out, only to discover later he'd fished them out of the trash bin. He often wore a sweat-stained old blue baseball cap embroidered "United

States Mounted Secret Service." It was only there out of sight of the media and the curious that he could be himself and really relax. Mike Deaver always said Reagan was utterly indifferent to fashion.[7]

In his first days of 1981, Reagan called Deaver into the Oval Office and said he'd been reviewing his schedule and saw no time included for the ranch. He told Deaver to fix this and then said, "The more I visit that Ranch, the longer I'm going to live."[8]

He so loved the ranch he even mentioned it in his farewell televised remarks to the nation on January 11, 1989. Reagan also mentioned the ranch in his farewell radio remarks.[9]

Later that year, Reagan was inducted into the National Cowboy and Western Heritage Museum in Oklahoma. He gave a speech there and said, "Western heritage has a special place in my heart . . . the spirit of the West is the spirit of America." During the campaign of 1980, Reagan gave an interview in Oklahoma in which he made fun of the eastern liberal establishment for not understanding "fly over country" and that they thought people who lived there were yahoos from "South Succotash."[10] For a time, South Succotash became a household phrase.

Historian Jon Meacham said that in many ways Reagan "was even more Jeffersonian than Jefferson. The ranch was a true retreat; Monticello was a big, bustling operation, with slaves and a constant stream of (usually unannounced) visitors."[11] Indeed, to get away by himself Jefferson went and hid out at "Poplar Forest," a small house southwest of Monticello where, he said, he could live the "solitude of a hermit."[12] On the other hand, the ranch was best described as adobe— plaster over brick—or "simple hacienda" kidded Marilyn Fisher, the staff historian at Young America's Foundation.[13]

Further, Meacham said, Monticello was only 800 feet above sea level while Rancho del Cielo was at an altitude of 2,240 feet—more than half a mile—and the road up was always arduous and sometimes impossible to traverse. (Originally named Tip Top Ranch, Reagan changed it to Rancho del Cielo—Ranch in the Sky—when he and

Nancy purchased it in 1974.)[14] Reagan's spread really was a breather from the world, unlike Monticello. Finally, Meacham noted that "Reagan probably did more manual work than Jefferson ever did." But, "the spiritual side is clearly something they had in common, and I suspect both men liked the idea that they could see more from their mountains than they could from the arena."[15]

At the last, unlike Jefferson, Reagan would make one final trip to Washington, though ironically, it was faster to travel three thousand miles via jet in 2004 than it was to travel less than two hundred miles via carriage in 1826. Jefferson's final days ended at his beloved little mountain just as he had hoped.

Reagan's sadly did not.

It was only at the ranch where Reagan could operate a vehicle (other than a golf cart at Camp David) during the presidency, the two jeeps, which he could drive at his leisure over the crude roads of the 688-acre spread. More than one agent came back shaken by Reagan's sometimes harrowing driving.

"Mornings usually meant riding his favorite horse, El Alamein. Afternoons usually were spent chopping wood, trimming trees or working on a project like building a fence," recalled Pete Souza. "Dressed in blue jeans, a work shirt and some sort of hat, Reagan could easily have been mistaken for one of his workers."[16] He'd made the patio in front of the house with flat sandstone rocks he'd dug up on the property. There was also a "pet cemetery" on the property, complete with carved headstones.[17]

But he sometimes went out for a late afternoon ride, once to the embarrassment of a female Secret Service agent. At least according to rumor.

She was posted to a remote part of the ranch and as such decided to sunbathe—with her blouse off. Reagan, riding in quiet, startled the young woman—now deeply red—but he had a good laugh. He was the first president to have a woman on his protective detail, and there was never any problem, except he kept insisting she go first through doors.[18]

The two jeeps—both standard transmissions—that were owned and used by President Reagan at Rancho del Cielo were the well-used red 1962 Willys model CJ-6 that still resides at the ranch, and the pristine blue 1981 Jeep Scrambler CJ-8.[19] (This is on permanent display in the Reagan Ranch Center in Santa Barbara.) The Scrambler had a 1985 Inaugural license plate that said, "GIPPER." He also showed off his sense of absurdity, putting up a fictitious movie poster of him as Clark Gable and Margaret Thatcher as a bosomy Scarlett O'Hara in the tack barn, and the "Kangaroo Crossing" sign he'd been given by an Australian women's club.[20]

Water supply was always a problem, which meant brushfires were always a problem, and though "Lake Lucky" contained some one million gallons of water, transporting or pumping it to a distant part of the ranch was impossible. But there was no way to adequately describe the spectacular beauty of the Santa Ynez Mountains where the ranch was located. Olive trees and Coast Live Oak trees bloomed there as did the Vladrone flower. There were Mountain Lilac and Black Sage and Toyon and White Sage and Yerba, all beautifully flowering exotic plants. The Coast Goldenbush was exquisite and the Hummingbird Sage was a gorgeous shade of deep red. A plant called Our Lord's Candle was spectacular, and the Meadow Barley and the Purple Needle grass when watered were spectacular. It was a horticulturalist's dream.

Wild animals were plentiful too. Everything from bobcats to foxes, California mule deer, mountain lions, black bears, and varmints like skunks and squirrels were there. In the air were ducks, woodpeckers, and hawks and slithering on the ground were all sorts of snakes, including the poisonous kind. There was an old television inside that got pretty good reception from Los Angeles. The house was only heated by the two fireplaces and many were a morning when Nancy Reagan did not want to get out of her warm bed and put a toe on the cold tiled floor.

Their bed in the tiny bedroom was actually two single beds shoved together. The kitchen was small and had only an oven and underpowered range. The dishes and utensils were unmatched, a mishmash collected over the years. Nancy Reagan must have laughed silently to herself when at the ranch as she thought of all those reporters and politicians who had attacked her as the "queen of Beverly Hills."[21] If she was the queen, she had no subjects to command, especially at Rancho del Cielo. Reagan had his own reminders of humility, including a copy of a Montgomery Ward catalogue that sat on a table there for years, perhaps to remind him of how he'd applied for a job in the sporting goods section with the chain department store in Dixon after graduating from Eureka, only to lose out to a local high school basketball player.[22]

At night, there was no ambient light from a neighboring town or from street lamps, only from the little house itself. Often the night sky was so brilliantly clear, shooting stars and the constellations filled the heavens. The air was bracing, clear, and quiet. Throughout his presidency the networks leased some land from a higher adjoining property, though at a great distance, and aimed their cameras down on the main house and surrounding land, which nonetheless perturbed the Reagans, who saw it as a violation of their privacy. Still, Reagan liked to jerk their chains, as he proved one day by facing the cameras and clutching his chest, feigning a heart attack.[23]

During his eight years in Washington, he spent approximately one entire year at Rancho del Cielo. (Because he didn't like Washington, he and Nancy also spent 183 weekends at Camp David.)[24]

Indeed, 333 Refugio Road was their official residence, and the Reagans were registered to vote there, as they did in 1984. It had been the Reagans' official residence since 1974. They'd sold the Pacific

Palisades home in 1981, the very house built for them by General Electric in the 1950s.[25]

Dennis LeBlanc said toward the end of Reagan's second term the temporary buildings for the helicopter, the military, and the doctors began coming down and finally, the only government building left was the Secret Service command post. LeBlanc had gone to Governor Reagan's detail fresh out of a new graduating class of California Highway Patrolmen. He quickly bonded with both Reagans, later going on the payroll of Deaver and Hannaford, handling security but also working closely for years with Reagan at the ranch. Sometimes it would be just the two of them there, working during the day, eating simply, and watching television in the evening.

Outside the family, LeBlanc was one of the very, very few who stayed overnight at the ranch. At the end of a hard day, Reagan would tell LeBlanc, "We did good today," and then discuss what he wanted to do the next day.[26] Up there Reagan almost never discussed politics, except in 1996 when he and LeBlanc were watching the Democratic Convention, where President Clinton was being renominated. Reagan got "irritated" according to LeBlanc. "He said, 'We can't let this happen. We have got to do something. What can I do, what can I do?"[27]

Toward the end of his presidency, Reagan called LeBlanc and said, "Dennis, you know I am going to be leaving office. I'm thinking about spending a lot of time up at the ranch." LeBlanc warned Reagan that his employer in 1988, Pacific Bell, liked the cache of one of their executives being close to the president of the United States but might be less willing to let him go work at the ranch if Reagan needed him after January 1989. Reagan asked LeBlanc for the name and phone number of his boss. Less than an hour later LeBlanc's boss, Art Latno, called the young man.

"How did he take it?"

"He took it very well and you should, too, because you are going to continue going up to the ranch."[28]

In the last months of his administration, Reagan's speechwriters, including Clark Judge, often inserted references to the ranch into Reagan's remarks. No doubt he really wanted to get back but also Judge and others knew Reagan felt it was important to signal to the world that he believed the peaceful transfer of power was a hallmark of the American government and that all presidents upon leaving office were merely private citizens once again.[29]

Like Jefferson, he also did a lot of writing and thinking at the ranch. Well-marked books on the many shelves there included several volumes by William F. Buckley, novels, and *How to Pitch* by Bob Feller.[30]

As he wrote in his autobiography, *An American Life*,

> As I rode Little Man around Rancho del Cielo during the spring of 1975, I thought a lot about the lost vision of our founding fathers and the importance of recapturing it and the voices from around the country who were pressing me to run for president. And I remembered something I'd said many years before: A candidate doesn't make the decision whether to run for president; the people make it for him.[31]

No doubt presidential biographies contain a bit of fluff and revisionism, but even so, it was clear that Reagan did decide to take on Ford, setting off a chain of events that altered the course of American and world history.

With Reagan's health failing in 1998, Nancy Reagan reluctantly sold the ranch to the Young America's Foundation for "nearly $6 million"[32] and for a time some family members, especially Michael, squawked. But their complaints faded when it became clear that the Foundation—headed by Ron Robinson—and the ranch—headed by Frank Donatelli, Reagan's old political director—had only good intentions and planned on using the ranch sparingly with high-dollar donors and as an inducement for high school and college students who wanted to study and learn about American conservatism and Reagan. Years later, Patti Davis wrote a charming article for *Town & Country* and while she couldn't get comfortable with their philosophy, she noted with pleasure that they had taken marvelous care of the ranch her parents had loved. "The ranch was my father's refuge, his sanctuary; it fed his soul."[33]

Donatelli handled much of the negotiations for the sale of the ranch on behalf of the Young America's Foundation, and later he said it was not true that Nancy did not like the ranch, as some had claimed.[34] It was the one place in the world she could have Ronnie to herself. Dennis LeBlanc agreed and said while at first the ranch was not "her cup of tea," Nancy ended up "really, truly enjoying her visits up at the ranch."[35]

Frankly, Mrs. Reagan needed the money. The care for her ailing husband was extraordinary and the cost to maintain the ranch was prohibitive. The Clinton administration failed to protect it as an historic site as had the state of California, and prior to the Foundation's purchase a wealthy liberal, Ron Burkle, had made his interests known. There had also been some talk about subdividing the property for development. Dennis had been there when the widow of Ray Kroc, the McDonald's hamburger king, looked over the property.[36] She, too, was a wealthy liberal even though her deceased husband was a Republican who'd known Richard Nixon and Reagan.

Real estate values in Santa Barbara had always been at a premium and the ranch, with its seclusion and spectacular views of the Pacific Ocean, would have been attractive for many of the rich and famous who wanted to have a second or third home. Sotheby's had the listing on the property. It was not unusual for a presidential home to fall into the wrong hands or disrepair as had happened to both Mt. Vernon and Monticello, which descended into rotting ruin for years until citizens stepped forward to save both of them.

In Reagan's case, neither the local, state, or federal government ever showed any interest in obtaining the historically important ranch.

Fortunately, the ranch was obtained by an organization with which Reagan had a long and warm relationship. The same was true with the Young Americans for Freedom, a once-affiliated organization. Donatelli, who had worked on all the campaigns and had produced the very first CPAC at which Reagan spoke, was also a top official with the Foundation and this was further evidence the ranch would not be abused.

Reagan had always had an extraordinary relationship with young people. But not all loved him, like at Berkeley, where thousands protested his election in 1980, burning and plundering the campus. Sponsored by Students for Peace, scores were arrested.[37] But many more did support him and now he'd created "a remarkable generation of conservatives," said CNN's Judy Woodruff.[38] For years, Reagan had a close relationship with the Young Americans for Freedom, serving on its board of advisors, and gave some of his most important policy speeches on college campuses.

Marc and Kristen Short were hired in 1998 by the new owners of the ranch to oversee its maintenance and begin to put together a program to attract young people to the conservative legacy of Ronald Reagan. The Shorts were newly married in their twenties, were young and photogenic, and had grown up as children of the Reagan Revolution. But before they could even get their feet wet, the first order of business was to meet Mrs. Reagan at the ranch.

As it turned out, they were there the last time Nancy was there. Similarly, Dennis LeBlanc was there the last time Nancy was there and the last time the Gipper was at the ranch. Suffice it to say, nobody was happy on either occasion. Nancy went up previously, accompanied by Dennis, to spend two days going through things including all the books, what she wanted to take, and what she wanted to leave. She gave

LeBlanc Reagan's set of signed Louis L'Amour novels. Nancy also gave LeBlanc a hand-carved duck decoy for his wife, who collected them. Over the years, the Reagans had given Dennis clothes and other gifts, and they never missed his birthday.[39]

After the ranch was sold, Nancy went back in the spring of 1998 and brought things she thought belonged to the ranch. Kristen remembered she wanted to bring back "things that . . . would add . . . personal touches to the house."[40] She also, according to LeBlanc, wanted to take some personal items. Arriving, she said to Dennis, "Boy, this brings back memories, but he's not the same man anymore. It's a different person."[41]

Nancy Reagan brought back to the ranch a bedspread, and she and Kristen made the master bed together. Since there was no one else around, Kristen and Nancy just went to work on other chores around the small house. As they worked together, Nancy reminisced. "It was just a poignant moment," Kristen recalled. "And she brought back some items of clothing . . . some of his riding things. A Secret Service jacket . . . given to him. Different boots and things . . ." All the time Nancy was telling Kristen about each item and memories about the ranch, and as they moved around Nancy repositioned furniture and items back to the way they'd had them.

"It was important for her that people would know who he was and what their life there was like. And she wanted to make sure that Marc and I understood that . . . because she knew that we would be telling that story, sharing that information with people . . ." As the afternoon wore on, Nancy warmed up to the Shorts, especially Kristen, and they walked the house and grounds together. They went into the guest-house and "she told us about Margaret Thatcher coming."[42]

But the Shorts also afforded Nancy Reagan some distance, allowing her time to reminisce and think alone. For two kids in their twenties, it was heady stuff. Marc Short reflected on her leaving the ranch for the last time. "This was kind of the real final end to that chapter. And . . . I think that there was a little bit of not quite yet wanting to let go." Mrs. Reagan, he recalled, "teared up at one point."[43] Alone with Dennis, "we both cried."[44]

LeBlanc said the last time Reagan was at the ranch no one actually knew it was the last time, so it had little of the sorrow as when Nancy knowingly left for the last time. But ranch hand Karl Mull wrote in his diary August 14–15, 1995,

> President and Mrs. R. up for 2 days. No riding-no work. President has obviously slowed down since his announcement that he suffers from Alzheimer's disease he is far less active than before. There will be no more horse riding and no more brush cutting or other rough work. Dennis drove him in blue jeep which he enjoyed [but] other than that there was no other activity. He is still very cordial as always but far less active.[45]

John Barletta went even deeper in his recollection of Reagan's last visit to the ranch, saying that he did not recognize the place, that he slept on the way there—unlike every other time—and that when he arrived, he thought he was at his Malibu ranch that he'd sold years earlier. Finally, Reagan exclaimed, "I thought we sold this place." Mrs. Reagan, crying, could not take it anymore. "I came here just to see about this, just to see his beloved ranch, and now even that's gone. What are we doing here?"[46]

Marilyn Fisher, curator of collections with the Young America's Foundation, said, "The entry on September 26 vaguely indicates last visit to the Ranch" for Reagan.[47]

In 1992, Steve Colo became head of Reagan's Secret Service detail after the calamity in Las Vegas, when a crazed left wing activist, Rick Springer, got on stage and smashed a glass eagle at the Gipper's feet. Colo was a popular and low-key career man with the Service and over the course of his time it fell to him to gently take away the more dangerous tools for Reagan's own safety, all with Mrs. Reagan's quiet approval. Even then, Reagan was telling jokes. "Hey, did you hear the story . . ." Reagan was still driving the jeeps around the property though, and Colo would sit in the passenger seat with his left hand gently on the wheel.[48]

He got to travel with Reagan in so-called retirement, as well, such as when the former president spoke at Oxford in 1992. "That's still kind of late in his career and he gave a marvelous speech . . . but after that he gave less and less . . ." He also accompanied the Gipper to a Stanley Cup game, to the Snake River, and to other locations and events. And to the Mayo Clinic in 1994. A doctor told him after examining Reagan, "You really need to understand that this is the onset of dementia, and that as you are protecting him, you and your team need to understand that there's going to be some changes."[49]

The analysis and arguments over Reagan's legacy continued. Presidential historian Michael Beschloss credited Reagan with popularizing conservatism and the idea of federalism—"moving power away from Washington."[50] But a sixty-year-old woman who'd gone to the mortuary two days earlier, Donna Glassman, simply said, "When I think of him, I think of America."[51].

Some, like Fred Ryan, embraced a "supply-side" approach and simply let a thousand flowers bloom when it came to the legacy, rather than trying to keep an impossible hold on it, as his predecessors at the Library had tried.

Still, there were sometimes private skirmishes and low warfare between some of the Reagan heritage entities. In the years since leaving the presidency, the fight over the Reagan legacy often was contentious and bitter. After all, he'd been preceded by failed or mediocre presidents and succeeded by failed or mediocre men and as the years went by, his shadow lengthened over the Republican Party, over the presidency, and over the country.

The difference between the Eastern Europeans' and the Western Europeans' response to the death of Reagan was astonishing. Basically, those who had freedom but had been threatened were coming down hard on his legacy while those who had no freedom until the victory over communism celebrated Reagan. The French dismissed him as a "cowboy *justicier*,"[52] while Mart Laar of Estonia said without Reagan he'd be somewhere in Siberia in chains.[53] Already, statues of Reagan had been going up where statues of Lenin and Stalin once stood, but more would be built in the years that followed.

Stories both good and bad were being recounted in the national media by the high, low, and middle about Reagan.

An indignant and thin-skinned Mario Cuomo told of how when he'd been introduced to Reagan by Senator Pat Moynihan, Reagan supposedly said, "You don't have to introduce me to Lee Iacocca!"[54] Cuomo, naturally, saw it as Reagan's *faux pas* instead of another perspective, which is he just didn't make much of an impression.

James A. Baker, his supremely competent first chief of staff, disputed that Reagan was a great compromiser, meeting his opponents halfway. Reagan, he said, "would much rather get 80 percent of what I want than to go over the cliff with my flag flying."[55] Some mistakenly said that Reagan said, "My 80 percent friend is not my 80 percent enemy." It was checked and rechecked and chased down and no one could really remember hearing Reagan say it, and it was never found in any of his interviews or writings. Still, the myth persisted, even when Reagan's longtime speechwriter and friend Peter Hannaford remarked, "Not only didn't he say it, I doubt he even thought it."[56] Reagan, as Baker accurately reflected, would negotiate for as much as he could but always wanted to go back and get more and eventually all.

The closest Reagan had come was in 1968 when he said, "I'm willing to take what I can get. You have to take what you can get and go out and get some more next year; that's what the opposition has been doing for years."[57]

Stories filled local newspapers of Reagan's passing from the local angle, and there were plenty. Everybody from Albany, New York, to Zamora, California, and points in between seemed to have a story about meeting Reagan or hearing him give a speech or some other type of personal contact. All told of his kindness and thoughtfulness, especially by those individuals often overlooked by politicians, like busboys, housemaids, cops, and firefighters. It was almost monotonous in that almost all warmly praised Reagan. Many stories opened using the name and the state and the phrase "love affair"[58] and Reagan. A retiree in Santa Monica said, "A lot of us out here have never met him, but we feel like we did."[59]

In 1984, Reagan's best state in the country was Utah, which he won with 75 percent of the vote. But it was not the greatest landslide there. That belonged to another populist from the Midwest, William Jennings Bryan, who carried the Beehive State (yes, you read it correctly) with a mindboggling 82 percent in 1896.

When Reagan hosted *Death Valley Days*, the opening narration was filmed in front of the Parry Lodge in Utah as he stood by a white horse. Reagan's death so infused the culture that a sports writer for the *Chicago Tribune*, Mike Downey, wrote a column, weaving together Reagan's love of horses with the winner of the Kentucky Derby and the Preakness, Smarty Jones, and the Downey's occasional correspondence with the Reagans over the years.[60]

Over the previous week some pretty important people had passed away, including Archibald Cox, ninety-two years old, the famed Watergate special prosecutor who was fired by Richard Nixon in 1973. Also Sam Dash, who was the counsel to the Senate committee investigating Watergate, had passed at the age of seventy-nine. William Manchester, historian and author of critically acclaimed biographies of John Kennedy, Winston Churchill, and Douglas MacArthur, perished at age eighty-two.

And Alberta Martin, ninety-seven years old, expired. She was widely believed to have been the last widow of a Civil War veteran.[61] In the early part of the twentieth century, there were plenty of "May-December" marriages between wizened old veterans of Blue or Grey that married sweet young things, who would, in turn, be cared for with a lifetime military pension. Fittingly, Alberta died in Enterprise—Alabama, that is.

The Bush-Reagan compare-and-contrast debate was percolating in the national media and was intensifying, becoming harsh. "After American troops seized Baghdad, President Bush donned a flight suit and landed by jet fighter on an aircraft carrier festooned with the words 'Mission Accomplished.' Mr. Reagan stopped wearing costumes when he left Hollywood."[62]

For some in the press, Reagan was now Pa Walton and Bush was Eddie Haskell. Many in the media, never respectful of Reagan, were now using Reagan to bash Bush. It was a scene often played out in the dens of the nation's broadcasting studios. From Barry Goldwater to Bob Dole to others they once excoriated by using other conservatives to bash them, they now used old conservatives to bash new conservatives. It was as familiar as it was predictable.

The major media were beginning to issue editorials and commentaries on the life and times of Ronald Reagan and many missed the point. The *New York Times* said the problems of Washington in 2004 could be traced to Reagan's term of office—sixteen years earlier. Words such as *flaws* and *slogan-driven foreign policy* littered the lead editorials, and it generally exhibited the most superficial understanding of Reagan and his life and times. Still, the editorialists got two things essentially right: "He will almost certainly be ranked among the most important presidents of the 20th century . . . Mr. Reagan's stubborn refusal to accept the permanence of communism helped end the Cold War."[63]

Letters to the editor of the *Grey Lady* were running generally more favorably toward Reagan than their columnists and editorial writers. The paper did print gracious columns by Mikhail Gorbachev and Bob Dole. Dole wrote,

> One of the first things he taught me was about loyalty: a few months after he took office, I was in the hospital recovering from kidney stone surgery. Much to my surprise, he took a helicopter to Walter Reed hospital to visit . . . By the time he left, I was ready to march up any hill, let alone Capitol Hill, for him. Ronald Reagan is smiling upon us today . . . [64]

David Brooks, a High Tory and neocon writer for the *New York Times*, nonetheless wrote a superb column accurately portraying Reagan as the quintessential Exceptionalist.[65] Clyde Haberman, another columnist with the paper, penned a piece ripping Reagan. He quoted Mario Cuomo saying Reaganism was "the triumph of persona over policy." Elaborating, Cuomo said, "The results [of Reaganism] made the denial of compassion respectable." Revealingly, Cuomo's old nemesis Ed Koch said of Reagan, "I thought he was a terrific president. I wish we had more like him."[66] Displaying his own form of compassion during the two campaigns Koch and Cuomo waged against each other, Cuomo operatives sent signs across New York City and the state that said "Vote for Cuomo, not the homo."[67]

Paul Krugman, a diminutive and longstanding Reagan basher, predictably wrote another column trashing him even in death. On a brighter note, Governor George Pataki said the state of New York would close their offices Friday, June 11, following suit of the national government as a day of mourning for Reagan. Many other states were closing down in remembrance of Reagan. But New York City mayor Michael Bloomberg announced that New York City would remain open because of the "complications" such a closing would do to the business of the city.[68] For years, the inflated and entitled metropolis felt itself apart and above the rest of the country. After September 11, there was some debate over whether New York City was even a part of the United States. Perhaps. Or perhaps the city was just dominated by left wingers.

The running joke was there were more communists on the Upper West Side of New York City than there ever had been in the politburo. Indeed, NYC had closed in memoriam for the deaths of Franklin Roosevelt, JFK, Martin Luther King, Jr., Robert Kennedy, and LBJ, but not for Ronald Reagan.

Bloomberg's indifference to the death of Reagan was typical for the cruel and indifferent city, as Kitty Genovese found out years earlier. In 1981, at a meeting of an ad agency, when news came of the shooting of Reagan by John Hinckley, the ad executives briefly looked at the TV news and then went back to their story boards, as their president's condition went without concern or regard by the masterminds of Madison Avenue.

The New York Stock Exchange, however, announced it would be closed the day of the Reagan funeral. The last time it had been closed for a president's death was for Richard Nixon in 1994. The Exchange, which had begun during the presidency of George Washington, did not close for all presidents and in fact, in the two-hundred-plus-year history of Wall Street, it had closed only thirteen times due to a president's death.[69]

The major publications also gave significant coverage to outside Reagan critics and not just their own in-house writers. One headline yelled, "Critics See a Reagan Legacy Tainted by AIDS, Civil Rights and Union Policies."[70] In fact, spending on AIDS research rose under Reagan, and his appointee Dr. C. Everett Koop as surgeon general became the world's leading advocate of AIDS prevention and research.

Both *Newsweek* and *Time* magazine issued commemorative

publications on the death of Reagan, both featuring the iconic photo of the Gipper taken some years earlier at the ranch. He looked like the rugged cowboy and naturally wore a white cowboy hat, a Stetson, size seven.[71] He wore a blue denim shirt. His eyes were crinkly, his lopsided smile familiar, curled up to the right. "Manly" was the way to describe the handsome photo, but point of fact Reagan was one of those lucky people who never took a bad photo, like JFK. Maybe it was their Irishness or their eternal optimism.

"We knew it might happen," said Jon Meacham, the managing editor of *Newsweek*.[72] Both magazines had to quickly dump their planned cover stories and scramble to paste together an entirely new magazine although, as with most elderly public officials, Reagan's obituary had been drafted sometime earlier but frequently updated to reflect current events and his changing status.

The cover photo had been taken after he'd lost the nomination to Gerald Ford, in 1976, by photographer Michael Evans, who in 1981 became the official White House photographer at Reagan's personal request. At the time, Evans was there at the ranch for a "shoot" for *Equus* magazine.

While there at Rancho del Cielo, Evans had also photographed Mrs. Reagan, clad in denim shirt and jeans, lying in a rattan hammock, looking downright appealing, her eyes alluring and red lips full. In 1980, the campaign was casting about for an official poster, and campaign operative Lorelei Kinder took it upon herself to come up with "Reagan Country" including this photo of the Gipper[73] surrounded by chintzy sketches of various town and country scenes; even though few at the time liked it, it became hugely popular and became one of the top-selling items at the Reagan Library gift shop.

The Nielsen Company, which tracked viewership on network and cable television, saw a sharp increase over the previous several days. Fox was up 11 percent, CNN was up 12 percent, and even MSNBC was up

5 percent. But more amazing was that among the key demographic, the 18 to 34-year-olds, CNN's viewership was up 27 percent and over at Fox, among 25 to 54-year-olds, viewership was up 17 percent.[74]

Even at the end, young Americans followed and understood Reagan better than many in their country.

Some of Reagan's most important speeches of his presidency were given on college campuses: Notre Dame, Eureka, Georgetown. He even spoke at Moscow State University under a giant bust of Lenin. To the children of Lenin and Stalin he said, "The key is freedom. A bird on a tether, no matter how long the rope, can always be pulled back." Elaborating, he spoke of "freedom of thought, freedom of information, freedom of communication,"[75] all notions for which men and women had been sent to gulags or disappeared into the night over the previous seventy years.

He never spoke at Harvard, because even though they had invited the president to speak at the 350th anniversary graduation, the egalitarians of the Yard refused to present President Reagan with an honorary degree. The Reagan White House politely told Harvard thanks but no thanks.[76]

At Eureka, a bust of him adorned what was called the "Peace Garden." All told in his career, Reagan had given thirteen speeches at the tiny school, according to John Morris, the school's director of development.[77]

Back in 1957, he was awarded an honorary degree from Eureka, and acknowledging his own indifferent academic record at the school said, "I always figured the first one you gave me was honorary."[78]

His last speech there was in 1992, giving the commencement address four years after leaving the presidency and sixty years after graduating from the school, one of forty-two seniors. It was his third and final commencement remarks, and he told the graduates there were other things besides politics to go into for a career, fearing the establishment of a permanent political class. He told the seniors instead to "get your own life . . ."[79] He was funny and poignant. Reagan opened by telling the smiling graduates, "I haven't heard such applause since the day I told the Washington media I was leaving town." He closed by telling them that years later "fond memories steadily will burn . . ."[80]

Along the way, an insufferable crowd of campaign consultants evolved—or devolved—from shadowy characters to bona fide celebrities. They became guests more and more frequently on the weekday cable shows and the weekend network shows. To complement the culture, a new documentary on the Discovery Channel about the consultants was airing. The days of the shadowy Mark Hanna and Louis Howe were long gone. The new power bosses in both political parties were the consultants. Reagan had never paid them much mind. He enjoyed being briefed on politics and policy and listened intently when his pollster Dick Wirthlin told him how he was doing and how Americans regarded his policies, but the last consultant who tried to tell Reagan what he could say and not say, John Sears in 1980, got a loud dressing down from Reagan and later almost a punch in the mouth, courtesy of the candidate.

The consultants of both the Bush and Kerry campaigns had decided that Ohio was going to be a battleground state. Ironically, Ohio had been a battleground state going back to the election of 1860.

Part of the cancellation of John Kerry's week included a large fund-raising event at the Walt Disney Hall in Los Angeles. Performances by Barbra Streisand and Neil Diamond and Billy Crystal were cancelled.[81] Hollywood had changed—radically, one might say—since Reagan's days. The New Deal had been replaced by the New Nastiness and the New Arrogance and, ironically, the New Entitlement.

There were New Deal Democrats (like Reagan) in the 1930s and

'40s, and there were political conservatives (like Reagan) and John Wayne and Robert Taylor and Arlene Dahl and many others. But the liberals and the conservatives mingled easily with each other in that era, and all were unified by their patriotism. By the time of Reagan's election in 1980, he had the support of just a handful of actors and actresses, most of them from his generation, like Jimmy Stewart and George C. Scott and a handful of younger actors like Michael Landon.

And a wall of unremitting hostility was being erected by the Hollywood Left against what remained of the Right in 1980. By 2004, there was very little *right* in Hollywood and those *left* met in hiding, like the opponents of Stalin who met in private, fearful for their lives and fortunes. Not to say the Hollywood left didn't enjoy celebrity, position, status, access, and riches that would embarrass Croesus. The compassionate liberals of Hollywood like George Clooney screeched from media stop to media stop, lecturing everybody else on how to live their lives and then hopped into a limousine and then onto a private jet—leaving behind an enormous carbon footprint that screamed hypocrisy.

Reagan had been of the Hollywood culture for many years and through his work as president of the Screen Actors Guild negotiated residuals for elderly actors from the studios, saving many from a lifetime of poverty, though this went unremarked and unnoted.

The newspapers were littered each day with stories about what a mess Iraq had become. Bush was in conference with European leaders in Sea Island, Georgia, including the interim president of Iraq, Sheik Ghazi Ajil al-Yawar.

He and Bush were enthusiastic about the future of a democratic Iraq.

Reporters probed more deeply into the complex relationship between the Reagan family and the Bush family. It was clear to all that George

H. W. Bush and Reagan had gotten over their mutual disdain that reached its peak in the primaries of 1980; a partnership of eight years, their weekly private lunches and Bush's grace and manners combined with Reagan's grace and manners helped two supremely self-confident men move beyond the old animosities. No such détente existed between Barbara Bush and Nancy Reagan. One former Reagan aide went on background to tell reporters that "Mrs. Bush felt she had been slighted by Mrs. Reagan. What I've found is that the wives of political people have long memories. They tend not to forget."[82]

In her book *My Turn*, Mrs. Reagan related a mild dustup she had with then–vice president Bush in 1987 over the controversial chief of staff Don Regan. She told Bush he needed to tell her husband to fire Regan. Bush brushed her off saying, "Nancy, that's not my role." To which she snapped, "That's exactly your role."[83]

In 1988, when Bush was giving his acceptance speech in New Orleans—a speech seen as a rebuke of Reaganism—the vice president told of a "kinder and gentler" approach to the world, and Nancy Reagan was overheard snapping, "Kinder and gentler than *whom?*"[84]

Ironically, while many so-called American political pathologists could not accurately see the role of Nancy Reagan, Mikhail Gorbachev never doubted her importance, saying she had encouraged her husband to pursue renewed relations with the Soviets. "She may have been the greatest influence in that regard because he truly believed her."[85] Gorbachev and Reagan had actually developed a deep friendship. It was not a public relations stunt. There was real affection between the two men, and anyone could see the former Soviet president was really saddened by Reagan's passing. Fred Ryan had been with Reagan when the two men met in Moscow, after Reagan's departure from the White House, and saw how with nothing to gain or lose they acted as friends and colleagues.

Another foreign leader was also "saddened" by the death of Reagan, but for different reasons. Libya's tin horn dictator, the unstable

Muammar Gaddafi, said, "I express my deep regret because Reagan died before facing justice for his ugly crime that he committed in 1986 against the Libyan children."[86]

It was also pointed out by the newshawks that the current President Bush had no relationship with Reagan whatsoever. Newspapers were filled with the self-serving quotes of GOP consultants going to extremes to make out the current President Bush to be the reincarnation of Reagan. Few took the consultants or their mythical observations seriously. The fact remained that the relationship between the two families was and would remain complicated.

Few knew what really constituted a state funeral. Betty Koed, a Capitol Hill historian, quipped, "You can lie in state without having a state funeral and you can have a state funeral without lying in state."[87]

FDR had a state funeral in Hyde Park but did not lie in state in the U.S. Capitol. Richard Nixon had a state funeral in Yorba Linda, California, and did not lie in state in the Capitol.

Generally, the rule for a state funeral relates to station in government. Presidents automatically qualified and five-star generals were made eligible for state funerals, although both Douglas MacArthur in 1964 and John Pershing in 1948 had to be granted such designations by presidents Johnson and Truman, respectively. Good for MacArthur, too, that he lived a long life because he probably never would have attained a state funeral designation from his mortal enemy Truman.

The Reagan funeral would be the biggest event in the city since the attacks of September 11, 2001, and because of the ongoing threat of terrorism, the event was officially designated a "national security special event," said John Ashcroft, U.S. attorney general, grimly.[88]

The city was a hubbub of activity as airmen, soldiers, sailors, and marines practiced for the first state funeral the city had seen in thirty-one years. Already, thousands were streaming into Washington but the media and the city paid them little mind. On Constitution Avenue twenty-one army howitzers were lined up to salute a fallen leader but even the nonchalant Washingtonians were stunned to hear the guns going off on Tuesday, practicing for the arrival and procession up to Capitol Hill the next day. To top that off, a squadron of thirteen Air Force F-15E Strike Eagles practiced thundering over the city at only one thousand feet in altitude.[89]

The eight military pallbearers practiced with a silver hearse and another practiced with a riderless horse and caisson. Actually, it was a small procession that began with the section chief in front, riding, followed by the caisson that was pulled by six horses with three riders seated only on the horses on the left, and followed at last by the riderless mount, led by a lone soldier. A caisson was used in war to transport ammunition. In peace, it was used to transport deceased commanders in chief.

City residents were warned to beware of increasing and heavy traffic, and hotels were already seeing an upswing in walk-in business and reservations, including hundreds of foreign visitors. Travelers along the East Coast were warned to avoid the Beltway around Washington because of the potential for congestion. City officials and Maryland bureaucrats were planning on closing dozens of streets in the metro area.

Crowds were already beginning to swell in Washington, especially on the Mall between the Capitol and the Washington Monument and under the leafy oak trees on a park bench. But thousands also ducked into any number of Smithsonian museum buildings or the National Gallery more for the air conditioning than to look at a Renoir on temporary loan or mechanical equipment on display at the National Museum of American History. Americans of all ages and all walks of life were streaming into the capital, drawn by curiosity, yes, but also by a chord that had been struck in many by their memories of Reagan. Feelings were evoked of times not so long ago, of a naïve pride in America, in being an American and not being ashamed when an American president spoke in a way that drew prideful tears.

Only in recent memory had FDR and JFK touched the deepest chords of the American psyche and hearts of the American citizenry. There was just something about this guy that made people want to sit up and take notice, even if they virulently disagreed with him.

Five honorary pallbearers had been announced. The number made some wonder why Paul Laxalt or Jim Baker or Ed Meese was not the sixth pallbearer, but to their credit they never said anything publicly.

As if American hearts were not already weary, more sad news arrived that week from Los Angeles with reports of the death of Ray Charles, America's beloved jazz and blues singer and pianist, at the age of seventy-three. Frankly, Charles had his own style and most people loved it. Charles had died of liver disease. In 1984, he appeared onstage the last evening of the Republican National Convention in Dallas to sing his tear-jerking happy rendition of "America, the Beautiful" in his own unique jazzy and evocative idiom.

Holding hands and singing along were the Reagans, the Bushes, and dozens of party dignitaries on stage. The floor of the Dallas Convention Center was jammed with thousands of people locked hand in hand, arm in arm, all crying, singing along with Charles and the president of the United States. The director of northeast fund-raising for the Republican National Committee—an agent of the Reagan-Bush reelection committee—was there with her husband, who was working on an independent effort supporting Reagan's reelection. Though it was against the law for agents of the reelection campaign to coordinate efforts with agents of independent committees supporting Reagan's reelection, their devotion to and support of Reagan was nonetheless coordinated. They, too, were crying tears of joy.

The Rotunda of the U.S. Capitol had been emptied of tourists and was now filled with technicians, aides, technical equipment, and lighting to broadcast the thirty-six hours during which Reagan would lie in state. The catafalque was stored in a room there called "Washington's Tomb." When the cornerstone of the U.S. Capitol was laid (by Washington in a Masonic ceremony and not a presidential ceremony) in 1793, plans were made for the construction of a room to hold the remains of the first president of the United States. But Washington demurred and the room went unused though it retained the name. It was there that the catafalque first used by Lincoln and then by more than two dozen others, including presidents and Unknown Soldiers, was stored and now would be hauled out for Ronald Reagan.[90]

The stupendous outpouring in Simi Valley and along the road transporting his remains to the Library on Sunday and then to the airport on Wednesday was duly noted by the national media, yet not dwelt upon. All along the way were seen the young and the old, men and women in uniform, saluting. Old men in walkers straightened up and saluted, too, as the Reagan procession passed. Children waved little American flags. Many were shedding not just tears of sadness but of pride as well, pride for the man who had been a part of their lives for so many years and who they believed so ably and effectively led their country.

The funeral entourage was winging its way to Washington now, with Reagan's coffin aboard, touchdown scheduled for late afternoon on June 9, with a procession to Sixteenth Street and Constitution Avenue set to begin at 6:05 p.m. There, the coffin would be hoisted onto the four-wheel caisson. From there, the motorcade would proceed slowly to the east, up Constitution Avenue to the Capitol.

Planes would fly over in several formations, including one missing man formation. At the foot of the Capitol, the army howitzers would fire a 21-gun salute before 7:00 p.m., and then Reagan's coffin would be tenderly carried up the front steps of the Capitol where a closed state funeral was scheduled to begin at 7:00 and end at 8:30 p.m.[91] Vice President Cheney was to give the eulogy there. Dignitaries from Congress, the Bush administration, the diplomatic corps, the Washington establishment, former Reagan administration officials, and corporate executives would attend. All in all, several hundred of the cream of the American power elite.

Then, the doors to the U.S. Capitol would open to the general public at 9:30 p.m. on the evening of Wednesday, June 9, to walk in a circular motion around the Reagan catafalque, solemnly and slowly paying their respects. As they departed, all would be handed a palm card memorializing the life of Ronald Wilson Reagan. Five guards representing the five service branches would guard the president's mahogany-stained, velvet-lined casket, covered by the American flag. They would rotate positions every thirty minutes.

The Rotunda was scheduled to stay open all night Wednesday, all day Thursday, all Thursday night, and would finally close Friday at 8:00 a.m., to begin the official day of national mourning for President Reagan.[92] But no one really expected that with all this time available to pay their respects that any wait of extended duration was in the cards. Of course, they hadn't thought it would take six hours for people to get a ride on the shuttle buses going up to the Library either.

For every individual who had or was planning to pay his or her respects in person to Reagan, there were millions watching on television in America and around the world. "But it's also true that the simple gesture of turning on a television today has become a way to share the communal grief . . ."[93] It was not the first time the American community held hands via the magic of the screen. The first time was the afternoon of November 22, 1963, and then for three awful days when millions sat with tears pouring down their faces as their young champion was laid to rest in Arlington Cemetery. Now an old champion was being laid to rest and though there was less painful grief for some, there was still a lot of love for this fallen president.

Even with the national attention mostly turned toward the Reagan day of mourning, Father's Day was still approaching, as well, and the newspapers and electronic media were filled with helpful suggestions for gifts for Dad. The electronics store Best Buy was touting DVD players for as little as $799.99 and a 50-inch plasma TV with "built in HD tuner" for $8,999.99.[94] Many fathers would have to dig deep into their pockets to pay for the gifts their families purchased for them on Father's Day. Other suggested gifts included the usual accoutrements of barbecue grills and hammocks and exercise equipment. Bill Clinton's autobiography, *My Life*, was selling for Father's Day but at a 40 percent discount.

One popular item on sale for Father's Day was *Big Russ and Me*, a small but touching book by *Meet the Press* host Tim Russert about his own father.[95] The father had been a blue collar laborer in Buffalo and his son never forgot the life lessons he learned about community, a parish paradigm of faith and family. Russert was a Democrat, having once worked for Mario Cuomo and Pat Moynihan, but he'd transformed into a consummate reporter and host and was well regarded for his balance and professionalism. *Meet the Press* had become a "must watch" show under his leadership and all foresaw a long and successful career for the popular and down-to-earth host and Buffalo Bills football fan.

Another book being ballyhooed as a Father's Day gift was one on advice and ethics entitled *Every Second Counts* by Lance Armstrong. The *New York Times* recommended the book in part because of the "peculiar problems that come with celebrity."[96] Other books being hyped for Dad included Suzanne Somers's *The Sexy Years*, about how "bioidentical hormone replacement therapy can promote fabulous sex . . ." and *Sarah*,[97] about one of the most famous if misunderstood women in the world, accused by some of being a Philistine, by others of being deceitful, and by still others of not being smart, though all agreed she was very attractive and also very controversial. She had an "Old Testament" view of the world.

With all the attention being focused on Reagan and his passing and his Library, overlooked was the impending opening of the Clinton Library in Little Rock. The ultra-modern design was inspired by Clinton's line, a "bridge to the future"[98] but locals joked that it looked more like a "doublewide to the future." It was located alongside Interstate 30 in an undeveloped industrial zone.

The cost had mushroomed to 175 million dollars and the size of the Library itself had doubled, too, from the original plans for 70,000 square feet to 152,000 square feet,[99] in direct contravention of the existing guidelines governing presidential foundations.

A Clinton aide said the former president was planning on staying in an apartment at the Library—once it was opened in the fall of 2004—a week or more each month. All presidential foundations were governed by and large by a federal law signed by Reagan in 1986 that had amended a previously established law signed by FDR.[100]

Behind the scenes, Clinton was proving to be a royal pain for the Reagan funeral organizers. All the former presidents and high-ranking government officials and rank and file Reaganites were, almost to a person, being polite and understanding about the unbelievable pressures that Joanne Drake, Fred Ryan, Rick Ahearn, Jim Hooley, and others were under. There were simply a thousand moving parts and the logistics were indescribable. All seemed to get this except Clinton, who as the week progressed kept up a steady drumbeat of internal pressure on the Reagan team to allow him to speak at the National Cathedral.

That schedule had been set long before. It would feature the current president, regardless of party; Reagan's former vice president and former president and friend George H. W. Bush; John Danforth of Missouri, an ordained Episcopal priest and U.S. senator; a video eulogy by Margaret Thatcher; and remarks by Brian Mulroney, the former Canadian prime minister. The schedule was packed, and if the plane was going to make it to California that afternoon in time for a sunset ceremony, then adding a long-winded and self-absorbed Clinton to the schedule invited all sorts of unnecessary risks. Clinton's minions kept up the pressure citing "bi-partisanship" and a "bi-partisan send-off." Finally Fred Ryan took the matter to Mrs. Reagan, who without hesitation said no.[101]

The fact was Clinton and Reagan barely knew each other. They'd met once or twice at White House functions when Clinton was governor, in late 1992 after Clinton was elected president, and at the Nixon funeral in 1994.

The 1992 visit to Century City by president-elect Clinton to see former president Reagan was pretty much a washout. First, Clinton was forty-five minutes late. Second, when he did show up, he made an unmistakable and crude pass at a young woman on Reagan's staff.[102] When they did meet, Reagan tried to give the younger man some advice about the presidency, but Clinton did not digest it. Reagan tried to get Clinton interested in the wasteful spending uncovered in the Grace Commission but Clinton was uninterested. Clinton was only a bit more interested when Reagan told him to salute the marines standing guard at Marine One.[103]

Also, during the 1992 campaign both Bill and Hillary Clinton repeatedly labeled the 1980s as a "Decade of Greed."[104] There was no love lost between the Reaganites and the Clintonistas.

As of Wednesday, some of the more thoughtful historical pieces delved into the story behind the story of Reagan's coming-out speech for Barry Goldwater in 1964 and how Reagan's brother Neil had a bigger hand in it than anyone knew. Also, the subject of the relationship between the two sons was covered. As children, their father had moved them around rural Illinois so often in search of employment, it was difficult for the youngsters to make friends, so they often played with each other; but even so, they were competitive and each sometimes let his more competitive side show. They hadn't spoken much as elderly men and Neil suffered from his own struggles with dementia. "Moon" died before "Dutch" in 1996 at the age of eighty-eight and was cremated.

President Carter had been at the Plains Baptist Church, teaching Sunday school, praising the life and times of his old adversary, Ronald Reagan, saying it was a "sad day for our country." Then with grace and charm, he told his class, "I probably know as well as anybody what a formidable communicator and campaigner that President Reagan was. It was because of him that I was retired from my last job."[105]

Three thousand miles away, the new minister at the Reagans' church in Bel Air, Reverend Roger Dermody, had told a capacity congregation two days earlier of the Reagans' generosity in donating food to the church and clothes each year for the poor. "We have a lot of homeless people in downtown LA walking around with RWR on their sleeves and not knowing what it means."[106]

Meanwhile, Nancy Reagan said her family's return to Washington was "surreal."[107]

# CHAPTER 6

# HOI POLLOI v. HOITY-TOITY

*"He came to Washington like an occupying army."*

In 1979, while preparing one last run for president, former California governor Ronald Reagan outlined his views on national defense and foreign policy and scrapping of the SALT treaties that had begun under Richard Nixon and continued under Gerald Ford and Jimmy Carter. His plan was to start over by building up America's defenses. Reagan saw the SALT treaties and the long negotiations with Moscow as fatally flawed and détente as a joke.

A nervous reporter suggested to Reagan that his plan might lead to an arms race with the Soviets, but Reagan replied, in essence, that maybe what was needed was an arms race. The establishment came down with a bad case of the vapors and went away convinced that he was a nutty nuclear cowboy who was going to wipe everybody out in an atomic war. Critics during his time in Sacramento said that California was the only state in the Union with its own foreign policy.[1]

Twenty-five years later, with the United States emerging victoriously from the Cold War and millions having escaped the nightmare of nuclear holocaust, with the fall of the Berlin Wall and the reunification of Germany, a handful of those very same liberal editorial critics were now praising his vision, his courage, and his program. "Against waves of 'expert opinion,' he pursued his belief that the Soviet Union would crack under the pressure of an accelerated arms race, and he lived to see the Soviet empire crumble and a degree of freedom and democracy come to Russia itself," said David Broder, an oft Reagan critic.[2]

Even then those who did credit him said he and Gorbachev "ended" the Cold War rather than Reagan and the West "won" it. It was an almost eighty-year contest of ideas, with freedom and the free market winning out over communism and economic collectivism, enslavement, and mass murder. More than a few eggs were broken by the Evil Empire.

Western Europe itself, however, was somewhat ambivalent about the passing of Reagan, even though his policies had steered their future away from nuclear war and toward peace and prosperity.

In 1990, Reagan, seventy-nine years old, returned to the scene of the communist crime and took a chisel and a hand sledge and chipped away at a bit of history for him and for eternity. As he took his own whacks at what was left of the Berlin Wall, there was a knowing smile on his face. The *Washington Post*, however, led their coverage with a *People* magazine–like commentary on his age, implying for the one-thousandth time he dyed his hair, and wrote smarmily "the famous ambling stride has been reduced to the shuffle of an old man."[3]

Typical for the *Post*, the article used the words *raspier* and *gaffe* and spent almost as much time reporting on the advance work of the Reagan staff as it did on the tremendous outpouring of support for Reagan among the West Berliners. Thousands turned out. Said a supportive city resident, "He had the most vision of any politician in recent times," saying what the *Post* failed to comprehend.[4]

Even as of 1991 and beyond, his letters to friends, fans, and colleagues were convivial, frank, informative, and clearly demonstrated an agile and contemplative mind. In a long missive to Lorraine

Wagner, he discussed going back to Dixon, his views on the Bible and Armageddon, the Strategic Defense Initiative, the Patriot missile, the presidential library, and Gorbachev.[5]

In 1991, Reagan was doing an interview with Lou Cannon for the revised edition of *Role of a Lifetime*, and the old scribe asked the older president what he thought about the fall of the Berlin Wall. Reagan, struggling, still gave a "thoughtful answer," Cannon said. Reagan told him he "thought it would happen, but he didn't realize that it was going to happen as quickly as it did."[6]

America was in its fourth day of mourning for Ronald Reagan and showed no signs of abating. Indeed, it was picking up momentum, and his passing had been front-page news for four consecutive days now and the outpouring from the American citizenry was only accelerating. Even so, much of the elite of the national media and the liberal establishment had come not to praise Reagan but to bury him. The American people had a different idea.

On Wednesday evening, June 9, the very first citizen in line for the viewing of Ronald Reagan lying in state in the U.S. Capitol was Carol Williams, a teacher at Strayer University located in Chesterfield, Virginia. That it was a woman, middle-aged, and a college professor was uniquely interesting. The intelligentsia for years had said those demographics despised Reagan.[7]

Williams arrived at 5:00 a.m. on Wednesday and waited for some sixteen hours in the stifling heat and humidity before being admitted into the cool and darkened Rotunda. There she would have only a few moments in which to move around the historic catafalque, upon which nine presidents had lain, to pay her respects. By the time Williams was admitted, thousands of Americans were lined up behind her, and it was just the beginning.

Ronald Reagan's seven-hundred-pound coffin arrived on schedule aboard SAM 28000 precisely at 5:00 p.m. (EST) at Andrews Air

Force Base in suburban Maryland. They'd left Point Mugu that morning at precisely 9:30 a.m. (PST). Mrs. Reagan, the Reagan children, and staff also were on the plane, including Joanne Drake. The plan was for her to stay at Mrs. Reagan's side for the week.[8] The Military District was following a 138-page playbook,[9] and the Reagan team of Jim Hooley, Rick Ahearn, Linda Bond, Robert Higdon, and dozens of others was following a slightly larger playbook of three hundred pages.[10] The Military District was issuing helpful press releases complete with phone number, routes, times, and places.

A group of spectators aware that the funeral motorcade, upon leaving Andrews Air Force Base, would take Suitland Parkway into the city, set up lawn chairs at a McDonald's along the way to watch.

Everything was moving along with military precision—a phrase not overused this week because everything, at least in public, was coming off without a hitch, or nearly so. Behind the scenes was another matter. For whatever reason, Mike Reagan was not pleased with the car he was assigned in the motorcade at Andrews. After a delay of ten minutes, and a loud and not happy discussion with Rick Ahearn in front of the live television cameras, he finally walked away and entered another car at the back of the motorcade.[11] Hundreds of thousands of people and a national television audience of millions were left wondering what the holdup was.

The motorcade was late in departing but eventually followed a preplanned route that took it across the Memorial Bridge and ultimately to Constitution Avenue and Sixteenth Street NW. Spectators began lining up as early as 10:00 a.m., securing choice shady positions under the few trees along the historic street. The procession would pass under the statue of General George Meade, the victor at Gettysburg and the first man to vanquish Robert E. Lee in battle. Parade organizers passed out fifty thousand small American flags to the spectators along Constitution Avenue.[12]

In the Rotunda shortly before the VIP ceremony at which

Vice President Cheney and House Speaker Denny Hastert (whose district covered Reagan's old Illinois stomping grounds) were scheduled to speak, alarms suddenly went off and the Federal Aviation Administration ordered the immediate evacuation of the Capitol. This was no drill. An unauthorized plane was heading into the restricted airspace over Washington and right for the U.S. Capitol. Memories of September 11 were still fresh and everyone knew but for the courage of the passengers of Flight 93 that plane would have likely plunged into the U.S. Capitol rather than a rural area of Pennsylvania.

At around 4:40 p.m. people were firmly and loudly told by the Capitol Hill police and other security personnel to run for their lives, and if women could not run in their high heels they were ordered to remove them and run stocking footed. Had it not been so serious and the day so serious, it would have been comical to witness power brokers like Ed Meese, Dan Quayle, Rupert Murdoch, Tricia Nixon Cox, and dozens of others, dignity askew, streaming out of the U.S. Capitol into the blistering heat all because of a false alarm. As it later became known, it was due to the broken transponder on the private state plane of the Kentucky governor Ernie Fletcher as he flew into Washington for the Reagan funeral.[13]

"Airborne threat! Four minutes out!" was heard through the halls of the Capitol.[14] Police told the VIPs to move as if their lives depended on it. The dignitaries had been gathered in a private room for a reception before the beginning of the ceremony in the Rotunda before their frenzied flight from the old building, shucking shoes and jackets, running and falling head over heels. "I didn't know Rupert Murdoch could run so fast," quipped Bob Colacello, who was a writer and close friend of Nancy Reagan.[15]

Joan Rivers was also observed running and for once was speechless as the police yelled, "Air Con Red! Air Con Red!" Linda Bond was yelling, "Run! Run!" She later saw Rivers walking around, shoes in hand, even after the alarm had passed. Bond said Jeane

Kirkpatrick refused to run, saying, "I've had a good life. I'm not running out there." Someone then threw Kirkpatrick over his shoulder and carried her out.[16]

The summer heat they ran into was stifling, and when they finally returned for the Rotunda event, all were drenched. Bond was impressed with Senator Bill Frist's calm demeanor through the false crisis; she was also impressed when they returned and she spotted Jack Kemp, his shirt damp with sweat, behind the bar helping to serve drinks. She noted Tricia Nixon Cox, whom she surmised was surprised to be invited to the VIP event, was humble and appreciative.

Bond was less than impressed that Al Haig objected to the protocol that held that George Shultz should go ahead of him.[17] Then again, Reagan had also taken note of Haig's super ego, writing in his diary the day he fired Haig that the only thing the two disagreed on was who was president.[18]

A young intern for Patrick Kennedy who had only been in Washington for a few days exclaimed that he'd been part of an evacuation and seen a presidential funeral and these "are the most historic things I've seen!"[19]

The police and security presence was felt everywhere in the city. Bomb-sniffing dogs were frequently spotted.

In story after story after story, many American citizens in chapter and verse told of their admiration for Reagan, their affection for Reagan, their esteem for Reagan, and their devotion to Reagan. Even from those who'd opposed him, there was respect. A black man from Memphis said that while Reagan was "sometimes-offensive . . . to African Americans . . . 'he definitely believed in freedom, and I certainly enjoy freedom.'"[20]

In Dixon, Illinois, a life-sized statue of Reagan atop a stone pedestal was quickly disappearing under flowers and other tributes. A group of Girl Scouts was photographed in a circle around the statue, holding hands, offering a prayer.[21] Social critics wrote lengthy pieces analyzing the meaning and significance of the grassroots shrines that came in to vogue with the death of Princess Diana. One or more sites of significance became makeshift memorials, and within a short period of time the locale became a heaping pile of florae and other memorabilia.

The little town of Dixon was overrun with camera crews and satellite trucks from nearby Midwestern cities, all in search of the not-so-elusive man on the street or woman on the street to discuss his or her thoughts and memories of Reagan. They knew they'd hit the mother lode, though, when on occasion they found someone who actually knew Ronald Reagan in the old days.

The state of Reagan's birth announced that a stretch of Interstate-88 from the Iowa border to Dixon would be designated "The Ronald Reagan Memorial Highway." The decision to do so was announced in an executive order by the governor of Illinois, Rod Blagojevich. However, the press release from the governor's office mistakenly said the Gipper's birthplace was Dixon, rather than Tampico.[22]

There was renewed public discussion about a Reagan monument on the Mall and issuing a RWR dime along with the FDR dime. Yet another proposal being floated was to put Reagan on the twenty-dollar bill.[23] As with nearly everything else, the Republicans on Capitol Hill got into a fight on how to commemorate Reagan. Grover Norquist knew the path of least resistance was right over the memory of Alexander Hamilton, who was not a president and who didn't have the lobbying muscle of supporters of Andrew Jackson, or John Kennedy, or FDR, and besides, as Norquist quipped, "Alexander was a bad shot."[24]

The irony about talk of a memorial on Washington's National Mall was that Reagan, as president, had signed a bill that designated a twenty-five year wait before anyone could be memorialized on the strip of land between the Capitol and the Washington Monument.[25] And Nancy Reagan had earlier opposed the likeness of her husband on the dime and in fact had issued a statement saying as much.[26] (Nancy Reagan had earlier received a handwritten note from Anna Eleanor Roosevelt, thanking her for wanting to keep FDR on the dime.)[27]

For Reagan, the mourning and memorializing continued in Tampico, in Dixon, at Eureka, in Washington, in Santa Barbara, at his Library in Simi Valley, at his home in Los Angeles, and at his star on the Walk of Fame in Hollywood. A condolences book was set out at the Nixon Library for Reagan mourners to sign, and Eureka College invited guests to a memorial service on the campus.[28] The *Peoria Journal Star* tracked down some former classmates from Eureka and all had vivid and fond memories of their friend. "He loved Eureka College and wasn't afraid to say so," said Aline Schrock. "He never showed any shame in graduating from such a small school."[29]

A year earlier Katherine Ashenburg had written *The Mourner's Dance*, and in an interview she said, "There was a reaction against the Victorians, who mourned so extravagantly. Now we're seeing the pendulum swinging back, and we see it especially with celebrities and public figures . . . It's ironic, but it's easier to have some kind of public expression of mourning for strangers than for someone in our own family." She noted that in people's own lives, after a death in the family they are expected to be back at work in a short period of time and that public expression for loved ones is "socially unacceptable."[30]

This, though, wasn't the mourning associated with the tragic deaths of Lincoln, FDR, and JFK. There was mourning for Reagan and plenty of tears but also celebration of a man who had done much for so many over numerous years. The tragedy wasn't that he was ninety-three years old at his death but that he and Nancy only had several years to themselves after the White House and before the onslaught of Alzheimer's.

The weather across the nation, especially in the east, was very hot and humid, well above ninety degrees. The temperature recorded that day at Reagan National Airport was ninety-two degrees—ten degrees above normal[31]—though it was hotter by far in the city with all the buildings and vehicles and congestion. The evenings were moist and still. No air was stirring. The heat and humidity were such that dozens of people passed out among the hundreds of thousands lining Constitution Avenue, in some places ten or more deep, waiting for the Reagan funeral procession. Fences lined the street all the way to the Capitol for crowd control.

Thoughtfully, the Capitol police distributed 150,000 bottles of water to the sweltering crowds.[32] Also, giant electric fans blew much-needed air onto the onlookers, and there were also cooling tents. Still, more than three dozen were taken by ambulance to local hospitals because of the extreme heat.

Sixteen blocks away, near the Ellipse that is situated between the White House and the Washington Monument, the mahogany coffin was gently placed on a carriage that had been built in 1918. The riderless black horse, with Reagan's worn but polished riding boots, was named Sergeant York. The horse was covered with a blanket called a "caparison."[33] When not in service, the horses were stabled nearby at Fort Myer in Arlington.

At Sixteenth Street and Constitution Avenue—between the White House and the Washington Monument—Mrs. Reagan got out of her black limousine to watch several young, tall, handsome uniformed men gently transfer her husband's coffin with care and tenderness. These men had been nothing more than children when Ron and Nancy occupied the White House. The crowd applauded her, and she could be seen mouthing a "silent thanks in return," responding with a wave or a smile.[34] As with everything else, the playbook developed over the years for the Reagan funeral planned for a small, ticketed VIP area at the location, so they could watch the movement of the casket from the hearse to the caisson.

Reagan's casket was handled by eight men in uniform: two army, two navy, two marines, one air force, and one coast guard. Because of the stifling heat and humidity and the many steps up the west front of the Capitol, a platoon system of several bands of brothers was used.

Often throughout the week, someone in a crowd yelled, "We love you, Nancy."[35] For the elites, it was yet another revelation. They'd more or less despised her—especially in the early days of the 1980s—when they thought she didn't measure up to Eleanor, Jackie, Lady Bird, Betty, and Rosalynn. She began to win over the American people after a bumpy first year, mostly because of the bashing she'd unfairly taken in the media. By the second term, she was as popular as any of her predecessors, but the snotty Georgetown society mavens and matrons still were contemptuous. The fact was, Nancy Davis could match them, class for class. She'd grown up in Chicago society and attended the highbrow Smith College, where she majored in English and drama.

She was born Anne Frances Robbins but after her mother and father divorced, Edith Luckett Robbins married Dr. Loyal Davis, a highly successful neurosurgeon; he adopted Anne and her name was changed to Nancy. They moved to Chicago in the 1930s, and it was possible that she and Ronald Reagan were in the same town at the time and conceivable that she'd heard him on the radio.

Incredibly, some in the national media were writing stories about the "New Nancy,"[36] as if the past ten years had been some public relations stunt rather than simply a woman taking care of the man she loved the best way she knew how. For the past week, she was deeply moved and impressed at the outpouring for Ronnie.

Only after the fall of 1994, with Reagan's announcement of his affliction, did the elites begin to understand what the American people knew. One of the few times Nancy left his side was in 2001 for the christening of the USS *Ronald Reagan* in Newport News. Carl Cannon, a writer, was there with his father, Lou, who'd covered Reagan for many years, and they saw Nancy. When asked if she was going to spend a few days on the East Coast, she blanched at the thought of being away from Ronnie for one second more than necessary.[37] She returned for the commissioning in 2003, but again only for a very short time.

Reagan was an accomplished horseman and was comfortable in both English and Western saddles. (His love of horses came from the 1930s, when he joined the army's Calvary Reserve in California.) Of course, horses were trained differently to respond; with English a squeeze of the thighs and knees was needed and with Western a kick of the rider's heels along with neck reining the horse. For the rider, too, the styles were drastically different. In 1966, a major magazine wanted to do a photo spread on Reagan riding horses at his ranch, getting ready to run for governor. Reagan was delighted and came out in jodhpurs and high boots, carrying an English saddle, looking like he was ready to mount and call "ta hounds."

Lyn Nofziger, his new press aide, knew this was all wrong and told him to go back in and change. Americans knew the cowboy Reagan and would be disappointed and maybe even angry to see him transformed into a country squire. Reagan changed and came back out in the proper Stetson, dungarees, cowboy boots, and a saddle with a pommel.[38] Later, as president, Americans came to see him as both types of horsemen and they liked it.

After the "horse episode," as he called it in 1989, he was touchy about the subject, writing to Lorraine Wagner, with whom he'd been corresponding for forty years. In no uncertain terms, he wrote, "I didn't fall off. Something spooked him . . . and he erupted. I was bucked off. I've some sore bruises but it's a miracle I broke no bones."[39]

It was those English riding boots, of which Robert Higdon had been given custody, that now adorned the saddle stirrups of "Sergeant York," the riderless horse that led the caisson. The boots faced backward, in ancient military tradition. Some said it was so the departed commander could see his troops in the afterlife and others said to signify that the commander would never ride again while still others said it was so the departed leader could say good-bye to their families. No one was really sure about the origins.[40] The worn boots had been given a light polish with saddle soap by Ahearn. Mrs. Reagan later noted her surprise and mild displeasure to General Jackman over her husband's cleaned-up boots.[41]

"Thus, on a warm June evening before throngs of perspiring citizens, was the former president transported for the last time to Capitol Hill, along the same streets and to the same sounds as other famed figures in an exquisite American ritual of mourning," wrote Michael E. Ruane of the *Washington Post*, in his own singular and exquisite prose.[42]

Slowly, the funeral procession made its way to Capitol Hill, past hundreds of thousands of Americans. It was followed by a lone soldier carrying the flag of the commander in chief, a blue field with a circle of fifty stars and the seal of the American president. The silence was astonishing. There was no breeze and little sound from the crowd either. All that could be heard was the "clomp, clomp, clomp" of the horses and the creaking of the wooden wheels on the carriage, the soft sound of drums. Broadcast live on national television, commentators knew it was best to keep their mouths shut and they did so for the most part. The caisson passed the buildings that housed the IRS and the EPA.

When Warren G. Harding passed away in August 1923, some ten thousand students from DC schools were enlisted to spread the petals of flowers along Pennsylvania Avenue between the White House and the Capitol. It was hot then, too—above 100 degrees—and, according to news reports at the time, two hundred people, including uniformed military, fell victim to the oppressive heat.[43]

As the procession approached the west façade of the Capitol, a sad looking Mrs. Reagan was now at the west entrance awaiting her husband's remains as military pallbearers took 116 steps from the carriage at the foot of the building all the way to the Rotunda. Heard playing was "Ruffles and Flourishes," "Hail to the Chief," and a "mournful rendition of 'The Battle Hymn of the Republic.'"[44] The ground shook and the quietude exploded at the 21-gun salute by the army howitzers. Three 75mm cannons fired seven times at five-second intervals.[45] Military commanders could be heard in the background shouting out orders.

The week and this event were dripping with ritual. Myth had it the 21-gun salute came from the total of the numbers 1, 7, 7, and 6; and "Hail to the Chief" from James Monroe, because he was so short that when he entered a room no one knew it. But the Military District of Washington said it was not clear where the 21-gun salute originated because in the 1840s the practice was for the number of reports to correspond with the number of states and America had twenty-six states, but the fire was cut back to twenty-one though it was not formalized until 1875.[46] There was symbolism and tradition everywhere.

Overhead flew twenty-one F-15 Eagle jet fighters from the air force. A single plane led the way, and it was followed by four formations of five planes—except the last, which had the familiar missing plane that symbolized the loss of Reagan. Military brass was everywhere and the rich and the famous were spotted occasionally among normal Americans. Margaret Thatcher was there, of course, as was George Shultz, Al Haig, and others; although the ticketing was controlled mostly by Congress, said Linda Bond, an attractive Washingtonian who had been "volunteered" by Robert Higdon to work on the impossible jobs of handling both the Rotunda ceremony and the National Cathedral funeral on Friday.[47] Higdon was low-key but a close, close friend of Nancy Reagan and Thatcher.

Finally, the U.S. Army Quintet played "Amazing Grace."[48]

"In the Rotunda, Reagan rested below the 'Apotheosis of Washington,' an 1865 painting [by Constantino Brumidi], designed to illustrate Washington's ascension into Heaven. The head of his casket faced East and was placed squarely in the Rotunda's center so the sunlight would illuminate it Thursday."[49] From the polished sandstone floor to the ceiling was 180 feet. The circular room, 96 feet in diameter,[50] was silent, and the statues of Washington and Hamilton and Jefferson looked on. The statue of Lincoln sculpted by Vinnie Ream was there too. Ream was a woman, and Lincoln posed for her, making her the first woman to create a watchful statue in the Capitol. The television cameras along the wall accompanied by lights mounted on tall posts were also watching.

Reagan would lie in state for more than thirty-four hours.

The last time Reagan had been in the Rotunda was his last day as president—and first day as a private citizen—on January 20, 1989. This was eight years after his last day as a private citizen and first day as president, following his unprecedented win over Jimmy Carter. He'd been reelected in a huge landslide, the second biggest in American history, exceeding his 1980 election, which was considered the third-biggest landslide in American history. The inaugural of January 1981 was downright balmy but the inaugural of 1985 was so cold—the wind chill was ten degrees below zero—the outdoor events were cancelled, including the parade, and Reagan was sworn into office in the Rotunda, the first president to do so. Still, his inaugural address was eloquent.

In the Rotunda nineteen years later, Cheney was uncharacteristically eloquent, even moving. "In this national vigil of mourning, we show how much America loved this good man and how greatly we will miss him." "'There's no question I am an idealist, which is another way of saying I am an American,'" he quoted Reagan as saying. He called Reagan's arrival on the international scene "providential" and closed by telling the assembled and the millions watching on television, "Fellow Americans, here lies a graceful and a gallant man."[51] Mrs. Reagan was spotted near tears several times during Cheney's remarks.

Fellow Illinoisan house speaker Denny Hastert also spoke well. "Ronald Reagan's long journey has finally drawn to a close."[52] Senator Ted Stevens, the president Pro Tempore of the Senate, was equally up to the task. Maybe it was because it was for Reagan, but for whatever reason, three generally low-key public speakers were articulate and even soaring at times in describing the fallen president. Significantly, none of the three men injected themselves into their eulogies. Each placed a wreath before the casket, one saying "Senate," another "House of Representatives," and the third "Executive Branch." The House chaplain Daniel Coughlin opened with a prayer, and the Senate's chaplain Barry Black concluded the service with a eulogy.

Nancy Pelosi kicked up a fuss that she and Democrats had not spoken at the Rotunda event even when it was explained to her it was not a political event. The government was in the hands of Republicans, and so they represented the government in the seat of government.

At the end, an army band played "God Bless America" and Mrs. Reagan stood alone at her husband's coffin and then knelt in silent prayer. As she rose, she ran her hand lengthwise along the American flag, as if smoothing it out a bit for Ronnie, making sure he was presentable, as she'd done for him for fifty years. She was dressed simply but elegantly in a two-piece black ensemble that buttoned on her right shoulder. Her wan smile would emerge very occasionally and mostly she remained silent, breaking only when she whispered to daughter Patti or son Ron or to her military escort, Major General Galen Jackman, the commander of the Military District of Washington.

Jackman, fifty-two years old, was six feet, two inches tall and stood ramrod straight, as did all the military this week. Jackman's career was anything but ceremonial, having spent much of his life in harm's way serving with the Special Forces, pursuing Colombian drug lords in the jungles of South America, commanding a Delta Squadron, and heading up tactics at the U.S. Army Infantry School, before assuming command of the Military District of Washington.[53]

Dick Cheney escorted Nancy Reagan slowly out of the Rotunda at the conclusion of the forty-minute memorial after she stole a few moments alone at the casket, again smoothing the flag, but this time she seemed to be saying something to Ronnie.

Departing, Margaret Thatcher curtsied in front of the bier and she, too, gently touched the flag. Again, all was televised and millions watched but the anchors and commentators let long moments go without saying a word, although there was the occasional inanity.

The planning for the Reagan funeral had begun more or less in 1981, changed and embellished over the years, much under the watchful gaze of Nancy Reagan. As Jim Hooley had been in charge of much of the advance and execution of the California end of things, his friend and fellow former Reagan White House advance man, Rick Ahearn, was in charge of many of the events in Washington. Like Hooley, Ahearn was also a large Irishman with an often pleasant demeanor doing his best for another large Irishman who had a pleasant demeanor.

Nancy Reagan did not control everything, however. The National Cathedral seated four thousand people but Congress controlled three thousand of the seats for the Friday funeral at the large, old church. The allocation of the three thousand seats was for foreign dignitaries, the Joint Chiefs, the Supreme Court, the Diplomatic Corps, and the like. Mrs. Reagan had to make do with the other one thousand to accommodate a lifetime of aides and friends and family.[54] For the normal American family, one thousand tickets to a funeral would have been hundreds more than enough, but for the Reagans it was a stretch.

There were people and friends and family from Chicago, Eureka, Dixon, Tampico, Des Moines, and Los Angeles; from Sacramento, Santa Barbara, Washington, London, Ottawa, Mexico City, and Grenada; from Moscow, Prague, Warsaw, Israel, and dozens of other places. Not to mention the staff and aides who were loyal to the couple at the beginning and at the end. Between the two of them, they had accumulated ten lifetimes of friends and associates. Her relatively small allotment of seats meant some Reaganites would sadly not be invited to the Cathedral. A couple of Reagan alumni groups made plans to have watching ceremonies.

After the services in the National Cathedral, at the Reagan Building in downtown Washington, the surviving members of the Reagan cabinet would hold one last meeting. Almost every former Reagan cabinet official gladly appeared. It was a warm and poignant event sponsored by Lou Cordia, head of the Reagan Alumni Association.

Ahearn was supervising dozens, including Linda Bond, who was supervising the ticket allocation and a thousand other details from the Mayflower Hotel, where thirty years earlier—in 1973—Reagan had spoken to the very first Conservative Political Action Conference organized by two young conservatives, Frank Donatelli, twenty-four years old, and Jim Roberts, twenty-seven years old, two of the most original of the original foot soldiers in the Reagan Revolution. They'd done so at the direction of Stan Evans and Tom Winter, two conservative writers, activists, and leaders. The star attraction at the very first CPAC was outgoing California governor Ronald Reagan. Demoralized by Richard Nixon's policies and then, for some, Watergate, conservatives needed something to be hopeful about again.

Reagan gave them hope in what became known in conservative circles as the "City Upon a Hill" speech. Conservatives and certainly many of the speechwriters knew countless Reagan speeches by shorthand—"Bold Colors" and "New Republican" and "The Speech," "City Upon a Hill," "Ash-bin of History," "Evil Empire," and "Tear Down this Wall" and "Challenger" and others. All were important in the annals of Reagan history, which made them important in the annals of American history. Conservatives kept track of Reagan speeches including his first at CPAC.

During the presidency, with accustomed modesty, he said "I don't really get to write my speeches these days—the fellas do."[55] But everybody knew better. Reagan was always his own best speechwriter, and from Ken Khachigian to Tony Dolan, all had their own humorous tale of over-writing and over-producing a draft, only to have it come back from the Oval Office with lines drawn through sentence after sentence, Reagan's handwritten rewrite, and always a kind note to the author saying thanks for his or her great efforts.

Oliver North, who had caused so much embarrassment for Reagan by nearly getting him impeached during Iran-Contra, was not invited.[56] Reagan had stormed in his private diaries that North had never been to Camp David to brief him on selling arms for hostages.[57] During the week of the funeral, North was quoted in the newspapers, claiming he was not going to attend because as a celebrity, his presence might have distracted attention. "When I walk into the cathedral, all the cameras go to Ollie North, and that's not what this is about."[58]

Those who knew, knew this was bull. Army general John Singlaub, who'd parachuted behind enemy lines into Nazi-occupied France, a Reagan man, an American hero, was never enamored of North. "But I knew better. There was a wide gap between the media image of Ollie North . . . and the sordid reality of his true character and performance."[59]

There had been an unofficial official "Do Not Admit" list to the Reagan White House that the Secret Service was aware of, as were most of those in charge of ticketing for all the events the week of the funeral. Some were people who had worked in the White House but had left or been forced out under a personal or ethical cloud. It was the job of those in charge of the events—from Andrews to the Capitol to the National Cathedral and all the others—to keep these people from gaining access and causing some disturbance or being an embarrassment.

Jim Hooley had already asked some volunteer advance men at Simi Valley to leave, as they were not helping and seemed to be there just to rubberneck and collect souvenirs. And they comported themselves more like yokels than as solemn professionals. Oddly, he also discovered that a square swatch of the black fabric backdrop had been neatly cut out by a tacky souvenir hunter.[60]

James Watt, who had been Reagan's very controversial secretary of the interior before being fired, also would not be attending the services at the Cathedral though he was invited; the reason cited was a family sickness.[61]

And there were a few others who were specifically not invited.

Seating in the massive National Cathedral would be an exercise in the proximity of power but for the sake of security, there really was no alternative, especially with the unique pew arrangement inside the church. In the front would be the honored guests including pallbearers; the band and chorus would be in their usual locations. Right behind the centrally placed coffin would be the former presidents and First Ladies on the left side of the aisle and the Reagan family in the first row on the right side. Seats were also set aside for the diplomatic corps, members of Congress, and Reagan cabinet members. The service was to begin at 11:30 on Friday morning.[62]

Letters to the Editor of the nation's newspapers continued to run heavily in favor of the Gipper, including one from the *chargé d'affaires* in Tehran during the Iranian Hostage Crisis, Bruce Laingen, praising Reagan for extricating himself from the Iran-Contra affair.[63] Another message from Susan Berger Kabaker of Glencoe, Illinois: "I think that the public is drawn to this state funeral in part because of the greatness of Ronald Reagan, but more because it draws us together as a people who love America and all that it stands for."[64]

Interestingly, letters to papers in the nation's heartland were more heartfelt than some of the heartless letters published in the broadsheets of New York, Washington, Boston, and Los Angeles. In one Midwest paper, missives were printed under the headings of "A great man," "high standard," and "American hero."[65] Said longtime Reagan press aide Mark Weinberg, "He was their president."[66]

In New York, charges against a mayor for performing a gay marriage ceremony were tossed out, though marriage between members of the same sex was illegal under state law.[67] Also in New York, Congressman Anthony Weiner, who was considered to be a mayoral candidate, sponsored a bill to "track and catalog asteroids that are dangerously close to Earth."[68]

Martha Stewart, having been railroaded by the government using false information, was understandably asking for a new trial in the hopes of clearing her name. She'd been convicted in part because of the perjured testimony of a witness who the government was now prosecuting—for perjury.[69]

Memories of Reagan continued to pour forth. A television producer, Steve Wark, who'd earlier been a part of the youth campaign for Reagan in 1984 and was with Reagan after the presidency shooting some public service commercials, noted that Reagan was still as good as ever. "He was a one-taker." At the end of the shoot one particular day, Wark was told by Reagan aides not to talk to the former president afterward, not to ask for autographs, and certainly no pictures. The crew quietly packed up until a quizzical, almost hurt, Reagan said, "Doesn't anyone want to take pictures?" With that he then spent the next half hour chatting with the film crew, telling stories, and taking pictures.[70]

Howard Baker, the kindly former senator from Tennessee and close friend of the Reagans who as much as any one man helped to right the administration after the twin second-term disasters of Don Regan and Iran-Contra, weighed in with his gentle thoughts on the Gipper. They had run against each other in 1980 for the GOP nomination, and had previously butted heads over the Panama Canal Treaties, but almost never did they criticize each other personally as there was real affection between the two men.

"While I had hoped very much to be president myself, even I had to concede that Ronald Reagan was exactly what the country needed in those critical years of the 1980s. Those qualities of stability, confidence, courage and optimism were the bedrocks of Ronald Reagan's own character, and he shared them with us when we needed them most." Baker concluded saying that "this remarkable man with a ready smile and a profoundly good heart emerged to lead us out of the darkness and into the light."[71]

George Will said, "He came to Washington like an occupying army."[72]

The esteemed veteran political columnist David Broder weighed in. Unlike his liberal brethren, he every so often wrote favorably about Reagan, going back to the time when Broder was writing for a small Midwest paper covering Reagan while he was on the rubber chicken circuit for GE or when he'd make an appearance at Eureka College. Broder's post mortem piece was softer toward Reagan than when he'd often been a burr under the saddle of the Reagan administration as one of the *Post*'s top political columnists and reporters; but his criticism was never personal.

He would criticize Reagan's philosophies, but Broder did so in an even-handed manner. When Jimmy Carter was at 1600 Pennsylvania Avenue NW, Broder regularly hit him over the head with a two-by-four. Broder called Reagan "The Great Persuader."[73] The scribe believed that he warranted the moniker because Reagan had persuaded himself of the righteousness of his positions, and would then go out and convince the American people. The column was typical of Broder. A praise here, a kick there. It was both honest and frank. It was why so many people read his work avidly.

Still another opinion came from Mark Weisbrot, the director of liberal Washington think tank the Center for Economic and Policy

Research. After faintly praising Reagan for shifting the political debate and changing "the world more than probably any American in the 20th Century," Reagan's economic policies, he wrote, "were mostly a failure." He wrote derisively of the Reagan legacy on tax cuts, a military buildup, and said the growth of the 1980s was the slowest since the end of WWII. He also leveled charges at Reagan for firing the air traffic controllers in 1981 because they had gone on a strike, which Weisbrot failed to note was illegal.

And "Reagan is often credited with having caused the collapse of the Soviet Union, but this is doubtful. He did use the Cold War as a pretext for . . . funding and support for horrific violence against the civilian population of Central America." Citing the United Nations as a source of reliable information, he wrote of the "genocide" inside of Guatemala and managed—through a couple of bank shots—to blame Reagan for this as well. But then bizarrely Weisbrot referred to the corrupt communist Ortega machine in Nicaragua as "democratically elected." He also laughingly compared the Cold War to the "war on terror."[74]

Others wrote extensively about the hangover of Iran-Contra; it was a black eye and an embarrassing episode that halted the momentum of the Reagan administration for more than a year in the second term, eating up precious time. The debate over the constitutionality of the Boland Amendment, which limited a president's ability to conduct foreign policy, never took place as operatives inside the Reagan White House took it upon themselves to break the very law many thought trampled on the presidency; so that became the focus of congressional investigators and an independent counselor, Lawrence Walsh. Reagan later testified before the grand jury in his post-presidency and got terrible reviews for fumbling and his inability (or unwillingness) to answer questions. The John Poindexter attorneys went to California to take his deposition and during the morning session he was sharp and clear; after lunch, and after talking to his attorneys, Reagan reverted to a not-so-cooperative style in the afternoon. Reagan was cleared in the final report issued by Lawrence Walsh, and some thought he simply resented having to testify in the first place.

Overlooked in all the coverage and all the obituaries was the fact that the farther one got away from the power centers of Washington and New York, the kinder and gentler the stories became. They tended to focus on the life and times of Ronald Reagan. However, some repeated the cruel falsehood issued by Washington access seller Clark Clifford, who once called Reagan an "amiable dunce."[75] Yet Clifford some years later became dumbly embroiled in one of the biggest banking scandals in history, causing many to think of him as an "amiable crook." Clifford's indictments were put on ice because of his age and poor health.[76]

Some of the stories and obituaries, however, contained factual mistakes. One often repeated was that the nickname "The Great Communicator" began when he gave the speech for Goldwater in 1964; in fact, it had been hung on him as a term of derision by Judy Bachrach of the defunct *Washington Star* during the 1980 campaign.[77] But it stuck and was embraced like "Yankee Doodle Dandy" by Reaganites, and even Reagan mentioned it in his farewell remarks in January 1989.[78]

Another mistake often made was misquoting Reagan's famous put-down of the Left that he made in his landmark speech for Goldwater. Reagan said, "The trouble with our liberal friends is not that they're ignorant; it's just that they know so much that isn't so."[79] Over the years, it had often been mangled by fans trying to quote him.

The media also erred when it wrote of "the Nancy gaze," which was incorrectly interpreted to mean she had no thoughts that weren't his; that she had no thoughts of her own. But in fact, they sometimes disagreed, and Pete Souza witnessed one instance in which they argued over whether Reagan should go to Bitburg in 1985 at the invitation of Chancellor Helmut Kohl. It had been revealed that

Nazi soldiers were buried in the cemetery there. A storm of protest ensued in the media and political circles and inside the Reagan White House. Mrs. Reagan also protested her husband's stubbornness, but he replied that he made a promise to another head of state and if he didn't keep that promise, "my word means nothing."

Reagan went, explained why, and was battered in the world press but the storm eventually passed. "Even the first lady couldn't change his mind." Souza said he only saw them argue "rarely" but if they did, "it inevitably concerned something that was hurting him politically."[80] Others had seen them argue over White House Chief of Staff Don Regan, who everybody—especially Mrs. Reagan—knew was hurting the president.

Souza was there in the Oval Office the last day of the Reagan presidency to record the moment for posterity. He later looked at his work and thought Reagan looked "almost sad." In the years that transpired, he would occasionally drop Reagan a note that was always promptly answered with a handwritten letter. Until "our correspondence ended when his Alzheimer's disease became apparent in 1993."[81]

The day before, June 8, had been another memorable day in American history. In 1948, the first of many corporate-sponsored television shows, the *Texaco Star Theatre*, began broadcasting on NBC with Milton Berle as the host. It was a forerunner to the *GE Theater* hosted five years later by Reagan on CBS. And it was twenty-two years earlier that President Reagan had addressed the British Parliament, the first American chief executive in history to do so. For some, the most important anniversary was the passing of the great Leroy "Satchel" Paige in Kansas City.[82]

It was the thirty-sixth anniversary of the capture in London of James Earl Ray, the man who'd been indicted in the assassination of Dr. Martin Luther King, Jr.[83]

Twenty-three years and several months earlier Reagan had himself nearly been shot dead. Of the six bullets fired by John Hinckley that day, four found the hard flesh of tough men, doing their damage. The first shot had been taken by District police officer Thomas Delahanty, the second hit Jim Brady in the head, the third hit McCarthy, the fourth went through a nearby window, Reagan took the fifth bullet, and the sixth and final shot went across the road.[84] McCarthy actually spread his torso and body in front of the car door to the limousine acting as a human shield, just the way he had been trained.

These men and Agent Jerry Parr, Agent Ray Shaddick, and others saved Reagan's life that day. To a man, they adored him and Mrs. Reagan—"Rawhide" and "Rainbow"—and the Reagan assignment was so popular agents actually argued over who would get to serve on the Reagans' detail. Stories were legendary about their kindnesses and thoughtfulness to the men and women of the Service and their families.

It was announced that Wall Street was making plans to honor the memory of Ronald Reagan.[85] Some went slack jawed. It had long been known that Reagan was not enamored with the titans of finance, nor they of him, a by-product of his populist upbringing. The New York markets would be closed on Friday along with the Chicago markets. Many leaders of Wall Street high finance praised Reagan in death, which was both curious and ironic. In the 1970s, these giants of banking used to routinely knock Reagan. Reagan had always been suspicious of oligarchies and plutocrats.

Stories were being written that seemed to track liberals' complaints about Reagan, as if the media thought they hadn't covered the Reagan critics enough over the previous several days. Reporters went to inner-city haunts like barber shops and spoke with blacks who had a low opinion of Reagan. But, it was also noted, "a substantial segment of the public also strongly disagreed with him on education, the environment, abortion and civil rights, views that now help to complete a fuller portrait of the 40th president."[86]

A nationally syndicated radio talk show hostess, Bev Smith, whose broadcast audience was largely African Americans, said that in a three-hour show, not one caller praised Reagan or said anything nice about him. Ralph Neas, president of People for the American Way, a liberal interest group, said, "As people start looking at the real record, we have been candid in saying Ronald Reagan had an absolutely abysmal record in terms of civil rights, the environment and reproductive freedom."[87]

One could only imagine newspaper editors yelling at their reporters to find things to say and write about the Reagan era, and the journalists followed their bosses' directives. "In terms of culture and style, the Reagan era was not as intellectual or refined as the patrician Kennedys', but it was just as glittering . . ."[88]

Even at this, the midpoint in the week of the Reagan funeral, newspapers were still finding things to hit Ronald and Nancy Reagan with. The *Chicago Tribune* complained that she'd made the Ritz-Carlton her favorite haunt and "instantly establishing its posh Jockey Club restaurant as prime gathering . . . for inveterate climbers." It also roughly reviewed Frank Sinatra's friendship with the Reagans, and that Washington became a tacky center of "showbiz" and an "adjunct to New York high society." And, "the Reagans were not much for art and art museums . . ."

It got worse. "But perhaps in deference to his age and the social awkwardness engendered by the president's hearing problems, the Reagans had a penchant for retiring unusually early. At one gathering for 330 foreign ambassadors, other diplomats and State Department officials, the Reagans shook every hand—then went immediately to bed." The story did manage to bury one sentence saying Nancy Reagan had been the best White House hostess since Jackie Kennedy. Not to let a slight go by, however, it continued, noting that Nancy Reagan and

Raisa Gorbachev had battled, then proceeded to criticize the Reagans' taste in music and performers.[89]

The criticisms and conjectures continued. Television executives wondered if they were devoting too much coverage to Reagan's death, even as cable ratings were "up 20 to 30 percent since Reagan died."[90] The networks, which were not covering the week of the Reagan funeral nearly as much as the cable cousins, had not seen their ratings budge upward an inch. As television had evolved into the nation's town hall, the men and women on and behind the camera were dissecting their role in covering the death of Reagan, and whether they should be respectful or judgmental. But like Narcissus, they were fascinated with themselves, loved to talk and gossip about themselves, and generally celebrated and revered themselves.

Phrases such as "His military successes had a price" and "costly misadventures"[91] filled the stories printed in the nation's newspapers, despite the fact that his military and foreign policies had been demonstrably successful in bringing down the Soviet Empire and relieving Americans from having Soviet nuclear missiles pointed at their children's heads. Still, the disaster of Lebanon was repeatedly reviewed, as was Iran-Contra. Again.

Standing in contrast were hundreds of stories of his thoughtfulness or kindness, the people who'd driven through the night just to stand in line for hours on the Mall. For each tale by the elites bashing Reagan were a hundred anecdotes about how people thought he'd saved the country, saved the world from nuclear war, or saved the future for their children.

For some of the liberal elites and columnists during the week of the Reagan funeral, there was never any such thing as a cease-fire. Molly Ivins was a feisty (some said mean spirited) pedestrian writer based in Austin who made a living and a habit of tormenting George W. Bush in rambling and disconnected pieces, and she did not disappoint. The day before Reagan was buried she accused Bush of wanting to cut off health care for American military veterans.[92] Watching the national fuss over Reagan, a professor from American University threw up his hands in exasperation and said, "He hurt the environment; there was double-digit inflation. I just don't get it."[93] He was wrong about the environment, and he was wrong about inflation, and he was dead wrong in not getting it.

So far, the hoped-for bounce for President Bush in the polls due to the death of Reagan was just that: hope. A new poll out from the *Los Angeles Times* had Kerry leading Bush nationally 48–42 and ahead in the battleground state of Ohio.[94] [94] Another Bush, number forty-one, however, was hoping not to bounce, as at the age of eighty he announced he would make another parachute jump to celebrate his birthday.[95] The relative success of his one-term presidency was being debated by historians and scholars but never debated was the courage and character of George Herbert Walker Bush. He was simply one of the most decent men to ever occupy the Oval Office.

The line grew as people continued to assemble, some arriving in the middle of the night, and despite being warned they most likely would not see the inside of the Capitol in time, they still did not leave. As of 11:00 p.m., the Washington Metro system was still full, still dislodging passengers at Union Station or Capitol South on Capitol Hill so people could walk over to the Mall for the privilege of standing in line for hours before going into the Rotunda. A commemorative card handed out said, in part, "In Final Tribute from a Grateful Nation" along with Reagan's birth date and death date.[96] Visitors clutched the keepsake closely.

One woman who departed the lighted and gleaming white structure said, "I'm just speechless. It was just wonderful, beautiful." People went through in shorts and tennis shoes and suits and dresses but all were quiet, somber, and respectful. Many had tears in their eyes and their own tales of Reagan, of once seeing him at a campaign rally or shaking his hand, or getting a letter from the White House. Many had driven for hours and were proud to say so. At the other end of the long, long, long line, it was another story. A man at the end of the line yelled if anyone ahead of him was for John Kerry, and "a dead hush fell over the crowd."

"Good," the man yelled again.[97]

# CHAPTER 7

# ASSAULT ON JENKINS HILL

*"It enrages them still, which is why they're so eager*
*to diminish him, to peel him, even in death."*

S he told me that as he neared death and it became evident it was
close, he opened his eyes and he gazed at her. His eyes were as
blue as ever and he closed them and died. She told me it was the greatest gift ever."[1] The day before the funeral of the fortieth president of
the United States, Joanne Drake related this emotional and deeply
personal story of Nancy Reagan's and Ronald Reagan's last moments
together to the American people, in the hopes they would understand
that in death he remained dignified.

Patti Davis echoed her mother's recollections but was surprised
how hard she was taking her father's passing. "I thought I was prepared. So many waves of grief crashed over me during these years."[2]

At his final breath she said, "At the last moment, when his breathing told us this was it . . . and looked straight at my mother. Eyes that
hadn't opened in days did, and they weren't chalky or vague. They were
clear and blue and full of love."[3]

Most commentators had noted by now that Reagan had been out
of the public eye for almost a decade. It had also been noted that Nancy

Reagan had not and would not make any public statements during the week leading up to the funeral, other than the short release announcing her husband's passing and thanking people for their support. The three children were scheduled to speak at the committal ceremony at Simi Valley but Mrs. Reagan would remain silent. She did tell her friend Merv Griffin, in confidence, of her surprise at the outpouring. "I thought they forgot Ronnie because nobody had seen him for 10 years."[4]

But even now, only five days after his passing, Ronald Reagan and his legacy were *still* being harshly knocked by some commenters and columnists alike, and on both sides of the Atlantic. Garry Wills, an erstwhile conservative writer for *National Review* and author of the book *Reagan's America*, said that Ronald Reagan played "the heart-warming role of himself."[5] When Wills left conservatism, many on the Right were not sorry to see him go. His thought patterns and writing style could best be described as "macaronic." Men and women of the Right said *Conservatism, si; Wills, no*.

Jet-set-celebrity-editor Tina Brown wrote a retrospective piece for a national paper about Reagan, and a photo shoot and another article in 1985. However, the article was more about her stewardship at *Vanity Fair* (from which she was long departed), though she did manage to get to the second sentence of her piece without using a first person pronoun.[6]

Even the history of Reagan was getting all tangled up. Glenn Kessler, a writer for the *Washington Post*, said Reagan won the election of 1980 with "a simple but devastating question: Are you better off than you were four years ago?"[7] This closing statement of his debate with Jimmy Carter was important to help close the sale with skeptical voters in 1980, but it was that and a thousand other things that helped or hurt Reagan and helped or hurt Carter, including the continuing hostage crisis in Iran, the bad economy, Reagan's new message of optimism, and the palpable sense of malaise in America.

To no one's surprise, the *Post*'s first editorial after his passing repeated the old shibboleth of his "inattentiveness to detail, as well as to some fairly major goings-on . . ." Iran-Contra was mentioned in the first paragraph but the victory over communism was relegated to the third paragraph, and then only as an allusion. The two-column, page-length editorial was typically and frequently tough on Reagan, shot through with words and phrases such as "his naiveté . . . dubious anecdotes . . . occasional confusion of reality with movieland myth." The editorial called his support for SDI "preposterous" and complained that permanent Washington never accepted a Reagan presidency including,

> people in government, journalism, think tanks, lobbying, law—whose frame of reference was never quite able, even after two administrations, to accommodate Ronald Reagan in the role of president. In the land of the quick, articulate and thoroughly briefed, Mr. Reagan seemed out of his depth from the day of his first press conference as president— obviously not conversant with the subject matter that was being thrown at him from all directions, evasive, fumbling, off-balance . . . Mr. Reagan will forever be seen by certain of his adversaries as an easily manipulated executive, something of a figurehead, fronting for the traditional interests of his party.[8]

It was his first press conference in early 1981 where Reagan eviscerated the Soviets causing the Washington insiders to get positively faint.

The frosty editorial conceded that Reagan was pretty good if he could be "alone in front of a camera and give a proper scripted speech." In passing, it noted his ability to connect with people but not without also hitting him again on the so-called budget cuts of the early 1980s, which "hurt" "a lot of people," and asserting that he lacked the conscience to be worried about those people. The *Post* also lauded Reagan for the massive tax increase of 1982, which he himself always regretted, feeling he'd been sold a bill of goods by Tip O'Neill and the Democrats. It also mentioned the arms deal with the Soviets of 1987 but did not recognize that it was Reagan's hard-line policies that brought the Kremlin to the negotiating table in the first place.

Throughout, the whisper of "poor" and minorities was faintly heard. In the end, the piece only grudgingly allowed that Reagan had a role in ending the Cold War but never once said he'd actually won the Cold War. Oddly, it did say he continued "the policy of his predecessor, Jimmy Carter" with regard to a military buildup.[9] The editorial was a classic study in liberal sophistication and was typical of the *Post*. A little grudging praise here—to give it a patina of fair-mindedness—but a lot of heavy criticism to reveal their real attitude toward Reagan, which was smarmy, unctuous, and condescending. However—and to the everlasting gratitude of conservatives everywhere—the *Post* never claimed that Reagan had "grown" in office as it often patronizingly said about politicians who moved from the Right to the Left.

Offsetting those harsh judgments of Reagan was a column by the *Post*'s E. J. Dionne that praised Reagan's abilities as a politician and political leader in part because the Gipper did not talk like a traditional Republican. "Reagan had the New Deal bred in his bones and could talk to Democrats like a Democrat, and in a way no Republican has matched since."[10] Adding his voice was another liberal scribe David Ignatius, who also positively described Reagan as the president who "mobilize[d] moralism and pragmatism in a way that eventually toppled the Soviet Union."[11]

Reagan's memory was warmly celebrated by people who did not read the *New York Times* or the *New Republic* at the Ropewalk Tavern in Baltimore, where there was a six-foot statue of him—outside the establishment—made reportedly out of bronze. Busts of the Gipper also were featured on the bars inside the establishment.[12]

Despite their public protestations to the contrary, the Bush reelection campaign was draping the image of Reagan all over its website. A faxed daily political newsletter *The Bulletin's Frontrunner* devoted day after day of coverage to the political ramifications of the death of Ronald Reagan and how the Kerry and Bush operations were denying their attempts to politicize the Gipper's passing—even as each side did their best to politicize his passing. "Kerry Says He Sees Personal Contrast Between Reagan, Bush" and "Bush Campaign Reworks Web Site to Prominently Feature Reagan."[13]

The campaigns weren't alone. "Effect of Reagan's Death on This Year's Presidential Campaign Examined," screamed one story touted in the *LA Times*. The *Philadelphia Inquirer* said all the Reagan "hagiography" could not be good for Kerry. But the *Chicago Tribune* brought up the 1978 House campaign in Texas, where a young George W. Bush sought the GOP nomination but was opposed by none other than former governor Ronald Reagan. It was the only primary that year in which Reagan took sides.[14]

*Newsweek* noted "neither Bush nor Kerry fares well alongside a president who entered the history books long ago."[15] It was not clear, however, if the editors thought Reagan great or the other two men small.

The line that had formed behind Carol Williams on Wednesday evening stretched into the oppressively warm night, snaking around the Capitol building, down the front sward, and along the Mall for as far as the eye could see. It streamed passed the Air and Space Museum a half mile away and beyond, all the way to Seventh Street. It was a twisting line that had gone back and forth and back and forth, snaking under the occasional shade of trees to escape the scorching daytime sun. Others held up umbrellas as they stood patiently following the route of metal fences hastily arranged to add some order to the procession.

Citizens had been advised not to bring purses, rucksacks, cameras, or food into the *sanctum sanctorum*, and all would be required to pass through a magnetometer. Outside, some carried flowers and a few signs that made political statements. Children fidgeted, understandably bored after many hours, but some took advantage of the time to study homework or just chat with their parents about Reagan or Washington or the U.S. Capitol building. There were many touching stories about fathers and daughters and grandmothers and grandsons driving long distances together and, along the way, bonding. In a sense, Reagan was once again uniting Americans. Ministers, priests, and rabbis were all seen waiting patiently in line.

"The Capitol Police estimated that 30,000 visitors had passed through by 9 a.m." on the morning after the private memorial service.[16] That was in twelve hours and overnight to boot. In all the time Lyndon Johnson laid in state only forty thousand came to pay their respects.[17]

The wait time was up to nine hours for citizens to make their way slowly up what was once known as Jenkins Hill to pay their respects to Ronald Reagan. Thomas Jenkins pastured his cows on the small rise that overlooked the rest of the new federal city in the last years of the 1700s, before the government acquired it for their new Capitol building. One woman was unfazed by the long wait. "I loved Ronald Reagan."[18]

Even in the late evening, the weather was almost unbearable. The sun had gone down hours before but the humidity was such that men and women were perspiring heavily, staining their clothes under their arms and down their backs. There was absolutely no breeze for respite. But nobody complained. The good news was that row upon row of portable toilets were available.

Standing in line were oldsters and youngsters and Boy Scouts and Girl Scouts and grandmothers and grandfathers and mothers and fathers holding the hands of children or pushing strollers. There were men and women in uniform and of all races, all ages. And they weren't just from Washington or the Virginia or Maryland suburbs either. They were from all over the country.

One eighty-five-year-old, Boydson Baird, had flown from Knoxville to Atlanta and there, after his son and grandson joined him, the three went on to Washington all for the privilege of standing in line for Reagan. An elderly couple drove from Florida in their motor home along with their cat. "If I can drive from Orlando to see him, I'm sure I can wait eight hours to see him." A construction worker sporting tattoos, Don Coles, also drove a long distance to pay his respects to the Gipper. He told reporters, "This is the way a good man should be buried."[19]

They were not unique. A blind couple was spotted waiting patiently in line. "Joanne and Harold Wilson, both blind, used their walking sticks to tap their way along the circuitous route . . ." "You feel the respect and the awe, the feel of the crowd, the historical moment," Joanne said.[20]

Sheryl Gay Stolberg, a talented writer for the *New York Times*, captured the moment perfectly. "The people came to the People's House, to honor a president many remember as a man of the people."[21]

Overhead in the night sky, a sliver of a moon danced in and out of the clouds and the thick, moist mist.

Also coming to pay their respects were President and Mrs. Bush, but so quietly and with so little fanfare that people were surprised to see the first couple. The Bushes were silent and simply and reverently approached the coffin, and Bush bowed his head and then reached out and touched the flag over the coffin. He gently smoothed it, which made for a memorable and historic moment.

Those in line behind the velvet ropes were admonished again not to take pictures while in the Rotunda and none did, respectful of the somber occasion. There was nary a sound as only the scuffing of shoe leather on the sandstone floor could be heard. Wisely, the lines went both ways, clockwise and counterclockwise, so twice as many people could move in a half-circular motion around the funeral bier, a flag-covered casket sitting atop a catafalque with a black velvet skirt.

The subject of the weight of the Reagan casket had been much debated during the week. One report had it as heavy as 735 pounds because it was lined with marble.[22] Three groups of military bearers had to rotate when taking the casket up the many stairs of the west front of the Capitol because of the heaviness, the heat, and the number of steps.

In an elaborate and thoroughly planned ceremony, the Honor guards standing at post around Reagan changed every half hour, but they were all on duty for fifteen-hour shifts. Six guards were always at post with four carrying M1s, though they did not have bullets or firing pins. They did have bayonets. A "supernumerary" was in charge. He inspected each of the other men but was also there in case one of them faltered. Four armed guards stood motionless at each of the four corners of the casket. The fifth, unarmed, stood at attention at the head of the coffin.[23] The changing of the guard was a long and beautifully choreographed ceremony, rich with ceremony and symbolism.

These men performed in parades and funerals and guarded the Tomb of the Unknown Soldier, even staying at their post through hurricane Isabel. They were not allowed to scratch, sneeze, smile, twitch, itch, drool, or pose for a camera. Never. They were not allowed to swat away mosquitoes or horse flies or fidget in any way. Their job was to march and stand at attention and only draw attention to the uniform and the service and the duty and not to themselves.[24] General Jackman used to sneak over the fence around Arlington in the early hours to inspect the lone soldier marching in the dark. He was never disappointed.[25] These soldiers did have a sense of humor though. When performing funerals, they said their unofficial motto was "The Last to Let You Down."[26]

Even as Wednesday night wore on into Thursday morning, which then wore into the wee hours of Friday morning, more and more people joined the back of the seemingly endless line hoping they could whisper a final good-bye and prayer for the Gipper. Former Soviet premier Mikhail Gorbachev entered the cool round room with no fanfare and he, too, silently paid his respects, and then he, too, gently placed his hand on the American flag on top of Reagan's coffin, as if to touch his former adversary and later good friend one last time. He looked very sad and moved with a slower gait. Backing away from the coffin, Gorbachev dipped his head. He was alone as his wife Raisa had died five years earlier.

Fred Ryan recalled they'd met in Moscow after Reagan was out of power, and as he walked through the doorway he attempted to embrace Gorbachev, who balked—it was bad luck in Russian culture to greet someone in an entryway. Reagan stepped inside the room and they embraced.[27]

Ironically, both men ended up unpopular in Russia, especially Gorbachev. But in some parts of the former Soviet Union—especially in the Baltics—Reagan had achieved a mythic status. So, too, in the Warsaw Pact countries like Poland and Hungary where there were memorial services going on for Reagan, candles being lit, and prayers offered. It was astonishing when one considered that just a few years earlier organized religion and the practice of religion had been suppressed, and now out in the open, because of Ronald Reagan, people were praying for Ronald Reagan.

When asked, the people standing in the line on the Mall had their own reasons for coming, but all had in some manner been touched by Reagan. A speech, a joke, his presidency, his confidence, his manliness, his integrity, his humor, his handsomeness, his humility, his place in history, somehow this man infused millions with their own special memories of him. Of all the presidents who had passed, it could only be said of Kennedy, FDR, Lincoln, and Washington that each American had his or her own reason for and way of cherishing the president at the time of his passing.

Wordlessly, funeral aides moved down the line over Wednesday,

Thursday, and early Friday morning looking for VIPs or at least identifiable Reaganites and silently took them out of line and moved them to the head of the procession in the Rotunda. Quietly in line was Sandra Day O'Connor, Reagan's first appointment to the Supreme Court. Same with Bob Dole, who also waited patiently.

There was no announced dress code for the procession into the Rotunda, and it was understandable that because of the oppressive heat many were in casual wear, but there were also plenty of men and women in dark suits and dark dresses, attired as they would be for any other funeral. Young boys were in blazers and young girls in dresses. And there were plenty of men and women in uniform. Some might have been tempted to jump into the fountains in front of the Capitol to cool off but none did.

On and on through Wednesday night and into Thursday night, American citizens came, and they came, and they came in the hot and humid day and in the hot and humid evening. Some had no plans whatsoever to go to Washington, thinking they'd be content to watch the proceedings on television. But then something came over them. Someone called. Or they called someone and they simply said, "Let's go to Washington—before it is too late."

No one needed to elaborate the whos and the whys. They simply got in their cars or trucks or minivans and drove to Washington, some never having been there before. Others took buses and planes and trains, but they came by the thousands first, then by the tens of thousands, then by the hundreds of thousands. It was nothing short of remarkable. During the 1980 campaign Reagan had often said, "We have to move ahead. But we can't leave anyone behind."[28] Now it seemed that no one wanted to be left behind in the streams of humanity making their way toward a shining city on a hill.

The high and mighty also spoke out.

A Senate resolution was passed unanimously, though two senators were missing. A House resolution was also passed unanimously, though dozens of Democrats chose not to vote. "Ronald Wilson Reagan— father, husband, actor and dedicated public servant—restored the pride, optimism and strength of the United States and earned the deep respect and affection of his fellow citizens."[29] Senator Ted Kennedy went even further. Of Reagan, the old liberal from Massachusetts said,

> He brought a special grace to the White House and the country in everything he did. We often disagreed on specific issues, but he had an undeniably unique capacity to inspire and move the Nation. On foreign policy, he will be honored as the President who won the cold war. It was more than the fact that he was a superb communicator. Some attributed at least part of his success to the fact that he had been an actor. But his deepest convictions were matters of heart and mind and spirit, and on them, he was no actor at all.[30]

Hundreds of other members of Congress also read statements on the floor of the House or the Senate, and they were later published in a book entitled *Ronald Reagan: Late a President of the United States. Memorial Tributes Delivered in Congress.* The book was more than three hundred pages long and cost one million dollars to be published.[31] From the most passionate conservative to the most dispassionate liberal, many paid tribute to the Gipper. Some chronic Reagan haters in Congress like Debbie Wasserman Schultz and John Lewis and Jim Moran chose not to include any praise of Reagan in the book, but they were in the minority. Truth be told, in their own party Wasserman Schultz and Moran were extremely unpopular and were known to have turnstiles in their Capitol Hill offices through which many staff members departed.

On the other hand, people like Nancy Pelosi had deeply poignant tributes to Reagan. No rancor, no politics, just a statement infused with "dignity" and "passionate" and "freedom" and "eloquence" and "grace" and "humor."[32] It was utterly moving.

John Boehner inserted not one but two statements of unvarnished praise for Reagan, including announcing that in his home district the "Ronald Reagan's Voice of Freedom Park" was so named in the Gipper's honor.[33]

The debate over his place in history continued without end and even increased as more and more people turned out to show their respect and affection for Reagan. Sean Wilentz, a pleasant, liberal professor from Princeton, bluntly said that Reagan "was not a great president. He was master at projecting a mood; he could certainly rally the country. He would have made a great king, a great constitutional monarch, but we do not have that form of government."[34] Wilentz had been a passionate defender of Bill Clinton during his impeachment and testified before Congress defending the not–fanatically married Arkansan.

The place of various presidents in history along with their ranking was on the lips and keyboards of many. Most, like Wilentz, would not even consider Reagan in the top ranks alongside Abraham Lincoln, Franklin Roosevelt, and George Washington. Most rated Lincoln a greater president than Washington even though the first president had been on the national stage for a quarter of a century while the man from Springfield, Illinois, was on the national stage for all of six years. Calvin Coolidge was the butt of many jokes told by liberal historians even though the economy grew and many progressive social causes were addressed, including his support for universal suffrage. Still, H. L. Mencken said of Coolidge, "There were no thrills while he reigned, but neither were there any headaches. He had no ideas, and he was not a nuisance."[35]

Coincidentally, a group of historians gathered in Washington to compare and contrast American presidents during the week of the Reagan funeral. When the subject of Woodrow Wilson came up, the American historians rated him highly, his hardwired racism notwithstanding. But the Australians said he was a "flop, largely because of his rigid and eventually counterproductive idealism." The American academics rated John Kennedy high but said Reagan had "achieved no such status overseas. His brand of radical conservatism . . . has achieved little success . . ."

American liberal historian Robert Dallek also slammed Reagan's legacy as being one of attacking government and separating the economic classes and casting poor people into permanent servitude. "Much of the country, including most of those who are physically, economically or otherwise disadvantaged, deeply resented and still resent his insistence that government is the problem, not the solution."[36]

Some liberal historians were typically blinded to the facts by their own ideology. In contrast, in 1951, Hannah Arendt wrote *The Origins of Totalitarianism*, and in it she audaciously compared Stalin and Hitler and their respective countries. The Left in America went nuts even in the face of the fact that communism and National Socialism were both forms of collectivism. Some American liberals could never accept that Hitler was a leftist.

Reaganites were incessantly accused of doing their utmost to push back against the assault on his legacy by liberal historians, but under the constant barrage, who could blame them? Gorbachev had a different and better appreciation for Reagan's legacy than did the liberal historians, saying that he wanted to go down in history as a "peacemaker."[37]

A singular and remarkable liberal historian John Patrick Diggins was in many ways the unofficial chronicler of the American Left in the twentieth century, having written numerous and important books about American liberalism. Of Reagan and Mrs. Reagan, Diggins reminded Americans of Michelangelo, who wrote, "Death and love are the two wings that bear the good man to heaven."[38] He later noted that up to the time of Reagan's passing nearly all the books written about the fortieth president had been harsh and even cruel, few giving him credit or the benefit of the doubt. Their titles were revealing: *Our Long*

*National Daydream* and *Sleepwalking Through History* and others deni-
grating the man and his time in office.

Another historian of the Left, the much-esteemed John Lewis
Gaddis, had also gone through his own evolution of thinking. Gaddis
was one of the best chroniclers of the Cold War and in an earlier time
had given Reagan short shrift, but by the time of Reagan's passing he
had come to the conclusion that Reagan was a giant of history, calling
him one of the "saboteurs of the status quo."[39]

The liberal columnists continued their criticism. Paul Krugman and
Bob Herbert, notably in the *New York Times*, on the day of the Reagan
funeral tastelessly savaged Reagan again. Krugman, not satisfied with
the facts, made up his own in challenging that Reaganomics worked or
that jobs were created in the eight years Reagan was in office. "For much
of the Reagan era, the economy suffered from very high unemployment.
There was, in short, nothing magical about the Reagan economy."[40]

That was true, of course, if you considered the eradication of the
double-digit inflation of the 1970s to be an unremarkable achievement.
Or if you thought the same of the drop in real interest rates from more
than 20 percent to below 7 percent,[41] or the real cut in federal spending and the cuts in government regulations, or that according to the
Bureau of Labor Statistics almost eighteen million jobs were created
during the 1980s.[42] Also, the Bureau did not count the self-employed
and the 1980s saw an explosion of entrepreneurship.

But it was Diggins who had the most interesting take on the
Reagan legacy—he beat the neocons about the head and shoulders.
"Not only did the neocons oppose Mr. Reagan's efforts at rapproche-
ment, they also argued against engaging in personal diplomacy with
Soviet leaders. Advisers like Richard Perle, Paul Wolfowitz and
Donald Rumsfeld . . ." Diggins said the neocons clung to the notion
that the Soviet Union was a thing of permanence, the Berlin Wall was
a permanent fixture in our lives, and the Cold War was unending. He
concluded, writing, "But many neocons came to hate Mr. Reagan . . .

Mr. Reagan gave us an enlightened foreign policy that achieved most of its diplomatic objectives peacefully and succeeded in firmly uniting our allies." In contrast, he said the foreign policy of George W. Bush and its architects like Rumsfeld had "lost its way and undermined valued friendships throughout the world."[43]

The neocons, of course, feared their loss of prestige more than anything else, and if the West actually transcended the Soviets they would be proven wrong and they would lose their status.

For many, even by 2004, the Cold War had almost faded into obscurity, seen as a relic of the past. The end of history so to speak. The terrors of the Soviets had nearly been forgotten. But not by everybody. A columnist John Kass wrote of his own father's experiences in the "old world" though it wasn't so long ago. "They repeatedly tried to kill him . . . They shot up the village and stole food from starving people at gunpoint and killed those who disagreed with them, including teachers, and used their politics as cover to settle disputes by gutting those they stole from."[44] Kass, too, ripped the Washington establishment and Jimmy Carter. "But," Kass wrote,

> . . . then came Reagan. He didn't care about satisfying the establishment by waxing on about shades of grey. He understood that there was good and evil in the world and that we weren't evil. The Soviets were evil because they squashed the individual in the name of the collective. Big central governments everywhere are determined to maintain themselves at the cost of the individual. This is the nature, the danger, of bureaucracies. Reagan understood this. He rebuilt the military, confronted the communists and broke them. This outraged the hand-wringers and the shades-of-grey crowd. It enrages them still, which is why they're so eager to diminish him, to peel him, even in death. And what happened in the world? They call it freedom. They call it the American Century. They don't call it the Soviet Century. Thank you, President Reagan.[45]

At the same time the leading neocon organization, the Council on Foreign Relations, was going through its own internal civil war over a report on Saudi Arabia and whether the royal dictatorship was helping or hurting in the war on terror. A leading member of the neocon group, Mallory Factor, was embroiled in the squabble, working with Bush White House aides to slow roll any criticism of the Bush White House. On the other hand, the draft report was written by former Clinton aides who were now advising John Kerry. Factor defended the Bush White House, saying they only wanted "factual changes" made in the report.[46] The bottom line was the truism that truth was always the first casualty in war and politics.

Still, the head of CFR Richard Haass agreed with Diggins on the Cold War. "Reagan's words mattered. He questioned the basic legitimacy of communism and the Soviet empire. When he called it an evil empire, this reverberated."[47]

Reagan the old Cold Warrior once recalled his last summit meeting with Gorbachev and addressing the press in Red Square, a sight unimaginable only a few months earlier. Later, he said, "Imagine the president of the United States and the general secretary of the Soviet Union walking together in Red Square, talking about a growing personal friendship . . . Quite possibly we are beginning to take down the barriers of the postwar era."[48]

All this debate and discussion was leading inevitably to a closer examination of Bush and Reagan and more sophisticated observers and commentators were coming rapidly to the conclusion there were more differences between the two presidents than there were similarities. Reagan never trusted government—or at least rarely did—whereas Bush was very much like his father in celebrating the bureaucracy. Bush, when running for president in 2000, never proposed the cutting or elimination of one federal program, a contrast to Reagan, who in 1980 made cutting and eliminating agencies such as the Department of Energy and the Department of Education a centerpiece of his message. Indeed, his closing remarks of the 1980 debate were to "take government off the backs of the great people of this country . . ."[49]

Bush saw himself as not a Reagan Republican but a Bush Republican, though Tom Brokaw of NBC said most in the party saw themselves as Reagan Republicans.[50] In his mind, he was not trying to pattern his presidency after Reagan but understandably wanted to leave his own mark. Reagan, for his part, never called himself a "compassionate conservative." The way they both entered Washington was dramatically different. Reagan was assuming the presidency of a broken country. Bush was assuming the presidency as the leader of a divided country. Reagan had won in a popular and electoral landslide in 1980. Bush lost the popular vote in 2000 but won the Electoral College 271–266.[51] Even as Bush was trying to distinguish himself his aides were bending over backward to compare the two presidents.

During the week of the Reagan memorial, dozens of unofficial dinners, receptions, and get-togethers materialized; most were unplanned and not listed in any schedule or newspaper. Some of the former Reagan speechwriters gathered to reacquaint and for some polite conversation with other veterans of the Reagan years. They met in the old Executive Office Building adjacent to the White House. They'd often worked together, been competitive with one another, and admired one another.

In the history of Ronald Reagan it had been overlooked that he himself was a very fine writer, as evidenced by his thousands of letters, columns, speeches, and radio commentaries. Presidents tend to attract like-minded people. FDR was interested in quick solutions and politics, so many of the men around him saw things in that fashion. JFK was intellectually curious and he attracted men who also cherished reason and knowledge. Richard Nixon attracted insecure and paranoid men like Bob Haldeman, John Ehrlichman, and John Dean because they, too, saw enemies where they should have seen potential converts.

Carter drew people like him—they were called the "Georgia Mafia"—and the same held true for Reagan. He was principled and kind and had a large worldview so he brought in (for the most part) men and women who thought in the same fashion, such as Ed Meese and George Shultz and Jim Baker and Fred Ryan and others. This held true for the Reagan White House speechwriters for the most part. Behind the scenes, they fought and argued and formed cliques and knocked one another over the years. Some basked in the glory of having written speeches for Reagan while others, lower key, moved on with their lives.

Landon Parvin was there with Reagan as was Ben Elliott, Tony Dolan, Peter Robinson, Mari Maseng Will, Peggy Noonan, Clark Judge, Dana Rohrabacher, Josh Gilder, John Podhoretz, and others. Ken Khachigian and Peter Hannaford held special status as two of Reagan's favorite speechwriters from the 1980 campaign, but Hannaford also went back with Reagan even farther to the early 1970s in Sacramento. Dolan was the only one who'd been with Reagan in the White House all eight years and on the 1980 campaign as well.

Reagan sent Dolan a note on the last day of the administration recognizing his sturdy longevity. "Tony, you were keeper of the flame . . ." Dolan was a terrific writer and had won a Pulitzer uncovering homegrown corruption for a local newspaper in Connecticut. He was also very well connected politically. Bill Buckley was his mentor, as was CIA chief Bill Casey. Casey had hired him only after surrendering to a flood of telegrams Buckley kept sending him, telling him to hire Tony.[52]

He was also close to Jim Baker via his brother Terry Dolan but also to Don Rumsfeld. Dolan had written the Evil Empire speech and each, like Judge, could point with pride to a singular or series of Reagan speeches they helped write. For Judge, it was the sequence of "Iron Triangle" remarks by Reagan at the end of 1988, taking on the media, K Street lobbyists, and Capitol Hill. For Robinson it was the Berlin Wall speech. Parvin worked with Reagan on a book of the Gipper's speeches. Peggy Noonan, of course, drafted the brief but powerful *Challenger* remarks. They all took pride in their work and the man for whom they worked. It truly was the greatest collection of speechwriters in White House history.

A column several days later by Noonan in the *Wall Street Journal* was warm and liquescent about the week while also harshly alluding to several of her colleagues who had gathered during the funeral. The article caused cold comment among the Reagan wordsmith brethren. One she referred to as "The Hack" and said he had a "greasy political style" and another as "haircut boy" and yet a third as "a malignant leprechaun."[53]

As far as the rest of the speechwriters, they were conservatives, and they were keepers of the flame, and many like Parvin and Elliott were restrained. A compulsive man of letters himself, Reagan identified with the speechwriters more than with any other department in his White House.

Ironically, few of Reagan's speechwriters had actually been political or policy writers before going to work for him. Nearly all said their time with Reagan was the most important and most enjoyable and most fun they'd ever had. When Reagan walked between the old Executive Office Building and the White House on West Executive Drive, the speechwriters and the secretaries would often go out on the balcony and cheer him on: Reagan ate it up.[54]

Another dinner and drinks gathering occurred that week at Sam & Harry's and included a small group of conservatives who worked on the 1976 Reagan campaign, including former Pennsylvania senator Richard Schweiker and his wife Claire. Schweiker had audaciously agreed to go on the ticket with Reagan three weeks before the convention in Kansas City even though Reagan was behind in the delegate count. He was not a conservative at the time but his voting record moved to the Right dramatically afterward. In taking the courageous gamble, Schweiker endeared himself to all Reaganites for all time.

Also spotted there at the "wakish" event were Kenny Klinge,

Frank and Becki Donatelli, Roger Stone, Judge Loren Smith, David Bufkin, Phil Alexander, Maiselle Shortley, Tony Dolan, Judge Bill Clark, Helene von Damm, Charlie Black, Paul and Kathy Russo, Dale and Jewell Duval, Neal Peden, Peter Monk, David Keene, Don Totten, and others, and a good if low-key time was had by all as they meandered down memory lane. Bufkin, who'd worked on fund-raising for Reagan, said, "The mood was definitely Irish 'wakish'—even celebratory—rather than the Protestant funeral gloom. It was kinda like a reassurance Reagan's greatness couldn't be taken from him now. The Left could not erase his success from history. We the insiders loved him . . . but now it was confirmed America loved him too."[55]

Reagan's manager from 1976 and 1980, John Sears, was invited repeatedly but he demurred. Many were not on the "A-List" of Washington hosts but all were on the "A-List" of courageous revolutionaries, and their Reagan credentials were impeccable. Working for Reagan against the incumbent Ford in 1975 and 1976 meant one was putting his or her career in GOP politics in jeopardy. These were the über-Reaganites, first among equals.

Curiously, most worked in the 1980 campaign, as well, but only a few made it into high-powered or high-profile positions in the Reagan administration. Most were serious about their conservatism and seriously dedicated to Reagan, but few were good self-promoters, unlike some others who arrived late and left early to cash in on their short stay with Reagan. But like Schweiker, the stalwarts, too, had gambled and won. The beloved Franklyn—"Lyn" to all—Nofziger was there as the leader of the pack. Of the group, he went back to 1966 with Reagan. Nofziger was an original in every way imaginable. He was the last of the old-style political operatives, a cigar-chomping and gin-drinking war hero. To many, Lyn was something special.

Nancy Reagan had been struggling to hold it together all week. It had now been six days since her husband's death and one blurry emotional roller coaster. She had one more long day to get through that would start early on Friday morning in Washington and end Friday night three thousand miles away in California. Her health had been generally good, though she'd broken some ribs a couple of years earlier.

Thursday was a less hectic day than the rest of the week. She and Patti and Ron were staying at the Blair House, which again attested to the kindness of President Bush. The house was usually off limits to all but visiting heads of state. Mike Reagan did not stay there, choosing instead to use a nearby hotel that the funeral staff had arranged for him.[56] Pam Ahearn, Rick Ahearn's wife, was handling many advance duties for the week including working the Blair House, which given the egos and VIPs and security, required someone with a lot of patience and fortitude.

There was a reception at Blair House—one more event for which Nancy Reagan had to summon the strength to present a brave front. President Bush and Laura Bush dropped by, as did Condoleezza Rice. Former president George H. W. Bush was there. Gorbachev attended and the old Russian and Nancy embraced. He wrote in the condolence book, "I convey my deep feelings of condolence to dear Nancy and the whole family." Also present were George Shultz and Howard Baker and Margaret Thatcher and a small gathering of other world power brokers. Thatcher wrote, "Well done, thou good and faithful servant."[57]

Brian Mulroney and his wife, Mila, stopped by, too, and wrote, "For Ron with affection, admiration and respect. The Gipper always came through!"[58] The festive spirit of the Mulroney entry was a testament to how many saw the funeral as a time to celebrate Reagan. It also typified an Irish funeral.

Most of the members of the Supreme Court stopped by as well, and each—John Paul Stevens, Sandra Day O'Connor, Anthony Kennedy, William Rehnquist, Antonin Scalia, Stephen Breyer—made long and heartfelt entries into the condolence book. Rehnquist said he'd admired Reagan since the time he'd seen him play "George Gipp in the movie." All except Scalia—the product of Catholic education—had lousy penmanship.[59]

Rick Ahearn, dog tired after elongated days and nights with one more to endure, was relieved to find a corner and have a couple of drinks to help unwind.[60] For the Reaganites, it was old home week. Everybody who'd worked in the campaigns or the White House or the bureaucracy was in Washington, and there were plenty of get-togethers. Most had done their crying in 1994 when the Alzheimer's had been revealed and then again on Saturday when Reagan's death was announced. Ed Meese and Bill Clark were seen, as was Jim Baker, Ken Duberstein, Howard Baker, and Mike Deaver. There were Reagan's two "body men," Dave Fischer and Jim Kuhn. There were receptions in Georgetown hosted by influencers for Reagan, and there were lots of cocktail receptions and dinner parties and campaign reunions.

The Mayflower Hotel was the unofficial headquarters for the Reagan funeral team where the phones were answered "Office of Ronald Reagan." At midnight, a large group of Reaganites was drinking and milling about the bar when they broke into "Happy Birthday" to Joanne Drake. She recalled how years earlier Reagan had sneaked up on her at the Hotel Cipriani in Venice and sang "Happy Birthday."[61] Earlier Mrs. Reagan, even with so much on her mind, still remembered Joanne's birthday and arranged for a party for her at Blair House.[62]

Little escaped Nancy's attention as her dedication to detail had been legendary. In the middle of it all she had someone on her staff call Lou Cannon to find out why he hadn't yet RSVP'd for the sunset service at the Library. Cannon, of course, attended but only found out later his invitation had been sent to the L.A. bureau of the *Post*, which no one there bothered to tell him.[63]

On Thursday those invited to the Friday funeral at the National Cathedral began to line up at the Mayflower Hotel to pick up their invitation, which was mantled with a black border. No one doubted for a moment that Mrs. Reagan—who in her years had seen it all, including the near murder of her husband—would hold up. She knew she had to do so not just for herself or for the memory of Ronnie, but for the American people.

Earlier, she'd told a story of Reagan in his years of struggling with Alzheimer's. He had gone out for a walk one day when he saw some roses growing in front of a house. He bent over to pluck one when the Secret Service agent gently told the president it was not his house. Reagan, "stricken," protested, "But I want to give it to my lady."[64]

Book piracy on the Internet was becoming a real problem as people were downloading entire volumes and printing them off, all without paying a retailer or publisher for the book itself. Certainly not the author.

Scientists were openly speculating that the twelve-thousand-year run of a gradually warming Earth had reached its conclusion, and that a new Ice Age could be in the offing. Some of the research included digging down into the Antarctic and reaching ice that was three-quarters of a million years old.[65]

Father's Day was just days away, and the newspapers featured ads for golf clubs and tennis rackets and outdoor grills. There were also plenty of helpful "how to" articles and columns chock full of suggestions for chores for Dad around the house on his own day, from plumbing to cleaning grills to painting concrete.

The Bush administration announced its endorsement of a plan by the United Nations to "end Iraq occupation."[66]

Clear Channel Communications had to pay a fine of almost two million dollars to the FCC because of the public comments by the erudite and sophisticated Howard Stern, aka Mr. Manners.[67]

The Direct Marketing Association announced that it was calling on its members to abide by a moratorium to refrain from sending e-mails or making phone calls on Friday, the national day of mourning for Reagan.[68] It may have been the first time someone used "OMG" in an e-mail.

In a show of petty mean-spiritedness, the AFL-CIO announced it would not close on Friday, the national day of mourning.[69] The first president to carry a membership card in a labor union—indeed, the first president to be the president of a labor union—would not be honored by the AFL-CIO. The organization had strayed a long way from the days of George Meany, who had admired Reagan's anti-communism and pro–working class views.

Gary Bauer, a veteran of the first Reagan administration, got off a good line on Reagan's passing when he said, "He took a party of accountants and added some heart and soul." Several days earlier, a website sponsored by the Young America's Foundation sprung up with the website named rememberronaldreagan.com, and people began posting their thoughts and recollections.[70]

Others were springing forth with their reminiscences. A young Capitol Hill intern Kristen Hudak, twenty-one years old, stood outside the White House in the rain, crying, saying the reason she'd gotten involved in politics was because of Reagan.[71]

It was duly noted three years earlier on October 11, 2001, and again this week that Reagan was the longest living former president, surpassing John Adams.[72] Billy Graham had issued a preliminary statement on the passing of Reagan but then followed up saying, "Ronald Reagan was one of my closest personal friends for many years."[73]

Other lesser-known figures were talking about Reagan and telling stories, many of which could not be read without weeping. In his dotage, Reagan had become a Saturday fixture at the Los Angeles Country Club where there were always elderly men looking for a "fourth" for their threesome. Chase Morsey was a member and had many happy—and sad—memories of playing golf with Reagan. At first, there were plenty of jokes and the general frivolity of a group of retired men, still with boyish mischievousness, happy to play nine. Jokes were welcomed but politics were not, which suited Reagan just fine. Stu Spencer said the same about his days playing golf with Reagan. He said the Gipper would try to tell a joke, "get halfway through it and just couldn't finish it."

Later, after the announcement of the Alzheimer's, Reagan continued to play golf each Saturday but often said little or nothing to the other men. Reagan kept going, though, in part because he clearly liked golf and because the doctors encouraged physical activity.

Steve Colo, who'd become the head of his Secret Service detail, recalled how whenever they went somewhere Reagan wanted to stop and help. If they saw a homeless man, Reagan wanted to stop and give him money. Once they saw a man fixing a flat tire and Reagan wanted to stop and help him, but Colo gently told Reagan that he, Colo, would provide the assistance, but the former president of the United States could not.[74]

Colo—like most agents—was tall and handsome in a rugged way, the archetypical agent. He grew close to the Reagans, and was briefed by doctors on Reagan's Alzheimer's. Mrs. Reagan would ask Colo to make sure her husband did not have too much dessert at lunch. Colo at the ranch had to gently take chain saws away. At the ranch the eighty-two-year-old man still cut brush, still hauled it away, and still drove the old red beat-up jeep around the property, even though it lacked power steering.[75]

At one point Colo had to take away a pistol that Reagan had kept in his briefcase for years—"I've been carrying this gun since I got shot," he told a surprised Colo. Colo later told Nancy Reagan that he'd confiscated the gun from the president and she exclaimed, "Oh, thank God."[76]

Once, Reagan and Colo had a brief conversation about the assassination attempt by John Hinckley and after saying he hoped Hinckley got help, Reagan exclaimed, "But you know, it hurt like [heck]!"[77]

Other stories tinged with sadness began making the rounds about Reagan's declining years. John Barletta told of how he'd drive Reagan to the Los Angeles Country Club and Reagan asked several times where it was they were going. Colo also related how it was he who tearfully told Reagan he could no longer go horseback riding.[78] Barletta also told Reagan, and it was possible they both informed Reagan given his state. Barletta, loyal, longtime horseback rider, also showed a temper. As Reagan sunk into his own personal world, he would sometimes repeat himself, asking the agents where they were going. At one point, an exasperated Barletta snapped at Reagan, "Now what?"[79]

It was in Houston where Reagan gave his last speech to the Republican National Convention. He'd been to every one since 1960 when he was part of "Democrats for Nixon." This Houston speech was one of his finest, and the Astrodome was filled with teary and crying delegates and guests. Two friends stood on the floor applauding, surprised to find they were both weepy. One asked the other, with a tinge of sarcasm, "What are you crying about?" and his friend replied, without sarcasm, "I think he's going back to California and we're never going to see him again."[80]

Previously, in late 1989 he returned to Washington for the unveiling of his official portrait (which he and Nancy did not like; it was later touched up); he testified for more than seven hours in the Iran-Contra trials, and in 1993 he returned again to Washington to receive the Medal of Freedom, awarded by President Bush. In May 1993, Reagan gave the commencement remarks at the graduation ceremonies at the Citadel in South Carolina, where twenty-five hundred cadets stood and saluted Reagan as he saluted them, recalled Fred Ryan.[81] He spoke in moving terms but also joshed them. "Yes, it's true that my alma mater—Eureka College—awarded me an honorary degree 25 years after my graduation. That only aggravated a sense of guilt I'd nursed for 25 years."[82]

His last official speech was at a birthday party for him in Washington, in February 1994, hosted by Haley Barbour and the Republican National Committee. Some noted his performance was not up to par but Barbour defended Reagan, saying the teleprompter operator had screwed up.[83] Still, his letter to Margaret Thatcher—who had attended and spoken at his birthday dinner, was bright and solicitous. The last handwritten letter he sent was at the end of the year to Barbour, right after he and Newt Gingrich guided the GOP to a historic takeover of Congress. A victory that was built on a campaign rooted in Reagan's themes of less government and more freedom.

"Congratulations on a great job for the Republican Party. I couldn't be happier with the results of the election. And please don't count me out! I'll be putting in my licks for Republicans as long as I'm able. Sincerely, Ronald Reagan."[84]

Even during the week in which the media was often harsh about the deceased former president, some wondered if the media was being too gentle with him or at least his legacy. One more clear-eyed writer for the *Washington Post*, media critic Howard Kurtz, reminded all of how Reagan was "widely portrayed as uninformed and uninterested in details . . . he was often described as lazy, 'just an actor,' a man who'd rather be clearing brush at his California ranch and loved a good midday nap." Kurtz's point was that Reagan was much more than the man often misreported on.

Incredibly, in 1988, a book was published titled *On Bended Knee* by Mark Hertsgaard, an ultra-leftist writer for *The Nation*, which pummeled the media for supposedly going easy on Reagan during his presidency.[85] This, too, came back up. Liberal historian Robert Dallek complained that the coverage of Reagan since his death amounted to a "hagiography."[86]

As if to refute Hertsgaard and Dallek—and consistent with the real story of the Reagan in death narrative—many articles recounted the "schisms" created in the country by the Reagan years and "nearly 16 years after he left office, some major interest groups . . . remain bitter about his legacy."[87] Even Bitburg cemetery, from nineteen years earlier, was dragged back up again. Some African American leaders, including Julian Bond, were harsh in their criticisms of Reagan, and the controversy over the launch of the 1980 campaign was also rehashed.

The main problem was their facts were wrong. Reagan's 1980 campaign did not begin at the Neshoba County Fair (where Jimmy Carter and Mike Dukakis made appearances) but instead at Liberty State Park in New Jersey. Of course they failed to mention Reagan's high approval numbers among African Americans as he was leaving the office. What they and seemingly most commenters did not fail to mention was Iran-Contra, a matter that was reexamined and re-debated even though Lawrence Walsh's own report, while extraordinarily tough, said there was "no credible evidence" that Reagan knew of the illegal and clandestine operation.[88] "The Reagan years were marred by scandals . . ." stated one over-the-top *Washington Post* story.[89]

On the other hand, there were a number of stories running in which every Republican quoted claimed to have *always* loved Ronald Reagan and claimed to have *always* supported him. Republican apparatchiks, who in the 1960s and 1970s thought Reagan was a certified yahoo, the George Wallace of the Republican Party, and who couldn't give him the time of day, were now pronouncing their lifetime devotion to him.

Between the extremes, future historians knew they would have their work cut out for them trying to find the real story about Ronald Reagan. And as economist Robert Samuelson pointed out, nearly none of the obituaries so far had even mentioned what many regarded as Reagan's greatest achievement—the eradication of the inflation of the 1970s that had been eating away at income, savings, investment, and equity—America's future.[90]

A recent Pew Research poll showed that a healthy percentage of Republicans did not trust the "mainstream media."[91]

Defying history and gerontology, Roger Clemens, age forty-one, won his first nine outings for the Houston Astros. Some called his efforts superhuman and a first-year election to Cooperstown was assured.

Sparked by the Reagan funeral, some politicians were stepping forward to claim that stem cell research was the solution to Alzheimer's, even as research doctors said that the chances were small the treatment could make any difference with the dreaded disease.

At 2:00 a.m. Friday, Park police officials, noting the length of the line, began telling new arrivals not to waste their time because the Rotunda would be closed in several hours for Reagan's trip to the National Cathedral.

Nothing doing said the late-arriving citizens. People were still coming from hundreds and even thousands of miles away, and though warned they had no chance to get into the Capitol, they insisted on waiting in line, which the Park police reluctantly allowed them to do.

Maggie Hall of rural Virginia was adamant and was a voice that spoke for many. "Even if I couldn't get in, I had to wait. I couldn't give up. [Reagan] was an optimist. So I was an optimist."[92]

# CHAPTER 8

# DO WE NOT HEAR THE CHIMES AT MIDDAY?

*"Ronald Reagan does not enter history tentatively;*
*he does so with certainty and panache."*

The world had mourned the death of Ronald Reagan for six days. By Friday, the public outpouring of emotion was so impressive that one observer, Dave Keene, quipped that the other former presidents should simply "mail it in"[1] when they died, because their state funerals would never come close to rivaling the Gipper's. Keene was a "lifer" when it came to conservatism, though he'd had his ups and downs with the Reagans over the years, supporting Nixon over Reagan in 1968, supporting Reagan over Ford in 1976, and supporting Bush over Reagan in 1980.

However, as the head of the annual Conservative Political Action Conference during the 1980s, Keene had made sure that the Gipper came each year, often fighting with truculent aides in the Reagan White House, who couldn't fathom why Reagan wanted to go each year to speak to a room full of young right wing nuts. Reagan, ever self-aware, told the CPAC audience of his staff's objections, and then he knocked it out saying he told his staff, you "dance with the one that brung ya."[2]

On top of everything else, the funeral schedulers continued to contend with Bill Clinton. He was making things difficult with his insistent badgering of anyone and everyone about allowing him to speak at the National Cathedral. Intermediaries and go-betweens kept calling repeatedly, asking, pleading, and begging for Bill to speak. "Bill Clinton has asked me to call."[3] Each time, they were told no again. Nancy Reagan had already decided. There was no way she was going to allow Bill Clinton to speak at her husband's funeral.[4]

In 1996, Clinton's reelection campaign had tastelessly aired commercials on gun control that included footage of the assassination attempt on Reagan. Clinton had politicized the event that nearly claimed the life of Ronald Reagan. Mrs. Reagan wrote Clinton at the White House to ask him to take them off the air but they were never taken down. In the weeks before the actual announcement of Reagan's affliction, then–president Clinton was speculating publicly about Reagan's condition, which also angered many Reaganites.[5] Many people around Reagan world regarded the Clintons as vainglorious. Still, Clinton would not go away, even when told the speakers had been selected well before—by Mrs. Reagan and Ronald Reagan.

The first "general mourning" in America had been for Benjamin Franklin in 1791.[6] The first state funeral in American history was for William Henry Harrison, who died of pneumonia one month after his inaugural in 1841 after giving a three-hour speech in the driving rain.[7] There was so much irony in the American presidency. Harrison had been the oldest man elected president. Until Reagan. Harrison's demise also began the twenty-year jinx for 140 years that had plagued the American presidency. Until Reagan.

From Harrison to Lincoln to Garfield to McKinley to Harding to FDR to JFK, all were elected at twenty-year intervals, and all had died in office, including four via an assassin's bullet. Reagan, through the grace and hand of God, the speed of his Secret Service detachment, the decision of Jerry Parr to go to George Washington Hospital rather than the White House, the skill of the attending physicians, nurses, and staff, and his own strength, stamina, and mental toughness, broke the curse; he did not succumb to the assassination intentions of John Hinckley aka Travis Bickle.

Always a man of devout faith, the experience of having narrowly escaped death drove Reagan's Christian faith even deeper into his character. And no one would really know his immense capacity for Christian forgiveness until 1983 after Hinckley's incarceration at St. Elizabeth's Hospital, a mental institution in Washington, DC.

Astonishingly, Reagan sought a meeting with Hinckley to tell him in person that he forgave the young man. Reagan had first raised the idea of talking to Hinckley with the White House physician Dr. Daniel Ruge one weekend at Camp David. After Ruge initiated the conversation, Reagan reached out to the head of psychiatry at St. Elizabeth's Hospital, Dr. Roger Peele. "Ruge said that Reagan would like to talk with me . . . ," Peele recalled. A call was arranged but "the striking thing for me was how modest they were. They were concerned about interrupting my schedule . . ."[8]

Reagan and Peele chatted amiably, and Peele said he recalled the kindness and professionalism of Reagan and his staff asking several times if he was being inconvenienced in any way. Further, he told of Reagan saying he wanted to pardon Hinckley, not legally but "personally"[9] and "in private."[10] But Reagan also made clear he wanted to do what was best for Hinckley. After a fashion and a good talk, Dr. Peele said such a meeting would not be an advisable course for his patient. He had already spoken with Hinckley's psychiatric team, and upon their advice Peele counseled Reagan against it, as he felt "Hinckley's sense of responsibility should not be reduced."[11]

He told Reagan that a pardon or a meeting would only empower the young man, whose ego was out of control and whose sense of guilt was nonexistent. Hinckley was a sociopath who did not feel the pain

of others but only his own. Indeed, Peele said Hinckley had four official diagnoses, including depression. At some point he said Hinckley
was "the only patient that ever came to St. E's and got four personality
disorders . . ."[12]

It was a principled decision by Peele and his team, as St. Elizabeth's
was underfunded, and telling Reagan to go ahead and meet with
Hinckley might have brought more federal dollars to the hospital.[13]

Peele said the phone call was anomalous because it seemed as
if Reagan was talking "from the clouds." He later found out to his
amusement that indeed, Reagan had been on Air Force One when he
made that call. He and Reagan parted warmly and later he was invited
to have lunch with Ruge in the White House Mess. Peele was deeply
impressed with the thoughtfulness of the Reagan White House.[14]
Dr. Peele and Reagan did have a good laugh together, though, when
it was suggested that the president could join his "treatment team."[15]

One of Hinckley's attorneys who helped develop the distinct
"innocent by reason of insanity" plea was Greg Craig, who later served
as counsel to Bill Clinton during his impeachment trial and, after that,
counsel to Barack Obama. In between, he'd also represented Fidel
Castro when the communist dictator of Cuba demanded the return
of the young political refugee Elian Gonzalez, and on Craig's advice,
Clinton surrendered the defenseless child to the island's communist
authorities, denying him a life of freedom. Over the years, Craig also
represented the *Washington Post* during Watergate and later when
Ted Kennedy was a witness in the rape trial of his nephew William
Kennedy Smith. He also served on the boards of various left wing
groups.[16] Only a cynic would suggest there existed a vast left-wing conspiracy though.

Quite apart from cynics, the *Washington Times* had deferentially
covered the week of the Reagan funeral with more accuracy than most
other papers in the country. The conventional wisdom among liberal journalists was that the motives of conservatives and wisdom of

conservatism were always to be questioned. Liberalism, however, was never to be questioned. All of that is for sociologists and historians and ethicists to sort out later, but the simple truth was the *Times* was the favorite paper of the Reagan White House, and Reagan read it avidly. It had a reliable conservative editorial policy and while the religious affiliation of the paper bothered many in Washington, they seemed less offended by the *Christian Science Monitor* or the *Deseret News*, owned by the Mormon Church.

Some of the reporting and opinion writing was nothing short of superb, and this week men and women who really knew Ronald Reagan, like Jack Kemp and Don Lambro and Don Feder, John Leo, Georgie Anne Geyer, and others wrote pieces that would be important to history's understanding of Ronald Wilson Reagan. Unlike the *Post* and its embarrassing and damaging Janet Cooke scandal, the *Times* suffered no major ethical embarrassments during the Reagan years. It also came to light that during the assassination attempt, the *Post* worked overtime to attempt to prove that the Reagan budget cuts had somehow endangered Reagan's life.

Nancy Reagan had never stipulated a certain kind of flower for the service at the National Cathedral, so the ladies of the church's flower guild went to work using thousands of "red and white roses and blue hydrangeas." All told, five thousand flowers were tastefully displayed throughout the church.[17]

The three networks, along with C-SPAN, FOX, CNN, et al., were planning live coverage of the funeral beginning with their programing at 7:00 a.m. (EST) and continuing through to 1:00 p.m. Then Fox and ABC would break back in at 7:30 p.m. (EST) for the interment ceremony in California. The day before, a conversation on air between Peter Jennings and George Stephanopoulos caused comment. Talking to Stephanopoulos, Jennings said, "And as you alluded . . . this morning . . . we haven't seen many African American faces up at the Presidential Library or this morning . . ."[18] It was sadly ironic, as Reagan was one of the most non-judgmental men to ever occupy the White House. As a child, his father refused to allow him to see the racist *Birth of a Nation*.[19] In chapter and verse, he'd shown himself to be color-blind before the phrase became popular.

Some presidents turned down state funerals. Andrew Jackson, out of character, was one who did and, in character, Calvin Coolidge was another. The funeral of Andrew Jackson at the Hermitage was flawed when his pet parrot had to be removed because it kept squawking out the profanity Jackson had taught the foul fowl.[20]

Harry Truman and Richard Nixon, both of whom agreed on nothing except their hatred for each other, separately agreed that neither would lie in state in the Capitol of that cursed city. At the end of their presidencies, both left Washington nearly run out of town on a rail. While Truman did not live to see his Phoenix-like rise in the estimation of historians and the American people, it was a lead pipe cinch that Nixon would never see any resurrection of his reputation. It was a funny country that way.

Truman grew up poor, had racist and anti-Semitic tendencies, came out of the corrupt Pendergast Democratic political machine, and was known to have a foul mouth. Still, he did some gutsy things as president. Nixon grew up poor, had racist and anti-Semitic tendencies, ran a corrupt White House, and was known to have a foul mouth. Still, he did some gutsy things as president. But, years later it was Truman who got the elevator and Nixon who got the shaft.

George Washington was terrified of being buried alive, so among his last requests was that he not be interred until two days after his death.[21] The custom of the day was to bury the deceased individual as soon as possible to stave off the chance for a diseased body to spread contagion.

The general who defeated the greatest standing army in the world; who then laid down his sword and went back to Mt. Vernon,

Cincinnatus style; who presided over the drafting and implementation of one of the greatest documents in history and then became the greatest president in American history, said he wanted to be buried "without parade or funeral oration."[22] It was completely in character with the man who rejected all the proposed titles as the nation's first chief executive and said he wished to be simply addressed as "Mr. President."

In fact, there was a tremendous outpouring for George Washington across the country; many made the pilgrimage to Mt. Vernon for his funeral, and in the days that followed many more came. Mock funerals for President Washington were also held around the fledgling country of which he was the father.

The funeral and public reaction to the death of a president can be a fascinating thing. Washington was always beloved, though in life he did have his critics, including some broadsheets and writers of the era. Abraham Lincoln was reviled by at least half the population below the Mason-Dixon line and by plenty of people above it as well. But after his assassination, the neck-straining turnaround in opinion that quickly became adulation was amazing. No president transformed more quickly from questionable to venerable than Lincoln. His re-election had been in doubt even as of the fall of 1864, even while he beat the Democratic nominee George McClellan by a solid 55–45 popular vote margin and an Electoral College landslide.

There were actually many funerals for Lincoln as his cortege train slowly—almost two weeks—made its way from Washington to Springfield, Illinois. Along the way, his coffin was opened for memorial services and public viewing in Baltimore, Philadelphia, and other locations.

Lincoln was the first chief executive to be embalmed, but even so a mortician accompanied his funeral train to "touch up the corpse several times." Lincoln was dressed in a black suit, white shirt, and tie as could clearly be seen in one surreptitious photo taken in New York—photos had been forbidden. Dwight Eisenhower was buried in a World War

II uniform—the tunic famously became known as the "Ike jacket." On his chest were only three decorations and he was buried in "a standard $80 military coffin."[23]

Eisenhower, like most presidents, was interred in his adopted home state—in Ike's case, Kansas—even though he'd actually been born in Texas. Reagan, of course, was from Illinois, and Lincoln's humble origins had begun in Kentucky. The only two presidents buried at Arlington were JFK and William Howard Taft. Woodrow Wilson was not buried in his birth state of Virginia or his adopted state of New Jersey but instead in the Washington National Cathedral. Monroe was actually buried in New York until Virginia forked over the money to have him disinterred and then reinterred in his beloved Commonwealth. Grant was buried in, well, Grant's Tomb.[24]

Reagan never talked much or wrote much about his own death and almost never used the *legacy* word. When he did talk about it, it was to poke fun at himself and his opponents, noting that he'd exceeded his expected years and that this greatly troubled[25] his political opponents.

It was only at the 1992 convention, four years out of office, that he addressed his passing in any meaningful way, at least until his letter to the nation two years later.

> And whatever else history may say about me when I'm gone, I hope it will record that I appealed to your best hopes, not your worst fears, to your confidence rather than your doubts. My dream is that you will travel the road ahead with liberty's lamp guiding your steps and opportunity's arm steadying your way . . . My fondest hope for each one of you—and especially for the young people here—is that you will love your country, not for her power or wealth, but for her selflessness and her idealism. May each of you have the heart to conceive, the understanding to direct, and the hand to execute works that will make the world a little better for your having been here.
>
> May all of you as Americans never forget your heroic origins,

never fail to seek divine guidance, and never lose your natural, God-given optimism.

And finally, my fellow Americans, may every dawn be a great new beginning for America and every evening bring us closer to that shining city upon a hill.

Before I go, I would like to ask the person who has made my life's journey so meaningful, someone I have been so proud of through the years, to join me. Nancy . . . My fellow Americans, on behalf of both of us, goodbye, and God bless each and every one of you, and God bless this country we love.[26]

It was one of Reagan's finest speeches and though he began slowly, as the faithful sounded their approval and ate up the shots at Bill Clinton, Reagan hit his stride in a few minutes and was that night the Reagan everybody loved and admired and had followed. At the end, thousands in the old Astrodome, a giant moldy petri dish, smiled. Some cried as they thought it would be the last time they would ever see him and certainly believed it was the last time they would ever see him at a Republican convention. It was in many ways the beginning of a long good-bye.

Friday morning. The day was overcast, grey, and humid. But it also was cooler. All day long it rained off and on. All in all a crummy day.

It was time for the funeral procession to move from the Rotunda to the National Cathedral. By the count of the Park police, 104,684 individuals stood in line to pay their last respects to Reagan in the Capitol. "This figure does not include 1,324 visitors admitted onto the West Front . . . lawn to observe the departure of former President Reagan. Over 200,000 bottles of water were distributed during the event."[27]

The Associated Press moved a heartrending photo on the wires of a young marine saluting Reagan's remains. The marine Corporal James E. Wright's right hand and left hand were missing.

Amid the solemnity of the ceremony there were numerous reminders of the sacrifices of young men and women. Even in the reality of death and the face of war, a college professor Gary Laderman of Emory University said from his own personal Ivory Tower of the Reagan funeral, "We're now in the realm of myth."[28]

The people who came represented a cross section of the American fabric. Elders and youngsters, polished shoes and casual sandals, American Indians in headdresses and seniors in walkers. Not all could touch the coffin or smooth the flag, but all had been touched by Reagan, by his words, or by his presidency.

Some who passed through weren't American citizens, including Mikhail Gorbachev, who once called Reagan "the preeminent anti-communist," which in his world (and on some American college campuses) was not a badge of honor. At their first meeting in Geneva in 1985, Gorbachev had told aides that Reagan was "a real dinosaur," but at the end Gorbachev had nothing but respect for Reagan.[29]

One report had it that three thousand people per hour were moving through the Rotunda.[30] The previous day, the Washington Metro subway system had its busiest day in its history to that point, transporting more than 850,000 people. It easily broke the record set the day of Bill Clinton's inaugural in 1993.[31] The heat and distance and the lines and the security may have kept tens of thousands more citizens away from seeing Reagan off.

Mist and light rain fell throughout the morning hours. Many thousands would have to be turned away despite their best pleas about the distance they'd traveled or how much they loved Reagan. Near the deadline, people who had to use the bathroom were allowed to leave the line and return, provided they knew the secret password that Park officials gave them, which was "yogurt."[32]

History may forever dispute who the last person in line was. According to the *Washington Post*, it was either Fred Miller, an office worker from NYC, who'd driven for hours and stood waiting for hours, or it may have been Brenda McGuirk, an office worker from Alexandria, Virginia, who'd driven minutes and stood waiting for minutes. She had snuck in as security temporarily deteriorated toward the end of the viewing.[33] The *Washington Times*, however, said it was Michael Golias of Fairfax, Virginia, who also got in just under the wire.[34]

As the final moments drew near, in order to accommodate the many thousands still in line, security encouraged, hurried, and cajoled the mourners to move quickly; for those who did not get in, many were also given a treasured copy of the palm card that had been distributed inside the Capitol on this and on previous days. The unwritten standing order from Mrs. Reagan to Fred Ryan to all the volunteers was maximum politeness and maximum courtesy and maximum patience. The man at the center of all this would have been overjoyed had he known how kindly citizens were being treated.

The events of the past several days had been nothing short of remarkable because some Reaganites had been working literally years on the planning and implementation of the state funeral for President Reagan, and none had been paid one cent. In fact, going back to early days of the post-presidency when the Reagans were traveling and giving speeches and doing the like, they still needed advance men and advance women to handle and plan things and smooth the way; all did it without being paid a penny more than the reimbursement for their out-of-pocket expenses said Ahearn.[35] Loyal Reaganites like Robbie Aiken and Matt Boland were volunteering and working at Ahearn's direction at the National Cathedral, juggling tasks and egos.

No one outside of politics knew how tough the job of an advance man was. These unsung men and women had to deal with people, weather, tempers, alcoholics, screwups, lines, waiting, corruption, their own luggage, and deportment. And then the thousand other things that would surface during the course of the week. They were like offensive linemen in football. If they did their jobs you never heard their names, but if they made a mistake their name was etched permanently in event-planning nightmares.

On the military side the logistics required were equal to none. Mike Wagner, the chief of state funeral planning at the Joint Force Headquarters said all told "there were about 5,000 military personnel . . . in support of the funeral. There were about 1,900 marchers, about six hundred members of the Joint Service Military Cordon, and several hundred air force personnel who were involved in supporting the flyover." And it was even more considering the bands and troops at various locations and behind-the-scenes support staff, Wagner said. The casket team alone had nine soldiers. Along with the eight pallbearers, there was the officer who commanded the team. But because of the heat and humidity, there were multiple casket teams that week and fresh teams were rotated in often.[36]

The schedule read, "Mrs. Reagan proceeds inside Rotunda alone for a private moment."[37] As it had been all week, when her husband was transferred from one location to another or from one mode of transportation to another, Mrs. Reagan was there as the casket was slowly marched out of the Rotunda and into a hearse for the unhurried trip to the National Cathedral at 3101 Wisconsin Avenue NW several miles away. Again, she reached with a hand to smooth the flag and then gently kissed it. She emerged, and as with the previous six days, she was once again escorted by General Jackman.

The entourage departed the Capitol at 10:45 a.m., arriving at the Cathedral less than an hour later at 11:25 a.m., with the services to begin at 11:30 a.m. The enormous, grey gothic structure had been closed for the week for security reasons and its fifty-seven acres cordoned off. The service was scheduled to conclude at 1:15 p.m.[38] "The atmosphere was cheerful, almost festive . . . then, 40 minutes before the ceremony, when the achingly beautiful music began, people sat quietly and somberly, some with tears in their eyes . . . ," said columnist Michael Barone of the mood in the Cathedral.[39]

The music selected was appropriately grand and featured pieces composed by Brahms, Mendelssohn, Bach, and Schubert's "Ave Maria." But American composers would not be overlooked, and a Reagan favorite, "The Battle Hymn of the Republic," written by Julia Ward Howe, was sung by the United States Armed Forces Chorus.[40]

Almost four thousand members of the Washington power elite gathered at the National Cathedral; many newspapers compared the funeral service to a reunion or family get-together. There were plenty of VIPs gathering in that holy place, however, who would have happily crucified more than a few of their enemies. While few Washingtonians ever engaged in actually plotting the murder of a political opponent, they did subscribe to Clarence Darrow's pithy observation that while he never wished for anyone's death, he did on occasion read an obituary with a great deal of pleasure.

Amid the arrangements at the Capitol and at the National Cathedral, Linda Bond had received a phone call a couple of days earlier from the world famous Soviet dissident Natan Sharansky meekly asking if a seat could be arranged for him at the Cathedral.[41] He hadn't been on the original invitation list, but a seat was hastily and happily arranged. He whispered to Bond, "I want to be there. The President saved my life. I wouldn't be alive if it weren't for Ronald Reagan."

Bond, like others, was busy and stressed with her responsibilities. It was only after the week was over it hit her. She realized Reagan had passed away, and only then did she break down, weeping uncontrollably over a newspaper article about the funeral.[42] She was not alone in experiencing a delayed reaction.

Another Soviet dissident, Aleksandr Solzhenitsyn, once said, "The line separating good and evil passes not through states, nor between classes, nor between political parties either—but right through every human heart."[43] Reagan had been taught since an early age that people were generally good.

The Washington National Cathedral—officially The Cathedral Church of Saint Peter and Saint Paul—sat atop the highest point in the nation's capital. When George Washington commissioned Pierre L'Enfant to design the capital city, he envisioned a "great church for national purposes," but it wasn't built until more than a century later. Teddy Roosevelt gave a speech during the laying of the cornerstone, and Dr. Martin Luther King Jr.'s last Sunday sermon was in the National Cathedral. Most presidents of the twentieth century had attended services at this venerated place of worship. The denomination was Episcopalian but over the years it had taken on the ecumenical cast.[44]

The Cathedral structure was draped in history and tradition. It was constructed mostly of limestone from Indiana. At the altar were ten stones that had been obtained from the Chapel of Moses at Mt. Sinai. These stones were representative of the Ten Commandments. There had been death services and prayer services for presidents and First Ladies there, including Eleanor Roosevelt. Helen Keller was buried in the church. President Wilson was buried there as was his second wife, Edith. So was Cordell Hull, former secretary of state. Eisenhower lay in repose there after his death in 1969.[45] It was cavernous, foreboding, and yet also so familiar. The acoustics were both intimidating and unambiguous.

People solemnly moved into the giant, grey stone structure. The color of the church matched the color of the low clouds, which matched the mood of the day. All were gathered to celebrate the life but also mourn the death of Ronald Wilson Reagan. Somewhere in the middle of light and dark was grey.

The grounds of the church were lined with a high chain-link fence temporarily installed for obvious security reasons. The streets around the church were closed off to civilian traffic, and congregants had to park some distance away. Much of the area around the Capitol, the White House, Blair House, and the National Cathedral had been barricaded since Monday.

The sidewalks were jammed with tourists and the merely curious. Many were peering through the fence to see if they could spot the famous and the powerful. Many were crying, holding rosaries, offering silent prayers. Some held umbrellas and listened to the services and news of the funeral proceedings on radios. Others sported cameras and video cameras poised to capture the images of Barbara Walters or Katie Couric or Bob Dole.

The following day in Washington, a Gay Pride Festival was scheduled, and some early arrivals mingled in the crowd but fewer mingled with those there for the Reagan funeral. Along with the gay activists came anti-gay activists and the usual sidewalk arguments ensued.

A tearful young woman standing in the crowd, Patty McGaughey, twenty-one years old, had an extra-special reason to be present as she was an undergraduate at Eureka College, Reagan's beloved alma mater. She'd come from Illinois with no special pass, no special access, just a special appreciation for the deceased man. "It's the least I could do for what he's done for me and other students at the college."[46] For her classmates, a service was planned at the school in the Ronald Reagan Peace Garden.

In recent memory only three American presidents made their fellow countrymen cry. John Kennedy when he was assassinated, Richard Nixon when he resigned, and Ronald Reagan any time he spoke of his beloved America. And now, at the last, Americans were crying as they spoke of their beloved president.

For those who were invited to the Reagan funeral, this was not an event or a day to show up "fashionably late" as so many in Washington did for social events. Make no mistake about it—funerals in Washington were social events, the kissing cousin to the Washington cocktail party. Both were opportunities to network and rubberneck.

For the Reagan funeral, egos were supposed to be checked at the door.

Given all the closed-off roads and fencing and guard dogs

and security personnel, a good number of the high and mighty of Washington arrived extra early, surprisingly, in order to get through security and find a good seat in their assigned area, which essentially went from the top of the power pyramid at the front of the church to the bottom of the pyramid at the back of the church. But any seat was a desired part of history.

Each ticket had a discrete, small round sticker on the backside. Those with yellow dots were first among equals, then red, then orange, and finally black. Those with black dots sat at the back of the Cathedral.

Linda Bond alerted Robert Higdon to the color-coded system she'd come up with, and asked him who was in charge of the ushers at the Cathedral. She was taken aback when Higdon informed her on the spot that she was now in charge of the ushers.[47] Bond had violated the old Bob Dole maxim: "Never ask a question unless you already know the answer."[48]

Senator John Danforth, an Episcopal priest, had been summoned to lead the funeral proceedings as Billy Graham's health had deteriorated. Graham personally told Reagan some years earlier that his health might not allow him to preside over the funeral. Still, Graham had the strength and wisdom to observe that "Reagan had a religious faith 'deeper than most people knew.'"[49]

Danforth was a gentle, sincere, and Midwestern kind of man— like someone else, some thought. Reagan had been more conservative in his political career but there was a great deal of admiration between the two men. Nancy Reagan really liked Danforth, and they spoke often over the phone in the years leading up to the funeral. Danforth had a voice that was both calming and commanding. He intoned, "If ever we have known a child of light, it was Ronald Reagan."[50] He was no latecomer to his faith or the collar. Reverend Danforth had already given homilies at the funerals of senators John Heinz, John Chafee, and *Washington Post* publisher Katharine Graham.[51]

So much history and so many men and women who had affected history were there in the National Cathedral. It was simply the largest gathering of past and present officialdom the world had seen in a long time, certainly since the funeral for JFK, and before that King Edward VII. "Twenty-five heads of state converged on the cathedral, and 11 former heads of state, and 180 ambassadors or foreign ministers."[52] Mikhail Gorbachev, the former leader of a regime that had occupied Poland, was seated near Lech Wałęsa, the former Polish shipyard welder who after a food price hike in 1980 would lead a strike that ended up changing the world. The collapse of communism had brought Gorbachev down and raised up Wałęsa, and along the way they both oddly collected Nobel Peace Prizes.

Two other Nobel Prize winners were present, former president Jimmy Carter and former vice president Al Gore, along with their wives, Rosalynn and Tipper. And there were Gerald and Betty Ford. And, of course, George and Barbara Bush as well as the president of the United States George W. Bush and the First Lady Laura Bush, and the vice president of the United States Richard Cheney and wife Lynne Cheney.

Gore, like Clinton, had also made himself a pain in the neck to the planners over being seated with the senators rather than at the front of the church with the grownups, Ahearn said. Gore did not seem to grasp that he was only a former senator and only a former vice president and thus was a creature of the legislative branch and not the executive branch. He was such a nuisance voices were raised and threats were made until Gore reluctantly promised to behave himself.[53]

Some commentators made catty comments about Barbara Bush's outfit, including Tom Shales of the *Washington Post*. "Barbara Bush . . . made the curious choice of wearing a comparatively bright gray suit, oddly jolly and casual attire for such a supremely solemn event."[54] It may have been the first time in the life of Barbara Pierce Bush that she'd been accused of not dressing to the occasion.

And there were Walter Mondale and Colin Powell and George Shultz and Dan Quayle. There were many, many of the children and grandchildren of presidents, from Julie and David Eisenhower to Tricia Nixon Cox and Edward Cox, Caroline Kennedy Schlossberg and husband Edwin, Lynda Bird Johnson Robb and her husband Chuck, and so many others. Unlike Gore, Mondale and Quayle did not squawk about their seating arrangements.

There were Bill and Pat Buckley and son Chris, Ed Meese, Dick Allen, and Jim and Sarah Brady, and Ed Koch, Valéry Giscard d'Estaing, and George and Mari Will. Laura Ingraham was there as was Caspar Weinberger, Reagan's first secretary of defense. Alan Knobloch, the president of Reagan's Eureka fraternity, was there as was Eureka student body president Jeremy LaKosh, and the president of the college Paul Lister. Reagan had been a TKE—Tau Kappa Epsilon—and the national office was in mourning. Reagan had served many years as a trustee of the beloved little college in rural Illinois. The school had written a private prayer for Reagan that they planned on giving to the family.[55]

Nearly all the living former cabinet members were in attendance as well as nearly all the White House staff, including Frank Donatelli, Reagan's political director, his wife Becki, and Ron Robinson and his wife Michelle Easton. Also present was Al Haig, with whom Reagan had clashed on more than one occasion, and David Stockman also surprisingly was in attendance. Bud McFarlane was there, unsurprisingly. There was Jack Kemp and Newt Gingrich, two of whom Tip O'Neill had often dismissed as "Reagan's Robots" because they had done such an effective job implementing the Reagan Revolution in the U.S. House. Their wives Joanne and Callista, respectively, accompanied them. Also the Supreme Court was there, sans robes, although a few foreign leaders were decked out in their own ceremonial robes.

Seated together were Reagan's four White House chiefs of staff, Jim Baker, Don Regan, Howard Baker, and Ken Duberstein. And there was Lyn Nofziger and Jeane Kirkpatrick and Larry Speakes, all Reagan White House veterans. Seen in an aisle seat was Jim Burnley, Reagan's last secretary of transportation. His first job in 1981 was supervising the dismantling of ACTION, a corrupt government boondoggle, and Burnley, aided by Mark Levin and Tom Pauken, both original Reaganites, tore the agency apart much to the joy of the Gipper.

Surprisingly, Carter and Clinton were spotted chatting with each other and seemed to be enjoying it. Everybody knowledgeable in politics knew the two Democratic men of the South despised each other and had for years. It wasn't quite the Hatfields and the McCoys, but the animus between the Carters and the Clintons had been thick for years.

Before the ceremonies had begun, Clinton had positioned himself in the driveway outside of the Cathedral, acting as some kind of national game show host, greeting every motorcade that arrived—and there were thirty-two of them—according to Ahearn. Some motorcades only had a couple of cars but others were long and extended affairs.[56] Of course, each former president was afforded his own motorcade. And there was Clinton, greeting all, in his syrupy and saccharine style. Some people actually fell for his act.

George H. W. Bush was seen animated in discussion with soon-to-be Democratic nominee John Kerry. Clinton also chatted up Italian prime minister Silvio Berlusconi, with whom he shared little in common politically but with whom he shared other things. Hillary Clinton stood off by herself with an alternately angry or bored look on her face. It had been known for years that she personalized politics and deeply despised anyone who was a Republican or conservative. The same look was on her face at the funeral for Richard Nixon several years earlier, and when former First Lady Pat Nixon had died in June 1993, First Lady Hillary Clinton snubbed the memory of Nixon's dead wife, refusing to attend her funeral. Instead, she hosted a fund-raiser for liberal candidate Mary Sue Terry, who was running for governor of Virginia.

It was well known Hillary Clinton hated the Reagans. She once said if you compare "Reagan's eight years with Bill's eight years, it's like night and day."[57] She also was known to make wildly exaggerated statements about Reagan and Clinton when it came to the economy and job creation.

President George W. Bush arrived and as he and Mrs. Bush were shown to their seats the band played "Amazing Grace," and then an astonishing thing happened. All the talking heads and nattering nabobs and Chatty Cathys and leakers and schmoozers and suck-ups and the like all shut up. The great grey hall went mostly silent for more than ten minutes as the nearly four thousand attendees waited for the proceedings to begin. They actually started five minutes ahead of schedule.

Some like Linda Bond ruefully noted later that there were empty seats along the wall on the other side of the stone columns that adorned the center hall of the National Cathedral. These seats had been reserved for Congress at the request of Speaker Denny Hastert but they'd never been distributed. Sadly, they could have gone to deserving Reaganites from the campaigns and Sacramento and the administration. "There were other people who would love to have been there." Still, she was pleasantly surprised when Bush's chief of staff Andy Card called her and offered to give back fifty tickets for the funeral service that had been reserved for the Bush White House staff. Bond immediately called Becky Norton Dunlop at the Heritage Foundation and Dunlop gladly took twenty-five of them to distribute to appreciative recipients.[58] Dunlop had, of course, been a Reaganite's Reaganite going back to 1976 and even before.

Television monitors placed around the sanctuary showed the hearse pulling up in front of the church via closed circuit. The crowd then heard the band play "Ruffles and Flourishes" and that was the signal that the funeral procession was to begin. As the procession entered the back of the church, the band played Brahms's "Requiem."

Just a few days earlier syndicated columnist Cal Thomas, a veteran of the religious wars, wrote movingly of the Gipper, "Reagan used to say that America's greatest days are ahead of it. Now it can be said, so are his."[59]

Mrs. Ronald Reagan and her family then entered at the back and walked slowly down the center aisle, thousands of eyes on her, pitying her, encouraging her, praying for her, envying her, and, for a few, detesting her. Some things in Washington never changed.

As the casket approached the front of the church, Jimmy Carter and others could be seen putting their hands over their hearts in reverence for the American flag that was covering the casket of President Ronald Reagan. Mrs. Reagan and her family were followed by the pallbearers, walking alongside the coffin as the U.S. Coast Guard band struck up a slow rendition of "Hail to the Chief." For a moment some thought it was for President Bush, until they realized it was for Reagan.

Reagan's remains were officially received by Reverend John Bryson Chane. Danforth celebrated the procession, the "collect for burial," the Homily, the Lord's Prayer, and the Commendation. As the men of the cloth moved slowly down the center aisle, Danforth read John 11:25. "I am the resurrection and the life . . ."[60] During the Collect Mrs. Reagan, Patti, Mike, and Colleen bowed their heads but Ron and Doria did not.

"Under gray, sprinkling clouds, a time capsule opened, and out stepped the men and women who strove and clashed, rose and fell, won and lost in an age that seems long ago and far away."[61]

The casket was carried again by eight uniformed young men from all the military branches and was led by three robed children, a girl and two boys, carrying candles and a cross. The Joint Chiefs marched slowly up the aisle in remembrance and in a final recognition of their fallen commander. Reagan's coffin was gently placed on a catafalque covered with red velvet at the center of the front of the church, just under the altar. Nancy Reagan was escorted by General Jackman to the front of the church.

President Bush stepped forward, smiled, and took Mrs. Reagan's arm gently from General Jackman. She looked up and seemed startled for a moment, and then smiled in return as Bush showed her to her seat in the front pew. The president then took a few steps to the other side of the aisle and sat down next to his wife, Laura. The entire church was silent.

The flag-covered casket, at the front center, was just a few feet away.

"The pomp was nearly unprecedented in American annals, more than two extraordinary hours of thundering organ, swelling chorus, haunting silences and eloquent prayers."[62] A passage from Matthew 5:14–16 ("Ye are the light of the world. A city that is set on an hill cannot be hid . . ."[63]) was read and the church choir sang "Jerusalem." A children's choir also sang.

There were pool cameras everywhere for the networks and the cable systems and there were some magnificent shots. But attendees never felt their presence, as they often did at other affairs of state.

The speakers finally selected by Mrs. Reagan, in addition to Danforth, were former president George H. W. Bush, former British prime minister Margaret Thatcher, former Canadian prime minister Brian Mulroney, and the president of the United States, George W. Bush. Supreme Court justice Sandra Day O'Connor was chosen to read from John Winthrop's "We Shall Be as a City upon a Hill," the Pilgrim's tract written upon his arrival in the New World and detailing his hopes for a brand-new world. Winthrop's observations often found their way into speeches by Reagan.

Also speaking was Rabbi Harold Kushner, who read from Isaiah in both English and Hebrew. "Even youths grow tired and weary, and young men stumble and fall; but those who hope in the LORD will renew their strength. They will soar on wings like eagles; they will run and not grow weary, they will walk and not be faint."[64]

Each in his or her own way summoned his or her best public speaking abilities, and each in his or her own way more than met the challenge, especially Thatcher. Thatcher was evocative of Churchill in her recorded annotations.

"With the lever of American patriotism, he lifted up the world. And so today, the world—in Prague, in Budapest, in Warsaw and Sofia, in Bucharest, in Kiev, and in Moscow itself, the world mourns the passing of the great liberator and echoes his prayer: God Bless America." In so doing, she bestowed a new moniker on the Gipper by calling him "The Great Liberator" to go along with "The Great Communicator."[65]

Like her intellectual and ideological predecessor, Thatcher pulled no punches when it was important to drive home a point. "I cannot imagine how any diplomat or any dramatist could improve on his words to Mikhail Gorbachev at the Geneva summit: 'Let me tell you why it is we distrust you . . .' His policies had a freshness and optimism that won converts from every class and every nation—and ultimately, from the very heart of the 'Evil Empire,'" Thatcher intoned.[66]

Her remarks, delivered in her neat and pleasing British accent, were truly stunning for a mostly American audience used to the bland platitudes of their recent leaders. She paid homage to Nancy Reagan, saying, "Reagan's life was rich not only in public achievement, but also in private happiness," and in speaking of Reagan she mostly focused on his role as world leader and the victor over Soviet Communism. Words like *daunting* and *invigorating* and *decisively* and *unyielding* infused her remarks.[67]

"We here still move in twilight, but we have one beacon to guide us that Ronald Reagan never had. We have his example."[68]

Ailing, Lady Thatcher was fortunately there at the funeral in person, escorted down the aisle by Prince Charles. She'd suffered from a series of small strokes, and the tape had been made some months earlier in anticipation that her declining health would prevent her from attending "Ronnie's" funeral. Very few people called Reagan "Ronnie" other than his two ladies—Nancy and Margaret. Thatcher was outfitted, of course, in the black dress and black hat and other accoutrements she'd been traveling with for a number of years in anticipation of Ronnie's demise.[69]

An Irish tenor Ronan Tynan sang "Ave Maria" and "Amazing Grace." Former Canadian prime minister Brian Mulroney, another Reagan favorite, spoke as well. But because of his galloping fear of heights, he did not speak from the pulpit high above the congregation in true Church of England and Episcopalian tradition, but from a lectern temporarily set up at floor level.[70]

"Ronald Reagan does not enter history tentatively; he does so with certainty and panache." He quoted from an Irish poet, Thomas D'Arcy McGee, and spoke in more personal terms than had Thatcher, speaking of Reagan as much as a lost friend as a world leader. But there was no doubt Mulroney recognized Reagan's greatness and said so, quoting French president François Mitterrand, who in an aside to Mulroney said, *"Il a vraiment la notion de l'état."* ("He really has a sense of the state about him.")[71]

Mulroney concluded that Reagan well understood the "difference between the job of president and the role of president."[72] As the Canadian spoke, Bill Clinton was spotted on television nodding off, and Hillary Clinton still looked sullen and morose, as if the funeral of Ronald Reagan was the last place on the face of the earth she wanted to be. The Carters looked respectful, as did the Fords, and the Cheneys, and certainly George and Barbara Bush. Through it all, Nancy Reagan was attentive, sometimes smiling, shaking her head sadly, often dabbing a handkerchief to her eyes. Patti sat close to Nancy doing the same, crying, laughing, and sad, and here all realized how much she looked like her mother.

The elder Bush spoke for the forlorn, talking about the Gipper in the most personal terms. Playing off a death notice about FDR in 1945 he said,

It will not take 100 years to thank God for Ronald Reagan. He was beloved, first, because of what he was . . . of what he believed. He believed in America so he made it his shining city on a hill. He believed in freedom . . . He believed in tomorrow . . . As his vice president for eight years, I learned more from Ronald Reagan than from anyone I encountered in all my years of public life.[73]

His voice quavered for a moment.

There wasn't a dry eye in the Cathedral by the time the former president's remarks concluded, even as he poked fun at himself over his age and told a couple of funny stories about Reagan, lightening the mood perfectly. Indeed, he had learned from Reagan. Bush was charming and presidential all at the same time.

The elder Bush's remarks had been handwritten. He spoke from the same lectern as Mulroney did. He spoke little of polity but mostly of personality and character. Not of nuclear arms but of nuclear families. Reagan and those darned squirrels. Reagan and the handwritten notes he'd left Bush in the White House. Reagan and Bishop Tutu. When Bush asked Reagan how a meeting had gone with the opinionated South African leader, Tutu, Reagan replied, "Tutu? . . . So-so." Everyone laughed. He jokingly called the Reagan children "kids."[74] Several times he choked up and struggled to maintain his composure. Many were laughing through their own tears. It was a revelation for many who'd never seen him display much emotion in public. Up until this day, his Episcopalian upbringing had forbidden it.

In a word, Bush was superb.

President Bush the son spoke for the nation doing so well, saying, "Ronald Reagan belongs to the ages now, but we preferred it when he belonged to us." His remarks were fittingly presidential, spoken from one president to another.

> When he saw evil camped across the horizon he called that evil by its name. There were no doubters in the prisons and gulags, where dissidents spread the news, tapping to each other in code what the American president had dared to say. There were no doubters in the shipyards and churches and secret labor meetings where brave men and women began to hear the creaking and rumbling of a collapsing empire.[75]

He also made several kind references to Nancy Reagan and her stoicism. Bush reviewed the high points of the life and times of his predecessor, and all agreed he did very well.

Bush also told of a delightful letter Reagan had written a young boy. The young author had written him asking for federal assistance to clean up his room after his mother had declared it a "disaster." Reagan mirthfully replied that the federal budget was pretty well tapped out but he recommended the boy "launch another volunteer program," and Bush had the crowd laughing.[76]

It wasn't a speech as in the case of a Pericles or a Roosevelt, but it was very thoughtful, and favorable comments rippled through the hall and across the networks.

> He often began his speeches by saying, "I'm going to talk about controversial things." And then he spoke of communist rulers as slave masters, of a government in Washington that had far overstepped its proper limits, of a time for choosing that was drawing near. In the space of a few years, he took ideas and principles that were mainly found in journals and books and turned them into a broad, hopeful movement ready to govern . . .
>
> In his last years he saw through a glass darkly. Now he sees his

Savior face to face. And we look for that fine day when we will see him again, all weariness gone, clear of mind, strong and sure and smiling again, and the sorrow of this parting gone forever.

May God bless Ronald Reagan and the country he loved.[77]

A blessing was offered by Bishop John Bryson Chane and the dismissal by Bishop Theodore Eastman of the Episcopal faith. Other participants included the Catholic archbishop of Washington, Theodore Cardinal McCarrick, and the archbishop of the Greek Orthodox Archdiocese of America, Demetrios.

The band also performed "Battle Hymn of the Republic" and "The Mansions of the Lord," which Rick Ahearn had recommended after watching *We Were Soldiers*.[78] The music was majestic and was majestically performed by the U.S. Marine Chamber Orchestra and was accompanied by the singers of the United States Armed Forces Chorus. Mrs. Reagan, chaperoned again by General Jackman, walked slowly but deliberately out of the church behind the coffin of her beloved Ronnie.

As the procession withdrew as directed by ushers—some had a plane to catch—the band played Beethoven's "Ode to Joy." The bells of the National Cathedral rang forty times, tolling for Reagan as America's fortieth president. The building of the National Cathedral had begun in 1907 and construction was halted many times for lack of funds. The bells had only been installed forty years earlier,[79] and now the forty-year-old bells tolled forty times for the fortieth president. At 1:15 p.m. (EST), the sound of bells rang from churches across the nation. They also tolled forty times.[80] Then, only the muffled sound of military drums could be heard as the crowd slowly made its way toward the door.

And then a remarkable thing happened.

As the uniformed funeral party proceeded through the doors of the back of the National Cathedral and started their way down the granite stairs, a bright ray of sunlight sliced through the grey, overcast sky to momentarily shine on the casket of Ronald Reagan.

On the day of his inauguration in January 1981, it had been an overcast day, but at an inspirational moment the clouds parted that day, too, and the sun shone on the platform where Reagan was speaking.

The same had happened to another man of Illinois, another man of God, Abraham Lincoln, at his inauguration in 1865.

The crowd filed out right after the ceremony—mostly silently—to the dour day and dozens of television cameras, but there was also a fair amount of handshaking and air kissing and networking and gawking. Henry Kissinger was in big demand by the camera crews, and he gladly complied with every interview request. It was clear who was there to mourn Reagan and who was there to celebrate Washington society. In contrast to Kissinger, when a reporter asked Bill Buckley for an interview he said, "No, I won't."[81]

Among the Reaganites it was different. They knew each other almost by instinct. From Sacramento, from the campaigns, from the White House, from the offices in Century City to the Library, and the rest of the post-presidency, they gathered in small clutches, touching, hugging, kissing, crying, many somber and sad. For them it wasn't just that a president had died. It wasn't just that a monumentally successful president had died. It wasn't just that a man of stunningly high character and good will had died. For the Reaganites, it was something deeper. For the Reaganites, it was more personal.

They had their own treasured stories of Reagan and Mrs. Reagan. Stories of speeches and events and meetings, of conversations and picnics and meals, of policies and jokes and tragedies and fights and primaries and elections, they went on and on. It was rarely one-upmanship either. Sure, some complained about Jim Baker or Dick Darman or an errant cabinet member, but more often than not they celebrated each other. They treasured and respected the others' stories and experiences of their cause of working for Ronald Reagan, the cause of saving Western Civilization, the cause of American intellectual conservatism. Though some might have experienced difficulty explaining it, they all understood it easily. They all believed in it. And they knew Ronald Reagan believed in it too.

His passing was the passing of an era.

He was their friend, their inspiration, their hero, their rock. They were Reaganites, had been Reaganites, and would always be Reaganites. They were proud of this and knew others were envious. Their obituaries would say they had worked for Reagan, and each was proud to have had that honor. Their lives had been defined by the Gipper, and their pride abounded.


Immediately after the services at the National Cathedral, the members of the Reagan Alumni Association gathered—five hundred strong—for a reception at the Reagan Building and the last meeting of the Reagan cabinet. It was an impressive event organized by the Association's longtime director Lou Cordia.

Present were UN Ambassador Jeane Kirkpatrick and Transportation Secretary Jim Burnley and Attorney General and Reagan confidant Ed Meese, Secretary of Energy Jim Edwards, U.S. Trade Representative Bill Brock, and National Security Advisor Bud McFarlane. All told, fifteen former Reagan cabinet members assembled at a long table in front of the audience and held forth. Also in attendance were Ann McLaughlin, a former Secretary of Labor, and Don Hodel, Energy Secretary. And a personal favorite of the Reagans, Richard Schweiker, former Secretary of Health and Human Services and the Gipper's foresworn running mate in 1976. Another personal favorite of the Reagans, Bill Clark, a former Secretary of the Interior, was also among the thousands gathered in the Cathedral and now at the last Reagan cabinet meeting.

The event had the feel of a high school reunion, everyone wondering how it was that everyone had gotten older except themselves. There was lots of catching up, sharing tales from those halcyon days of almost twenty years earlier, and lots of gossip. Some had moved away from Washington but many had not. Many had become a part of the permanent Washington they had vowed never to join back in 1980 and 1981, more than thirty years earlier. Still, it was for most of them a glorious and tumultuous time. They never doubted what their mission was or doubted the commitment of the man who led them on that mission.

Dick Allen, one of the original Reaganites, along with Marty Anderson, spoke to the audience. There was a moment of silence for three recently departed members of the Reagan circle, Don Regan, Sam Pierce, and Malcolm Baldrige. Meese told the bittersweet gathering, "We came to change a nation, and we changed the world."[82]

The legacy talk accelerated. Some doubted the success of Reaganomics, the policy about which Reagan had once quipped, "The best clue that our program is working is our critics don't call it Reaganomics anymore."[83] Of the economy, it was true that Reagan had added to the national debt, but the annual deficit was falling in his last years in office and discretionary federal spending as a percentage of the GDP fell. He did substantially increase military spending but many said if this was the price to free millions of people and win a Cold War, America got off cheap. On the matter of the size and scope of government, the overall size escaped the budgetary knife, but the growth in the size of the private economy under Reagan had multiplied at a faster rate and pace, thus diminishing the influence of the national government.

More importantly, petty and cumbersome regulations had been rolled off the backs of the American entrepreneur. All in all, Reagan had put a fence around the government, protecting the private citizen from its unethically long reach. But the phrase "supply-side" and "Laffer Curve" would always be conjoined with the word *controversial* in the minds of the nation's journalists.[84] It was reported that a Bush aide said supply-side economics was the work of "charlatans and cranks."[85]

Regarding controversy, the long analysis of Reagan's career in the *Chicago Tribune* said George W. Bush had been a "more consistent" ideologue than Reagan. No wonder conservatives at the time liked to josh, "Why do you think they call them 'stories'?" The writer Jon Margolis cited the breaking of treaties by Bush as evidence of conservatism. He claimed that the growth of executive authority in the presidency was part of conservatism, which any first-year college student at Hillsdale would say was nonsense. He ascribed some of Reagan's successes to "luck." He also mistakenly claimed that "large majorities" disagreed with Reagan's policies. It was true that while often during his presidency Reagan was more personally popular than some of his policies, those goals and programs nonetheless enjoyed wide support.

The "analysis" by Margolis went downhill from there: "In fact, the impression of Reagan as an extremely popular president is a myth carefully orchestrated by that conservative political apparatus, which is still at it, attempting to establish Reagan memorials all across the country . . ."[86]

And the old chestnut that "Reagan exacerbated inequality" was pulled out and thrown at his legacy without substantiation, natch. The long, harsh, gratuitous piece over which Margolis had labored concluded, "Reagan started his adult life as an entertainer, and he never stopped performing."[87]

Others were debating anew the "Reagan on the money" matter.[88] Some said it was too soon. But others pointed out that FDR was tooled on the dime the year after he died, Kennedy appeared on the half dollar the year after his death,[89] and Eisenhower had gone on the one dollar coin two years after his passing. Jennifer Harper, a top journalist with the *Washington Times*, reported that as of June 2004, some "62 sites around the globe" are "named for former President Ronald Reagan—with more in the works."[90]

Fortunately, some unexpected but favorable comments about the Reagan presidency were coming from Richard Neustadt at Harvard, who said, "Mr. Reagan restored the presidency to 'a place of popularity, influence and initiative . . . both pacesetter and tonesetter, the nation's voice to both the world and us . . .'" At the University of California, another liberal historian Samuel Kernell said Reagan had "cast a long shadow" and compared him favorably to FDR, courageous talk from Ground Zero for Reagan bashing. And from Cornell came yet another historian, Walter F. LaFeber, who said his "contribution to ending the Cold War" was his greatest achievement and that it "would have been very difficult for a Democrat to have done that."[91]

Only Reagan could go to Moscow.

Jeff Greenfield was not a historian but he was a well-regarded political commentator and writer. He had cut his teeth in liberal politics working for Robert Kennedy and Democratic causes. Still, "Communism fell on his watch, and we know from his letters this guy was a lot more than a well-spoken actor."[92]

Another aspect of the Reagan legacy was told by columnist Mark Shields, who interviewed an old Eureka football teammate Franklin Burghardt, who told of the story in 1930 when he and another black player could not stay at a "whites only" hotel, and Reagan took the two to his home where his parents warmly greeted them for the evening. Still, Shields could not understand how Reagan had once opposed the Civil Rights Bill. (He did so on the basis of privacy and the right of association guaranteed in the First Amendment.) Shields blamed Reagan for homelessness. But he credited him with setting a new standard for presidential debates, in that Reagan did not duck debating Walter Mondale in 1984 even as he was coasting to his reelection, unlike LBJ in 1964 and Richard Nixon in 1972. Reagan's courageous and risky decision would force all future occupants to debate regardless of their standing in the polls.[93]

Joanne Drake had a first-row place on American history, and as a valued member of the inner circle, she had many responsibilities for the week. But she also had many memories. She remembered how the Secret Service agents refused to ride in cars, despite the heat and humidity. They walked even though the director informed them they could ride. "They adamantly put their foot down," she said of the agents.[94]

Another poignant memory was the trip from the National Cathedral back to Andrews Air Force Base through the run-down, poorer parts of Washington, which included Anacostia, and through the poorer suburbs in Maryland. Unexpectedly, thousands of citizens turned out here as well. One rider said, "You pass by all of those homes. Those old homes . . . These are middle-class Americans of every color, of every age, of every size, of every economic stature. Scout troops, people in uniforms, veterans, children, mothers, fathers, students . . . I was in tears."[95]

Michele Woodward, riding in the same motorcade, had similar recollections, a similar front-row seat to history. "And there were African American women with their hands over their hearts. There were African American firefighters and Asian firefighters and Hispanic firefighters." Woodward was helping with press advance. For a man who was supposedly old-fashioned, Reagan had many women in positions of authority over the many years. Still, Woodward said as they sped through Anacostia, "I was boo-hooing like a baby."[96]

Reagan's longtime press aide Mark Weinberg summed up what was on the minds of the people lining the streets that week.

He made peoples' lives better. He made the world better. He made the world safer. He gave them hope and opportunity. Jobs were better, incomes were better, homes. Things were better, and they missed that. And they wanted to thank him, I think as best they could. If you could stand there and wave a flag as the hearse passed by, it's your way of saying thank you.[97]

As with everything this week, the hearse and motorcade arrived on schedule at Andrews Air Force Base and Reagan's coffin was discretely and gently placed on the plane at the back on the catafalque, secured in place.

The crowd watched, knowing he would never be in Washington again. They watched, knowing they'd never see him again. The finality of it all crushed many, silent tears streaming down their faces in the cool, grey, overcast day.

At the foot of the jet ramp, Nancy Reagan had paused for a long time to thank many of the people who'd worked so long and hard over the past week, and she was seen smiling, clearly grateful for the work done. Michele Woodward recalled that Nancy Reagan had arranged for the unpaid, sleep-deprived core group, who had planned seamlessly the week's events, to be there as "departure greeters" much to their surprise.[98] And then Nancy went through, one by one, and thanked each for his or her dedication and tireless work. They were deeply touched.

Mrs. Reagan walked slowly up the ramp of the big plane, and at the top turned to give a long and generous wave to the mostly weeping crowd, a wan smile on her face. Then she blew a light kiss and disappeared into the plane, the low rumble of the engines primed for takeoff.

The band played Antonín Dvořák's "Going Home."[99] Dvořák was a Czech composer who had spent a summer in Iowa—Reagan's neck of the woods—drawing inspiration from the American heartland while working in New York as the director of the National

Conservatory. While in Iowa he composed "The American String Quartet Op. 96."[100] There was something lyrical, symmetrical, about the connection between Dvořák, who supported the liberation of his countrymen from the Austro-Hungarian Empire, with that of Reagan's opposition to a later empire, supporting another Czech artist, a playwright, Václav Havel, in another struggle for Czech freedom.

Maybe the real music of the world was human freedom.

Ronald Reagan left Washington for the very last time. His signature song was "California, Here I Come." And so it was.

The big plane gathered speed and hurtled down the runway, it lifted easily into the air, gaining altitude, to the applause of the crowd on the tarmac, and then quickly disappeared into the overcast sky. This last group in Washington to see Reagan off did not disperse quickly, as if they wanted to hold on to this moment for as long as they could.

The jet raced across the heartland and left behind the dreary weather of the East Coast. Flying above the Midwest a couple of hours later, it dropped altitude over Tampico, Illinois, Reagan's birthplace. There was nary a cloud in the sky.

The pilot then dipped his wings, a final salute to the folks there in Reagan's hometown.

# CHAPTER 9

# "SIGNAL: RAWHIDE'S LAST ARRIVAL"

*"I know in my heart that man is good, that what*
*is right will always eventually triumph, and there*
*is purpose and worth to each and every life."*

F or the first time, a week under the unceasing glare of the international spotlight, and only at the very end, Nancy Reagan finally broke down. Crying uncontrollably over the loss of her husband, over his coffin, over his gravesite. Shoulders rounded, the tiny woman was weeping, stricken, and could be clearly seen whispering, "Oh, Ronnie, Ronnie, Ronnie." She touched his coffin lightly.

"Former first lady Nancy Reagan, stoic through nearly a week of somber rituals, surrendered to her grief after being handed the flag that had covered her husband's coffin."[1]

As she gently laid her head on the newly flagless casket, her hands caressing it, Ron and Patti stood forlornly on either side of her and Michael stood sadly behind her. Each individually and together a picture of acute sadness. They were a small family that had just become smaller. All tenderly touched Nancy, letting her know they were there and she was not alone.

Then Nancy leaned to her right, clutched the folded American flag with her left hand, covered her face partially with the other, and pressed on son Ron's chest. Patti protectively closed in toward her mother and Mike tried to hold it together, a stricken look on his face too.

The four of them were alone at the tomb. As the world watched in silence, the Reagans were now oblivious to all. This was not a stage. This was not a performance. This was not an act. This was a grieving widow saying good-bye to her husband for the last time. This was three sad and fatherless children saying good-bye to their father for the last time. Long before he was president of the United States and Leader of the Free World, he was "Ronnie" and "Dad" and before that "Daddy." Even during and after his eight monumental years in the White House he was always Ronnie and Dad.

This was the first time they were referred to as "the Reagans" without him.

The strength of will with which Nancy had carried herself for the past week—the past ten years, the past many years—had finally drained away, and she was just another disheartened and saddened and lonely widow. Their fifty-three years together had been far, far better than worse but at the last, death had indeed finally parted them.

She whispered a farewell "I love you."

Later, Nancy was heard to say, repeatedly, "I can't believe he's gone." As one observer that day remarked, "She had been expecting his death, but not really preparing for it."[2]

A few hours earlier, the big silver, blue, and white plane had actually been a few minutes early landing at Naval Air Station Point Mugu, and the party on board dallied a bit after landing so as to get the timing to ensure Reagan could be buried right at sunset. As the coffin and the small group of passengers were off-loaded, a marine band performed "Ruffles and Flourishes" four times and then "Hail to the Chief." The

Military District of Washington explained in a flurry of helpful press releases, "Ruffles are played on drums and flourishes on bugles. They are sounded together, once for each star of the general officer being honored . . . Four ruffles and flourishes are the highest honor and are played for presidents."[3]

All of this was broadcast live on C-SPAN, as so much of the Reagan funeral had been broadcast on the reliable cable system, most of it without commentary. Nancy Reagan, escorted yet again by General Jackman, was seen gently waving with a surprised smile on her face as the large crowd waved and yelled praises to her.

There were five family limousine cars, the first carrying Nancy, Patti, Ron, and his wife, Doria. Michael and Colleen Reagan and their children Cameron and Ashley were in the second. In the third was Maureen's widowed husband, Dennis Revell, and his fiancée, Diana Wilson; and on Nancy's side of the family, the Davis family members in the fourth; and Peterson family members in the fifth. Other cars in the motorcade carried VIPs such as Fred Ryan and his wife, Genevieve; Mike and Carolyn Deaver; Reverend John Danforth and his wife, Sally; Dr. John Hutton; and columnist Hugh Sidey, among others.[4]

Some thirty miles away at the top of a small foothill in the Santa Susana Mountains that overlooked the blue Pacific, some seven hundred people waited patiently, exchanging pleasantries and introductions. Some were helped along by the wine being served, though most stuck to water or soda pop or iced tea. Like most funerals, there was always nervous energy and awkwardness before the actual ceremonies began. Mawkishness was frowned upon but so, too, was excessive laughing or humor.

The entire week had been scripted and practiced and rehearsed and polished and planned out and thought out, and while the planners thought there would be a respectful turnout of the American people, who knew? They'd gotten a pretty good inkling the first day Reagan lay in repose in the lobby of the Library five days earlier, when more than one hundred thousand people showed up and then, as Reagan lay in state in the U.S. Capitol, again there was a larger-than-expected turnout, with hundreds of thousands sweltering in line for hours on end to pay their last respects. But nothing prepared them for the spontaneous outpouring they were about to encounter for the entire thirty miles from the Point Mugu naval base all the way to Simi Valley.

When the motorcade arrived at the Library, the call went out over the agents' and staff's radios, "Signal: Rawhide's last arrival." This sent all who heard the broadcast into renewed quavers of tears. Along each stop and start for the past week, and for his presidency, the Secret Service and advance team always said, "Signal: Rawhide arrival" and "Signal: Rawhide departure."[5]

Over the years, the media had reported sometimes that the Reagan children were fighting with their parents or with each other or disagreed with his politics, and Reagan confided in his diary the couples' intermittent exasperations with their children.[6] Truth be told, though, many presidents, like many citizens, had problems with their children and their families. John Adams's son Charles was a drunk and the black sheep of the family. James Madison's stepson John Payne Todd was an inveterate gambler and cost his mother her beloved *Montpelier* because of his debts. Lincoln had his hands full with son Robert and his own wife, Mary Todd. (No relation to John Payne Todd is believed.)

FDR's children often said they never really knew their parents. The tales of Alice Roosevelt Longworth and the headaches she caused her father, Theodore Roosevelt, were legion. Eisenhower's son John was a WWII vet but also a philanderer, and other presidents had more than their share of problems with ne'er-do-well children and family members. Billy Carter was a bad news buffet all by himself. Both Johnson and Nixon were troubled by brothers who never measured up, associated with shady characters, and nary a month but what it seemed a new Clinton relation was discovered. The Reagan children's problems seemed pretty tame by comparison.

By the time of the announcement of their father's affliction, each had—for the most part—become responsible individuals, and all had reconciled more or less with their father and mother and stepmother.

Both Maureen's death and their father's Alzheimer's had brought them together, and the public squabbling had ceased. In Reagan's death his family had found life together, as a page was turning in history.

"The man who once declared it morning in America was laid to rest at sunset Friday."[7]

Magnolias encircled the gravesite where Reagan was now and Mrs. Reagan would one day be buried. Patti later said the week of mourning had not been a burden but helpful as "all of it kept us above the waterline."[8]

At noon that day, at every U.S. military base in the world, there was a 21-gun salute in honor of the Gipper. At dusk on Friday, June 11, there was a 50-gun salute at every American military base in the world.[9] The television ratings were off the scale, but that was the way it often was with Reagan. Indeed, the funeral of Ronald Reagan would be one of the ten most watched events in broadcasting history, drawing nearly twenty-one million viewers according to Nielsen Media Research.[10]

Said Lou Cannon, "This was a genuine outpouring of feelings for somebody they cared about who had died."[11] President of the Alzheimer's Association Sue Tatangelo was taken aback when she overheard a Secret Service agent "weep and quietly step out into the aisle where he could grieve alone."[12] Cannon was astonished at Nancy Reagan's physical and emotional endurance over the past week and indeed, the past ten years. Cannon was also close to Joanne Drake, and over the years he'd get calls about stories regarding Reagan's condition and he'd call Joanne, who was confident to share anything new with him knowing he'd keep it confidential or handle it diplomatically. Cannon and Nancy had known each other for years, and for him she felt comfortable wearing old clothes, so comfortable she once told the scribe, "There's times that I don't know him. That I can't get beyond that barrier."[13]

By now the often harsh reportage and commentary over the past week—and the past fifty years—had nearly melted away. No one was mocking "the Gaze" now, but rather universally applauding Nancy Reagan for her courage, her fortitude, her grace under pressure, and all she'd done for the cause of Alzheimer's research.

There could be no doubt that the sheer gravity of the outpouring from average American citizens, those who showed up in California and Washington and a hundred other places in America and around the world to give respect to the Great Egalitarian, made a lasting impression on the Great Elites. Nor was there any doubt they also came to support Nancy. Thousands of citizens took the time to write letters to the editors of newspapers and make themselves heard on the Internet and on talk radio. Most of the letters were not from the elderly but from the young Americans who wished to pay tribute to the wise and grandfatherly and consequential man they knew as their president. Others wrote praising the courage and dignity of Nancy Reagan.

As Fred Ryan noted, each time someone criticized Reagan on the network or cable shows earlier in the week the "switchboard would light up" with people telling the commentators to knock it off.[14]

Numerous times during the week network anchors had complained about the "over-coverage" of the Reagan funeral, according to Gail Shister of the *Philadelphia Inquirer.* Oddly, Dan Rather had quoted darkly from Shakespeare, "To paraphrase Mark Antony, I think, by and large, that the good that men do should live after them, and the evil should be interred with their bones."[15] It was so oddly incongruous, but it was not unusual for Rather to say the wrong thing at the wrong time.

Tom Brokaw was more rational, saying that journalists had an obligation to put Reagan's life in perspective, "to put his whole life and his political career in context."[16]

Six days earlier the elites were out of sync with the citizenry, but by the day of the Reagan committal some had changed their tune and a few were even singing Reagan's praises. Even the cartoonists, who'd been especially vicious in their treatment of the Gipper over the years, had grown respectful, even kind. Mike Luckovich of the *Atlanta Journal-Constitution* depicted on one panel a Republican elephant and a Democratic donkey in boxing shorts and boxing gloves, pummeling each other. But in the next panel they stood side by side, arms at their sides, heads bowed, at a flag-covered casket bearing the name "Reagan."[17]

Even the organized Left was mostly silent. No doubt there was grousing and complaining on college campuses and in the drinking salons of American liberalism and leftism. A small group gathered at the trendy Visions Bar Noir in Washington to drown their sorrows at the national grief for Reagan. They just couldn't understand how anybody ever supported this yahoo to begin with. He wasn't like them; he actually liked the country and her people, and never subscribed to their favorite elixirs of cynicism and sameness.

A writer described these sullen liberals as the "evil twins of Alex P. Keaton of 'Family Ties.'" *Family Ties* was a popular comedy of the 1980s that depicted two aging lefties from the 1960s raising a son who was a Reagan conservative. Other Reagan haters who gathered drank drinks named the Gipper and the Bonzo, ate jelly beans, and watched *Bedtime for Bonzo* and *The Killers*, and though their group was most definitely in the minority, they consoled themselves with the belief that they cared more.[18]

Also, some gays gathered and they, too, were outspoken critics of Reagan, somehow blaming him for AIDS. As reported in the *Washington Post*, a gay pride festival was going on in Washington. "The braless women were marching along 17th Street, near DuPont Circle, shouting 'What do you want? Dyke Rights! When do you want it? Now!'" In a bar in DC, a gay man told a reporter, "I think it's kind of fitting. He gets buried on the night we're all here."[19]

Musicians also were down on Reagan as many songs and bands of the 1980s and 1990s ripped him, including those performed by the Dead Kennedys, Ramones, and the Violent Femmes.[20]

Other than that, there had been very few organized protests against Reagan, and it wasn't due just to the heat. Some on the Left had truly mixed feelings about Reagan, who was in his heart a classical liberal. John Patrick Diggins, a longtime liberal and academic, had opposed Reagan his entire life, including his days at Berkeley while Reagan was in Sacramento, but had later in life come around to appreciate Reagan.

The debate over the legacy had only begun, including the meaning of the "Reagan Doctrine." What was never debated was Reagan's faith. He invoked it often and said in his inaugural remarks of 1981 his belief that God intended man to be free. "We are a nation under God, and I believe God intended for us to be free."[21] Reagan was infused with both natural law and natural rights.

In sharp contrast with some other liberals, former Clinton White House chief of staff Leon Panetta said of the Reagan remembrance, "It was good for the country to go through something like this. It was an important time out for us to recognize that, for all the problems we face in the country, we have some incredible strengths as a people and to a large extent Reagan represented that kind of larger picture about what this country is all about."[22]

The *LA Times* had no front-page coverage the day of the Reagan funeral. While Fox and ABC planned extensive coverage of the evening committal ceremonies, NBC would abbreviate their coverage, and CBS chose not to cover the ceremonies in favor of regularly scheduled programming that included *JAG* and *48 Hours*.[23]

David Nyhan, longtime liberal writer for the longtime liberal *Boston Globe*, said derisively of Reagan, "He demonstrated for all to see how far you can go in this life with a smile, a shoeshine and the nerve to put your own spin on the facts."[24]

But at the other end of the spectrum, Cal Thomas gently wrote, "He lingered too long for his own good, but not long enough for his beloved Nancy and the many others who loved and admired him."[25]

The immediately recognizable blue-and-white Boeing 747 plane—Air Force jet call sign "SAM 28000"—had departed Washington earlier that day and was heading for California through the thick mist above Andrews Air Force Base. The strains of "Going Home" being played echoed in the ears of any who were in its proximity.[26] As with the entire week, this last ceremonial event was open to the media. The only exception would be the plane trip back to California.

The flag-draped coffin bearing Reagan's remains was secured near the rear of the plane. The manifest was not nearly filled and people easily moved about the cabin as it winged its way back toward the West Coast. The official count, not including crew, was fifty-three with all the principal players, including the Reagan family, the honorary pall-bearers, and staff.[27]

Seated at the back with Reagan's remains was his military detail, including General Jackman. Nancy Reagan and the children wandered back from time to time, each taking the occasion to smooth the flag over the casket. The flight took approximately five hours back to Point Mugu, where it seemed like an eternity ago they had departed for Ronald Reagan's last political tour of America. Now he was heading back home, back to the California hills he loved so much, once and for all.

The motorcade in California was pretty much the same as in Washington, only in Reagan's final journey Mike Reagan and his family had their own car and Nancy Reagan's stepbrother Dr. Richard

Davis and his wife, Patricia, and their son Geoffrey also had their own limousine.[28] It was estimated the drive from Point Mugu to the Library would take about forty-five minutes—moving at twenty miles an hour.

Reagan was on the final leg of his last journey. It would be memorable and unforgettable for all. The week of public mourning for the passing of the fortieth president had impacted and impressed everyone, but this last spontaneous demonstration truly blew everyone away, including Nancy Reagan. Beginning at the gates of Point Mugu and for the thirty miles to the Library, hundreds of thousands of people turned out to pay their respects, to wave flags, to shed tears, and to honor a president all had grown to respect and many had grown to love. The funeral planners had hoped to have some citizens to line Presidential Drive up to the Library but this was way far beyond what any had imagined.

"The 101"—as the divided highway was called—was a parking lot for the entire route as the funeral cortege passed slowly by on the other side. The national media had never before witnessed a similar, spontaneous outpouring, and it was broadcast live on national television. Joanne Drake said, "I've never seen so many people in my whole life."[29] Drake was a strong woman, but even the old actor Fess Parker noted "tears flowing down [her] face, wiping them away . . ."[30]

The younger Jim Lake, son of Reagan's old press aide Jim Lake and one of the principal advance men on Jim Hooley's team, was in charge of this portion of Reagan's return home. The younger Lake had grown up marinated in national politics and as a child being patted on the head by every Republican office holder. As an adult, he'd worked on the Reagan campaigns and in the administration, seeing history up close and personal, such as being at Reykjavik for the summit between Reagan and Gorbachev.[31]

He, like everyone else, was stunned. "The farm workers in the fields who stopped working and stood in silence with their hats held over their hearts." Overpasses had fire engines displaying giant American flags, and firefighters saluting and crying, and police officers saluting and crying, and Mexican farm workers saluting and crying, and housewives, and blue-collar workers and white-collar workers, and the elderly and the young—just an amazing outpouring of Americans from all walks of life—all brought together by their respect and affection for Ronald Reagan. Lake saw an old ranch hand holding up a sign, "All Cowboys Return Home. Welcome Home Mr. President."[32]

Lake cried like a baby. He was not alone.

At the presidential library, the exclusive list of around seven hundred guests[33] was beginning to gather. Several places for lemonade and iced tea had been set up and the weather had cooled since earlier in the week. This list was almost exclusively Nancy and Ronald Reagan's friends, dinner companions, and acquaintances from Hollywood and entertainment, but also some folks who had worked for and with the Reagans over the years. Nancy's friends—"The Girls"—were there, including Betsy Bloomingdale, Marion Jorgensen, and Jane Dart; Wayne Newton was there as was Mickey Rooney, and Kirk Douglas, and Norman Lear, and Bo Derek, and Tommy Lasorda. And Tom Selleck and Governor Arnold Schwarzenegger and Maria Shriver, former governor Pete Wilson, Frank Sinatra's widow Barbara, Wayne Gretzky, and George Shultz were there.

It was an eclectic crowd and notably not terribly political. Reagan's doctor from Yellowstone Neurosurgical, Dr. John Moseley, who'd removed the subdural hematoma the Gipper had suffered after being thrown from a horse in Mexico and hitting his head, was there. Moseley and his wife Cheryl, in attendance, had also gone by the funeral home and took note of the people who "put up their own little memorials, cards and memorabilia . . . people from Africa, Central America, Poland, etc. . . ."[34]

If the Cathedral and the week had been for President Reagan, this last event was in many ways for Nancy Reagan. She was heard sadly saying, "I can't leave him here."[35]

Next to and terraced slightly above the Library facilities were two large parking lots filled with dozens and dozens of satellite trucks and microwave antennas. There were also hundreds of print reporters, radio reporters, and photographers. The media turnout that included so many Reagan critics brought to mind what Bill Buckley once said when Eleanor Roosevelt passed away: "Some came to pay their last respects, others to make sure."[36]

Around the nation more people wrote of the times they remembered meeting the Gipper. An entertaining columnist with the *Peoria Journal Star* wrote of meeting Reagan in 1975 at a press conference in which Jerry McDowell was the only member of the press in attendance. "His words weren't particularly memorable although . . . Reagan could make you misty-eyed talking about what he had for dinner the night before." Reagan had just given a speech in Peoria and was playing coy about the possibility of taking on the incumbent Gerald Ford, but McDowell recalled, "There was a certain connection that Reagan could make, the eye contact, the honesty of a smile, that would carry him far beyond a chance meeting of a reporter and politician in the winter 29 years ago."[37]

All week Reagan staffers had been conducting interviews with the media, and the press staff was happily encouraging them to do so. Better to have them on the record celebrating the life and times of Ronald and Nancy Reagan, adding to the pages of history rather than Reagan bashers and wounded opponents trying to make their own history. Hooley had never done a television interview in his life but now someone with the Library's public relations staff asked him to do an interview with CBS. He replied, "I don't do those things," and the staffer said, "Jim, I think you should do this one. It's ok. You're not going to get in trouble." He complied, but later said of the interview, "I never saw it." Hooley also recalled that in the early planning of the Reagan funeral there was an aide who wanted to make it into a fundraiser, but he was long gone by June 11.[38]

The Library was awash in flowers and cards and letters and telegrams, each expressing condolences. Fashion maven Gloria Vanderbilt wrote, "People talk of closure . . . there is never closure, there is nothing left but acceptance and the courage to go on." Sending their commiserations were Bobby Short, Brooke Astor, Tish Baldrige, Henry Grunwald, George McGovern, George Steinbrenner, Ron Lauder, and Ambassador Evan Galbraith and his wife "Bootsie." Also, Micky Roosevelt wrote, "When he entered a room, he brought sunshine with him."

Respected journalist Hugh Sidey, who'd grown up in the Midwest listening to Dutch Reagan broadcast Cubs games, sent a tender letter. And Katie Couric, Barbara Walters, Norman Lear, John Travolta, Howard Keel, Larry King, Bob Colacello, William Kristol, Chris Matthews, and other celebrities and media noteworthies sent notes. And Andy Williams and Joanna Carson, Carol Burnett, Burt Bacharach and Phyllis George, Lorna Luft, Suzanne Somers, Don Rickles, Kathryn Crosby and Pat Lawford, David Niven, Jr., and Tony Danza, and thousands of others. The entire Sinatra family sent notes, including Nancy Sinatra and her brother Frank Jr.[39] So did Rich Little, who'd entertained at the Reagan White House five times and who had exchanged impressions of John Wayne and Jimmy Stewart (Reagan was awful according to Little) and Truman Capote (Reagan was excellent according to Little) with Reagan.[40]

From the administration and friends of the administration, there were notes from George Shultz and Rudy Giuliani, Rupert Murdoch, and Bob and Maria Tuttle. Lyn Nofziger wrote Nancy a kindhearted note: "Just let me say there are two things I am convinced of; He would not have been president if it had not been for you and the world is surely a better place because he was president."[41] For all the guff Nancy had taken over the years, people were coming to recognize that she was far more than just the fashion maven she'd been mercilessly caricatured as being. In fact, she was tough. She was tough because she had to be tough. While tough, she was also thoughtful and kind, which so many who had received phone calls each year on their birthdays would come to know. Mike Deaver, Jim Baker, Dennis LeBlanc, and many, many others got calls and cards and gifts over the years.

Historian and conservative chronicler Lee Edwards wrote a thoughtful note. So did Kathy Osborne, Reagan's longtime secretary, as did Peggy Grande and Dick and Claire Schweiker, and Mark Weinberg and Mark Rosenker. Even Ann Regan, the wife of the late Don Regan, who had been unceremoniously fired as Reagan's chief of staff and denounced Nancy Reagan before he left, penned a note. Their disagreement was all in the past now. Another voice from the past writing a sympathetic letter was Jane Wyman, Reagan's first wife. Jamie Lee Curtis, David Hyde Pierce, Christopher Reeve, and other actors sent either notes or letters.[42]

By week's end, there were hundreds of thousands of letters and notes. And each would eventually be answered. All were read and some were answered personally by Mrs. Reagan. And gifts by the thousands, many of which spoke to Reagan's loves. There were cowboy hats and books and American flags of all sizes, and jars and jars of jelly beans. There were framed pictures of Reagan, bordered by red, white, and blue or black crepe. There were Bibles and poems. Marilyn A. Hayes sent a poem "escribed on a plaque" titled, "Your Ronnie."

A letter written by Boy Scouts and lots of candles were sent as gifts. There were all sorts of flowers, real and imitation. Roses and dried flowers and wreaths. Someone thoughtfully sent horseshoes. There were "Beanie Babies" and a "rose porcelain tea pot and cup for one person" left by a Tommy Nichols. There were campaign buttons, and a "National Defense Medal," and a sign that proclaimed "Heaven is Reagan Country." There was a Notre Dame cap and images of Jesus and "24 Christmas cards one for each day in dec. [sic] addressed to Nancy." There were "Christmas tree napkins" and an "Uncle Sam snow globe that plays God Bless America."

A gift was sent by "Mrs. Mason's Kindergarten Class" and "Boy Scouts troop 007 and 99" and a gift of signed condolence books from the Nixon Library, married couples, and families and individuals.[43] Most of the gifts were from Americans but all were from people who were both mourning and celebrating the life and times of Ronald Reagan.

Some of the most heartfelt notes to Nancy Reagan came from political rivals like Jimmy and Rosalynn Carter. "President Reagan was one of our nation's greatest treasures, and we have admired his commitment to his values, his sense of humor and his consummate leadership . . . The courage and strength with which he faced his illness are further testaments to his character," wrote the former president and First Lady.[44]

Tony Blair, President and Laura Bush, Dick and Lynne Cheney, Queen Elizabeth, James A. Baker III, Margaret Thatcher, Donald Rumsfeld, Sandra Day O'Connor, Anthony Kennedy, Jack Kemp, Mitt Romney, Gray Davis, the famous and powerful political leaders of America and the foreign dignitaries of the world, by the hundreds, sent notes to Nancy Reagan.[45]

Baker said with heartfelt grief to Nancy, "Let me say again how proud I am of having had the privilege of serving this truly beautiful human being . . . because of who he was and the principles he believed in he changed America—and the world."

Presidential daughters Julie Nixon Eisenhower and Luci Baines Johnson were fulsome. Eisenhower shared a poem, which began: "Do not stand at my grave and weep, I am not there, I do not sleep . . ." and Johnson spoke of the bond between all presidential families and the special kind of pain they feel. Former president Bush simply wrote, "I loved your man, my president. I really did."[46]

After the departure ceremonies at Point Mugu, the motorcade began the almost thirty-mile trip to Simi Valley and Reagan's final resting place. Bob Boetticher, the funeral director, again was behind the wheel of the hearse carrying Reagan. He was the chief embalmer of the Reagan and Gerald Ford funerals.

As they made their way, at first it was just a pedestrian or two waving or saluting or placing their right hand over their hearts. Many were making the Catholic sign of the cross. But the trickle quickly became a flood of humanity. Thousands upon thousands upon thousands of men and women of all ages, all creeds and races, all economic backgrounds, lined the interstate Route 101 waving American flags, cheering for him, cheering for her, welcoming Ron and Nancy Reagan home. It was astonishing. It was a natural, but unplanned, outpouring of emotion that was not one of the details ever considered by the funeral planners.

Migrant workers in sweaty shorts and dirty overalls stood in the flatbeds of rusted pickup trucks, their hats off in deference to the most successful president many of them had ever known. The roads were clogged with people, so much so that traffic stopped but no one complained. They got out and cheered and applauded and put their hands over their hearts, and Mrs. Reagan asked the driver to slow down so she could wave to the thousands and draw strength from the last and final spontaneous outpouring for her husband. But it was also for her, for Nancy Reagan. Many of the signs mentioned her, as in "God Bless you, Nancy," and "Our Prayers are with you, Nancy." They cheered her and applauded her.

A man stood in the sweltering heat for hours with his little children. When asked why, he replied, "I want my kids to see a real hero, to be a part of history, and to remember this day when a great man was honored like no other."[47]

The hearse pulled up in front of the Library. The casket was carried inside and gently placed for a moment on the catafalque while the family gathered and the dignitaries could be escorted to their seats.

The honor guard shouted, "Pre—sent Arms!"[48] Then the flags of the three branches of the military were lowered with only the flag of the president of the United States still upright. A gentle breeze stirred the banners.

Then the military pallbearers went through the next ceremony at the Library that was the playing of "Presidential Honors," also known as "Ruffles and Flourishes"—played only for a president—and then "Hail to the Chief," which was the last time it was ever performed for Ronald Reagan.[49]

The arrangements for the final interment had always called for a late afternoon or evening sunset service so the timing was critical for the funeral cortege to arrive at the right time. The planners had come up with an ingenious system whereby nearly everything was adjusted quickly so as to keep the sun in the right position, regardless of where it was, so the stage, the chairs, the entire proceedings rotated. The final staging was elegantly framed by the magnolia trees.

As the coffin was carried to the grey granite half-circle crypt, a sole bagpiper, Eric Rigler, played "Amazing Grace" leading "the casket to the dais."[50] Only moments before, the American flag covering Reagan's coffin had been folded by U.S. servicemen in tri-corner fashion, some said to remind citizens of the three-pointed hat worn by Americans during the Revolutionary War. The thirteen folds that went into the ceremonial retiring of the flag were steeped in both Christian and American history and tradition, fathers, mothers, and family. The thirteen folds, of course, represented the original thirteen colonies, and the ceremony itself was reserved for men and women who wore the uniform for their country—including police and firefighters—and, of course, commanders in chief, though Reagan had also been active duty in the army as a captain during World War II. As cannons fired, military personnel had to take care to ensure that brushfires were not started on the hillside.

Captain James A. Symonds, commander of the USS *Ronald Reagan*, presented the flag from the Reagan coffin, and bending to his knee, repeated the phrase to Nancy Reagan that was painfully familiar to countless other widows of fallen soldiers and sailors, "On behalf of the president of the United States, the United States Navy, and a grateful nation, please accept this flag as a symbol of our appreciation for your loved one's honorable and faithful service." Symonds could barely control his own grief. Nancy used her handkerchief. Symonds had practiced the simple but all-important ceremony repeatedly because he kept breaking down crying.[51] A lone bugler played "Taps."

Those attending the small ceremony and those millions watching on television did likewise. The flag given her was the same that had flown over the U.S. Capitol on January 20, 1981, the day he'd been sworn in as the fortieth president of the United States. The crew of the USS *Ronald Reagan* had earlier dedicated a wreath to the memory of the man who was the inspiration for the giant, nuclear-powered projection of American power and purpose.[52] The naming of the super carrier was the first time an American naval vessel had been so designated after a living individual.

It seemed as if the funeral planners had left absolutely nothing to chance. Everything about the week had meaning, substance, irony, and poignancy. Even those things beyond the ken of the planners only added to the richness of the seven days of Reagan.

In Las Vegas, the lights along the strip of the "City of Lights" were dimmed for three minutes, not for Reagan the Vegas performer who had bombed there years earlier, but for Reagan the president and world leader, who had wowed the audience. The dimming of the lights was a signal honor as it had only been done for John Kennedy, Frank Sinatra, Dean Martin, Sammy Davis, Jr., and George Burns.[53]

At the grave, the Reagans' pastor, Reverend Michael Wenning of the Bel Air Presbyterian Church, said, "We began this day and it seemed the heavens were weeping. We have come from sea to shining sea to the soil he loved so much and where his body will remain."[54] Four F-14s then thundered overhead. (One small flap was Wenning went on too long and the over flight had to be waved off until he finished.[55])

Reagan's remains were covered in blue fabric and placed on the stage before the seated audience. The setting sun and the Pacific served as background behind the lectern at the rear of the Library, in the out of doors, facing west.

All three of the Reagan children spoke—approximately five minutes each. All aroused some memory of their father's ability to stir, to move, and to inspire a crowd, as well as make them laugh through their tears. Ron spoke of his father's grace and charm, Michael spoke of his father's kindness toward he and other children, and Patti spoke of the lessons of life and death and renewal he'd taught her. "My father never feared death. He never saw it as an ending."[56] In a piece she'd just penned for *Newsweek*, Miss Davis wrote, "No one ever saw all of him. It took me nearly four decades . . . to sit silently with him and not clamor for something more." Before coming to terms with him on his terms, she wrote, "I resented the country at times for its demands on him, its ownership of him."[57]

In his eulogy, Mike said, "I knew him as dad." His comments were sweet but also tinged with a bit of loneliness. He'd floated between Jane Wyman's world and his father's world ever since the divorce. Still, he was gracious. "Last Saturday, when my father opened his eyes for the last time, and visualized Nancy and gave her such a wonderful, wonderful gift." He also mentioned his departed and beloved sister Maureen.[58]

For all the contretemps over the years, Ron had once said his father was the guy who didn't just watch boys playing football in the backyard, he was the father who went out and played with them. In his encomium he said that his father loved to pull on earlobes and that his father was a gentleman and gave his son lessons in being a gentleman. He told a funny story about how his father gave the thumbs-up signal, and how he wanted it to catch on in the country, and how a protester used "an entirely different hand gesture. Dad saw this and without missing a beat turned to us and said, 'You see? I think it's catching on.'"[59] The audience chuckled.

But Ron assumed a political edge when he said his father "never made the fatal mistake of so many politicians wearing his faith on his sleeve to gain political advantage,"[60] and some people shifted uncomfortably in their seats.

Patti remembered the tenderness her father showed when one of her pet goldfish died and how together they dug a tiny grave. "He told me that my fish was swimming in the clear blue waters in heaven and he would never tire and he would never get hungry . . . He was free." After hearing how wonderful heaven was for her departed goldfish, "I suggested that perhaps we should kill the others so they could also go to that clear blue river and be free."[61] Again, the audience chuckled. She made reference to her father's eyes opening at the end. Her grief was powerful. "Ultimately, I lost him as a woman who had asked his forgiveness but still couldn't quite forgive herself for the wounds she'd inflicted," she said.[62]

Mike talked about a note his young son received from his grandfather. "Some guy got $10,000 for my signature. Maybe this letter will help you pay for your college education."[63] The Gipper added a postscript to the note reminding his grandson that he was president of the United States, Mike told the appreciative crowd. He told of how his father never brought up the topic of adoption, but of the good times of riding and swimming together. Mike was the adopted son but had also known his father longer than nearly anyone present, including Nancy. Ron said his father was "honest, compassionate, graceful, brave."[64]

Each in his or her own way was charming, evocative of their father's grace and ability to move an audience.

Nancy Reagan sat in the front row watching, but noticed that the seat behind her she'd reserved for Dennis LeBlanc was empty. The seating at the event had been tightly controlled and each seat had a premium. All assignments were personally approved by Nancy Reagan or by Fred Ryan and Joanne Drake. The Reagans often gave Dennis gifts and never forgot his birthday. Few men had spent as much intensely personal time alone with Reagan, and in those nearly thirty years Dennis almost never heard Reagan say anything derogatory about anyone.[65]

Like Mike Deaver, Dennis was also a surrogate son, who worked with the Gipper at the ranch cutting trees, getting on the roof to repair the old tiles, building, tearing down, moving, hauling, just the two of them for hours on end, neither speaking much except to ask for a tool or an opinion. Reagan liked the serenity and normalcy of the ranch and appreciated Dennis's discreet company. When they ate together they said even less, food flying, and sometimes Nancy would ask Dennis to eat slower in the hopes of inducing her husband to eat slower. In 1976, Reagan took an old trailer from Hollywood to the ranch for Dennis to sleep in while they worked there.[66]

Despite his California surfer boy good looks, marked by his tousled reddish-blond hair, he was quiet and reserved. Their closeness had lasted for years and had only deepened, and he was there the last time Reagan was at the ranch in 1997 and Dennis cried then. So there was a good reason why he was not there at Simi at the end of the day, as the sun was setting over the life of Ronald Reagan. Dennis could not take it. The former California Highway Patrolman—a tough and capable man—was home, weeping uncontrollably, stricken beyond words at the loss of his old workmate and ranch friend and father figure.[67]

The ceremonies concluded just as the sun was setting over the Pacific with an orange hue, and the moment was too powerful for all present, even touching the most stoic military officer or police officer or Secret Service agent. In the words of the theater, there wasn't a dry eye in the house.

After Nancy departed from the funeral proceedings, guests were allowed to form a line to pass by Reagan's casket and pay their final respects. Mike Deaver was sobbing and crying and grabbed Jim Hooley and hugged him. Deaver later sent Hooley a note saying, "Jim, I apologize. It brought it all home when I saw you, and I lost it."[68]

Reagan's casket was slowly moved to his final resting place at the top of the hill at the back of the Library. At the top of the hill the sun was starting to set just as there was one last 21-gun salute.

Per tradition, three of the spent rounds, cartridges, were put inside the folded flag given to Nancy. "The cartridges signify duty, honor, and sacrifice."[69] The 21-gun salute was reserved only for presidents, former presidents, and foreign heads of state. Their firing in three volleys was punctuated by five-second intervals.

The number three was significant. In Roman times, dirt was cast three times on the grave to symbolize the end of the ceremonies; in later years, three volleys of twenty-one muskets meant a battlefield funeral was over and the fighting could resume.[70]

Episcopalians also threw dirt on the coffin as did some evangelicals and Catholics, but Methodists did not.

It was all too much for even the most cynical, and seven hundred guests all cried tears of sorrow without shame. Millions more around the country and around the world—in living rooms and firehouses and dormitories and churches and community centers and embassies and public housing—were also crying tears of joy, pride, and sorrow. Reagan had always had that effect on people; in life and in death, he still evoked powerful emotions.

For seven days, the eyes of the world had remained fixed on Nancy Reagan. She was videotaped constantly, photographed constantly, commented on constantly, written about constantly, and watched constantly. She was holding up remarkably well, but as mentioned earlier, was often seen wearing glasses, which in an earlier time neither she nor Ronald Reagan wore in public. It wasn't anything unusual. Bill Clinton used reading glasses, as did Richard Nixon and JFK. George H. W. Bush had often been seen in public wearing glasses, as was Dwight Eisenhower, as was Lyndon Johnson. It was a matter of taste.

She'd personally asked former president Bush to speak at the funeral, and like much of the previous week her imprimatur was on most everything. Jackie Kennedy, who had passed away almost exactly ten years earlier, had an equally direct hand in the planning of her husband's funeral. At the time of the Reagan funeral, Nellie Connally was the only figure still alive in 2004 who was in the presidential car in Dallas that day, the other three having died prematurely. It was also Nellie Connally's voice that was probably the last thing Kennedy heard when she said, "Mr. President, you certainly can't say that Dallas doesn't love you."[71] Some people were recalling the grace with which Jackie Kennedy handled herself during her husband's funeral as they witnessed Mrs. Reagan's quiet and elegant comportment, and comparing the two women favorably.

Simi Valley ranges from seven hundred feet to one thousand feet above sea level and the Reagan Foundation property covered about one hundred acres. Chaparral plants covered the nutrient-starved sandy soil. The original intended location for the Reagan Library with some had been Stanford University, in part because the Hoover Institution was there, but for a variety of reasons—most especially because Reagan didn't want his library at Stanford, said Robert Higdon, and four years of fighting over politics, of course—the site was later moved to Simi, which was nice for the Reagans as it was approximately halfway between Los Angeles and the ranch near Santa Barbara. They had looked at as many as twenty different locations for the Library before Simi became available because of a generous donation by an admirer who had absolutely no relationship to Reagan.[72] Reagan had deeply fond memories of Eureka College but it was never considered for the presidential library, in part because it was far away from where he lived in California.

The land in Ventura County had been donated by developers Donald Swartz and Gerald Blakeley, and it looked out over the Pacific, about twenty miles to the west, just like the ranch. Its address was 40 Presidential Drive. Swartz was hoping to build a hotel or hotels nearby to support the visitors to the Library. The design of the Library was evocative of the ranch, California Mission style, with the signature curved tile roof and spackled white exterior walls. But while the ranch was tiny—not more than eighteen hundred square feet—the Reagan Library was the largest of all the presidential libraries, with plans for even greater expansion, including an auspicious and enormous pavilion to house the soon-to-be acquired Air Force One.

The plane had been retired from service, but the Reagan Foundation and Fred Ryan eventually scooped it up knowing what a draw it would be. This Air Force One had gone into service under Richard Nixon and "flew more than a million miles, served seven presidents from . . . Nixon to George W. Bush, and Reagan accounted for 211 of its 445 flights," according to Duke Blackwood.[73]

The Library cost approximately fifty-seven million dollars to build, and was opened in 1991 with a huge gala that included George Bush, Richard Nixon, Gerald Ford, and Jimmy Carter, along with all the former First Ladies, including Lady Bird Johnson and excepting Jackie Kennedy Onassis.[74] It also housed a full-scale facsimile of the Oval Office as it appeared when Reagan was president, down to the carpeting, the shim under the Resolute desk so Reagan could get his legs into the well, the photos on the credenza, and the little leather saying on his desk, "It can be done."[75] Also, the Remington statues of cowboys and mountain men were in the same locations on either side of the office.

When the Library was built, the architects wanted to maintain a clear roofline that was not as high as the real White House Oval Office at eighteen feet, six inches. Rather than raising the roof they dug down, so to access the Oval Office at the Reagan Library one had to step down.

The Reagan Library was nearly as expensive to operate as the Kennedy Library in Boston. Fund-raising was always at a premium in order to keep the doors open and to have sufficient funds for programs and the like, such as centers for learning, a new restaurant, and other amenities.

Melissa Giller was a pert, popular, and valued longtime member of the Reagan Library staff who knew her subject cold, and when asked if there was anything about Reagan and his first wife, Jane Wyman, at the Library she reportedly quipped, "Somewhere, I know there's a picture."[76]

With all the attention focused on the events in Washington for the last day of the Reagan funeral, it was completely overlooked that it was also the twenty-fifth anniversary of the passing of his old friend John Wayne. They'd never made any movies together—after all, he was the "Duke"—but a cowboy buddy film featuring the two would have been fascinating. Still, the men were with different studios and while WWII slowed Reagan's celluloid career, it only accelerated Wayne's.

Already, demand for Reagan memorabilia was heating up on the Internet. His posters had always been popular collector items and became more so after his election in 1980, but now people were bidding for autographs and buttons and photos and statues. A whole industry based on Reagan collectibles was growing.

The House and the Senate passed resolutions commending the life of President Ronald Reagan, although the House vote was 375–0, which meant sixty members did not vote, and the Senate fell two votes short at 98–0.[77] So in neither body was it a unanimous vote.

It was a busy day in history. It was the anniversary of Margaret Thatcher's election to a third term as prime minister. It was the anniversary of Jeannette Rankin's birthday, the first woman elected to the U.S. House, from Montana, even before universal suffrage had passed the Congress, with the support of the Republican Party and the widespread opposition of the Democratic Party.[78]

"So ended the nation's farewell to a man judged by fans and critics alike to have ranked among the most consequential presidents of the past century, a man credited by former British prime minister Margaret Thatcher yesterday with having 'won the Cold War.'"[79] She also painted a verbal picture of the man she had eulogized, saying, "That cloud has now lifted. He is himself again."

Some were tossing around a very profound sentence from her eulogy of earlier in the week that Reagan had also dedicated himself to "the great cause of cheering us all up."[80] Most also felt she gave the best speech but, given the horse race nature of the national media, that was to be expected. Plus, some of them liked to stick it to Bush. "Neither of the Bush men is known as a spellbinding speaker, to put it mildly, but nothing makes Bush the elder look more impressive than being on the same roster with son George," Tom Shales of the *Post* acidly wrote.[81] He also took a petty shot at Fox News, finding fault in of all things the size of its graphics.

Mulroney's comments were also being favorably received. Few before that morning knew what a marvelous speaker and phrase maker he was. No wonder the Irishman Mulroney and the Irishman Reagan got on so well.

Some in the West during the early 1980s believed communism and democracy were equally valid and viable. This was the school of "moral equivalence." In contrast, Ronald Reagan saw Soviet communism as a menace to be confronted in the genuine belief that its squalid underpinning would fall swiftly to the gathering winds of freedom. And we know now who was right.[82]

He'd done that and more but that was all in the past, all subject to earthly and eternal debates by historians and political scientists and politicians. Reagan had other things on his mind when he left office. In his farewell letter to the American people in late 1994, he'd spoken of going "home"[83] in a sweet and tender reference to heaven and eternal life. For Reagan, going to the mountaintop was not just a phrase but an ideal. Going to the mountain had great meaning to his mother, Nelle, active in the Disciples of Christ, and to his father, Jack, a devout Catholic. All Christians believed in going to the mountain, in going home.

When he thought of or was at his home at the ranch, he'd often quoted Psalm 121:1: "I will lift up mine eyes unto the mountains."[84] Reagan's favorite poet may have been Robert Service, a big handsome man who wrote manly prose about the West and about mountains. Reagan could quote him verbatim. Indeed, Service had written "The Mountain and the Lake." "I know a mountain . . . my lake adores my mountain."[85] Ron Reagan said in his eulogy, "He is home now."[86] Everybody knew what the prodigal son meant. His daughter Patti wrote, "My father always believed in going home."[87]

Ronald Wilson Reagan had finally gone home.

Early the next morning, long, long after the reception following the sunset ceremony and after Nancy Reagan had gone home and after the media and television cameras were gone and all was quiet and still, a small group of Reagan's devoted advance men drank and made several toasts to the Gipper. They broke out cigars and encircled the crypt, over which had been engraved across a curved stone, "I know in my heart that man is good, that what is right will always eventually triumph, and there is purpose and worth to each and every life."[88] The only other etching was the seal of the president of the United States. Later, a small stone would be added with his name and year of birth and death.

Reagan probably would have appreciated the lightness and solemnity of the moment. He'd joked often about his age and when the tombs were being built at the Library for him and Nancy, he'd point it out to friends and visitors: "See that over there? That is where I am going to be buried. Not too soon."[89]

Several years earlier, there had also been some laughs among the staff over what phrase Reagan would choose to have engraved over his gravesite. Some joked it would be "There you go again" or "Tear down this wall" or another one of his memorable or jokey lines.[90] Reagan would have been right there, laughing.

The advance men had arranged for ultra-strong spotlights to shine out from the plaza toward the area where remaining camera crews might be set up to blind them as to the post-memorial happenings. Even at the end, the old advance men wanted no attention on themselves and for the focus to be on the president. It was fitting, as it was and as it had always been. Reagan was the star.

They lit up cigars, had some second drinks, and sat outside the party, unwinding after stressful and sweaty days and sleepless nights. And they reminisced about the past week, the past ten years, and for some the past thirty-plus years, going back to the campaign of 1980 and even before.

Hours later, after nightfall, the casket was still where Mrs. Reagan had left it, in front of the gravesite. A post-ceremony reception had been held inside the Library but that, too, had been over for hours by now. "A larger group of people—mostly former full time and volunteer White House advance—stayed fairly late into the night enjoying cocktails on the balcony off of the private quarters and telling many, many stories about President Reagan, the 'old days' and the memorable events of the previous week," recalled Gary Foster.[91]

The script called for the media to be herded out around 8:30 p.m. A private reception with Mrs. Reagan had begun at 7:30 p.m. in the "Private Quarters" and called for her to leave the Library no later than 10:00 p.m. There was also a larger reception in the auditorium, which began at 7:35 p.m. At midnight, the "last guest departs Library" and the "Dig Begins" at 12:10 a.m., again according to the plan.[92] One solitary individual had the responsibility for this last and lonely act.

With most mainstream faiths, it was common practice to have a committal ceremony and then let the family and friends depart. Then the coffin was interred in private. With some Baptists, the gathering remained as the casket was lowered into the ground. Reagan's funeral would follow tradition and his interment was planned to be a private one. JFK, a Catholic, was interred in private. Long after midnight, nearly everybody was gone, and at the last the planned program was way behind schedule. The military guard had left as had the crowd, and it was now late in the evening and the responsibility for the final ceremony was going to be left to a gravedigger. After the final ceremony, the casket had not yet been placed in the sarcophagus, as the plan had been to inter Reagan in private after everybody had departed.

The advance men were startled to discover that Reagan's remains were to be left alone. "What if someone comes in and steals it? Do you want that?" they stormed to the military and Secret Service. "So you guys are telling me that the president of the United States is going to be out there alone?" But an agent relented and said, "I'll be there. We won't leave until the tomb is sealed."[93] The final six Reagan advance men were Gary Foster, Joe Brennan, Grey Terry, Andrew Littlefair, Rick Ahearn, and Jim Hooley. Also present was Duke Blackwood, the head of the archives for the Library. As Foster recalled,

Duke approached Jim Hooley on the day of the sunset ceremony and asked that he and several of the former White House staff members who had worked on the funeral—at Jim's choosing—stay to witness the casket lowered down to the mausoleum entrance. Duke wanted to rule out any chance of "conspiracy theories" of a stolen body . . . and he thought it was appropriate to have the people who had worked for President Reagan . . . be there for the last event.

The workers were escorted in . . . and began to dig the hole to the opening of the tomb. We watched as they finished digging the hole and then opened the large concrete door to the tomb. Duke earlier had expressed concern about the condition of the tomb because it had never been opened since it had been built . . .[94]

The old advance men looked inside the crypt and saw some muddy water, so efforts were made to clean it out before the casket was placed inside. It was not a high-tech process. The plan was for the casket to be rolled into place on logs, and as Ahearn said, just like a pharaoh some four thousand years earlier.[95] It was now around 2:00 a.m.

"We watched as they lowered the casket down . . . ," Foster said.[96]

After reciting the Lord's Prayer—led by Ahearn—they formulated their own impromptu ceremony and each threw a small cup of dirt onto the casket. Hooley felt bad they hadn't planned ahead to have a silver cup to use instead of a Styrofoam cup but it was devised at the last, as advance men often had to do, and somehow seemed appropriate.[97] "When the Lord calls me home . . . ," Reagan had written in his Alzheimer's letter ten years earlier.[98]

There was something so poignant and romantic about the advance men who prepared the way for Reagan in life now preparing the way for Reagan into eternity. All—Foster, Brennan, Terry, Littlefair, Ahearn, and Hooley—were too grief stricken to say what was on their minds, but they were all thinking the same thing, and besides, as advance men they had been taught to say little in formal or intimate circumstances.

Discretion was their watchword but so was devotion.

Hooley, Ahearn, and their colleagues, most Irish, and those not were honorary Irishmen all this evening, had a private Irish wake for the Irishman they had happily devoted their lives to and whom they adored. Hooley whispered to his associates, "We took him home."[99]

Foster was also filled with emotions. "To me, it was an incredible honor to be asked to witness the occasion with this group." Their "deep loyalty and fondness for President Reagan were unquestionable," he said.[100]

"Then we turned and left, and I remember the sound of equipment starting up," Hooley said.[101] The now former Reagan advance men were not drunk but they were into their cups and that was of little consequence. These were naturally friendly and gregarious guys. They believed, as did Reagan, that the Irish poet was right when he said, "There are no strangers here; only friends you haven't yet met."[102]

Still, it might have been the Bard, not William Butler Yeats, who offered the most appropriate quote—from *Richard II*—to speak to this time. "His body to that pleasant country's earth, and his pure soul unto his captain Christ, under whose colours he had fought so long."[103]

## CHAPTER 10

# A PRAYER IN SPRING

*"Reagan is indisputably a part of America and he*
*may become a part of American history."*

A couple of hours after Jim Hooley and company left, workers quietly sealed the tomb of Ronald Reagan. "Reagan's body was entombed at the Simi Valley library site shortly before 3 a.m. Saturday," said Duke Blackwood, executive director of the Library and Ronald Reagan Memorial Foundation.[1]

After a week of public mourning there was a solitary ending. There was no ceremony, no pomp, no religious statement, just the Lord's Prayer whispered in near silence. There was only the perfunctory task of a burial. It was all very anticlimactic, very undramatic. "It was not a public event," Blackwood remarked. Even the family was not present.[2]

The limestone gravesite was "a curved wall adorned with shrubbery and ivy."[3] All told, the vault and casket weighed four thousand pounds. Later, a headstone of "Georgian gray granite" was added with his birth and death dates.[4]

"The solid mahogany casket was sealed within a bronze-lined vault, seven feet underground inside the crypt, which also includes space for Nancy Reagan."[5] The whole thing was so discreet it was not even entered into the planning book for the week, save a single reference to a solitary person performing a lonely ritual. Instead, the very last line of the playbook created for the implementation of the Reagan funeral ended with one sentence. "9:00 a.m. Library re-opens for business."[6]

Seven hours after the final entombment, tourists were solemnly, respectfully, and quietly gazing at and taking pictures in Simi Valley, California, of the ossuary of Ronald Wilson Reagan, fortieth president of the United States.

Simi Valley had once been ancient American Indian territory, occupied by the Chumash. The tribe thrived off of small game and fish and were adept at cave painting, building canoes, and weaving baskets. Some believed the name Simi was derived from the Chumash Indian word for "little white clouds."[7] Later, the area was occupied by the Spanish and even later, settlers. The Spanish considered the Chumash to be the most sophisticated of all California's American Indian tribes.

Tracks were then laid for the railroad, which helped in the transformation of the area and benefited the citrus farmers that needed to ship their lemons and grapefruit to market. Located in Ventura County, it later became a bedroom community to Los Angeles. Its ruggedly beautiful topography made it ideal for cowboy-and-Indian movies, and Reagan had filmed a number of movies there himself.

Reagan may well have lasted longer than ninety-three years had it not been for the scourge of Alzheimer's, but perhaps only God will ever know for sure. Certainly his quality of life—a trendy phrase in 2004—would have lasted longer, and certainly the strain and stress put on Nancy Reagan would have made those ten years vastly different. Still, Reagan was the longest living president, besting John Adams by almost three years. Even the day after his funeral, the *Washington*

*Times* was reporting about a breakthrough in the understanding of the "'genetic signature' of aging in the human brain."[8]

His affliction helped to launch a national discussion and millions in increased funding for research for the dreaded infirmity. Cures were pursued aggressively and most researchers were hopeful that a cure or a vaccine would one day be found. Mrs. Reagan threw herself into the cause of Alzheimer's research, doing as much for it as any First Lady or former First Lady has done for any cause. Her efforts were never appreciated by activists, and those who would never miss a chance to criticize Nancy or the president.

When she went into the White House, the gentlewomen of the press derided her for not having a cause, as all First Ladies should, don't you know? She had worked with former POWs from Vietnam and foster grandparents. She made strides with her anti-drug campaign, which again the elites poked fun at on occasion but which did some very good work based on the evidence. Over wine and cheese, the matrons of Georgetown snarkily said the anti-drug campaign was really about her public relations. But no one questioned her work with Alzheimer's research. At the time, it was estimated that four million Americans suffered from the affliction. The ongoing research was focused on both a cure and prevention.

The diagnosis was devastating, but Reagan took it calmly. To a person, no one ever came forward and said Reagan ever felt sorry for himself, ever asked God, "Why me, Lord?" He never got down in the dumps, never moped around, simply accepting and working around it and maintaining his uncanny optimism. Mrs. Reagan, as always, took his lumps upon herself, and she more than once asked God, "Why?"

Part of the debate over Reagan was whether he suffered from Alzheimer's while he was still in the White House, a notion that his own son Ron advanced in a much-criticized book. Yet the people who knew him best—the staff and close friends—said they saw the same Mr. President. He went to the Mayo Clinic each year to undergo a battery of physical and mental tests and passed each with flying colors. Don Lambro, a nationally syndicated columnist said,

> Over the course of my journalism career, I had many interviews with Reagan in the '70s and '80s, two of them in the Oval Office. In both, he was knowledgeable and fully in command of the issues, as he was in the many news conferences he held in prime-time—when he was pummeled with tough questions, not the softballs President Obama gets from a compliant White House press corps.[9]

More would be aware of the troubles by the spring of 1994 when the Republican Party held its annual dinner hosted by its chairman Haley Barbour, when Reagan did not seem himself at all. He had difficulty delivering the speech, and while in New York before going to Washington for the GOP dinner had exhibited a behavior that worried Fred Ryan.[10]

Mike Deaver, one of Reagan's closest aides, wrote a frank account of his last meeting with Reagan in 1997, including the painful fact that the Gipper no longer recognized him.

> His disease was progressing, and Nancy was circling the wagons. Soon, only family and those who were tending to the president would be allowed to see him. He looked great . . . but it didn't take long to realize that Ronald Reagan had no idea who I was, or any interest in why I had walked into his office. A book was in his hands; his attention to it was total. Finally, I slipped over to his side to see what it was. He was reading a picture book about Traveller, Robert E. Lee's famous horse. I was heartbroken.[11]

Deaver concluded that he'd heard rumors but "I won't include the grim details here. Suffice to say that a man who has done so much for America can now do so little for himself."[12]

A lot of things happened in American history on June 12. For one thing, it was the birthday of President George H. W. Bush, who'd been born in 1924. To celebrate, he was going to make two parachute jumps so he'd have five total and get a pin from the Golden Knights of the U.S. Army. Barbara Bush could only shake her head and tell her husband, "You don't need any more pins or any more plaques."[13]

It was the ten-year anniversary of the murder of Nicole Brown Simpson and Ronald Goldman.

Gasoline had spiked to more than $1.50 per gallon.[14]

And in 1939, the National Baseball Hall of Fame had opened in Cooperstown, the hometown of Abner Doubleday, who ironically was not the father of American baseball. George Washington had written about a game his troops played during the Revolution called "Town Ball" that featured a batted ball and base running. But it was the anniversary of regular season interleague play between the National League and the American League beginning in 1997. Some purists thought it was the end of Western civilization.

On the other hand, in defense of Western civilization, it was also the anniversary of Reagan's historic trip to Berlin where he stood in front of a barricade and told a communist dictator to "tear down this wall."

Nancy Reagan stipulated that she never wanted to be known as Mrs. Nancy Reagan, the polite way of letting society know a woman was a widow. She made clear to all that she was Mrs. Ronald Reagan and would always be known as such; some women made such choices. Their marriage would be everlasting, even in death.

His bedroom has been turned back into her den, from where she writes letters, pictures of him all around. Even years later she still slept on one side of their bed, the other side where he slept for more than fifty years unmarked and unwrinkled. The bed is smaller now, but his presence is everywhere.[15] The living room goes largely unused. But now, according to Patti, the smells of the house—lavender, bath oils—are all Nancy's.

Immediately after the funeral, Reagan memorabilia went up for auction on the eBay website and other Internet sites. Odd trinkets as well as traditional collectibles were also sold at antique stores around the country. The palm cards given out at the Rotunda were already fetching twenty-five dollars and upward, while the programs from the National Cathedral were going for 250 dollars.

Reagan's signature had been rising in value for years, and depending on the signed document or item was attracting hundreds and even thousands of dollars. Movie posters, statuettes, record albums, books, fan magazines, buttons, campaign posters, and other Reagan memorabilia were all becoming prized items. Ronald Reagan's image was eventually issued on three different U.S. postage stamps, and the popular items sold out quickly. Richard Nixon stamps were issued and quickly destroyed—hundreds of thousands of them—because no one wanted to send a letter through the mails with the Trickster's image.[16]

As much as the talking heads talked, they had become more and more quiet as the previous week wore on, letting their viewers drink in the momentous events of the week of the funeral, letting the signifying events reflect the death of a significant American president. The silence of the talking heads was remarkable, but no less so was the coverage because of the networks' and cable channels' cessation of advertising, especially on Friday. "But when it came to the day's centerpiece, the actual funeral for Reagan at the Washington National Cathedral, television transmitted the pictures, words and music, but not its own employees' interpretations, to a public looking to honor the man, be part of American history or both."[17]

Reagan had been the most dominant figure over the long haul on American television, from 1953—when he signed the deal with GE *Theater* on CBS—to his passing more than fifty years later—when he was covered by all networks and all cable systems. Even ESPN explored Reagan the athlete, and C-SPAN rebroadcast old speeches and press conferences, and local television stations broadcast old Reagan movies.

Other historical figures—such as Richard Nixon or John F. Kennedy—had their moments, but no one in the history of the country or the medium of television so ruled the national debate for the length of time Reagan had. Even in the past ten years, during his seclusion as he descended into the black pit of Alzheimer's, his name, his policies, and his persona governed the national debate. No political figure in American history—save maybe Abraham Lincoln—was invoked in the national debate of ideas and ideologies as much or as often as Reagan. And none was referenced—not even Lincoln—more within the conservative movement and the Republican Party. Indeed, though the sixteenth president was hailed as the founder of the GOP (which wasn't true; Lincoln's old adversary John C. Frémont was the first nominee in 1856), Reaganism was becoming rightly recognized as a legitimate political philosophy, overlapping American conservatism and American populism.

Frank Fahrenkopf, close friend and confidant of Paul Laxalt, who in turn was close friend and confidant of Reagan's, noticed several years ago as he was walking through an airport terminal that President Obama was on all the television sets giving a speech or a press conference, and yet the travelers continued walking, talking, milling about, utterly and completely ignoring Obama. Fahrenkopf contrasted that with a time twenty-five years earlier, when Reagan was president, and how everybody in a terminal would stop and want to watch and hear what their president was saying when he was on television.

Laxalt was a master politician in his own right and a master of knowing men and what made them think. He said that Reagan's belief in himself as a "citizen-politician" was not a "pose." "Much of life is psychological, and it is Reagan's genius that he convinced himself and others that he was not really a politician, which inspired unbelievable trust in him."[18]

Ronald Reagan was simply one of the most compelling men in American political history. The course of politics changed because of him. Politicians used to routinely denounce television, as if it was some parlor novelty. Richard Nixon often spoke derisively of television, Eisenhower tolerated it, Truman was awful on it. And LBJ was too hot for it, Ford was too oblivious, Carter was too ill defined. Only Reagan and John Kennedy recognized the power of the little box in people's living rooms and put it to good use. But they were also among those lucky few men who almost never took a bad photograph. It was seemingly impossible to catch either man looking bad because in almost any pose, their rugged good looks shone. Unlike Nixon, who almost never looked good on television even when he was smiling and jovial, which wasn't often.

Life was moving on.

Bill Clinton released his memoirs and while desperate to claim a comparison to Ronald Reagan, no one was having it. The only debate ever held regarding Reagan's conduct in the Oval Office was whether he had entered the presidential office without a tie and jacket. He sometimes did, but mostly on a Saturday morning to tape his weekly radio address before heading to Camp David. In fact, there was no comparison between the two men or their administrations. Not in any way, shape, or form could one be drawn between the two men. They had absolutely nothing in common as men, husbands, fathers, or politicians. Clinton's longtime advisor Paul Begala had at one point wanted to write a book favorably comparing the two men, but was talked out of it by sane friends.

The weekly reports of DVD sales had *Miracle* at number one but among rentals, the movie *Paycheck* was number one. The more popular television programs were *The Bernie Mac Show*, *The West Wing*, *NCIS*, and *Friends*. Also *Law and Order* in its twenty-eight flavors.

Mikhail Gorbachev for a time resisted acknowledging that the Soviets had lost the Cold War and resisted even harder admitting that the West—and Reagan—had won. But he did not hesitate crediting Reagan with having core principles. "He was a person committed to certain values and traditions. For him the American dream was not just rhetoric. It was something he felt in his heart. In that sense he was an idealistic American."[19]

Bill Buckley, whom Reagan had known for years—long before ever meeting Gorbachev—said, in his typical understated fashion, "Reagan is indisputably a part of America and he may become a part of American history."[20]

Joanne Drake said it took six months to send thank you notes to everybody they had heard from when Reagan passed away.[21] A little more than a month after the funeral, Nancy Reagan hosted a sumptuous private dinner and reception for the staff who worked such long hours, days, and years planning and implementing the funeral. It took place at the Hotel Bel Air, where she often liked to have lunch with "the girls" in her circle of friends. The invitation said, "With heartfelt gratitude for your service, sacrifice and dedication."[22] Nancy Reagan within weeks sent handwritten and tender notes to the honorary pallbearers.[23] She also wrote a letter to the citizens of Simi Valley, thanking them for their patience,[24] and one to former president Bush, whom she called "George," in which she wished him a happy birthday and celebrated his parachute jump. "I want to thank you from the bottom of my heart for the beautiful tribute you gave to Ronnie . . . Please give my love to Barbara."[25] She also wrote a letter to the American people on July 4, thanking them.[26]

Reagan's fraternity Tau Kappa Epsilon was writing letters,

mourning a fallen brother.[27] Randall Wallace, who wrote the lyrics to the song "Mansions of the Lord," wrote Nancy a sweet note, telling her he thought that Reagan was "among the greatest of our presidents" and how delighted he was that the song had been a part of the funeral at the National Cathedral, and how he'd written the lyrics in the wake of his own father's death.[28]

Diane Disney Miller wrote a letter to Joanne Drake thanking her for being invited to the Simi Valley ceremony. "I was . . . so proud of the fact that my father was a personal friend of Ronald Reagan's."[29] Reagan was one of three hosts chosen by Walt Disney for the opening of Disneyland in July 1955.

Finally, Reagan was perhaps the most consistent and conscientious writer of the presidency—speeches, books, diary entries, notes, letters, and radio commentaries. These and so many other historical records refute the nonsense that he was "unknowable."

Reagan, the oldest president and oldest former president, was the first president to die in the twenty-first century. Yet he once said, "As you look to the future, always remember the treasures of our past."[30]

# AUTHOR'S NOTE

*"They wrote Truman off as a little haberdasher from Missouri
and they wrote off Reagan as a B-grade actor . . ."*

While highlighting with a yellow magic marker each time the word *Reagan* appeared in research documents for my book about the 1980 campaign, *Rendezvous with Destiny*, our then nine-year-old son Mitchell looked up from his work and asked, "Dad, has anyone ever done a book on Reagan after he was president?" I thought for a moment and then said, "No."

That was the birth of *Last Act*.

I did not proceed incautiously however. The reporting of any death and funeral must be handled delicately and the passing of a president ever more so, especially Ronald Reagan, about whom so much disinformation has been reported.

I consulted books about the passing of Thomas Jefferson, the funeral of Abraham Lincoln, the last years of Woodrow Wilson, the last years of Richard Nixon, the last year of FDR, and the death of JFK and James Garfield in order to get perspective. Each author handled the topic respectfully but truthfully as well. There was little gloss. Gene Smith wrote *When the Cheering Stopped* about the last years of

Woodrow Wilson, Monica Crowley penned the excellent *Nixon in Winter,* Jim Bishop wrote *FDR's Last Year,* Alan Pell Crawford produced *Twilight at Monticello,* William Manchester labored over the exquisite *TheDeath of a President,* James L. Swanson put in writing the prized *Manhunt* about the death of Lincoln and the pursuit of John Wilkes Booth, and the well-regarded Candice Millard authored *Destiny of the Republic,* about the shooting and demise of James Garfield.

Each of these scholars rescued their subjects from myth and half-truths, thus protecting the real history. But this is not typical in accounts of Ronald Reagan's death and such is the case with his post-presidency. The shorthand is he left Washington, announced he had Alzheimer's, and died, but in fact, there was a lot of living in those fifteen plus years he and Mrs. Reagan had together after the presidency.

Part of the reason is that Reagan, like Eisenhower, did not obsess about his legacy for the rest of his life. He left a heritage of which he was very proud but the presidency alone did not define all of Reagan's life to him, unlike say Richard Nixon or Jimmy Carter. He saw himself through many prisms, which may have explained why he was particularly fond of the phrase by Thomas Paine, "We have it in our power to begin the world over again,"[1] which was a quintessentially American conservative concept. Paine, Thomas Jefferson, and other Founders and Framers believed that man controlled his own destiny, and there were no forgone conclusions, and the dignity of the free and private individual was the essential expression of American conservatism.

June 5 was an important day in American history. It was the day planned for the invasion of Europe in 1944, which was pushed back to June 6 because of weather. June 5 was the anniversary of the shooting of Robert F. Kennedy in California, just after winning the Democratic primary there. June was also the anniversary of the births of Adam Smith in 1723 and John Maynard Keynes in 1883. Even 160 years apart, these two economists would become synonymous with two competing economic theories: one championed by the Right, the other by the Left. That they were born in the same month did not do the word *ironic* justice.

It was the anniversary of George Marshall's speech in 1947 in which he outlined a strategy to prevent the Soviet Union from taking over or dominating more European countries that later became known as the "Marshall Plan." It was also the anniversary of the birth of Pancho Villa in 1878, and in 1884 William Tecumseh Sherman told the Republican convention, "I will not accept if nominated, and will not serve if elected."[2] In 1981, five gay men in Los Angeles were diagnosed with what was thought to be pneumonia. Later, it was discovered they had a new and deadly virus, Acquired Immunodeficiency Syndrome, which shortly would become known as AIDS. In 1993, the great Conway Twitty died, again on June 5.

June 5 was a big day in American and world history but with the passing of Reagan it was about to become even bigger.

Reagan never planned on going into elective politics. He wrote this in his own autobiography *An American Life* and indeed, emphatically told a group of wealthy Southern California businessmen after the 1964 Goldwater campaign—the soon to be known "Kitchen Cabinet"—"no" repeatedly. To the point of seeming to be angry.[3]

He affected lives big and small and some of these stories only came out in the years after he'd left Washington. A boy in Orlando had his life saved by Reagan when he intervened as president to help the one-year-old get a liver transplant in 1985. Nineteen years later the boy, Ryan Osterblom, was appreciative, as were his parents. "I owe my son's life to him," said Karen Osterblom.[4]

"I admired him because he was genuine in showing respect to all people—whether it was a head of state or a White House butler," said Pete Souza.[5]

Reagan, while president, had established a pen-pal friendship with a young African American boy in Washington, DC.[6] The Reagans—with no fanfare—went to his house for dinner, and the writing between the two continued into Reagan's late years and only stopped when his life became enveloped and then darkened by Alzheimer's.

He touched so many and even years later many staff and friends tear up when they talk about Reagan. His young friend and aide Dennis LeBlanc, who knew the Reagans before, during, and after the White House years, can't reminisce too long without getting emotional. The same held true for so many other Reaganites.

Reagan changed conventions, especially in his own party, even in the face of great opposition from the established elites of the GOP in 1976 and 1980. The noted writer John Fund first met Reagan back in California during the gubernatorial days and was struck by how well he connected with young people. Until Reagan, young Americans had little use for the GOP and those who did were seen as nerds and losers by their peers in the 1960s and 1970s. By the 1980s, young conservatives were seen as hip and cool. Being pro-freedom and anti-communist was sophisticated. "In 1980, Democrats outnumbered Republicans among voters under 30 years old by a margin of 2 to 1. Now, the parties are virtually even," wrote E. J. Dionne in October 1988.[7]

He had an extraordinary political philosophy, one based on the Framers. His old aide Fred Ryan noted that "the only position the Constitution recognizes . . . being of greater importance than the presidency, that of private citizen."[8] Reagan believed fervently in the private, spiritual, but also joyous individual.

Another old friend George Shultz said, "I think you have to realize—he was fun."[9]

No one calls themselves a Bush Republican or a Nixon Republican but many call themselves Reagan Republicans, including those who have no idea what Reagan was about. Phyllis Schlafly said at the time of her friend's passing, "Conservative politicians will want to call themselves Reagan Republicans forever."[10]

If it hadn't been for Reagan, would there have ever been a President George Bush elected in 1988, the Gingrich Revolution of 1994, or the Bush forty-third presidency of 2000? Would Bill Clinton have ever uttered the phrase, "The era of big government is over"?[11] Would an evil empire have toppled?

By the time of his death, many of his so-called radical ideas in 1980 had become conventional thinking, including the resurrection and redefinition of American conservatism as being centered on the freedom and dignity of the private individual.

Mara Liasson of NPR, no conservative herself, still saw this. "Back then, some of the smartest thinkers in America thought communism would be around forever and that Star Wars, Reagan's plan for a missile shield around the U.S., was a nutty idea. But by 1989, the Soviet Union had collapsed, the Berlin Wall had fallen . . ."[12]

The opening of the Reagan Library came at a point in time when there were five American presidents still alive, which was rare in American history even though presidents tended to live longer than the average American male. It was not the first presidential library in California—Richard Nixon had that honor—but it was the first to host all five.

Like Nixon, whose library was turned away by Duke, Reagan saw Stanford turn up its nose at his presidential library. Plus, he didn't see the point to having his library so far away from his homes in Los Angeles and Santa Barbara. So land was donated by Donald E. Swartz and Gerald W. Blakeley just a little over an hour north of Los Angeles.[13]

Even years after his passing, his presidential library continues to host thousands more guests every year than does those of his contemporaries. Even JFK fares poorly when compared to Reagan. In 2014, the Reagan Library drew 383,000 while the Kennedy Library drew 296,000. The Nixon Library drew 85,000 and the Carter Center drew 52,000.[14]

In the days after his passing, many newspapers ran timelines of Reagan's life, but when they got to the end they simply said he announced he had Alzheimer's in 1994 and died in 2004. But in fact, there was a lot of living and a lot of action in those years between leaving the presidency and passing away. This book does not cover all of it down to the smallest details, but it does try to give the reader a better understanding of Reagan's life out of the glare of the international spotlight.

He'd gone far—farther than anyone else—from the soybean and cornfields of the flat Midwest. It was his good looks that got the young man in many a door, but his charm and voice and intelligence are what got him invited for a second cup of coffee. It was said of his voice that it "recedes at the right moments, turning mellow at points of intensity. When it wishes to be most persuasive, it hovers barely above a whisper so as to win you over by intimacy, if not by substance . . . He likes his voice, treats it like a guest . . . it was that voice that carried him out of Dixon and away from the Depression."[15]

Reagan wasn't "discovered" in Hollywood. He wanted to be an actor and worked to get an appointment with a talent agent. Serendipitously Louella Parsons, the famed and feared gossip columnist, was also from Dixon and she bent over backward to promote Ronnie and his career. Reagan was a good actor who may have become a great actor if fate had worked differently. His wholesome good looks probably worked against him a bit. Many of the big actors of the era—Humphrey Bogart, Cary Grant, Jimmy Stewart, Orson Welles, John Wayne, Clark Gable, and Henry Fonda—had some sort of distinguishing characteristic—even a nervous tic or odd way of talking or walking— that made them *them*. Reagan was just as wholesome as fresh milk. And, of course, the dark film noir of the 1950s was not his style at all. Marlon Brando and Montgomery Clift and Robert Mitchum, yes, but never Reagan.

But in fan polls, he always rated high, and in 1941 Warner Bros. said he along with Errol Flynn received more fan mail than anyone else on the studio lot.[16] And he was popular with his leading ladies, including Barbara Stanwyck, Olivia de Havilland, and Doris Day. He signed a contract with Warner Bros. for two hundred dollars per week in 1937 but at the peak he was pulling down around thirty-five hundred dollars per week. He was actually pretty good at light comedy and some of his films like *Brother Rat* became classics. He also had some good dramatic moments in *Desperate Journey* and *Storm Warning*. "Reagan was set to play opposite Ann Sheridan in a World War II melodrama called 'Everybody Goes to Rick's.' But when Ingrid Bergman suddenly was signed for the female lead, the film moved from 'B' status to a definite 'A' list position and was recast, with Reagan losing out to Bogart and the project given a new title: 'Casablanca.'"[17]

His favorite role wasn't just Drake McHugh in *King's Row* but also George Gipp in *Knute Rockne, All American*. He knew the story cold having recounted it many times as a radio broadcaster in the Midwest. When he signed with Warner in 1937, Max Arnow of the studio said Reagan would be the "next Robert Taylor."[18]

Film historian Leonard Maltin defended Reagan's film career saying, yes he began in B pictures but ended up in A movies, even if he wasn't the leading man. "Nobody sneered at him as an actor until he became a politician."[19]

When he and Jane Wyman were divorced, she complained of "extreme mental cruelty" because of his growing passion for politics and leading the Screen Actors Guild.[20] After the divorce, alone and lonely in London making a movie and complaining about the lousy British food, he made a half-hearted pass at his co-star Patricia Neal.[21]

But it was friend Jimmy Stewart who summed it up nicely as far as Nancy Reagan and her devotion to her husband—and Reagan's developing talent. "If Nancy Reagan instead of Jane Wyman had been Ronald Reagan's first wife, he never would have gone into politics.

Instead, she would have seen to it that he got all the best parts, he would have won three or four Oscars and been a real star."[22]

Part of the Reagan legacy is not only what he did but also what he didn't do. Three times in the nation's history between 1929 and 2006 the economy went into a tailspin created by Wall Street. In 1929, Herbert Hoover panicked and created new bureaucracies, issued new regulations, and generally did everything possible to make the situation even worse. In 2006, when again the felonious knights of Wall Street drove the American economy into a ditch, George Bush allowed Henry Paulson, secretary of Goldman Sachs, to cover the markers of his buddies on Wall Street to the tune of billions of dollars, sticking Middle America with the bill. Wall Street, via its enablers in the Bush administration, was bailed out for their own lawlessness and yet not one investigation by the New York attorney general's office or any of the investigatory or law enforcement agencies of Washington showed even the most minor interest. No one jumped from a building, disappointing many.

But Reagan, in 1987, was faced with his own "Black Monday" when the market lost 22 percent of its value in one afternoon. The Chicken Littles were out in force, squawking, crying, chirping, and whining that Reagan needed to do this and Reagan needed to do that and Reagan needed to panic like the rest of them. Reagan simply said, "No."

Within days, the markets calmed down and in less than a year, nearly all investors recovered their temporary losses. By not panicking like Hoover and Bush, the wiser Reagan left well enough alone and everything became well again. Bush during his panicky moments told the American people that the marketplace no longer worked. Reagan never would have said such a thing. Politicians fail and policies fail but freedom and free markets are quite another matter.

He wasn't just a successful president. When he left the California governorship, the Field Poll, famous in the Golden State's politics, showed that 71 percent of Californians thought he'd done a "fair" or "good" job.[23] And that was in 1974 when the Republican brand was about as popular as botulism. Democratic pollster Stan Greenberg said, "Ronald Reagan confounded the Democrats, not just because he won. Because the way he won."[24] The origin of the phrase "Reagan Democrat" is credited to writer Peter Goldman.

Reagan never intended on going into politics nor did anyone ever think of "grooming" him for elected office. As far as he was concerned, grooming was a part of personal hygiene.

What has been often overlooked about the Reagan campaigns in high school and college, for president of the Screen Actors Guild, for governor of California in 1966 and 1970, and then for president in 1968, 1976, 1980, and 1984 is that there was no hint or odor or suggestion of wrongdoing or deceit or cheating. In the hundreds of political contests in which he'd been involved, not one was ever anything but an honest effort by an honest man who was surrounded by honest people.

The American people always seemed to sense this in the man. In 1967, his first year as governor, he went to Orange County, California, to dedicate the new airport there and one hundred thousand people showed up. He launched his reelection campaign there in 1984 at a large outdoor park, Mile Square Regional Park, and nearly sixty thousand people squeezed in. According to the *Orange County Register*, "20,000 people were turned away." Some had shown up as early as 5:00 a.m. to attend the launch of Reagan's last campaign. A local party official had warned Mike Deaver that they could never fill it. Deaver never worried about Reagan's drawing power.[25]

It was in Orange County in 1962 where, at an event, he was challenged by a woman as to why he was still a Democrat, so he called the woman up on stage, who was a Republican Party registrar. "I'd like to change that," she told Reagan. In front of the cheering crowd, he signed the papers and switched his registration right there, according to Maureen Reagan.[26]

When the Reagans arrived in Washington, they were not

welcomed with open arms, to say the least. Generally, the women of the press corps despised Mrs. Reagan for unreasoned reasons of politics and culture. They were from California, they were conservative, they preferred California wines to French wines, and though both looked great in formal wear, they could move easily between the worlds of the well-to-do and the downtrodden; but the sophisticates of Georgetown looked down their noses at the Reagans. And while Nancy Reagan went to the socially acceptable school of Smith College, Reagan had gone to some little religious college in the Midwest called Eureka. Plus, he'd once made a living as an actor. So much for celebrating diversity.

"Political critics characterize him as banal and shallow, a mouther of right-wing platitudes, delight in recalling that he co-starred with a chimpanzee in 'Bedtime for Bonzo,'" said a prince among Washington's Beautiful People, Howell Raines of the *New York Times*.[27]

The Style section of the *Post* was even harder on Mrs. Reagan.

Within a short time, Mrs. Reagan was telling jokes in private at the expense of the media, including her personal favorite. Playing on the long established stereotypes of the *New York Times*, the *Wall Street Journal*, and the *Washington Post*, Mrs. Reagan would ask her guests if they know how each would report the impending end of the world. "The headline of the *New York Times* would say, 'World Ends Tomorrow. See page 37 A for details.' And the headline of the *Wall Street Journal* would say, 'World Ends! Stocks Plunge!' and the headline of the *Washington Post* would say, 'World Ends Tomorrow. Poor and Minorities Hardest Hit.'" Mrs. Reagan always got big laughs at her tweaking of the unctuous *Post*.

The attempted obliteration or rewriting of Ronald Reagan and his legacy continues. Many in the mass media and academia continue the assault on the legacy, attacking both Reagan personally and his accomplishments. Liberals like Congressman Jim Moran of Virginia have vowed for years to take the Gipper's name off of the airport there, and Congresswoman Dina Titus of Nevada has been working overtime to prevent a mountain there from being named after Reagan, even as dozens of mountains throughout the United States are named after other presidents.

What is remarkable about Moran and Titus is their un-remarkableness. Both came from the casting call for clichéd, knee-jerk liberals. A pattern emerges. The more unoriginal the liberal, the more calumny they heap on Reagan's legacy. Some have gone so far as to call him an occultist and during the frenzy over the fiftieth anniversary of the assassination of JFK, two enterprising conspiracy theorists suggested that because Reagan had given a speech critical of Kennedy's policies, this somehow contributed to a "right wing climate of hate" that inspired the pro-Soviet, pro-Castro, procommunist Lee Harvey Oswald to pull the trigger.

Reagan haters have falsely smeared him so many times, it bears reminding that even years after his death Reagan still stirs passions. But some more remarkable on the Left such as Mikhail Gorbachev praised Reagan even as he was bringing Gorbachev and the collectivist state of the Soviet Union to its knees.

Few can underestimate the personal relationship between Reagan and Gorbachev. When he was being briefed for the summit in Geneva, Reagan started asking Dimitri Simes about Russian soccer and Simes thought to himself, "This was not a good use of his time." But afterward, Gorbachev told his people how impressed he was with Reagan because he even knew Gorbachev's favorite players. After that meeting, Gorbachev told people he'd "underestimated" Reagan.[28] The Soviets—who know about such things—said the American media vastly underestimated Reagan's negotiating skills.

The contempt among the elites for Reagan is national and international. Millions across the globe live in freedom because of him and yet Mikhail Gorbachev was awarded the Nobel Peace Prize for losing the Cold War. This was akin to Cornwallis being given the game ball even though Washington beat him at Yorktown. However, Reagan's reward was more long lasting than a simple medallion gathering dust in a forgotten antechamber.

Reagan from a longer perspective is important. History up close is often myopic. After their tours of duty, aides such as Larry Speakes and Don Regan wrote books about Reagan that were sometimes harsh and imbalanced.

He remains one of the most misunderstood men in American politics. The week of the Reagan funeral, guest after guest on the cable and network shows fell back on the he-was-a-nice-guy-who-told-funny-jokes oratory. Of course, he had a sense of humor, best when it was aimed at himself. "Preparing me for a press conference was like reinventing the wheel. It's not true. I was around when the wheel was invented, and it was easier."[29] Years before he told an audience that Al Smith was once an actor. "What a president he would have made!"[30]

His humor goes to the deeper issue of his character and geniality though he had a temper, too, and was known to swear although almost never take the Lord's name in vain. That was another commandment he abided by. Dr. Kiron Skinner, who edited several important books of Reagan's correspondence, understood the man as well as anyone and better than most. "I think there's a political evolution between 1975 and 1979. And you see his ideas and his themes becoming increasingly more sophisticated over time. His understanding of the Cold War, of the Soviet Union, of U.S. grand strategy, of the economic challenges. He becomes increasingly more sophisticated, and thoughtful, and elegantly reductionist over those years."

Concerning his views on the Soviets she said, "They seemed like heresy at the time. Many Sovietologists disagreed straight through his presidency until the Soviet Union fell apart."[31] Reagan, she said, believed the American system was economically, technologically, and spiritually superior to the Soviet system. Part of his new sophistication was an understanding that to defeat the Soviets the United States had to defeat the Soviet system, not the Soviet people.

A former Soviet spokesman Gennady Gerasimov confirmed Dr. Skinner's views. "Reagan bolstered the U.S. military might to ruin the Soviet economy, and he achieved his goal. Reagan's SDI [Strategic Defense Initiative] was a very successful blackmail. The Soviet Union tried to keep up pace with the U.S. military buildup, but the Soviet economy couldn't endure such competition."[32]

Unlike his hero Franklin Roosevelt, Ronald Reagan was able to see the world he'd changed and made infinitely better. Roosevelt— and Winston Churchill—truly saved the world by leading the Allies in the defeat of the evil of Nazism and Japanese Imperialism. The Soviet Union was no less evil, but while FDR passed away in April 1945, just weeks before the German surrender and months before the Japanese surrender, Reagan was able to witness shortly after his presidency the fall of the Berlin Wall and the collapse of Soviet communism. The wall fell and the evil empire surrendered because of Reagan, and he knew it and was proud of it.

Ron Pearson, an official with the Young America's Foundation and lifetime Reaganite, said,

> President Reagan's love of his Rancho del Cielo shows how he was a practical man and solid conservative. His working the land shows his love of the land and the importance to him of individual responsibility from building fences on his ranch to clearing brush. For Reagan his love of his ranch was much like his love of the United States: places to preserve, protect and improve.[33]

The ranch was no act for Reagan, despite the critics. He did some of his "best thinking" there, said longtime aide Peter Hannaford.[34]

He was pro-life and said so repeatedly. He wrote an essay in 1983, "Abortion and the Conscience of the Nation," that spelled out in crisp and concise detail why he believed in life. He quoted the British philosopher Malcolm Muggeridge who said, "However low it flickers or fiercely burns, it is still a divine flame which no man dare presume to put out, be his motives ever so humane and enlightened." It was overlooked in his famous "Evil Empire" speech, but in addition to denouncing the Soviet Union, he also denounced abortion in America. After his presidency, he confided to his old friend Bill Clark that he wished he could have done more to advance the pro-life cause during his presidency.[35] Let there be no mistake: Reagan believed in the sanctity of all human life.

John Hinckley was never sentenced to death or a prison term because he successfully mounted an "innocent by reason of insanity" defense. So he was institutionalized at what was once known as the St. Elizabeth's Government Hospital for the Insane. Hinckley, thirty-four years after the attempt on Reagan's life, continually and successfully petitioned the court, which granted him more and more freedom. Hinckley was never declared cured, never showed any remorse, and to this day is still obsessed with actress Jodie Foster. Further, Hinckley was caught lying to his psychiatrists over seeing prohibited movies and was only caught because he'd been under surveillance by the Secret Service. All this in the face of letters signed previously by Mrs. Reagan asking that Hinckley not be granted parole, calling his actions "atrocious."[36]

Where does Reagan rank in the history of the American presidency? Most polls of university professors are dubious because they have become so politicized that some ranked Barack Obama higher than Reagan, even though Obama had only been in office a couple of years. When Reagan left office, a 1990 Siena Research Institute sampling of professors and historians put Reagan twenty-second out of forty, in the bottom half. But twelve years later—after the presidencies of George H. W. Bush and Bill Clinton—these same academics placed the Gipper at sixteenth, a giant leap forward.[37] Even so, this only puts him in the middle of the pack. Most academic polls are useless because the professors are hopelessly liberal and anti-intellectual.

But according to liberal historian John Patrick Diggins, Reagan was one of the four greatest presidents because like Washington, Lincoln, and FDR, Reagan saved or freed many, many people. James MacGregor Burns, a leading FDR historian, said he would put Reagan in the great or near-great category.

Presidents are often known for their famous lines—government is a "terrible master"; "endowed by their creator with certain unalienable rights"; "four score and seven years ago"; "the only thing we have to fear is fear itself"; "ask not what your country can do for you." With Reagan, there are many lines associated with him, etched deeply in the American psyche, from "you and I have a rendezvous with destiny . . ." to "community of shared values" to "there you go again" to "government is the problem" to "There is no question I am an idealist, which is another way of saying I am an American" to "Mr. Gorbechev, tear down this wall!"

As has been noted by historians, the true measure of a great president is whether the problems he was elected to solve still existed at the end of his term of office. When Reagan was elected inflation was out of control, interest rates were out of control, the economy was spiraling down, the national mood was described as a "malaise," and the West was losing the Cold War to the East.

When he left office, inflation had been all but eliminated, interest rates were low, the economy was booming, unemployment was at 5.4 percent,[38] gasoline prices had fallen dramatically, the national mood was confident once again, and the Soviet Union was in the final stages of losing the Cold War. "Ronald Reagan needs no one to sing his praises," said Antonin Scalia.[39] And yet thousands and maybe millions did.

"They wrote Truman off as a little haberdasher from Missouri and they wrote Reagan off as a B-grade actor, but in reality both have done a huge amount to lock in the freedoms that so many countless tens of millions . . . take for granted around the world," said John Anderson, Australian transportation minister.[40]

French president François Mitterrand told German chancellor Helmut Schmidt, in his best Gallic snobbery but also insight: "This is a man . . . without culture . . . But beneath the surface you find someone who isn't stupid, who has great good sense and profoundly good intentions. What he does not perceive with his intelligence, he feels by nature."[41]

On the other hand, of the American presidency Mitterrand also said it is not just a job, "it is a role."[42]

And the better ones like Ronald Reagan understood this.

CRAIG SHIRLEY

LANCASTER, VIRGINIA

# ACKNOWLEDGMENTS

First and foremost all gratitude to my wife and my best friend, Zorine, to whom I turn for all advice, all counsel, and all criticism. All I have, all I am, I owe my beloved Zorine. She and our children are my Alpha and Omega. Mitch, Taylor, Andrew, and Matt, thank you.

Thank you to Mrs. Ronald Reagan for all her support and encouragement. Her letters over the years, kind invitations to participate in Reagan Library events, and making sealed files at the Library available to me for exclusive research purposes has been both tremendous and invaluable, and I am forever grateful.

Thank you also to John Heubusch, Joanne Drake, Fred Ryan, Melissa Giller, Barbara Garonzik, Kirby Hanson, and Jennifer Mandel of the Reagan Library. They are all wonderful friends, have been very supportive, and are magnificent stewards of the Reagan legacy. I will always be in their debt.

Thank you to Dr. David Arnold, president of Eureka College, and also John Morris and Mike Murtagh of Eureka for their friendship and appreciation for the importance of Eureka to the development of

Reagan. Thank you deeply to Ron Robinson, Frank Donatelli, Andrew Coffin, Ron Pearson, and Marilyn Fisher with the Reagan Ranch, who also cherished the Reagan legacy. Also thanks to Lou Cordia, president of the Reagan Alumni Association Project. And to Mark Joseph and to Mike Reagan, thank you as well. Chuck Muth has been laboring for several years to name a mountain in Nevada after Reagan, but he still found the time to offer advice. Thank you, Chuck.

Borko Komnenovic has been at my side for years, working tirelessly on all four Reagan books as well as my other books *Citizen Newt* and *December 1941*. His dedication is only surpassed by his faith and his patriotism. He has become almost like family to Zorine and me. Thank you, Borko.

My friends Chris Ashby, Teresa Hartnett, and Bridget Matzie are always there to give valued counsel and advice. Stewart McLaurin is in a category all his own, as are Gay and Stanley Gaines, Joanne Herring, and, of course, my cherished friend and business partner Diana Banister, who is first among equals.

Lou Cannon, who is as much the official Reagan biographer as anybody, is my friend and my inspiration. Each time we speak I learn something new, and for an historian that is a wonderful thing. Newt Gingrich, to whom I often turn for frank advice, has also been generous with his time and advice. Thank you, Newt.

A special thank you goes to Candy Gadke Bhappu for her extraordinary research work at the Reagan Library and Foundation. Candy spent a week at the Library, thanks to the gracious support and help of Joanne Drake, going through box after box of confidential files, and came up with terrific heretofore unseen material for this book. I owe her a lot and not just because she is my sister-in-law, but also because Candy is the consummate professional researcher. Thank you, Candy.

Some of Reagan's men and women, including Tom Pauken, Jeff Lord, Roger Stone, Ed Meese, Jim Baker, Dick Allen, Stu Spencer, Jim Hooley, Ernie Angelo, Jim Pinkerton, Rick Reed, Pat and MJ Pizzella, Rick Ahearn, Robbie Aiken, Michele Davis, Larry and Judy Kudlow,

Mark Levin, Laura Ingraham, Tom Reed, Dennis LeBlanc, Jim Lake, Marty and Annelise Anderson, Ken Cribb, Andrew Littlefair, Gary Foster, Faith Whittlesey, Peggy Noonan, Dan Quiggle, Haley Barbour, Landon Parvin, Becky Norton Dunlop, Ed Feulner, Jim Watt, Don Hodel, Ed Rollins, David Bufkin, Alex Castellanos, Gary Hoitsma, Jim Burnley, Tony Dolan, Jim Pinkerton, Peggy Grande, Stephen Colo, Mark Tapscott, Jim and Linda Cherry, Ken Duberstein, Clark Judge, Robert Higdon, Linda Bond, Karen Roberts, Eileen Doherty, James Kuhn, Mark Weinberg, Cindy Tapscott, and others have been very supportive.

My publisher Thomas Nelson, ably manned by Brian Hampton, Kristen Parrish, Belinda Bass, Katherine Rowley, and Janene MacIvor, has been just great as have friends and writers Joel Miller, Jed Donahue, John Persinos, Jennifer Harper, Quin Hillyer, Peter Hannaford, Vic Gold, Steve Bannon, Lee Edwards, Howard Fineman, Fred Barnes, Margot Morrell, Fred Barbash, Tucker Carlson, Matt Lewis, Pat Dorinson, Tony Lee, Bill Kristol, Carl Cannon, Jen Kuznicki, and Maureen Mackey.

Also thanks to historians Jon Meacham, Doug Brinkley, Michael Beschloss, Michael Duffy, Paul Kengor, Jane Hampton Cook, Curtis Patrick, and Kiron Skinner for their friendship. American historical scholarship is better because of them.

And my family, including my mother, Barbara Shirley Eckert; my in-laws Roshan and Perin Bhappu; my brother-in-law Ross Bhappu and his and Candy's daughters, Katie and Elizabeth; my brother and sister-in-law Dan and Soonalyn Jacob and children, Jinnyn, Dan III, Corey, and Raymond; my brother-in-law Manek Bhappu; my sister and brother-in-law Rebecca and Humam Sirhal and their children Michelle, Stephanie, Laura, and Ethan; and my sister-in-law Ellen Shirley and my nephews Nathan, Eric (with his wife, Margaret, and their son Lincoln), and Todd (with his wife, Ruth, and their children Dylan, Evan, Blake, and Timothy); my step-sister and her husband, Elaine and David Eckert. Thank you.

And in no particular order but all friends, including Paul and Carol Laxalt, Tom Loringer, Adam Laxalt, James Golden, Dick and Lynn Cheney, Gary Maloney, Chris Ruddy, Brent and Norma Bozell, Shannon and Sheldon Bream, Jenny Beth Martin, James Rosen, Georgette Mosbacher, Christian Josi, Bill Pascoe, Ed Jenkins, Callista Gingrich, John Sacharanski, Chuck Todd, Torrance and Buff Harman, Rick and Sue Johnson, Bruce and Rhonda Baker, David Patten, Susan McShane, Jay Test, Mark Allen, Kevin McVicker, Dan Wilson, Tish Leonard, Linda Emery, Ryan Hughes, Mike Rudin, Mike Wagner, Kevin and Chris Kabanuk, Sam Harrod, Peter Wehner, Nikki West, Jim and Sue Scarborough, Tom Cole, Bob and Elizabeth Dole, John McLaughlin, Jim McLaughlin, Pattye and Tom Meagher, Cheri Jacobus, Mark Rosenker, Steven Scully, Neil Freeman, Richard Viguerie, Fred Barbash, Becki Donatelli, Garrett Graff, Tim Hyde, Karen Spencer, Paul Bedard, John Schmidt, Ken Rudin, John Grotta, Grover Norquist, Stuart Stevens, General Galen Jackman, Wayne and Lilly Holland, Jeff and Patty Goodman, Kyle and Stephanie Fugate, Hank and Carol Steininger, Michele Woodward, Kathleen Patten, Dr. Roger Peele, James Rosebush, Larry Cirigano, Fran Coombs, Jennifer Hickey, General P. X. Kelley, Dave and Lynn Swenson, Marc and Kristen Short, Tom and Lyn Finnigan, Jeff and Alethea Haas, Sameer and Shirley Shammas, Jim and Dana Jarvis, Chris and Peggy White, Mary Snyder, Jack and Dorian Schramm, David and Margaret Mary Howell, Charlie Pratt, Mary-Beth Cooper, John White, Fred Eckert, and Karin Andrews.

Thank you all.

# NOTES

## PREFACE

1. Ardeshir Zahedi to Nancy Reagan, Ronald Reagan Presidential Library, Simi Valley, CA.
2. *New York Times*, "Theater Directory," June 5, 2004, B14.
3. Dan Gilgoff, "Why Critics Are Still Mad As Hell," *U.S. News & World Report*, June 21, 2004, 136, no. 22, 50.
4. Steven V. Roberts, "Reagan's Final Rating Is Best of Any President Since 40's," *New York Times*, January 18, 1989, A1.
5. Thomas Carlyle, *On Heroes, Hero-worship and the Heroic in History* (London, UK: Chapman and Hall, 1840), 34.
6. Editorial, "The Reagan Legacy," *Wall Street Journal*, January 19, 1989.
7. *Blaze*, "Blaming Bush Is Getting Old; Let's Blame Reagan," March 2013, 6.
8. Dan Balz, "Reagan Events Put Race on Brief Hold," *Washington Post*, June 8, 2004, A6.
9. Wesley Pruden, "The Virulent Venom of Frustrated Rage," *Washington Times*, June 8, 2004, A4.
10. Kevin Phillips, *The Politics of Rich and Poor: Wealth and the American Electorate in the Reagan Aftermath* (New York: HarperPerennial, 1991), xvii.

11. Rich Lowry, "The New Decade of Greed," *Townhall*, June 27, 2003, http://townhall.com/columnists/richlowry/2003/06/27/the_new_decade_of_greed/page/full.

12. Pruden, "The Virulent Venom of Frustrated Rage."

13. Gilgoff, "Why Critics Are Still Mad As Hell."

14. Craig Shirley, *Rendezvous with Destiny: Ronald Reagan and the Campaign That Changed America* (Wilmington, DE: Intercollegiate Studies Institute, 2011), 593.

15. Ronald Reagan, "Remarks at Eureka College in Eureka, Illinois," February 6, 1984, www.reagan.utexas.edu/dtSearch/dtisapi6.dll?cmd=getdoc&DocId=3662&Index=*efd0fee5343905cffa0f0158ab4a751e.

16. Peter Hannaford, in discussion with the author.

17. Ronald Reagan, "Remarks at a Conservative Political Action Conference Dinner," February 26, 1982, www.presidency.ucsb.edu/ws/index.php?pid=42213.

18. Al Neuharth, "The Gipper Gave Us What Most Wanted," *USA Today*, January 20, 1989, 15A.

19. Heather Cox Richardson, "How the GOP Stopped Caring About You," *Washington Post*, September 19, 2014, www.washingtonpost.com/opinions/how-the-gop-stopped-caring-about-you-how-the-republicans-became-selfish/2014/09/17/7fe87a70-3dc5-11e4-9587-5dafd96295f0_story.html.

20. David A. Stockman, *The Triumph of Politics: How the Reagan Revolution Failed* (New York: Harper & Row, 1986), 119.

21. Shirley, *Rendezvous with Destiny*, 599.

22. *Onion*, "Doctors Say Reagan's Dementia Increasingly Hilarious," September 23, 1997, www.theonion.com/articles/doctors-say-reagans-dementia-increasingly-hilariou,945/.

23. Associated Press, "Benetton's Latest Shocker: Reagan As AIDS Victim," June 25, 1994.

24. Lawrence K. Altman, "A Recollection of Early Questions About Reagan's Health," *New York Times*, June 15, 2004, F5.

25. Martin Anderson and Annelise Anderson, *Reagan's Secret War: The Untold Story of His Fight to Save the World from Nuclear Disaster* (New York: Crown Publishers, 2009), 2.

26. Gilgoff, "Why Critics Are Still Mad As Hell."

27. Charles Krauthammer, "Scandal Time," *Washington Post*, April 12, 1987, D7.

28. Susan Page, "A 'Folklore' President Who Led a Revolution," *USA Today*, January 20, 2011, 1A.

29. Letter from Ronald Reagan to Cal Thomas, January 5, 1990, Private Collection of Cal Thomas.

30. Steve Johnson, "Coverage of Funeral Best When Anchors Kept Silent," *Chicago Tribune*, June 12, 2004, 25.

31. *Washington Post*, "Big-Ticket TV, By the Numbers," April 29, 2011, C4.

32. Lou Cannon, in discussion with the author, November 28, 2014.

33. Steven V. Roberts, "Reagan's Final Rating Is Best of Any President Since 40's," *New York Times*, January 18, 1989, A1.

34. Calvin Woodward and Jeff Wilson, "High Pageantry and Talk of the Common Touch as Capital Mourns Reagan," Associated Press, June 9, 2004.

35. Stephen Hunter, "Reagan in Hollywood, Warming Up for Bigger Roles," *Washington Post*, June 6, 2004, D1.

36. Ronald Reagan, *Reagan: A Life in Letters*, eds. Kiron K. Skinner, Annelise Anderson and Martin Anderson (New York: Free Press, 2003), 837.

37. Hunter, "Reagan in Hollywood, Warming Up for Bigger Roles."

38. Shirley, *Rendezvous with Destiny*, 337.

39. Vernon Scott, "Hollywood Considers Reagan's New Role," United Press International, November 5, 1980.

40. Ann Gerhart, "The Leading Man," *Washington Post*, June 6, 2004, D1.

41. Jay Tolson and Justin Ewers, "The Reagan Legacy," *U.S. News & World Report*, June 21, 2004, 136, no. 22, 46.

42. Ronald Reagan to Paul Michael Glaser, December 3, 1994, Ronald Reagan Presidential Library, Simi Valley, CA.

43. Steven Petrow, "'Fearbola' Reminds Me of the Early AIDS Panic," *Washington Post*, October 19, 2014, B1.

44. Merriam-Webster, www.merriam-webster.com/dictionary/infamous.

45. *Washington Times*, "Today's Talking Heads," June 12, 2004, A3.

46. Lewis L. Gould, "History in the Remaking," *Washington Post*, June 13, 2004, B1.

47. Mark Perry, "All the Presidents' Books," *Washington Post*, June 13, 2004, B3.

48. Steve Johnson, "Coverage of Funeral Best When Anchors Kept Silent," *Chicago Tribune*, June 12, 2004, 25.

49. Editorial, "The Reagan Legacy."

50. Larry Kudlow, in discussion with the author, April 10, 2014.

51. Ibid.

52. Joseph Demakis, *The Ultimate Book of Quotations* (Lulu.com, 2011), 181.

## CHAPTER 1 MORTAL COIL

1. Robert Higdon, in discussion with the author, May 30, 2014.

2. Jim Hooley, in discussion with the author, August 1, 2013.

3. Ronald Reagan, "9th Annual CPAC Conference," February 26, 1982, http://reagan2020.us/speeches/The_Agenda_is_Victory.asp.

4. Sherwin B. Nuland, *How We Die: Reflections on Life's Final Chapter* (New York: Vintage Books, 1994), 91.

5. Ronald Reagan, "Proclamation 5110—National Alzheimer's Disease Month, 1983," September 30, 1983, www.reagan.utexas.edu/archives/speeches/1983/93083D.htm.

6. Alzheimer's Association, "Seven Stages of Alzheimer's," www.alz.org/alzheimers_disease_stages_of_alzheimers.asp.

7. Lou Cannon, in discussion with the author, March 27, 2014.

8. Tom Raum, "Former President's Health Said to Decline," Associated Press, June 5, 2004.

9. Roger Cohen, "On Omaha Beach Today, Where's the Comradeship?" *New York Times*, June 5, 2004, A8.

10. Evan Berland, "9/11 Family Members to Hear Audio Tapes at Closed-Door Briefing," Associated Press, June 4, 2004.

11. Linda Deutsch, "O.J. Simpson Says the Media Have Convinced the American Public He Is Guilty," Associated Press, June 4, 2004.

12. John O'Connor, Associated Press "Blagojevich Wants to Close Pontiac Prison," *Peoria (IL) Journal Star*, June 5, 2004, A1.

13. John Chase, "Cheney Goes to Bat for Ryan," *Chicago Tribune*, June 5, 2004, 18.

14. Louis Uchitelle, "Healthy Growth of 248,000 Jobs Reported in May," *New York Times*, June 5, 2004, A6.

15. Hillel Italie, "Left, Right Appear at Chicago Book Expo," Associated Press, June 5, 2004.

16. Rebecca F. Johnson, "Last Bee Is the Best Bee for Spelling Champ," *USA Today*, June 4, 2004, 2A.

17. Archives, "Knute Rockne's 'Win One for the Gipper' Speech," University of Notre Dame, http://archives.nd.edu/research/texts/rocknespeech.htm.

18. Patti Davis, *The Long Goodbye* (New York: Knopf, 2011), x.

19. Robert Higdon, in discussion with the author, May 30, 2014.

20. Charlie LeDuff, John M. Broder and Dean Murphy, "First a Private Farewell, Then a Public Outpouring," *New York Times*, June 8, 2004, A23.

21. Ronald Reagan, "Election Eve Address 'A Vision for America,'" November 3, 1980, www.reagan.utexas.edu/archives/reference/11.3.80.html.

22. U.S. Bureau of Labor Statistics, "Unemployment Rate," accessed December 15, 2014, http://data.bls.gov/pdq/SurveyOutputServlet.

23. Jonathan Weisman, "Bush, Kerry Chasing Oil Impossible Dream?" *Washington Post*, June 4, 2004, A9.

24. *Ronald Reagan: Rendezvous with Destiny*, directed by Kevin Knoblock (Washington, DC: Citizens United Productions, 2009), DVD.

25. Ronald Reagan, "Farewell Address to the Nation," January 11, 1989, www .reagan.utexas.edu/archives/speeches/1989/011189i.htm.

26. Editorial, "The Reagan Years," *Washington Post*, January 20, 1989, A26.

27. Ibid.

28. Ronald Reagan, "Republican National Convention Acceptance Speech," July 17, 1980, www.reagan.utexas.edu/archives/reference/7.17.80.html.

29. Robert Higdon, in discussion with the author, May 30, 2014.

30. Ronald Reagan, "Remarks to Administration Officials on Domestic Policy," December 13, 1988, www.reagan.utexas.edu/archives/speeches /1988/121388a.htm.

31. Ronald Reagan, "Proclamation 5933—America Loves Its Kids Month, 1989," January 12, 1989, www.reagan.utexas.edu/archives/speeches /1989/011289d.htm.

32. Ronald Reagan, "Proclamation 5893—Fire Safety at Home Day— Change Your Clock, Change Your Battery, 1988," October 28, 1988, www.reagan.utexas.edu/archives/speeches/1988/102888d.htm.

33. Ronald Reagan, "Proclamation 5922—National Burn Awareness Week, 1989," December 8, 1988, www.reagan.utexas.edu/archives/speeches /1988/120888f.htm.

34. Barry Goldwater to Ronald Reagan, November 11, 1988, Ronald Reagan Presidential Library, Simi Valley, CA.

35. Ronald Reagan, *Reagan: A Life in Letters*, eds. Kiron K. Skinner, Annelise Anderson and Martin Anderson (New York: Free Press, 2003), 695.

36. Ronald Reagan Presidential Foundation, *Ronald Reagan: 100 Years: Official Centennial Edition* (New York: Harper Design, 2010), 197.

37. Peter Schifando and Jonathan Joseph, *Entertaining at the White House with Nancy Reagan* (New York: Harper Collins, 2007), ix.

38. Gerald F. Seib and Dennis Farney, "GOP Conservatives, After 8 Years in Ascendancy, Brood Over Lost Opportunities, Illusory Victories," *Wall Street Journal*, August 17, 1988.

39. Ronald Reagan, "Remarks to Administration Officials on Domestic Policy," December 13, 1988, www.reagan.utexas.edu/archives/speeches /1988/121388a.htm.

40. Jeraldine Saunders, "Today's Horoscope," *Washington Post*, June 4, 2004, C11.

41. Jim Hooley, in discussion with the author, August 1, 2013.

42. Ibid.

43. Ibid.

44. Ibid.

45. Ibid.

46. Ibid.

47. Ronald Reagan, *The Reagan Diaries*, ed. Douglas Brinkley (New York: Harper Collins, 2007), 692.

48. Ibid.

49. Jim Hooley, in discussion with the author, August 1, 2013.

50. Edmund Morris, *Dutch: A Memoir of Ronald Reagan* (New York: Random House, 1999), 652.

51. Jim Hooley, in discussion with the author, August 1, 2013.

52. Ibid.

53. James Kuhn, in discussion with the author, September 3, 2014.

54. Elisabeth Bumiller, "Between 2 First Families, A Complicated Rapport," *New York Times*, June 9, 2004, A1.

55. Jim Hooley, in discussion with the author, August 1, 2013.

56. Ibid.

57. Fred Ryan, in discussion with the author, July 31, 2013.

58. Lou Cannon, in discussion with the author, March 27, 2014.

59. Lou Cannon, "Bittersweet Trip for the Reagans," *Washington Post,* January 21, 1989, A1.

60. Jim Hooley, in discussion with the author, August 1, 2013.

61. Thomas Ferraro, United Press International, January 20, 1989.

62. Laurie Becklund, "Reagans Easing Into Private Life As Californians," *Los Angeles Times,* November 19, 1988, 1.

63. Ferraro, UPI, January 20, 1989.

64. Ibid.

65. Jim Hooley, in discussion with the author, August 1, 2013.

66. Ibid.

67. Ibid.

68. Ibid.

69. Ronald Reagan, "Announcement of Alzheimer's Disease," November 5, 1994, http://reagan2020.us/speeches/announcement_of_alzheimers.asp.

70. Ronald Reagan, *The Reagan Diaries,* ed. Douglas Brinkley (New York: HarperCollins, 2007), 693.

71. Mike Allen, "Bush 'Willing to Cooperate' with Leak Probe," *Washington Post,* June 4, 2004, A11.

72. Steven Ginsberg, "Bag Screening to Start in Union Station Lines," *Washington Post,* June 4, 2004, B1.

73. Steven Pearlstein, "How Accenture Seized Tomorrow," *Washington Post,* June 4, 2004, E1.

74. Nell Henderson, "Price Pinch Unlikely to Halt Economic Growth," *Washington Post,* June 4, 2004, E1.

75. United Press International, "Rumsfeld: Al-Qaida active in Iraq," June 5, 2004.

76. Thomas Childers, "Monumental Struggle," *Washington Post,* June 6, 2004, T10.

77. Edmund Morris, "5 Myths about Ronald Reagan," *Washington Post,* February 6, 2011, B2.

78. Morris, *Dutch,* 210.

79. Ira R. Allen, "Reagan Stump Speech Taking Shape," United Press International, October 22, 1983.

80. Michael K. Deaver, *A Different Drummer: My Thirty Years with Ronald Reagan* (New York: HarperCollins, 2001), 11–12.

81. Fred Ryan, in discussion with the author, July 31, 2013.

82. Ronald Reagan Presidential Foundation, *Ronald Reagan: 100 Years: Official Centennial Edition* (New York: Harper Design, 2010), 226.

83. Ibid., 221.

84. Fred Ryan, in discussion with the author, July 31, 2013.

85. Dana Priest and Walter Pincus, "Tenet Resigns As CIA Director," *Washington Post*, June 4, 2004, A1.

86. Evelyn Nieves, "'Take Back America' Aims at Left," *Washington Post*, June 4, 2004, A8.

87. Colman McCarthy, "Reagan: Not His Age, His Staleness," *Washington Post*, January 20, 1980, E5.

88. Joel Achenbach, "Progressives, Preparing to Advance in One Direction," *Washington Post*, June 4, 2004, C1.

89. *Washington Post*, "Nation In Brief," June 4, 2004, A7.

90. *Washington Post*, "Metro In Brief," June 4, 2004, B3.

91. Neil Irwin, "Businesses Look to Slow Rising Health Care Costs," *Washington Post*, June 4, 2004, E3.

92. *New York Times*, "Weather Report," June 5, 2004, B16.

93. Stuart Spencer, in discussion with the author, February 4, 2014.

94. Special Report, ABC News Transcripts, June 5, 2004.

95. Reagan Library Tour, C-SPAN, December 7, 1999, www.c-span.org /video/?153719–1/reagan-library-tour.

96. Tom Raum, "Former President Reagan's Health Said to Decline," Associated Press, June 5, 2004.

97. Robert Jablon, "Former President Reagan's Health Said to Be in Decline; Children at Bedside," Associated Press, June 5, 2004.

98. Robert Higdon, in discussion with the author, May 30, 2014.

99. Patti Davis, *The Lives Our Mothers Leave Us: Prominent Women Discuss the Complex, Humorous, and Ultimately Loving Relationships They Have with Their Mothers* (New York: Hay House, 2009), 10.

## CHAPTER 2 THE DEATH OF THE HIRED MAN

1. John Barletta, *Riding With Reagan: From the White House to the Ranch* (New York: Citadel, 2005), 208.

2. Patti Davis, *The Long Goodbye* (New York: Knopf, 2011), xii.

3. Ronald Reagan, "Farewell Address to the Nation," January 11, 1989, www.reagan.utexas.edu/archives/speeches/1989/011189i.htm.

4. Ed Meese, in discussion with the author.

5. Fred Ryan, in discussion with the author, July 31, 2013.

6. Fred Ryan, in discussion with the author, January 17, 2014.

7. Joanne Drake, in discussion with the author, January 17, 2014.

8. Peggy Grande, in discussion with the author, July 2, 2012.

9. Mark Weinberg, in discussion with the author, April 4, 2014.

10. Fred Ryan, in discussion with the author, July 31, 2013.

11. Ibid.

12. Ibid.

13. CBS News Special Report, "Death of Former President Ronald Reagan," CBS News Transcripts, June 5, 2004.

14. Fred Ryan, in discussion with the author, March 5, 2014.

15. CBS News Special Report, "Death of Former President Ronald Reagan," CBS News Transcripts, June 5, 2004.

16. Laurie Becklund, "Reagan Turns Raconteur at Jaycee Lunch," *Los Angeles Times*, July 11, 1991, B1.

17. www.dailymail.co.uk/news/article-2649948/Reagan-set-tone-D-Day -observances.html.

18. Ronald Reagan, "Message to the Senate Transmitting a Protocol to the 1949 Geneva Conventions," January 29, 1987, www.reagan.utexas.edu /archives/speeches/1987/012987b.htm.

19. Janie McCauley, "Rockies 11, Giants 2," Associated Press, June 5, 2004.

20. Confidential interview with the author.

21. Special Report, ABC News Transcripts, June 5, 2004.

22. Anick Jesdanun, "CNN Blames Human Error for Releasing Web Mock-Ups of Obits," Associated Press, April 17, 2003.

23. Special Report, ABC News Transcripts, June 5, 2004.

24. Patti Davis, *The Lives Our Mothers Leave Us: Prominent Women Discuss the Complex, Humorous, and Ultimately Loving Relationships They Have with Their Mothers* (New York: Hay House, 2009), 5.

25. Robert Jablon, "Reagan's Children Gather at His Bedside," Associated Press, June 5, 2004.

26. CNN Breaking News, "Former President Ronald Reagan Dies at Family Estate in California," CNN, June 5, 2004.

27. Sheldon Alberts, "Ronald Reagan Dead at 93; Beloved Former President and Conservative Icon Succumbs to Alzheimer's Disease," *Edmonton Journal* (Alberta), June 6, 2004, A1.

28. Davis, *The Long Goodbye*, 184–193.

29. Ibid., 192.

30. Ibid., 191–193.

31. Paula Zahn Now, "Ronald Reagan Dies," CNN, June 5, 2004.

32. Davis, *The Long Goodbye*, 192.

33. Special Report, ABC News Transcripts, June 5, 2004.

34. Jeff Wilson and Terence Hunt, "Ronald Reagan, 40th President of United States, Dies at Age 93," Associated Press, June 5, 2004.

35. Jim Hooley, in discussion with the author, August 1, 2013.

36. Memorandum by Duke Blackwood, "Entire Timeline Done in Pacific Standard Time," May 25, 2004, 20, Ronald Reagan Presidential Library, Simi Valley, CA.

37. Fred Ryan, in discussion with the author, March 5, 2014.

38. Ron Reagan, *My Father at 100: A Memoir* (New York: Penguin, 2011), 125.

39. William F. Buckley Jr., *The Reagan I Knew* (New York: Basic Books, 2008), 4–5.

40. Joanne Drake, in discussion with the author, January 17, 2014.

41. Ibid.

42. Michael K. Deaver, *A Different Drummer: My Thirty Years with Ronald Reagan* (New York: HarperCollins, 2001), 222.

43. Fred Ryan, in discussion with the author, March 5, 2014.

44. Special Report, ABC News Transcripts, June 5, 2004.

45. CNN Breaking News, "Former President Ronald Reagan Dies at Family Estate in California," CNN, June 5, 2004.

46. John Aloysius Farrell, "Reagan's 'Revolution' Left Enduring Legacy," *Denver Post*, June 6, 2004, A1.

47. Nancy Reagan, *I Love You, Ronnie: The Letters of Ronald Reagan to Nancy Reagan* (New York: Random House, 2000), 112.

48. Ibid., 2.

49. Ronald Reagan, *Reagan: A Life in Letters*, eds. Kiron K. Skinner, Annelise Anderson and Martin Anderson (New York: Free Press, 2003), 822.

50. Special Report, ABC News Transcripts, June 5, 2004.

51. Mike Feinsilber, "Reagan: Champion of Conservative Politics," Associated Press, June 5, 2004.

52. Special Report, ABC News Transcripts, June 5, 2004.

53. Ronald Reagan, *The Reagan Diaries*, ed. Douglas Brinkley (New York: HarperCollins, 2007), 149.

54. Tom Curry, "Ronald Reagan, 1911–2004," NBCNews.com, June 5, 2004,

www.nbcnews.com/id/3638299/ns/us_news-the_legacy_of_ronald
_reagan/t/ronald-reagan—/#.VCoWjhbisSs.

55. Ibid.

56. Ibid.

57. Special Report, ABC News Transcripts, June 5, 2004.

58. NPR News Special Report, "Reagan Revolution," National Public Radio, June 5, 2004.

59. Fred Ryan, in discussion with the author, July 31, 2013.

60. Ibid.

61. Ibid.

62. Ronald Reagan, "Announcement of Alzheimer's Disease," November 5, 1994, http://reagan2020.us/speeches/announcement_of_alzheimers.asp.

63. Fred Ryan, in discussion with the author, July 31, 2013.

64. Ibid.

65. Dr. Oliver H. Beahrs, Dr. Leslie Weiner, Dr. James R. Blake, General John Hutton, Dr. Ronald Petersen, "Physicians' Explanation of Ronald Reagan's Alzheimer's Diagnosis," www.reagan.utexas.edu/archives/reference /alzheimerphys.html.

66. *People*, "The Long Goodbye," December, 4, 2003, www.people.com /people/article/0,628278,00.html.

67. Brian Krans, "Study: Concussions May Lead to Alzheimer's Brain Plaques," *Healthline*, December 26, 2013, www.healthline.com/health -news/mental-concussions-linked-to-alzheimers-plaques-122613.

68. John Barletta, *Riding with Reagan: From the White House to the Ranch* (New York: Citadel, 2005), 235.

69. Jamie Tarabay, "Past and Present World Leaders Pay Tribute to Ronald Reagan," Associated Press, June 5, 2004.

70. *Santa Barbara (CA) News-Press*, "California Forecast," June 5, 2004, B14.

71. Associated Press, "North Carolinians Mourn the Loss of Reagan," June 5, 2004.

72. Billy Graham to Nancy Reagan, June 5, 2004, Ronald Reagan Presidential Library, Simi Valley, CA.

73. Associated Press, "North Carolinians Mourn the Loss of Reagan."

74. Special Report, ABC News Transcripts, June 5, 2004.

75. CBS News Special Report, "Death of Former President Ronald Reagan," CBS News Transcripts, June 5, 2004.

76. Fred Ryan, in discussion with the author, March 5, 2014.

77. Associated Press, "Bush Comments on Reagan Death," June 5, 2004.

78. Jerry Harkavy, "Bush: Former Political Opponent Became a Good Friend," Associated Press, June 5, 2004.

79. CNN Breaking News, "Reagan Dies," CNN, June 5, 2004.

80. Harkavy, "Bush: Former Political Opponent Became a Good Friend."

81. Special Report, ABC News Transcripts, June 5, 2004.

82. Elisabeth Bumiller, "Between 2 First Families, A Complicated Rapport," *New York Times*, June 9, 2004, A21.

83. *Peoria (IL) Journal Star*, "Former President, Tampico Native Never Abandoned Eureka College Roots," June 6, 2004, A1.

84. Ibid.

85. Peter Slevin, "In Illinois, Memories of a Favorite Son," *Washington Post*, June 7, 2004, A8.

86. Special Report, ABC News Transcripts, June 5, 2004.

87. Fred Ryan, in discussion with the author, March 5, 2014, and July 31, 2013.

88. Special Report, ABC News Transcripts, June 5, 2004.

89. Ed Meese, in discussion with the author, March 19, 2014.

90. Special Report, ABC News Transcripts, June 5, 2004.

91. Ibid.

92. Ibid.

93. Ibid.

94. Ibid.

95. Ibid.

96. William Shakespeare, *The Tragedy of Hamlet, Prince of Denmark*, Act 2 Scene 2, in Isaac Reed, ed., *The Plays of William Shakespeare* (Boston: Charles Willliams, 1813).

97. Ronald Reagan, *An American Life: The Autobiography* (New York: Simon and Schuster, 1990), 393.

98. Davis, *The Long Goodbye*, 179.

99. Special Report, ABC News Transcripts, June 5, 2004.

100. Paula Zahn Now, "Ronald Reagan Dies," CNN, June 5, 2004.

101. Ibid.

102. David Stockman, *The Triumph of Politics: Why the Reagan Revolution Failed* (New York: Harper & Low, 1986), 329.

103. Lou Cannon, "Now the Real St. Ronald vs. the Rhetorical Dragon," *Washington Post*, February 18, 1981, A4.

104. *Paula Zahn Now*, "Ronald Reagan Dies," CNN, June 5, 2004.

105. Craig Shirley, *December 1941: 31 Days That Changed America and Saved the World* (Nashville: Thomas Nelson, 2011), 10–11.

106. Robert D. Novak, *The Prince of Darkness: 50 Years Reporting in Washington* (New York: Crown Forum, 2007), 270.

107. Breaking News, "Former President Ronald Reagan Dies at Family Estate in California," CNN, June 5, 2004.

108. Bosley Crowther, "Kings Row (1941) The Screen; 'Kings Row,' With Ann Sheridan and Claude Rains, a Heavy, Rambling Film, Has Its First Showing Here at the Astor," *New York Times*, February 3, 1942, www.nytimes.com /movie/review?res=9903E2DE143BE33BBC4B53DFB4668389659EDE.

109. *Las Vegas Review-Journal*, June 6, 2004.

110. *Paula Zahn Now*, "Ronald Reagan Dies," CNN, June 5, 2004.

111. Ibid.

112. Special Report, ABC News Transcripts, June 5, 2004.

113. Fred Ryan, in discussion with the author, July 31, 2013.

114. Special Report, ABC News Transcripts, June 5, 2004.

115. Ibid.

116. CNN Breaking News, "Former President Ronald Reagan Dies at Family Estate in California," CNN, June 5, 2004.

117. Elisabeth Bumiller and Elizabeth Becker, "Down to the Last Detail, a Reagan-Style Funeral," *New York Times*, June 8, 2004, A1.

118. Ronald Reagan, "Address Before a Joint Session of the Congress Reporting on the State of the Union," January 26, 1982, www.presidency .ucsb.edu/ws/?pid=42687.

119. CNN *NewsNight with Aaron Brown*, "Ronald Reagan Dies," CNN, June 5, 2004.

120. Elisabeth Bumiller, Carl Hulse, Todd S. Purdum and Sheryl Gay Stolberg, "Reagan Team, a Bit Grayer, Gathers Again," *New York Times*, June 10, 2004, A1.

121. Mark Rosenker, in discussion with the author, February 26, 2014.

122. CNN Breaking News, "Reagan Dies," CNN, June 5, 2004.

123. Rick Orlov, "State Politicians Fondly Remember 'Humble Patriot,'" *San Bernardino (CA) Sun*, June 5, 2004.

## CHAPTER 3 TO BURY REAGAN

1. University of California, Berkeley, "Life Expectancy in the USA, 1900–98," http://demog.berkeley.edu/~andrew/1918/figure2.html.

2. Ronald Reagan, "Address at Republican National Convention," CNN, August 17, 1992, www.cnn.com/SPECIALS/2004/reagan/stories/speech.archive/rnc.speech.html.

3. Michael Barone, "He Stands in History," *U.S. News & World Report*, June 21, 2004, 136, no. 22, 59.

4. Alessandra Stanley, "Once Again, Reagan Lands the Big Television Moment," *New York Times*, June 7, 2004, A18.

5. Memorandum by Duke Blackwood, "Entire Timeline Done in Pacific Standard Time," May 25, 2004, 20, Ronald Reagan Presidential Library, Simi Valley, CA.

6. Chris Field, "Sunday's Front-Page Reagan Headlines," *Human Events Online*, June 7, 2004.

7. Diane Scarponi, "Naval Submarine Jimmy Carter Christened at Connecticut Shipyard," Associated Press, June 5, 2004.

8. *Washington Times*, "Friends, Foes Remember," June 6, 2004, A5.

9. Editorial, "Ronald Reagan, Revolutionary," *Chicago Tribune*, June 6, 2004, 8.

10. Harold Meyerson, "Class Warrior," *Washington Post*, June 9, 2004, A21.

11. Karen Rubin, "'Dutch' Made Impression on Locals, Great and Small," *Pasadena (CA) Star-News*, June 5, 2004.

12. Special Report, ABC News Transcripts, June 5, 2004.

13. Jeff Wilson, "Ronald Reagan, 40th President of United States, Dies at Age 93," Associated Press, June 6, 2004.

14. Rick Ahearn, in discussion with the author, March 25, 2014; Fred Ryan, in discussion with the author, July 31, 2013.

15. Jim Hooley, in discussion with the author, August 1, 2013.

16. Memorandum by Duke Blackwood, "Entire Timeline Done in Pacific Standard Time," May 25, 2004, 2, 5, 6, 11, Ronald Reagan Presidential Library, Simi Valley, CA.

17. Ibid., 5–6.

18. Ibid., 11.

19. Fred Ryan, in discussion with the author, March 5, 2014.

20. Memorandum by Duke Blackwood, "Entire Timeline Done in Pacific Standard Time," May 25, 2004, 8–9, 15, Ronald Reagan Presidential Library, Simi Valley, CA.

21. Jim Hooley, in discussion with the author, August 1, 2013.

22. Ibid.

23. Patti Davis, *Angels Don't Die: My Father's Gift of Faith* (New York: HarperCollins, 1995), 9, 11.

24. Tazewell Shepard Jr., *John F. Kennedy: Man of the Sea* (New York: W. Morrow, 1965), 13.

25. Davis, *Angels Don't Die*, 12.

26. Larry J. Sabato, *The Kennedy Half-Century: The Presidency, Assassination, and Lasting Legacy of John F. Kennedy* (New York: Bloomsbury, 2013), 362.

27. Craig Shirley, *Rendezvous with Destiny: Ronald Reagan and the Campaign That Changed America* (Wilmington, DE: Intercollegiate Studies Institute, 2011), 579.

28. United Press International, December 8, 1987.

29. Michael McGough, "Reagan to Have State Funeral, Private Burial," *Toledo (OH) Blade*, June 7, 2004, A1.

30. United Press International, "Ronald Reagan, 40th U.S. President, Dies," June 5, 2004.

31. Jeff Wilson, "Post–White House Reagan: The Gipper Gradually Faded from Public Eye," Associated Press, June 6, 2004.

32. Michael Kilian, "Family Life Full of Joy, Frustration for Reagans," *Chicago Tribune*, June 6, 2004, 10.

33. Michael K. Deaver, *A Different Drummer: My Thirty Years with Ronald Reagan* (New York: HarperCollins, 2001), 212–214.

34. United Press International, "Ronald Reagan, 40th U.S. President, Dies."

35. Jeff Wilson, "Nancy at Reagan's Side Until the End," Associated Press, June 5, 2004.

36. Betsy Streisand, "Memories of a Friend in the Park," *U.S. News & World Report*, June 21, 2004, 136, no. 22, 57.

37. John Barletta, *Riding with Reagan: From the White House to the Ranch* (New York: Citadel, 2005), 217.

38. Ibid.

39. *Paula Zahn Now*, "Ronald Reagan Dies," CNN, June 5, 2004.

40. CBS News Special Report, "Death of Former President Ronald Reagan," CBS News Transcripts, June 5, 2004.

41. Larry King Live, "Friends and Family Pay Tribute to Ronald Reagan Ahead of His 89th Birthday," CNN, February 4, 2000.

42. Lou Cannon, in discussion with the author, March 27, 2014.

43. Lewis Carroll, *Alice's Adventures in Wonderland* (Boston: Lee and Shepard, 1920), 19.

44. Lou Cannon, *President Reagan: The Role of a Lifetime* (New York: Public Affairs, 1999, 2000), 193.

45. Edmund Morris, *Dutch: A Memoir of Ronald Reagan* (New York: Random House, 1999), 402, 395, 670.

46. Confidential interview with the author.

47. John Podhoretz, "'Dutch' Is No Treat: So-Called Reagan Bio Is a Fictionalized Flight of Foolishness," *New York Post*, October 3, 1999, http://nypost.com/1999/10/03/dutch-is-no-treat-so-called-reagan-bio-is -a-fictionalized-flight-of-foolishness/.

48. *Washington Post*, "Once Upon a Time . . . From Beginning to Happily Ever After, the Reagan Years," January 17, 1989, B1.

49. Lyn Nofziger, in discussion with the author; Peter Hannaford, in discussion with the author.

50. Morris, *Dutch*, 587.

51. John O'Sullivan, "Not the Authorized Biography," *National Review*, October 25, 1999, www.nationalreview.com/articles/210947/not -authorized-biography-john-osullivan.

52. CBS News Special Report, "Death of Former President Ronald Reagan," CBS News Transcripts, June 5, 2004.

53. Morris, *Dutch*, 587.

54. Special Report, ABC News Transcripts, June 5, 2004.

55. CNN Breaking News, "Former President Ronald Reagan Dies at Family Estate in California," CNN, June 5, 2004.

56. Ed Rollins, in discussion with the author, May 2, 2014.

57. Ibid.

58. Special Report, ABC News Transcripts, June 5, 2004.

59. Ronald Reagan Presidential Foundation and Library, "Nancy Meets Ronald Reagan 1944–1966," www.reaganfoundation.org/details_t .aspx?p=PE40002PGE&tx=1189.

60. Special Report, ABC News Transcripts, June 5, 2004.

61. Jody Rosen, "A Century Later, She's Still Red Hot," *New York Times*, August 30, 2009, 1.

62. Ronald Reagan Presidential Foundation and Library, "Nancy Meets Ronald Reagan 1944–1966," www.reaganfoundation.org/details_t .aspx?p=PE40002PGE&tx=1189.

63. Special Report, ABC News Transcripts, June 5, 2004.

64. *Hellcats of the Navy*, directed by Nathan Juran (1957).

65. Special Report, ABC News Transcripts, June 5, 2004.

66. Lou Cannon, "Actor, Governor, President, Icon," *Washington Post*, June 6, 2004, A28.

67. General Electric Company, "A Legacy Of Progress," www.youtube.com /watch?v=GPfZ74TesSc.

68. *New York Times*, "About Politics: The Battle of Campaign Quotations Is On," July 24, 1980, A17.

69. Gerald C. Lubenow, Martin Kasindorf, Frank Maier and James Doyle, "Ronald Reagan Up Close," *Newsweek*, July 21, 1980, 36.

70. Michael Reagan, "Ronald Reagan's Son Remembers the Day When GE Fired His Dad," *Investors Business Daily*, February 4, 2011, http://news .investors.com/ibd-editorials-viewpoint/020411–562237-ronald-reagans -son-remembers-the-day-when-ge-fired-his-dad.htm.

71. *New York Times*, "About Politics: The Battle of Campaign Quotations Is On," July 24, 1980, A17.

72. Ibid.

73. Ibid.

74. CBS News Special Report, "Death of Former President Ronald Reagan," CBS News Transcripts, June 5, 2004.

75. Ibid.

76. Ken Kusmer, "Reagan Remembered as Giant Whose Policies Resounded Strongly Here," Associated Press, June 7, 2004.

77. Ronald Reagan, "Address at Commencement Exercises at the University of Notre Dame," May 17, 1981, www.reagan.utexas.edu/archives/speeches /1981/51781a.htm.

78. Ronald Reagan, "Remarks at the Unveiling of the Knute Rockne Commemorative Stamp at the University of Notre Dame in Indiana," March 9, 1988, www.reagan.utexas.edu/archives/speeches/1988 /030988a.htm.

79. Jan Dennis, "Reagan's Hometown Remembers, Mourns 'Dutch' Reagan," Associated Press, June 5, 2004.

80. Associated Press, "Reaction to the Death of Former President Ronald Reagan," June 5, 2004.

81. Del Quentin Wilber, *Rawhide Down: The Near Assassination of Ronald Reagan* (New York: Macmillan, 2011), 223.

82. Jon Margolis, "Reagan Revolution Stronger Now than During Presidency," *Chicago Tribune*, June 6, 2004, C1.

83. Ronald Reagan, *Reagan, In His Own Hand: The Writings of Ronald Reagan That Reveal His Revolutionary Vision for America*, eds. Kiron K. Skinner, Annelise Anderson and Martin Anderson (New York: The Free Press, 2001), xiii.

84. Ronald Reagan, *Reagan's Path to Victory: The Shaping of Ronald Reagan's Vision: Selected Writings*, eds. Kiron K. Skinner, Annelise Anderson and Martin Anderson (New York: The Free Press, 2004), 7.

85. John Barletta, *Riding With Reagan: From the White House to the Ranch* (New York: Citadel, 2005), 202.

86. Associated Press, "Missouri Republicans Honor Reagan," June 5, 2004.

87. Samira Jafari, "Alabama's GOP Leaders Credit Reagan for Democrats' Shift to GOP," Associated Press, June 5, 2004.

88. Daily News Wire Services, "World Leaders React to Loss," *San Bernardino (CA) Sun*, June 5, 2004.

89. Karen Rubin, "'Dutch' Made Impression on Locals, Great and Small," *Pasadena (CA) Star-News*, June 5, 2004.

90. Thomas M. DeFrank, Maggie Haberman and Jere Hester, "After a Long Struggle, Gipper Is Dead at 93: Former President Loses Fierce Battle with Alzheimer's," *Daily News (NY)*, June 6, 2004, 2.

91. Harry Levins, "The Great Communicator Ronald Reagan 1911–2004," *St. Louis Post-Dispatch*, June 6, 2004, A1.

92. *Las Vegas Review-Journal*, June 6, 2004.

93. Confidential interview with the author.

94. Paul Laxalt, "Laxalt: Nice Guys Can Finish First," *Human Events*, June 11, 2004, http://humanevents.com/2004/06/11/emreagan-tribute-exclusiveembrlaxalt-nice-guys-can-finish-first/.

95. CNN Breaking News, "Former President Ronald Reagan Dies at Family Estate in California," CNN, June 5, 2004.

96. Martin Weil, "Reagan's Legacy Honored at D.C. Vigil," *Washington Post*, June 7, 2004, B6.

97. Associated Press, "An Outpouring of Emotion to the News of Ronald Reagan's Death," June 5, 2004.

98. Associated Press, "Senators, Governor, Ex-President Praise Reagan's Leadership," June 5, 2004.

99. David Ammons, "State Leaders Mourn Loss of 40th President," Associated Press, June 5, 2004.

100. Special Report, ABC News Transcripts, June 5, 2004.

101. CNN Breaking News, "Former President Ronald Reagan Dies at Family Estate in California," CNN, June 5, 2004.

102. Associated Press, "Reaction to the Death of Former President Ronald Reagan," June 5, 2004.

103. David S. Broder, "Reagan Wounded by Assailant's Bullet," *Washington Post*, March 31, 1981, A1.

104. Elisabeth Bumiller, "Between 2 First Families, A Complicated Rapport," *New York Times*, June 9, 2004, 21.

105. Associated Press, "An Outpouring of Emotion to the News of Ronald Reagan's Death," June 5, 2004.

106. CBS News Special Report, "Death of Former President Ronald Reagan," CBS News Transcripts, June 5, 2004.

107. Mike Feinsilber, "Reagan: Champion of Conservative Politics," Associated Press, June 5, 2004.

108. CNN Breaking News, "Ronald Reagan Dies at 93," CNN, June 5, 2004.

109. CNN Breaking News, "Reagan Dies," CNN, June 5, 2004.

110. CNN Breaking News, "Former President Ronald Reagan Dies at Family Estate in California," CNN, June 5, 2004.

111. NPR News Special Report, "Hans Johnson of the Washington Post Discusses Ronald Reagan," National Public Radio, June 5, 2004.

112. Cannon, "Actor, Governor, President, Icon."

113. David E. Hoffman, "Hastening an End to the Cold War," *Washington Post*, June 6, 2004, A1.

114. Cannon, "Actor, Governor, President, Icon."

115. Doug Willis, "As Governor, Reagan Honed Conservative Message, Political Skills," Associated Press, June 6, 2004.

116. Marilyn Berger, "Ronald Reagan Dies at 93; Fostered Cold-War Might and Curbs on Government," *New York Times*, June 6, 2004, 1.

117. CNN Breaking News, "Reagan Dies," CNN, June 5, 2004.

118. Jafari, "Alabama's GOP Leaders Credit Reagan for Democrats' Shift to GOP."

119. Ronald Reagan, "Acceptance of the Republican Nomination for President," July 17, 1980, www.cnn.com/SPECIALS/2004/reagan/stories/speech .archive/nomination.html.

120. Peter Roff, "UPI's White House Watch," United Press International, June 11, 2004.

121. Special Report, ABC News Transcripts, June 5, 2004.

122. Suzanne C. Ryan, "Amid heat, CBS Pulls Reagan Film," *BostonGlobe*,

November 5, 2003, www.boston.com/news/nation/articles/2003/11/05
/amid_heat_cbs_pulls_reagan_film/?page=full.

123. Polly Anderson, "Reagan's Film Career Included Comedy 'Bedtime for Bonzo,' Searing Drama 'King's Row,'" Associated Press, June 5, 2004.

124. Ronald Reagan, "A Time for Choosing," October 27, 1964, www.reagan.utexas.edu/archives/reference/timechoosing.html.

125. Jeff Wilson and Terence Hunt, "Ronald Reagan, 40th President of United States, Dies at Age 93," Associated Press, June 5, 2004.

126. Berger, "Ronald Reagan Dies at 93; Fostered Cold-War Might and Curbs on Government."

127. Wilson, Hunt, "Ronald Reagan, 40th President of United States, Dies at Age 93."

128. Ibid.

129. Ted Anthony, "Mourning in America: The Great Communicator Remembered," Associated Press, June 5, 2004.

130. Special Report, ABC News Transcripts, June 5, 2004.

131. Kenneth T. Walsh, "An American Story," U.S. News & World Report, June 21, 2004, 136, no. 22, 34.

132. Ronald Reagan, The Reagan Diaries, ed. Douglas Brinkley (New York: HarperCollins, 2007), 227, 512.

133. New York Times, "The 1994 Campaign: Virginia; Mrs. Reagan Denounces Oliver North on Iran Affair," October 29, 1994, www.nytimes.com/1994/10/29/us/the-1994-campaign-virginia-mrs-reagan-denounces-oliver-north-on-iran-affair.html.

134. Marc Lavine, "Former US President Reagan Falls to Ravages of Alzheimer's," Agence France Presse, June 6, 2004.

135. Jamie Tarabay, "Past and Present World Leaders Pay Tribute to Ronald Reagan," Associated Press, June 5, 2004.

136. Daily News Wire Services, "World Leaders React to Loss," San Bernardino (CA) Sun, June 5, 2004.

137. Vladimir Isachenkov, "Reagan Remembered for Ending Soviet Rule," Associated Press, June 5, 2004.

138. Marie Horrigan, "Ronald Reagan, 40th U.S. President, Dies," United Press International, June 5, 2004.

139. Gay Gaines, in discussion with the author.

140. Fred Ryan, in discussion with the author, March 5, 2014.

141. World News Tonight, ABC News Transcripts, November 4, 1983.

142. Scott Lindlaw, "Bush Says Reagan Helped Save the World," Associated Press, June 5, 2004.

143. Ronald Reagan Presidential Library, "Air Force One 27000 Historical Fact Sheet," Simi Valley, CA.

144. Ronald Reagan Presidential Library, "Entrepreneur Boone Pickens Donates Ten Million Dollars to Reagan Library," Simi Valley, CA.

145. Neil A. Lewis and Eric Schmitt, "Lawyers Decided Bans on Torture Didn't Bind Bush," *New York Times*, June 8, 2004, A1.

146. Robert Burns, "Guard, Reserve Death Toll Rising in Iraq," Associated Press, June 8, 2004.

147. Lawrence Van Gelder, "Film Opening Postponed," *New York Times*, June 8, 2004, E2.

148. Mike Feinsilber, "Reagan: Champion of Conservative Politics," Associated Press, June 5, 2004.

149. Bernadine Healy, M.D., "A Patron Saint," *U.S. News & World Report*, June 21, 2004, 136, no. 22, 56.

150. Ronald Reagan, "1992 Republican National Convention," August 20, 1992, http://reagan2020.us/speeches/RNC_Convention.asp.

## CHAPTER 4 ROUGH REQUIEM

1. Aleksandr Solzhenitsyn, "A Special Message," *National Review*, June 28, 2004, 26.

2. George F. Will, *Washington Post*, February 22, 1974.

3. Craig Shirley, *Reagan's Revolution: The Untold Story of the Campaign That Started It All* (Nashville: Thomas Nelson, 2005), 44.

4. United Press International, Legion Chief Rips Peace Plan, *Pittsburgh Press*, October 12, 1972, 18.

5. Ronald Reagan, "1992 Republican National Convention," August 20, 1992, http://reagan2020.us/speeches/RNC_Convention.asp.

6. Jeff Wilson, "Ronald Reagan, 40th President of United States, Dies at Age 93," Associated Press, June 6, 2004.

7. Vincent J. Schodolski and Michael Martinez, "Quiet Moment, Public Sorrow," *Chicago Tribune*, June 8, 2004, 1.

8. Rene Sanchez, "Hail, Farewell to the Chief," *Washington Post*, June 8, 2004, A1.

9. Charlie LeDuff, John M. Broder and Dean Murphy, "First a Private Farewell, Then a Public Outpouring," *New York Times*, June 8, 2004, A23.

10. Vincent J. Schodolski and Michael Martinez, "Quiet Moment, Public Sorrow," *Chicago Tribune*, June 8, 2004, 1.

11. Memorandum by Duke Blackwood, "Entire Timeline Done in Pacific Standard Time," May 25, 2004, 6, 21, 22, Ronald Reagan Presidential Library, Simi Valley, CA.

12. Ibid., 9.

13. Jeff Wilson, "Nation Begins Farewell to Ronald Reagan with Service at Library," Associated Press, June 7, 2004.

14. LeDuff, Broder and Murphy, "First a Private Farewell, Then a Public Outpouring."

15. *NewsNight Aaron Brown*, "Reagan Illness, Death Brought Family Close Together; Reagan Democrats Caused a Political Shift in Michigan," CNN, June 7, 2004.

16. William Booth, "In California, a Community of Mourners," *Washington Post*, June 8, 2004, C1.

17. Rene Sanchez, "Hail, Farewell to the Chief," *Washington Post*, June 8, 2004, A1.

18. David Brooks, "Reagan's Promised Land," *New York Times*, June 8, 2004, A25.

19. Joanne Drake, in discussion with the author, February 20, 2014.

20. Jim Hooley, in discussion with the author.

21. Liz Sidoti, "Kerry Calls Reagan 'Likable Guy,' To Pay Respects at Presidential Library," Associated Press, June 8, 2004.

22. David M. Halbfinger, "Kerry Pays Respects to Reagan, but Takes a Swipe at Bush," *New York Times*, June 9, 2004, A20.

23. John M. Broder and Charlie LeDuff, "100,000, One by One, Pay Tribute to a President," *New York Times*, June 9, 2004, A1.

24. Andrew Littlefair, in discussion with the author, April 28, 2014.

25. Jim Hooley, in discussion with the author, March 7, 2014.

26. Broder and LeDuff, "100,000, One by One, Pay Tribute to a President."

27. Schodolski and Martinez, "Quiet Moment, Public Sorrow."

28. Elisabeth Bumiller and Elizabeth Becker, "Down to the Last Detail, a Reagan-Style Funeral," *New York Times*, June 8, 2004, A1.

29. Joint Congressional on Inaugural Ceremonies, "President's Swearing-In Ceremony," www.inaugural.senate.gov/days-events/days-event/presidents-swearing-in-ceremony.

30. Architect of the Capitol, "Lying in State," www.aoc.gov/nations-stage/lying-state.

31. Architect of the Capitol, "Lying in State," www.aoc.gov/nations-stage /lying-state.

32. Bumiller and Becker, "Down to the Last Detail, a Reagan-Style Funeral."

33. *New York Times*, "No Campaign Ads on Day of Reagan Rites," June 8, 2004, A23.

34. Jill Zuckman, "Kerry Calls Off Events, Gives Praise to Reagan," *Chicago Tribune*, June 7, 2004, 14.

35. Sarah Lyall, "Thatcher to Attend Funeral," *New York Times*, June 8, 2004, A23.

36. Bumiller and Becker, "Down to the Last Detail, a Reagan-Style Funeral."

37. Ibid.

38. Ibid.

39. Charlie LeDuff and John M. Broder, "Shrines Show Reagan's Reach; Services Will Attest to Historic Heft," *New York Times*, June 7, 2004, A19.

40. Grover Norquist, in discussion with the author.

41. Marilyn Berger, "Ronald Reagan Dies at 93; Fostered Cold-War Might and Curbs on Government," *New York Times*, June 6, 2004, 1.

42. Ibid.

43. CNN Breaking News, "Ronald Reagan Dies at 93," CNN, June 5, 2004.

44. Alzheimer's Association, "Alzheimer's Association Mourns Ronald Reagan," Jun 12, 2004, www.apfn.net/messageboard/06–12–04/discussion .cgi.14.html.

45. *New York Times*, June 11, 2004, A17.

46. Jeff Wilson and Terence Hunt, "Ronald Reagan, 40th President of United States, Dies at Age 93," Associated Press, June 5, 2004.

47. Berger, "Ronald Reagan Dies at 93; Fostered Cold-War Might and Curbs on Government."

48. Ronald Reagan, "Announcement of Alzheimer's Disease," November 5, 1994, http://reagan2020.us/speeches/announcement_of_alzheimers.asp.

49. Jeff Wilson, "Nancy at Reagan's Side Until the End," Associated Press, June 5, 2004.

50. Joanne Drake, in discussion with the author, January 29, 2014.

51. Berger, "Ronald Reagan Dies at 93; Fostered Cold-War Might and Curbs on Government."

52. CNN, "Small Town to Tinseltown," www.cnn.com/SPECIALS/2004 /reagan/stories/bio.part.one/index.html.

53. Rick Pearson, "Things That Made Him President Were Begun Right Here in Dixon," *Chicago Tribune*, June 7, 2004, 13.

54. Special Report, ABC News Transcripts, June 5, 2004.

55. Ibid.

56. Ibid.

57. Nancy Reagan and Ronald Reagan, *I Love You, Ronnie: The Letters of Ronald Reagan to Nancy Reagan* (New York: Random House, 2002), xii.

58. Special Report, ABC News Transcripts, June 5, 2004.

59. Ibid.

60. Michael Kilian, "Family Life Full of Joy, Frustration for Reagans," *Chicago Tribune*, June 6, 2004, C10.

61. Ronald Reagan, *The Reagan Diaries*, ed. Douglas Brinkley (New York: HarperCollins, 2007), 217.

62. Michael Reagan, *On the Outside Looking In* (New York: Zebra, 1988).

63. Kilian, "Family Life Full of Joy, Frustration for Reagans."

64. Ann Gerhart, "The Leading Man: Writing Their Own Script, They Loved Happily Ever After," *Washington Post*, June 6, 2004, D1.

65. Berger, "Ronald Reagan Dies at 93; Fostered Cold-War Might and Curbs on Government."

66. Paul Kengor, *God and Ronald Reagan: A Spiritual Life* (New York: HarperCollins, 2004), 331.

67. Certificate of Death: Ronald Wilson Reagan, June 10, 2004, County of Los Angeles, State of California, Ronald Reagan Presidential Library, Simi Valley, CA.

68. Lou Cannon, "Actor, Governor, President, Icon," *Washington Post*, June 6, 2004, A28.

69. Fred Ryan, in discussion with the author, March 5, 2014.

70. Lawrence K. Altman, "A Warm Smile, a Vacant Stare, and One Last House Call," *New York Times*, June 8, 2004, A23.

71. Audrey Hudson and Stephen Dinan, "Ronald Reagan Dead at 93," *Washington Times*, June 6, 2004, A1.

72. Ronald Kotulak, "Seeking Origins of Alzheimer's," *Chicago Tribune*, June 7, 2004, 1.

73. Fred Ryan, in discussion with the author, July 31, 2013.

74. Fred Ryan, in discussion with the author, March 5, 2014.

75. Dennis Lythgoe, "One-Time Secrecy about U.S. Presidents' Health Shifts to Overconcern," *Deseret News*, January 13 1992, http://www.deseretnews.com/article/204099/ONE-TIME-SECRECY-ABOUT-US-PRESIDENTS-HEALTH-SHIFTS-TO—OVERCONCERN.html?pg=all.

76. Dick Snyder, in discussion with the author.

77. Arthur M. Schlesinger Jr., *Robert Kennedy and His Times* (Boston: Houghton Mifflin Harcourt, 1978), 13.

78. AJ Garfein and AR Herzog, "Robust Aging Among the Young-Old, Old-Old, and Oldest-Old," *The Journals of Gerontology Series B Psychological Sciences and Social Sciences*, 04/1995; 50(2):S77–87. DOI: 10.1093/geronb /50B.2.S77.

79. Special Report, ABC News Transcripts, June 5, 2004.

80. Ibiblio.org, "Nell[i]e Clyde Wilson (1883–1962)," University of North Carolina at Chapel Hill, www.ibiblio.org/sullivan/CNN/RWR/album /Familytree/Nelle.html.

81. Lou Cannon, *Reagan* (New York: G.P. Putnam's Son, 1982), 20.

82. Thomas P. O'Neill Jr., *Man of the House: The Life and Political Memoirs of Speaker Tip O'Neill* (New York: Random House, 1987), 335.

83. *Ronald Reagan Presidential Foundation, Ronald Reagan: 100 Years: Official Centennial Edition* (New York: Harper Design, 2010), 224.

84. Special Report, ABC News Transcripts, June 5, 2004.

85. Jeff Wilson, "Nancy at Reagan's Side Until the End," Associated Press, June 5, 2004.

86. Nancy Reagan and William Novak, *My Turn: The Memoirs of Nancy Reagan* (New York: Random House, 1989), 60.

87. Nancy Reagan and Ronald Reagan, *I Love You, Ronnie: The Letters of Ronald Reagan to Nancy Reagan* (New York: Random House, 2000), 184.

88. Special Report, ABC News Transcripts, June 5, 2004.

89. Reagan, *I Love You, Ronnie*, 184.

90. Bernard Weinraub and Elisabeth Bumiller, "Her Home Silent, Nancy Reagan Found a Voice," *New York Times*, June 7, 2004, A1.

91. LeDuff and Broder, "Shrines Show Reagan's Reach; Services Will Attest to Historic Heft."

92. Vincent J. Schodolski and Michael Martinez, "Nation Mourns with Gestures Simple, Grand," *Chicago Tribune*, June 7, 2004, 1.

93. Frank Donatelli, in discussion with the author.

94. *NewsNight with Aaron Brown*, "Ronald Reagan Dies," CNN, June 5, 2004.

95. Pete Souza, "Along for the Ride of a Lifetime," *Chicago Tribune*, June 7, 2004, 1.

96. Adam Nagourney, "Reagan Legacy Looming Large Over Campaign," *New York Times*, June 7, 2004, A1.

97. Donald M. Rothberg, "Failed Rescue Mission Casts Cloud Over Presidential Campaign," Associated Press, April 25, 1980.

98. Tucker Carlson, "The Decline and Fall of the Republican Party," *Cato's Letter*, Spring, 2006, 4, no. 2.

99. Jodi Wilgoren, "Deferring to Reagan, Kerry Quiets Campaign for Week," *New York Times*, June 7, 2004, A14.

100. Nagourney, "Reagan Legacy Looming Large Over Campaign."

101. Weinraub and Bumiller, "Her Home Silent, Nancy Reagan Found a Voice."

102. Ibid.

103. Altman, "A Warm Smile, a Vacant Stare, and One Last House Call."

104. Ibid.

105. Ibid.

106. Ibid.

107. Arthur M. Schlesinger Jr., *Journals: 1952–2000* (New York: Penguin, 2007), 204–205.

## CHAPTER 5 A RANCH IN THE SKY

1. Thomas Jefferson, *The Jefferson Papers 1770–1826* (Boston: Massachusetts Historical Society, 1900), 144.

2. Ronald Reagan, *Reagan: A Life in Letters*, eds. Kiron K. Skinner, Annelise Anderson and Martin Anderson (New York: Free Press, 2003), 812.

3. Ibid., 815.

4. Ronald Reagan, *The Reagan Diaries*, ed. Douglas Brinkley (New York: HarperCollins, 2007), 693.

5. Dan Riehl, "Exclusive: Young America's Foundation Presents New Reagan Documentary," Breitbart.com, February 2, 2011, www.breitbart .com/Big-Hollywood/2011/02/02/Exclusive—Young-Americas -Foundation-Presents-New-Reagan-Documentary.

6. Stuart Spencer, in discussion with the author, February 4, 2014.

7. Michael Deaver, in discussion with the author.

8. *Libertas*, "The More I Visit the Ranch . . . ," 27, no. 3, 14.

9. Ronald Reagan, "Farewell Address to the Nation," January 11, 1989, www.reagan.utexas.edu/archives/speeches/1989/011189i.htm.

10. John Greiner, "Reagan Often Hit Trail in Oklahoma," *Oklahoman*, June 6, 2004, 13A.

11. Jon Meacham, in discussion with the author, January 10, 2014.

12. Travis Lively, "Route to Poplar Forest," July 14, 2010, monticello.org, www.monticello.org/site/research-and-collections/route-to-poplar-forest.

13. Marilyn Fisher, in discussion with the author, September 23, 2014.

14. Peter Hannaford, *Presidential Retreats: Where the Presidents Went and Why They Went There* (New York: Threshold Editions, 2012), 261.

15. Jon Meacham, in discussion with the author, January 10, 2014.

16. Pete Souza, "Along for the Ride of a Lifetime," *Chicago Tribune*, June 7, 2004, 1.

17. Sunday Morning, "Remembering Reagan; Ranch in Southern California Where Ronald Reagan's Spent Much of His Time," CBS News Transcripts, June 6, 2004.

18. Confidential interview with the author.

19. Marilyn Fisher, in discussion with the author, April 4, 2014.

20. Memorandum by Marilyn Fisher, "Fun Facts: Ronald Reagan/Ranch," January 16, 2014, Reagan Ranch and Ranch Center, Santa Barbara, CA.

21. Thomas P. O'Neill Jr., *Man of the House: The Life and Political Memoirs of Speaker Tip O'Neill* (New York: Random House, 1987), 151.

22. Memorandum by Marilyn Fisher, "Fun Facts: Ronald Reagan/Ranch," January 16, 2014, Reagan Ranch and Ranch Center, Santa Barbara, CA.

23. Steven F. Hayward, *The Age of Reagan: The Conservative Counterrevolution, 1980–1989*, (New York: Crown Publishing Group, 2010), 396.

24. Robert A. Rankin and Ron Hutcheson, "'The Great Communicator' Was Architect of an Era," *Kansas City Star*, June 6, 2004, 1.

25. Dennis LeBlanc, in discussion with the author, May 31, 2012.

26. Ibid.

27. Dennis LeBlanc, in discussion with the author, October 1, 2014.

28. Dennis LeBlanc, in discussion with the author, May 31, 2012.

29. Clark Judge, in discussion with the author.

30. Memorandum by Marilyn Fisher, "List of Books in Reagan Ranch Library Bearing Inscriptions to Ronald Reagan or Signatures by Authors," May 30, 2012, Reagan Ranch and Ranch Center, Santa Barbara, CA.

31. Ronald Reagan, *An American Life: The Autobiography* (New York: Simon and Schuster, 1990), 199.

32. Jeff Wilson, "Post–White House Reagan: The Gipper Gradually Faded from Public Eye," Associated Press, June 5, 2004.

33. Patti Davis, "Happy Trails," *Town & Country*, November 2012, www.townandcountrymag.com/society/tradition/patti-davis-on-reagan-family-rancho-del-cielo.

34. Frank Donatelli, in discussion with the author, February 20, 2014.

35. Dennis LeBlanc, in discussion with the author, May 31, 2012.

36. Ibid.

37. Wallace Turner, "Anti-Reagan Protests Continue for 3d Day on California Campus," *New York Times*, November 7, 1980, A16.

38. CNN Breaking News, "Reagan Dies," CNN, June 5, 2004.

39. Dennis LeBlanc, in discussion with the author, May 31, 2012.

40. Marc and Kristen Short, in discussion with the author, March 28, 2014.

41. Dennis LeBlanc, in discussion with the author, May 31, 2012.

42. Marc and Kristen Short, in discussion with the author, March 28, 2014.

43. Ibid.

44. Dennis LeBlanc, in discussion with the author, May 31, 2012.

45. Memorandum by Marilyn Fisher, "Karl Mull's Diaries," September 26, 2014, Reagan Ranch and Ranch Center, Santa Barbara, CA.

46. John Barletta, *Riding With Reagan: From the White House to the Ranch* (New York: Citadel, 2005), 215.

47. Ibid.

48. Steve Colo, in discussion with the author, June 3, 2014.

49. Ibid.

50. Marilyn Berger, "Ronald Reagan Dies at 93; Fostered Cold-War Might and Curbs on Government," *New York Times*, June 6, 2004, 1.

51. Rene Sanchez, "A Nation and the World Pay Tribute to Reagan," *Washington Post*, June 7, 2004, A1.

52. Todd S. Purdum, "An Impact Seen, and Felt, Everywhere," *New York Times*, June 7, 2004, A18.

53. Nicole Hoplin, "Cold War–Era European Leaders Reflect on Reagan and the Impact of Freedom," *Libertas*, Spring 2009, 30.

54. Purdum, "An Impact Seen, and Felt, Everywhere."

55. Ibid.

56. Peter Hannaford, in discussion with the author.

57. Lou Cannon, "Actor, Governor, President, Icon," *Washington Post*, June 6, 2004, A28.

58. Robert Perez, "Reagan Is in Country's Hearts," *Orlando Sentinel*, June 10, 2004, H1.

59. Rene Sanchez, "In Calif., Admirers Gather at Museum, Chapel," *Washington Post*, June 6, 2004, A27.

60. Mike Downey, "Reagan Was Hero, Just Like Smarty," *Chicago Tribune*, June 6, 2004, C1.

61. *Chicago Tribune* "Deaths Last Week," June 6, 2004, D4.

62. Alessandra Stanley, "Once Again, Reagan Lands the Big Television Moment," *New York Times*, June 7, 2004, A18.

63. Editorial, "Ronald Reagan," *New York Times*, June 7, 2004, A26.

64. Bob Dole, "Forever the Optimist," *New York Times*, June 7, 2004, A27.

65. David Brooks, "Reagan's Promised Land," *New York Times*, June 8, 2004, A25.

66. Clyde Haberman, "Reality Check During a Time of Mourning," *New York Times*, June 8, 2004, B1.

67. *New York Times*, "Cuomo and Koch Face Off in a War of Printed Word," April 18, 1984, B1.

68. Michael Cooper, "State but Not City Will Close on Friday to Honor Reagan," *New York Times*, June 9, 2004, B2.

69. Bloomberg News, "Shares Are Modestly Higher, Up in a Short Trading Week," *New York Times*, June 11, 2004, C5.

70. Robin Toner and Robert Pear, "Critics See a Reagan Legacy Tainted by AIDS, Civil Rights and Union Policies," *New York Times*, June 9, 2004, A20.

71. Marilyn Fisher, in discussion with the author, February 24, 2014.

72. David Carr, "2 Weeklies' Covers Separated by a Common Reagan Picture," *New York Times*, June 8, 2004, C1.

73. Craig Shirley, *Rendezvous with Destiny: Ronald Reagan and the Campaign Tthat Changed America* (Wilmington, DE: ISI Books, 2009), 603.

74. Jacques Steinberg, "Viewership of Cable News Is Up, Barely," *New York Times*, June 10, 2004, A20.

75. Ronald Reagan, "Remarks and a Question-and-Answer Session with the Students and Faculty at Moscow State University," May 31, 1988, www.reagan.utexas.edu/archives/speeches/1988/053188b.htm.

76. Elizabeth Kastor, "Harvard's 350th: Pomp and a 600-Foot Rainbow," *Washington Post*, September 4, 1986, A1.

77. John Morris, in discussion with the author.

78. Vincent J. Schodolski, "Reagan Dies," *Chicago Tribune*, June 6, 2004, C1.

79. Eureka College, "Commencement Ceremony," May 9, 1992, www.youtube.com/watch?v=96ybZulnXtc.

80. Ibid.

81. Jill Zuckman, "Kerry Calls Off Events, Gives Praise to Reagan," *Chicago Tribune*, June 7, 2004, 14.

82. Elisabeth Bumiller, "Between 2 First Families, A Complicated Rapport," *New York Times*, June 9, 2004, A21.

83. Nancy Reagan and William Novak, *My Turn: The Memoirs of Nancy Reagan* (New York: Random House, 1989), 315.

84. Maureen Dowd, "Epitaph and Epigone," *New York Times*, June 10, 2004, A27.

85. Thom Shanker, "Gorbachev Honors His Enemy and Friend," *New York Times*, June 11, 2004, A25.

86. Jeffrey Fleishman and David Holley, "The Reagan Legacy," *Los Angeles Times*, June 7, 2004, A11.

87. David Stout, Carl Hulse and Glen Justice, "Washington, Accustomed to Ceremony, Focuses on Logistics for a Rare State Funeral," *New York Times*, June 9, 2004, A21.

88. Ibid.

89. Ibid.

90. David Stout and Carl Hulse, "Cannons Echo as Washington Drills for Reagan's State Funeral," *New York Times*, June 8, 2004, www.nytimes.com/2004/06/08/politics/08CND-PREP.html.

91. *New York Times*, "The Funeral Procession," Wednesday, June 9, 2004, A21.

92. Ibid.

93. Caryn James, "Good Grief: The Appeal of Public Sorrow," *New York Times*, June 10, 2004, E1.

94. *New York Times*, June 9, 2004, B10.

95. *New York Times*, June 10, 2004, E8.

96. Ibid.

97. *New York Times*, June 10, 2004, E9.

98. Fred A. Bernstein, "Archive Architecture: Setting the Spin in Stone," *New York Times*, June 10, 2004, F1.

99. Ibid.

100. Ibid.

101. Confidential interview with the author.

102. Ibid.

103. Fred Ryan, in discussion with the author, [date?].

104. Scott Shepard and A.L. May, "Boos on the N.Y. Campaign Trail Jews Upset with Brown, Wall Street with Clinton," *Atlanta Journal and Constitution*, April 3, 1992, A5; George F. Will, "The Gifts of 'Greed,'" *Washington Post*, January 23, 1992, A25.

105. Vincent J. Schodolski and Michael Martinez, "Nation Mourns with Gestures Simple, Grand," *Chicago Tribune*, June 7, 2004, 1.

106. Ibid.

107. Memorandum, Aboard Air Force One, "NR's Feelings & Family RE: AF1 Returning to Wash. D.C.," June 9, 2004, Ronald Reagan Presidential Library, Simi Valley, CA.

## CHAPTER 6 HOI POLLOI v. HOITY-TOITY

1. Steven F. Hayward, *The Age of Reagan: The Fall of the Old Liberal Order, 1964–1980* (New York: Doubleday, 2009), 692.

2. David S. Broder, "The Great Persuader," *Washington Post*, June 7, 2004, A23.

3. Marc Fisher, "The Old Warrior at the Wall," *Washington Post*, September 13, 1990, D1.

4. Ibid.

5. Ronald Reagan, *Reagan: A Life in Letters*, eds. Kiron K. Skinner, Annelise Anderson and Martin Anderson (New York: Free Press, 2003), 821.

6. Lou Cannon, in discussion with the author, March 27, 2014.

7. Todd S. Purdum, "The Capital Pays Homage to 'a Graceful and a Gallant Man,'" *New York Times*, June 10, 2004, A20.

8. Memorandum, "Outline of Funeral Events in Honor of Ronald Wilson Reagan," Ronald Reagan Presidential Library, Simi Valley, CA.

9. Bob Kemper, "Ronald Reagan: 1911–2004: Funeral Steeped in Protocol," *Atlanta Journal-Constitution*, June 8, 2004, 7A.

10. Elisabeth Bumiller and Elizabeth Becker, "Down to the Last Detail, a Reagan-Style Funeral," *New York Times*, June 8, 2004, A1.

11. Rick Ahearn, in discussion with the author, March 25, 2014.

12. Lewis L. Gould, "History in the Remaking," *Washington Post*, June 13, 2004, B1.

13. Elisabeth Bumiller, Carl Hulse, Todd S. Purdum and Sheryl Gay Stolberg, "Reagan Team, a Bit Grayer, Gathers Again," *New York Times*, June 10, 2004, A1.

14. Purdum, "The Capital Pays Homage to 'a Graceful and a Gallant Man.'"

15. Bumiller, Hulse, Purdum, Stolberg, "Reagan Team, a Bit Grayer, Gathers Again."

16. Linda Bond, in discussion with the author, April 15, 2014.

17. Ibid.

18. Ronald Reagan, *The Reagan Diaries*, ed. Douglas Brinkley (New York: HarperCollins, 2007), 91.

19. David Von Drehle, "A Day of Ritual and Remembrance," *Washington Post*, June 10, 2004, A1.

20. Ibid.

21. *New York Times*, June 10, 2004, A21.

22. Christi Parsons, "2nd Highway Named for Reagan," *Chicago Tribune*, June 9, 2004, 22.

23. Jim Abrams, "Reagan Supporters Want to See Their Hero on U.S. Money," Associated Press, June 8, 2004.

24. Grover Norquist, in discussion with the author.

25. Abrams, "Reagan Supporters Want to See Their Hero on U.S. Money."

26. Memorandum by Joanne Drake, Office of Ronald Reagan, "Statement by Nancy Reagan Regarding Legislation to Put Ronald Reagan's Face on the Dime," December 5, 2003, Ronald Reagan Presidential Library, Simi Valley, CA.

27. Letter from Anna Eleanor Roosevelt to Nancy Reagan, January 25, 2004, Ronald Reagan Presidential Library, Simi Valley, CA.

28. Memorandum by Robert Garcia, Nixon Library, "Reagan Remembered at Nixon Library Public Invited to Sign Memorial Books, View Exhibit," June 7, 2004, Ronald Reagan Presidential Library, Simi Valley, CA.

29. Claire Jellick, "Classmates, Lawmaker Remember Reagan's Charisma," *Peoria (IL) Journal Star*, June 6, 2004, A17.

30. Caryn James, "Good Grief: The Appeal of Public Sorrow," *New York Times*, June 10, 2004, E1.

31. Michael E. Ruane, "A Somber Procession of Present and Past," *Washington Post*, June 10, 2004, A21.

32. Jim Drinkard, "Along Caisson's Route, a Sea of Admirers," *USA Today*, June 10, 2004, 4A.

33. Vincent J. Schodolski and Michael Martinez, "Flood of Reagan Admirers Pay Tribute," *Chicago Tribune*, June 9, 2004, 18.

34. Purdum, "The Capital Pays Homage to 'a Graceful and a Gallant Man.'"

35. Ruane, "A Somber Procession of Present and Past."

36. Muriel Dobbin, "Nancy Reagan: Looking Past Final Days of 'Long Goodbye,'" *Sacramento Bee*, June 9, 2004, E1.

37. Carl Cannon, in discussion with the author.

38. Lyn Nofziger, in discussion with the author.

39. Ronald Reagan, *Reagan: A Life in Letters*, eds. Kiron K. Skinner, Annelise Anderson and Martin Anderson (New York: Free Press, 2003), 813.

40. *Auxiliary*, "The Riderless Horse," May 2013, 32.

41. Galen Jackman, in discussion with the author, May 14, 2014.

42. Ruane, "A Somber Procession of Present and Past."

43. David Stout, "From Lincoln on, a Time of Grieving Has Been One of Reconciling," *New York Times*, June 11, 2004, A24.

44. Purdum, "The Capital Pays Homage to 'a Graceful and a Gallant Man.'"

45. Ruane, "A Somber Procession of Present and Past."

46. Military District of Washington, "Origins of the 21-Gun Salute," www .usstatefuneral.mdw.army.mil/military-honors/21-gun-salute.

47. Linda Bond, in discussion with the author, April 15, 2014.

48. Jeff Zeleny, Michael Tackett, Mike Dorning, Rudolph Bush and Vincent J. Schodolski, "Solemn Capital Turns Out for Reagan," *Chicago Tribune*, June 10, 2004, 1.

49. Ibid.

50. Architect of the Capitol, "Capitol Rotunda," www.aoc.gov/capitol-buildings /capitol-rotunda.

51. Associated Press, "Reagan Cheney Text," June 9, 2004.

52. Associated Press, "Reagan Hastert Text," June 9, 2004.

53. Mary Beth Sheridan, "Varied Career Prepared General for High-Profile Assignment," *Washington Post*, June 10, 2004, A22.

54. Fred Ryan, in discussion with the author, March 5, 2014.

55. Pete Souza, "Along for the Ride of a Lifetime," *Chicago Tribune*, June 7, 2004, 1.

56. Vicki Kemper, "Farewell to a President," *Los Angeles Times*, June 11, 2004, A12.

57. Ronald Reagan, *The Reagan Diaries*, ed. Douglas Brinkley (New York: HarperCollins, 2007), 474.

58. Mike Allen, "Reagan Veterans Bring Back the '80s," *Washington Post*, June 11, 2004, A31.

59. John Singlaub, *Hazardous Duty* (New York: Simon and Schuster, 1991), 19.

60. Jim Hooley, in discussion with the author, March 7, 2014.

61. Allen, "Reagan Veterans Bring Back the '80s."

62. Guy Taylor and Deb McCown, "Worldwide Congregation Will Attend Reagan Funeral," *Washington Times*, June 11, 2004, A1.

63. Bruce Laingen, "As the Nation Bids Farewell to a President," *New York Times*, June 11, 2004, A26.

64. Susan Berger Kabaker, "As the Nation Bids Farewell to a President," *New York Times*, June 11, 2004, A26.

65. *Chicago Tribune*, "Voice of the People," June 7, 2004, 20.

66. Mark Weinberg, in discussion with the author.

67. Thomas Crampton, "Court Says New Paltz Mayor Can't Hold Gay Weddings," *New York Times*, June 8, 2004, B6.

68. Jennifer Steinhauer, "Manhattan: Debt vs. Asteroids," *New York Times*, June 11, 2004, B5.

69. Constance L. Hays, "Stewart Prosecution Witness Pleads Not Guilty to Perjury," *New York Times*, June 17, 2004, www.nytimes.com/2004/06/17 /business/stewart-prosecution-witness-pleads-not-guilty-to-perjury.html.

70. *Las Vegas Review-Journal*, June 6, 2004.

71. Howard Baker, "A Political Life with President Reagan," *Chicago Tribune*, June 8, 2004, 23.

72. Special Report, ABC News Transcripts, June 5, 2004.

73. Broder, "The Great Persuader."

74. Mark Weisbrot, "A Critical Look at Reagan's Legacy," *Chicago Tribune*, June 8, 2004, 23.

75. Lou Cannon, "Actor, Governor, President, Icon," *Washington Post*, June 6, 2004, A28.

76. Marilyn Berger, "Clark Clifford, a Major Adviser to Four Presidents, Is Dead at 91," *New York Times*, October 11, 1998, www.nytimes .com/1998/10/11/us/clark-clifford-a-major-adviser-to-four-presidents-is -dead-at-91.html.

77. Judy Bachrach, "Reagan Tries Hard to Avoid Communicating," *Washington Star*, October 3, 1980, A4.

78. Ronad Reagan, "Farewell Address to the Nation," January 11, 1989, www .reagan.utexas.edu/archives/speeches/1989/011189i.htm.

79. Ronald Reagan, "A Time for Choosing," October 27, 1964, www.reagan .utexas.edu/archives/reference/timechoosing.html.

80. Souza, "Along for the Ride of a Lifetime."

81. Ibid.

82. *Chicago Tribune*, "Almanac," June 8, 2004, 6.

83. Ibid.

84. Carmen Greco Jr., "Agent Who Took Bullet Recalls Reagan's '81 Brush with Death," *Chicago Tribune*, June 8, 2004, 18.

85. *Wall Street Journal*, "Following Tradition, Markets Will Close for Reagan's Funeral," updated June 8, 2004, www.wsj.com/articles /SB108662286940130507.

86. Mike Dorning and Rudolph Bush, "Liberals May Mourn Man, but Not the Reagan Years," *Chicago Tribune*, June 9, 2004, 1.

87. Ibid.

88. Michael Kilian, "Reagans Replaced 'Malaise' with Mink," *Chicago Tribune*, June 9, 2004, 23.

89. Ibid.

90. Steve Johnson, "Networks Fear Burnout of 'Wall to Wall' Story," *Chicago Tribune*, June 9, 2004, 24.

91. Stephen J. Hedges, "His Military Successes Had a Price," *Chicago Tribune*, June 10, 2004, 19.

92. Molly Ivins, "Pay Close Attention to Bush's Backsliding," *Chicago Tribune*, June 10, 2004, 25.

93. *Washington Post*, "4:45 p.m. Outside Andrews," June 10, 2004, A24.

94. *Chicago Tribune*, "Kerry Edges Ahead," June 10, 2004, 10.

95. Michael Graczyk, "Former President George H.W. Bush to Mark 80th Birthday with Parachute Jump," Associated Press, June 13, 2004.

96. Thomas Sattler, "A Mass of Humanity," *Newsday* (NY), June 11, 2004, A51.

97. Rudolph Bush, "A Time to Remember," *Chicago Tribune*, June 11, 2004, 1.

## CHAPTER 7 ASSAULT ON JENKINS HILL

1. Hope Yen, "Michael Reagan Speaks Lovingly of Father, Mrs. Reagan Receives Long Line of Dignitaries," Associated Press, June 10, 2004.

2. Ann Gerhart, "A Widow's Heartfelt Farewell," *Washington Post*, June 11, 2004, A27.

3. Ibid.

4. Ibid.

5. Frank Rich, "First Reagan, Now His Stunt Double," *New York Times*, June 13, 2004, B1.

6. Tina Brown, "Dancing Into Hearts and History," *Washington Post*, June 10, 2004, C1.

7. Glenn Kessler, "Right-Leaning Policy Won a Nickname: Reaganomics," *Washington Post*, June 6, 2004, A27.

8. Editorial, "Ronald Wilson Reagan," *Washington Post*, June 6, 2004, B6.

9. Ibid.

10. E. J. Dionne Jr., "The New Dealer," *Washington Post*, June 8, 2004, A23.

11. David Ignatius, "Protean Leader," *Washington Post*, June 8, 2004, A23.

12. *Washington Post*, "Tributes in Word and Deed," June 11, 2004, A28.

13. *The Bulletin's Frontrunner*, June 9, 2004, 4, Ronald Reagan Presidential Library, Simi Valley, CA.

14. Ibid.

15. Ibid.

16. Sheryl Gay Stolberg and Courtney C. Radsch, "After Long Distances and Long Waits, Everyday Admirers Say Their Goodbyes," *New York Times*, June 11, 2004, A24.

17. David Stout, "From Lincoln on, a Time of Grieving Has Been One of Reconciling," *New York Times*, June 11, 2004, A24.

18. David Von Drehle, "Bushes Return to Honor Reagan," *Washington Post*, June 11, 2004, A1.

19. Stolberg, Radsch, "After Long Distances and Long Waits, Everyday Admirers Say Their Goodbyes."

20. Ibid.

21. Ibid.

22. Ibid.

23. Joel Achenbach, "In a Most Moving Setting, a Guard's Steadfast Presence," *Washington Post*, June 11, 2004, C1.

24. Ibid.

25. Galen Jackman, in discussion with the author, May 14, 2014.

26. Achenbach, "In a Most Moving Setting, a Guard's Steadfast Presence."

27. Fred Ryan, in discussion with the author, March 5, 2014.

28. Robert D. Novak, *The Prince of Darkness: 50 Years Reporting in Washington* (New York: Crown Forum, 2007), 349.

29. Associated Press, "Congress Mourns, Remembers Reagan with Resolutions in Tribute," June 9, 2004.

30. Ronald Reagan, *Memorial Services in the Congress of the United States and Tributes in Eulogy of Ronald Reagan, Late a President of the United States* (Washington, DC: Government Printing Office, 2005), 242–3.

31. Ibid., iii.

32. Ibid., 9–10.

33. Ibid., 175.

34. R. W. Apple Jr., "Legacy of Reagan Now Begins the Test of Time," *New York Times*, June 11, 2004, A1.

35. Ibid.

36. Ibid.

37. Thom Shanker, "Gorbachev Honors His Enemy and Friend," *New York Times*, June 11, 2004, A25.

38. John P. Diggins, *Ronald Reagan: Fate, Freedom, and the Making of History* (New York: W. W. Norton & Company, 2007), xiv.

39. John Lewis Gaddis, *The Cold War: A New History* (New York: Penguin, 2006), xxix.

40. Paul Krugman, "An Economic Legend," *New York Times*, June 11, 2004, A27.

41. The World Bank Group, "Real Interest Rate (%)," http://data.worldbank.org/indicator/FR.INR.RINR?page=5.

42. U.S. Bureau of Labor Statistics, "Labor Force Statistics from the Current Population Survey," http://data.bls.gov/pdq/SurveyOutputServlet.

43. John Patrick Diggins, "How Reagan Beat the Neocons," *New York Times*, June 11, 2004, A27.

44. John Kass, "Reagan Taught Us to Stand Tall as Americans," *Chicago Tribune*, June 11, 2004, 2.

45. Ibid.

46. Timothy L. O'Brien and David D. Kirkpatrick, "Nonpolitical Study of Terror Is Caught Up in Politics," *New York Times*, June 12, 2004, A6.

47. R. C. Longworth, "End of the Cold War," *Chicago Tribune*, June 6, 2004, 11.

48. Ibid.

49. *New York Times*, "Transcript of the Presidential Debate Between Carter and Reagan in Cleveland," October 29, 1980, A26.

50. *Hardball with Chris Matthews*, MSNBC, May 3, 2007.

51. "2000 Presidential Election; Electoral Vote Totals," www.archives.gov/federal-register/electoral-college/votes/2000.html.

52. Tony Dolan, in discussion with the author, April 1, 2014.

53. Peggy Noonan, "The Ben Elliott Story," *Wall Street Journal*, June 14, 2004, http://online.wsj.com/articles/SB122460039897754255.

54. Tony Dolan, in discussion with the author, April 1, 2014.

55. David Bufkin, in discussion with the author, March 13, 2014.

56. Rick Ahearn, in discussion with the author, March 25, 2014.

57. Calvin Woodward, "Tens of Thousands View Reagan Casket; Friends Close Ranks Around Mrs. Reagan Before Funeral," Associated Press, June 10, 2004.

58. Ibid.
59. Memorandum, "In Memoriam," Ronald Reagan Presidential Library, Simi Valley, CA.
60. Rick Ahearn, in discussion with the author, March 25, 2014.
61. Mike Allen, "Reagan Veterans Bring Back the '80s," *Washington Post*, June 11, 2004, A31.
62. Joanne Drake, in discussion with the author, March 19, 2014.
63. Lou Cannon, in discussion with the author, March 27, 2014.
64. Vincent J. Schodolski and Michael Martinez, "Nation Mourns with Gestures Simple, Grand," *Chicago Tribune*, June 7, 2004, 1.
65. Andrew C. Revkin, *New York Times* News Service, "Antarctic Data: New Ice Age Far Off," *Chicago Tribune*, June 10, 2004, 14.
66. Peter Slevin and Robin Wright, "U.N. Backs Plan to End Iraq Occupation," *Washington Post*, June 9, 2004, A1.
67. Peter Johnson, "What Will Stern Do if FCC Cracks Down on His Radio Show?" *USA Today*, June 14, 2004, 8D.
68. *Washington Post*, "Tributes in Word and Deed," June 10, 2004, A22.
69. Ibid.
70. Jeff Zeleny, John McCormick, William Neikirk, Michael Tackett, Rick Pearson, Richard Wronski, Imran Vittachi and Rick Jervis, "Sad Hour in the Life of America," *Chicago Tribune*, June 6, 2004, 12.
71. Ibid.
72. Associated Press, "Text of State Resolution Honoring Reagan," June 9, 2004.
73. *Good Morning America*, "Reverends Billy and Franklin Graham Condolences for the President," ABC News Transcripts, June 6, 2004.
74. Steve Colo, in discussion with the author, June 3, 2014.
75. Ibid.
76. Ibid.
77. Ibid.
78. Ibid.
79. John Barletta, *Riding with Reagan: From the White House to the Ranch* (New York: Citadel, 2005), 219.
80. Bill Schulz, in discussion with the author.
81. Fred Ryan, in discussion with the author, July 31, 2013.
82. Ronald Reagan, "Keepers of the Peace," The Citadel, The Military College of South Carolina, May 15, 1993, www3.citadel.edu/pao /addresses/reagan.htm.

83. Haley Barbour, in discussion with the author, January 21, 2014.

84. Ronald Reagan, *Reagan: A Life in Letters*, eds. Kiron K. Skinner, Annelise Anderson and Martin Anderson (New York: Free Press, 2003), 834.

85. Howard Kurtz, "15 Years Later, the Remaking of a President," *Washington Post*, June 7, 2004, C1.

86. Eric Pianin and Thomas B. Edsall, "Schisms from Administration Lingered for Years," *Washington Post*, June 9, 2004, A1.

87. Ibid.

88. David Johnston, "The Iran-Contra Report: The Overview," *New York Times*, January 19, 1994, A1.

89. Pianin, Edsall, "Schisms from Administration Lingered for Years."

90. Robert J. Samuelson, "Unsung Triumph," *Washington Post*, June 9, 2004, A21.

91. Howard Kurtz, "Fewer Republicans Trust the News, Survey Finds," *Washington Post*, June 9, 2004, C1.

92. Cheryl Wetzstein, Monique E. Stuart and Megan Fromm, "Braving the Line for a Last Goodbye," *Washington Times*, June 12, 2004, A6.

## CHAPTER 8 DO WE NOT HEAR THE CHIMES AT MIDDAY?

1. David Keene, in discussion with the author.

2. Ronald Reagan, "Remarks at the Annual Dinner of the Conservative Political Action Conference," March 1, 1985, www.reagan.utexas.edu /archives/speeches/1985/30185f.htm.

3. Confidential interview with the author.

4. Rick Ahearn, in discussion with the author, March 25, 2014.

5. Michael K. Deaver, *Nancy: A Portrait of My Years with Nancy Reagan* (New York: William Morrow, 2004), 196.

6. Military District of Washington, "The Evolution of State Funerals," http://mdwhome.mdw.army.mil/evolutionofsf.htm.

7. Michael Kilian, "Since 1841, Nation Has Had Many State Funerals," *Chicago Tribune*, June 10, 2004, 18.

8. Roger Peele, in discussion with the author, May 9, 2014.

9. Roger Peele, "Ronald Reagan's Magnanimity," *Washington Post*, June 11, 2004, A24.

10. Roger Peele, in discussion with the author, May 9, 2014.

11. Peele, "Ronald Reagan's Magnanimity."

12. Roger Peele, in discussion with the author, May 9, 2014.

13. Ibid.

14. Ibid.

15. Peele, "Ronald Reagan's Magnanimity."

16. Skadden, "Gregory B. Craig," www.skadden.com/professionals/gregory -b-craig.

17. Caryle Murphy, "Cathedral Flower Guild Gets Chance to Bloom," *Washington Post*, June 11, 2004, A33.

18. Special Report, ABC News Transcripts, June 9, 2004.

19. Peter Hannaford, *Reagan's Roots: The People and Places That Shaped His Character* (Bennington, VT: Images from the Past, 2012), 50.

20. Mark Cheathem, "Andrew Jackson's Profane Parrot," *Jacksonian America: Society, Personality, and Politics* (blog), April 16, 2012, http:// jacksonianamerica.com/2012/04/16/andrew-jacksons-profane-parrot/.

21. Don Higginbotham, *George Washington Reconsidered* (Charlottesville, VA: University of Virginia Press, 2001), 256.

22. Benson John Lossing and Rufus Wilmot Griswold, *Life of Washington: A Biography, Personal, Military, and Political* (London, UK: Virtue and Company, 1860), 542.

23. Marylou Tousignant, "Two Hundred Years of Presidential Funerals," *Washington Post*, June 10, 2004, C14.

24. Ibid.

25. Ronald Reagan, "Address at Republican National Convention," CNN, August 17, 1992, www.cnn.com/SPECIALS/2004/reagan/stories/speech .archive/rnc.speech.html.

26. Ibid.

27. Sgt. Contricia Sellers-Ford, "Lying in State for Former President Reagan," United States Capitol Police, June 11, 2004, www.uscapitolpolice.gov /pressreleases/2004/pr_06–11–04.php.

28. Connie Cass, "Nancy Reagan Showed How to Touch Casket," Associated Press, June 11, 2004.

29. Robert G. Kaiser, "Gorbachev: 'We All Lost Cold War,'" *Washington Post*, June 11, 2004, A1.

30. Eric Rich and Allan Lengel, "Long Line Leads to a Letdown," *Washington Post*, June 12, 2004, A29.

31. Tarron Lively and Jeffrey Sparshott, "Funeral Procession Fuels Record Usage of Metro," *Washington Times*, June 11, 2004, A12.

32. Rich, Lengel, "Long Line Leads to a Letdown."

33. Ibid.

34. Cheryl Wetzstein, Monique E. Stuart and Megan Fromm, "Braving the Line for a Last Goodbye," *Washington Times*, June 12, 2004, A6.

35. Rick Ahearn, in discussion with the author, March 25, 2014.

36. Michael Wagner, in discussion with the author, March 24, 2014.

37. Memorandum, "The State Funeral of President Ronald Reagan," June 11, 2004, 9, Ronald Reagan Presidential Library, Simi Valley, CA.

38. Ibid., 11–12.

39. Michael Barone, "The 'Great Communicator' Was the FDR of the 1980s," *Chicago Sun-Times*, June 15, 2004, 39.

40. Office of the Director of Music, "Preludial Music & Texts of the Anthems, Hymns & Solos Performed During the Funeral Service for Ronald Wilson Reagan at Washington National Cathedral," Washington National Cathedral, June 10, 2004.

41. Robert Higdon, in discussion with the author, May 30, 2014.

42. Linda Bond, in discussion with the author, April 15, 2014.

43. Aleksandr I. Solzhenitsyn, *The Gulag Archipelago, 1918–1956: An Experiment in Literary Investigation III–IV* (New York: Harper & Row, 1975), 615.

44. Washington National Cathedral (cathedral.org), "Cathedral Timeline," www.cathedral.org/about/timeline.shtml.

45. Nps.gov, "National Cathedral," www.nps.gov/nr/travel/wash/dc5.htm.

46. Jeff Zeleny, "Reagan Laid to Rest," *Chicago Tribune*, June 12, 2004, 1.

47. Linda Bond, in discussion with the author, April 15, 2014.

48. Bob Dole, in discussion with the author.

49. Richard N. Ostling, "Scholar Says Ronald Reagan's Religion Was Strongly Evident, but Ambiguity Remains," Associated Press, June 10, 2004.

50. Jeff Wilson and Calvin Woodward, "Homage and Song Form a Lingering Goodbye for Reagan," Associated Press, June 11, 2004.

51. Hanna Rosin, "John Danforth, Churchman for a State Occasion," *Washington Post*, June 11, 2004, C1.

52. David Von Drehle, "Reagan Hailed as Leader for 'the Ages,'" *Washington Post*, June 12, 2004, A1.

53. Rick Ahearn, in discussion with the author, March 25, 2014.

54. Tom Shales, "Moving Pictures of a Stately Send-Off," *Washington Post*, June 12, 2004, C1.

55. Carrie Kepple, "Eureka Trio to Attend Private Burial," *Peoria (IL) Journal Star,* June 11, 2004, A15.

56. Rick Ahearn, in discussion with the author, March 25, 2014.

57. Charlie Rose, "An Hour with Hillary Rodham Clinton, Former Secretary Of State," PBS, July 16, 2014, www.charlierose.com/watch/60419259.

58. Linda Bond, in discussion with the author, April 15, 2014.

59. Cal Thomas, " Reagan Replaced Despair With Hope Former President Was Eternal Optimist," *Spokesman Review (WA),* June 8, 2004, 4.

60. John 11:25.

61. Von Drehle, "Reagan Hailed as Leader for 'the Ages.'"

62. Ibid.

63. Matt. 5:14 KJV.

64. Isa. 40:30–31.

65. Margaret Thatcher, "Eulogy for President Reagan," Margaret Thatcher Foundation, June 11, 2004, www.margaretthatcher.org/document/110360.

66. Ibid.

67. Ibid.

68. Ibid.

69. Robert Higdon, in discussion with the author, May 30, 2014.

70. Rick Ahearn, in discussion with the author, March 25, 2014.

71. *Washington Post,* "Text of Former Canadian Prime Minister Brian Mulroney Eulogy of Former President Reagan," June 11, 2004, www .washingtonpost.com/wp-dyn/articles/A34365–2004Jun11.html.

72. Ibid.

73. Associated Press, "Text of George Bush Tribute to Reagan," June 11, 2004.

74. Ibid.

75. *Washington Post,* "Transcript: President Bush Eulogizes Ronald Reagan," June 11, 2004, www.washingtonpost.com/wp-dyn/articles/A34393 –2004Jun11.html.

76. Ibid.

77. Ibid.

78. Rick Ahearn, in discussion with the author, March 25, 2014.

79. Washington National Cathedral, "About the Cathedral's Carillon," www .nationalcathedral.org/arts/carillonHistory.shtml.

80. Jeremiah Marquez, "Thousands Endure Hours to Pay Respects to Ronald Reagan," Associated Press, June 9, 2004.

81. Tony Dolan, in discussion with the author, April 1, 2014.

82. Roxanne Roberts, "The Gipper's Team," *Washington Post*, June 12, 2004, C1.

83. Ronald Reagan, "Remarks at the Biennial Convention of the National Federation of Republican Women in Louisville, Kentucky," October 7, 1983, www.reagan.utexas.edu/archives/speeches/1983/100783d.htm.

84. John Balzar, "Laffer Learning the Economics of Seeking Office," *Los Angeles Times*, April 24, 1986, 3.

85. Jon Margolis, "Reagan Revolution Stronger Now than During Presidency," *Chicago Tribune*, June 6, 2004, 1.

86. Ibid.

87. Ibid.

88. *Miami Herald*, "Reagan on the Money," June 13, 2004, 4L.

89. Jim Abrams, "Reagan Supporters Want to See Their Hero on U.S. Money," Associated Press, June 8, 2004.

90. Jennifer Harper and William Glanz, "Naming Efforts Get Renewed Push," *Washington Times*, June 9, 2004, A10.

91. Donald Lambro and Ralph Z. Hallow, "He Lifted Up the World," *Washington Times*, June 12, 2004, A1.

92. Ibid.

93. Mark Shields, "Reagan's Fairness Legacy," *Washington Post*, June 12, 2004, A21.

94. Joanne Drake, in discussion with the author, March 19, 2014.

95. Ibid.

96. Michele Woodward, in discussion with the author, March 26, 2014.

97. Mark Weinberg, in discussion with the author, April 4, 2014.

98. Michele Woodward, in discussion with the author, March 26, 2014.

99. Jeff Wilson and Calvin Woodward, "Homage And Song Form a Lingering Goodbye for Reagan," Associated Press, June 11, 2004.

100. Don Michael Randel, ed., *The Harvard Biographical Dictionary of Music* (Cambridge, MA: Harvard University Press, 1996), 235.

## CHAPTER 9 "SIGNAL: RAWHIDE'S LAST ARRIVAL"

1. David Von Drehle, "Reagan Hailed as Leader for 'the Ages,'" *Washington Post*, June 12, 2004, A1.

2. John Barletta, *Riding with Reagan: From the White House to the Ranch* (New York: Citadel, 2005), 234, 232.

3. Military District of Washington, "Military Honors for Former Presidents," http://mdwhome.mdw.army.mil/militaryhforfpresi.htm.

4. Memorandum, "The State Funeral of President Ronald Reagan," June 11, 2004, Ronald Reagan Presidential Library, Simi Valley, CA.

5. Jim Hooley, in discussion with the author, December 5, 2014.

6. Ronald Reagan, *The Reagan Diaries*, ed. Douglas Brinkley (New York: HarperCollins, 2007), 107.

7. Vincent J. Schodolski and Michael Martinez, "As Sun Sets, Last Respects Paid to 40th President," *Chicago Tribune*, June 12, 2004, 19.

8. Patti Davis, *The Long Goodbye* (New York: Knopf, 2011), 197.

9. Calvin Woodward and Jeff Wilson, "Private Moments Mark End of Weeklong Reagan Tribute," Associated Press, June 12, 2004.

10. Nielsen Media Research, "Big-Ticket TV, By the Numbers," *Washington Post*, April 29, 2011, C4.

11. Lou Cannon, in discussion with the author, March 27, 2014.

12. Memorandum by Sue Tatangelo, 3, June, 2004, Ronald Reagan Presidential Library, Simi Valley, CA.

13. Lou Cannon, in discussion with the author, March 27, 2014.

14. Fred Ryan, in discussion with the author.

15. Gail Shister, "Network Anchors See Excess in Reagan Funeral Coverage," *Philadelphia Inquirer*, June 8, 2004, E1.

16. Ibid.

17. *Dallas Morning News*, June 11, 2004, 31A.

18. Hank Stuever, "Weathering Reagan: A Low in the '80s," *Washington Post*, June 12, 2004, C1.

19. Jose Antonio Vargas, "Gays Recall a Silent Great Communicator," *Washington Post*, June 13, 2004, D1.

20. David Segal, "Pop's Reagan Record: Sound & Fury," *Washington Post*, June 13, 2004, D1.

21. Ronald Reagan, "Inaugural Address," January 20, 1981, www.reagan.utexas.edu/archives/speeches/1981/12081a.htm.

22. Donald Lambro and Ralph Z. Hallow, "He Lifted Up the World," *Washington Times*, June 12, 2004, A1.

23. *Peoria (IL) Journal Star*, "Tonight's Television/Friday, June 11," June 11, 2004, C8.

24. David Nyhan, "The 'Don't Blame Me' President," *Boston Globe*, December 28, 1988, 11.

25. Cal Thomas, "Reagan Replaced Despair with Hope Former President Was Eternal Optimist," *Spokesman Review (WA)*, June 8, 2004, 4.

26. Memorandum, "The State Funeral of President Ronald Reagan," June 11, 2004, 16–17, Ronald Reagan Presidential Library, Simi Valley, CA.

27. Memorandum, "28000 DC to CA Final Manifest," June 11, 2004, Ronald Reagan Presidential Library, Simi Valley, CA.

28. Memorandum, "The State Funeral of President Ronald Reagan," June 11, 2004, Ronald Reagan Presidential Library, Simi Valley, CA.

29. Joanne Drake, in discussion with the author, March 19, 2014.

30. Letter from Fess and Marcy Parker to Joanne Drake, Fespar Enterprises, June 18, 2004, Ronald Reagan Presidential Library, Simi Valley, CA.

31. Jim Lake, in discussion with the author, September 24, 2014.

32. Ibid.

33. Woodward and Wilson, "Private Moments Mark End of Weeklong Reagan Tribute."

34. Letter from John I. Moseley, M.D. to Michael Reagan, Yellowstone Neurosurgical Associates, September 29, 2004, Ronald Reagan Presidential Library, Simi Valley, CA.

35. Davis, *The Long Goodbye*, 197.

36. Lowell Ponte, "Memories of William F. Buckley Jr.," Newsmax.com, February 28, 2008, www.newsmax.com/LowellPonte/William-Buckley/2008/02/28/id/323027/.

37. Jerry McDowell, "My Cafeteria Chat with a Longshot Reagan," *Peoria Journal Star*, June 12, 2004, B1.

38. Jim Hooley, in discussion with the author, March 7, 2014.

39. Memorandum, "Condolence Notes, Letters, Card to NR," June 2004, Scrapbooks, Funeral Boxes, Ronald Reagan Presidential Library, Simi Valley, CA.

40. Rich Little, in discussion with the author.

41. Memorandum, "Condolence Notes, Letters, Card to NR," June 2004, Scrapbooks, Funeral Boxes, Ronald Reagan Presidential Library, Simi Valley, CA.

42. Ibid.

43. Memorandum, "Reagan Funeral Gifts," Ronald Reagan Presidential Library, Simi Valley, CA.

44. Ibid.

45. Ibid.

46. Ibid.

47. Barletta, *Riding with Reagan*, 233.

48. Jim Hooley, in discussion with the author, December 5, 2014.

49. Ibid.

50. Memorandum, "The State Funeral of President Ronald Reagan," June 11, 2004, Ronald Reagan Presidential Library, Simi Valley, CA.

51. Jim Hooley, in discussion with the author, December 5, 2014.

52. Michael Astor, "US Aircraft Carrier Crews Pays Tribute to Ronald Reagan," Associated Press, June 11, 2004.

53. Associated Press, "Lights of Las Vegas Strip to Dim to Honor Ronald Reagan," June 11, 2004.

54. Vincent J. Schodolski and Michael Martinez, "As Sun Sets, Last Respects Paid to 40th President," *Chicago Tribune*, June 12, 2004, 19.

55. Jim Hooley, in discussion with the author, December 5, 2014.

56. Associated Press, "Text of Remarks by Patti Davis at Father's Burial Service," June 11, 2004.

57. Patti Davis, "The Gemstones of Our Years," *Newsweek*, June 14, 2004, 42.

58. Associated Press, "Text of Michael Reagan's Remarks at Father's Burial Service," June 12, 2004.

59. Associated Press, "Text of Ron Reagan Jr.'s Remarks," June 12, 2004.

60. Ibid.

61. Associated Press, "Text of Remarks by Patti Davis at Father's Burial Service."

62. Patti Davis, "One Woman's Travels with Alzheimer's," *Time*, October 25, 2010, http://content.time.com/time/magazine/article/0,9171,2025638,00.html.

63. Associated Press, "Text of Michael Reagan's Remarks at Father's Burial Service."

64. Associated Press, "Text of Ron Reagan Jr.'s Remarks."

65. Dennis LeBlanc, in discussion with the author, May 31, 2012.

66. Ibid.

67. Dennis LeBlanc, in discussion with the author.

68. Jim Hooley, in discussion with the author, August 1, 2013.

69. *Auxiliary*, "Three-Rifle Volley and 21-Gun Salute," May 2013, 32.

70. Military District of Washington, "Military Honors for Former Presidents," http://mdwhome.mdw.army.mil/militaryhforfpresi.htm.

71. Mimi Swartz, "The Witness," *Texas Monthly*, November 2003, www.texasmonthly.com/story/witness?fullpage=1.

72. Fred Ryan, in discussion with the author, July 31, 2013.

73. Michael Martinez, "40th President's Lofty Burial Site Boasts Expansive View," *Chicago Tribune*, June 11, 2004, 18.

74. Lou Cannon, "Five Presidents and a Place in History," *Washington Post*, November 5, 1991, B1.

75. Ronald Reagan Presidential Foundation and Library, "Oval Office," www.reaganfoundation.org/DETAILS_F. ASPX?P=LM2022EXPG&H1=7&H2=3&LM=LIBRARYAND MUSEUM&ARGS_A=CMS&ARGS_B=32&ARGSB=N&TX =15&SW=15.

76. Martinez, "40th President's Lofty Burial Site Boasts Expansive View."

77. Associated Press, "Congress Mourns, Remembers Reagan with Resolutions in Tribute," June 9, 2004.

78. *History, Art & Archives: United States House of Representatives*, "Rankin, Jeannette," http://history.house.gov/People/Listing/R /RANKIN,-Jeannette-(R000055)/.

79. David Von Drehle, "Reagan Hailed as Leader for 'the Ages,'" *Washington Post*, June 12, 2004, A1.

80. Margaret Thatcher, "Eulogy for President Reagan," Margaret Thatcher Foundation, June 11, 2004, www.margaretthatcher.org/document /110360.

81. Tom Shales, "Moving Pictures of a Stately Send-Off," *Washington Post*, June 12, 2004, C1.

82. Associated Press, "Text of Mulroney's Tribute to Reagan," June 11, 2004.

83. Ronald Reagan, "Announcement of Alzheimer's Disease," November 5, 1994, http://reagan2020.us/speeches/announcement_of_alzheimers.asp.

84. Psalm 121:1 ASV.

85. Robert W. Service, *The Collected Verse of Robert Service* (Boston: Digireads, 1960), 112.

86. Associated Press, "Text of Ron Reagan Jr.'s Remarks."

87. Patti Davis, *The Long Goodbye* (New York: Knopf, 2011), xvi.

88. Amanda Covarrubias, "Reagan Grave Draws Crowd," *Los Angeles Times*, June 15, 2004, 5.

89. Fred Ryan, in discussion with the author, March 5, 2014.

90. Fred Ryan, in discussion with the author.

91. Gary Foster, in discussion with the author, November 3, 2014.

92. Memorandum by Duke Blackwood, "Entire Timeline Done in Pacific

Standard Time," May 23, 2004, 20, Ronald Reagan Presidential Library, Simi Valley, CA.

93. Jim Hooley, in discussion with the author, March 7, 2014.

94. Gary Foster, in discussion with the author, November 3, 2014.

95. Rick Ahearn, in discussion with the author.

96. Gary Foster, in discussion with the author, November 3, 2014.

97. Jim Hooley, in discussion with the author, October 30, 2014.

98. Ronald Reagan, "Announcement of Alzheimer's Disease," November 5, 1994, http://reagan2020.us/speeches/announcement_of_alzheimers.asp.

99. Jim Hooley, in discussion with the author.

100. Gary Foster, in discussion with the author, November 3, 2014.

101. Jim Hooley, in discussion with the author, October 30, 2014.

102. John McKnight and Peter Block, *The Abundant Community: Awakening the Power of Families and Neighborhoods* (ReadHowYouWant.com, 2011), 205.

103. William Shakespeare, "The Life and Death of Richard the Second," Act 4, Scene 1, in Isaac Reed, ed., *The Plays of William Shakespeare* (Boston: Charles Willliams, 1813).

## CHAPTER 10 A PRAYER IN SPRING

1. Calvin Woodward and Jeff Wilson, "Private Moments Mark End of Weeklong Reagan Tribute," Associated Press, June 12, 2004.

2. Ibid.

3. Jeff Wilson, "Reagan's Death Brings Tributes from World Leaders, Ordinary Folk," Associated Press, June 6, 2004.

4. Ryan Pearson, "Reagan's Body Entombed at Calif. Library," Associated Press, June 13, 2004.

5. Ibid.

6. Duke Blackwood, "Entire Timeline Done in Pacific Standard Time," May 25, 2004, 25, Ronald Reagan Presidential Library, Simi Valley, CA.

7. Strathearn Historical Park & Museum, "History of Simi Valley," www .simihistory.com/#!history/c161y.

8. Rick Callahan, Associated Press, "Study Finds Gene Changes in Aging Brains," *Washington Times*, June 10, 2004, A6.

9. Donald Lambro, "Lambro: Misreading Reagan," *Washington Times*, January 18, 2011, www.washingtontimes.com/news/2011/jan/18 /misreading-reagan/.

10. Fred Ryan, in discussion with the author, July 31, 2013.

11. Michael K. Deaver, *Nancy: A Portrait of My Years with Nancy Reagan* (New York: William Morrow, 2004), 174–5.

12. Ibid.

13. Mike Allen, "Sky's No Limit," *Washington Post*, June 13, 2004, D1.

14. U.S. Energy Information Administration, "Weekly U.S. All Grades All Formulations Retail Gasoline Prices (Dollars per Gallon)," www.eia.gov/dnav/pet/hist/LeafHandler. ashx?n=PET&s=EMM_EPM0_PTE_NUS_DPG&f=W.

15. Patti Davis, *The Lives Our Mothers Leave Us: Prominent Women Discuss the Complex, Humorous, and Ultimately Loving Relationships They Have with Their Mothers* (New York: Hay House, 2009), 7.

16. Craig Shirley, *Rendezvous with Destiny: Ronald Reagan and the Campaign That Changed America* (Wilmington, DE: Intercollegiate Studies Institute, 2011), 599.

17. Steve Johnson, "Coverage of Funeral Best When Anchors Kept Silent," *Chicago Tribune*, June 12, 2004, 25.

18. Lou Cannon, "Actor, Governor, President, Icon," *Washington Post*, June 6, 2004, A28.

19. Robert G. Kaiser, "Gorbachev: 'We All Lost Cold War,'" *Washington Post*, June 11, 2004, A1.

20. Associated Press, "Text of Bush's Tribute to Reagan," June 11, 2004.

21. Joanne Drake, in discussion with the author, March 19, 2014.

22. Nancy Reagan, Invitation, "Ronald Wilson Reagan, February 6, 1911 to June 5, 2004," July 14, 2004, Ronald Reagan Presidential Library, Simi Valley, CA.

23. Nancy Reagan to Charles Z. Wick, Ronald Reagan Presidential Library, Simi Valley, CA.

24. Nancy Reagan to the Citizens of Simi Valley, June 18, 2004, Ronald Reagan Presidential Library, Simi Valley, CA.

25. Nancy Reagan to Honorable George H.W. Bush, June 15, 2004, Ronald Reagan Presidential Library, Simi Valley, CA.

26. Nancy Reagan, "Ronnie Touched So Many of Us," *Los Angeles Times*, July 4, 2004, 4.

27. Timothy L. Taschwer to Joanne Drake, June 25, 2004, Ronald Reagan Presidential Library, Simi Valley, CA.

28. Randall Wallace to Nancy Reagan, June 28, 2004, Ronald Reagan Presidential Library, Simi Valley, CA.

29. Diane Disney Miller to Joanne Drake, June 21, 2004, Ronald Reagan Presidential Library, Simi Valley, CA.

30. Ronald Reagan, "Address at Commencement Exercises at the United States Air Force Academy in Colorado Springs, Colorado," May 30, 1984, www.reagan.utexas.edu/archives/speeches/1984/53084a.htm.

## AUTHOR'S NOTE

1. Ronald Reagan, "Ronald Reagan's Announcement for Presidential Candidacy," November 13, 1979, www.reagan.utexas.edu/archives/reference/11.13.79.html.

2. William Sherman, *Memoirs of General William T. Sherman* (Carlisle, MA: Applewood, 2008), 543.

3. Ronald Reagan, *An American Life: The Autobiography* (New York: Simon and Schuster, 1990), 145–6.

4. Associated Press, "As President, Reagan Helped Save Life of Orlando-Area Boy," June 5, 2004.

5. Pete Souza, "Along For the Ride of a Lifetime," *Chicago Tribune*, June 7, 2004, 1.

6. Associated Press, "Southeast Man Remembers Exchanging Letters with Reagan as a Boy," June 6, 2004.

7. E. J. Dionne Jr., "G.O.P. Makes Reagan Lure of Young a Long-Term Asset," *New York Times*, October 31, 1988, A1.

8. Fred Ryan, in discussion with the author, July 31, 2013.

9. Susan Page, "A 'Folklore' President Who Led a Revolution," *USA Today*, January 20, 2011, 1A.

10. Michael Tackett and Jeff Zeleny, "Reagan Still Looms Large within GOP," *Chicago Tribune*, June 7, 2004, 13.

11. *New York Times*, "Prepared Text for the President's State of the Union Message," January 24, 1996, A14.

12. NPR News Special Report, "Imprint Left by Ronald Reagan on the American Political Landscape," National Public Radio, June 5, 2004.

13. Sam Enriquez, "Ventura County Site Picked for Reagan Library," *Los Angeles Times*, November 14, 1987, 1.

14. *Washington Post*, "Presidential Library Museum Attendance," February 23, 2015, A4.

15. Roger Rosenblatt, "Out of the Past, Fresh Choices for the Future," *Time*, January 5, 1981, 13.

16. Edwin Schallert, "Mary Martin Chosen Outdoor Music Star," *Los Angeles Times*, December 2, 1941, 10.

17. Vincent J. Schodolski, "Reagan Dies," *Chicago Tribune*, June 6, 2004, 1.

18. Ibid.

19. Robert K. Elder, "All-American Appeal Carried Him to Heights," *Chicago Tribune*, June 6, 2004, 17.

20. Ibid.

21. Chuck Conconi, "Personalities," *Washington Post*, September 16, 1987, D3.

22. Elder, "All-American Appeal Carried Him to Heights."

23. Schodolski, "Reagan Dies."

24. NPR News, "Imprint Left by Ronald Reagan on the American Political Landscape."

25. Dena Bunis, "Ronald W. Reagan; At Home in O.C.," *Orange County (CA) Register*, June 6, 2004.

26. Maureen Reagan, *First Father, First Daughter: A Memoir* (Boston: Little, Brown, 1989), 118.

27. Howell Raines, "From Film Star to Candidate: Ronald Wilson Reagan," *New York Times*, July 17, 1980, A1.

28. R. C. Longworth, "End of the Cold War," *Chicago Tribune*, June 6, 2004, 11.

29. *NewsNight with Aaron Brown*, "Ronald Reagan Dies," CNN, June 5, 2004.

30. James R. Dickenson, "Carter and Reagan Parry Politely at an Al Smith Dinner Encounter," *Washington Star*, October 17, 1980, A1.

31. *NewsNight with Aaron Brown*, "Ronald Reagan Dies," CNN, June 5, 2004.

32. Vladimir Isachenkov, "Reagan Remembered for Ending Soviet Rule," Associated Press, June 5, 2004.

33. Ron Pearson, in discussion with the author, November 14, 2014.

34. Peter Hannaford, *Presidential Retreats: Where the Presidents Went and Why They Went There* (New York: Threshold Editions, 2012), 264.

35. William P. Clark, "For Reagan, All Life Was Sacred," *New York Times*, June 11, 2004, A27.

36. Letter from Nancy Reagan to U.S. Attorney General John Ashcroft, Office of Nancy Reagan, September 11, 2003, Ronald Reagan Presidential Library, Simi Valley, CA.

37. Mallie Jane Kim, "Survey Ranks Obama 15th Best President, Bush Among Worst," USNEWS.com, July 2, 2010, www.usnews.com/news /articles/2010/07/02/survey-ranks-obama-15th-best-president-bush -among-worst.

38. U.S. Bureau of Labor Statistics, "Unemployment Rate," accessed December 15, 2014, http://data.bls.gov/pdq/SurveyOutputServlet.

39. Ted Anthony, "Mourning in America: The Great Communicator Remembered," Associated Press, June 5, 2004.

40. Ted Anthony, "U.S. and the World Mourn Reagan's Death," Associated Press, June 5, 2004.

41. Harry Levins, "The Great Communicator Ronald Reagan 1911–2004," *St. Louis Post-Dispatch*, June 6, 2004, A1.

42. David Von Drehle, "Reagan Hailed as Leader for 'the Ages,'" *Washington Post*, June 12, 2004, A1.

# BIBLIOGRAPHY

## BOOKS

Anderson, Martin and Annelise Anderson. *Reagan's Secret War: The Untold Story of His Fight to Save the World from Nuclear Disaster*. New York: Crown Publishers, 2009.

Baker, James A., III, with Steve Fiffer. *"Work Hard, Study . . . and Keep Out of Politics!": Adventures and Lessons from an Unexpected Public Life*. New York: G. P. Putnam's Sons, 2006.

Barletta, John R. *Riding with Reagan: From the White House to the Ranch*. New York: Citadel, 2006.

Baxter, Terry. *November's Gladiators: Inside Stories of White House Advancemen, the Road Warriors of Presidential Campaigns*. Minneapolis: Langdon Street Press, 2014.

Berlinski, Claire. *There Is No Alternative: Why Margaret Thatcher Matters*. New York: Basic Books, 2008.

Bishop, Jim. *FDR's Last Year: April 1944–April 1945*. London, UK: Hart-Davis MacGibbon, 1975.

Bishop, Jim. *The Day Kennedy Was Shot*. New York: Funk & Wagnalls, 1968.

Brinkley, Douglas, ed. *The Reagan Diaries*. New York: HarperCollins, 2007.

Buckley, William F., Jr. *The Reagan I Knew*. New York: Basic Books, 2008.

Bushkin, Henry. *Johnny Carson*. New York: Eamon Dolan/Houghton Mifflin Harcourt, 2013.

Cannon, Lou and TIME contributors. *The Reagan Paradox: The Conservative Icon and Today's GOP*. New York: TIME Books, 2014.

Cannon, Lou. *Governor Reagan: His Rise to Power*. New York: PublicAffairs, 2003.

Cannon, Lou. *President Reagan: The Role of a Lifetime*. New York: PublicAffairs, 2000.

Cannon, Lou. *Reagan*. New York: G. P. Putnam's Sons, 1982.

Cannon, Lou. *Ronnie & Jesse: A Political Odyssey*. New York: Doubleday, 1969.

Carlyle, Thomas. *On Heroes, Hero-Worship, and the Heroic in History*. London, UK: Chapman and Hall, 1840.

Carroll, Lewis. *Alice's Adventures in Wonderland*. Boston: Lee and Shepard, 1920.

Cohen, David Elliot and Peter Robinson. *Ronald Reagan: A Life in Photographs*. New York: Fall River Press, 2010.

Colacello, Bob. *Ronnie and Nancy: Their Path to the White House—1911 to 1980*. New York: Warner Books, 2004.

Crawford, Alan Pell. *Twilight at Monticello: The Final Years of Thomas Jefferson*. New York: Random House, 2009.

D'Souza, Dinesh. *Ronald Reagan: How an Ordinary Man Became an Extraordinary Leader*. New York: Free Press, 1997.

Dallek, Matthew. *The Right Moment: Ronald Reagan's First Victory and the Decisive Turning Point in American Politics*. New York: Oxford University Press, 2000.

Dallek, Robert. *Ronald Reagan: The Politics of Symbolism, With a New Preface*. Cambridge, MA: Harvard University Press, 1999.

Davis, Patti. *Angels Don't Die: My Father's Gift of Faith*. New York: HarperCollins, 1995.

Davis, Patti. *The Lives Our Mothers Leave Us: Prominent Women Discuss the Complex, Humorous, and Ultimately Loving Relationships They Have with Their Mothers*. New York: Hay House, 2009.

Davis, Patti. *The Long Goodbye*. New York: Knopf, 2011.

Davis, Patti. *The Way I See It: An Autobiography*. New York: G.P. Putnam's Sons, 1992.

Davis, Patti. *Two Cats and the Woman They Own: Or Lessons I Learned from My Cats*. San Francisco: Chronicle Books, 2006.

Deaver, Michael K. *A Different Drummer: My Thirty Years with Ronald Reagan*. New York: HarperCollins, 2001.

Deaver, Michael K. *Nancy: A Portrait of My Years with Nancy Reagan*. New York: William Morrow, 2004.

Demakis, Joseph. *The Ultimate Book of Quotations*. Lulu.com, 2011.

Diggins, John Patrick. *Ronald Reagan: Fate, Freedom, and the Making of History*. New York: W. W. Norton & Company, 2007.

Edwards, Anne. *Early Reagan: The Rise to Power*. New York: William Morrow, 1987.

Edwards, Anne. *The Reagans: Portrait of a Marriage*. New York: St. Martin's Press, 2003.

Edwards, Lee. *The Essential Ronald Reagan: A Profile in Courage, Justice, and Wisdom*. Lanham, MD: Rowman & Littlefield, 2005.

Eliot, Marc. *Reagan: The Hollywood Years*. New York: Three Rivers Press, 2008.

Ericson, Edward E., Jr. and Daniel J. Mahoney, eds. *The Solzhenitsyn Reader: New and Essential Writings, 1947–2005*. Wilmington, DE: Intercollegiate Studies Institute, 2006.

Evans, Thomas W. *The Education of Ronald Reagan: The General Electric Years and the Untold Story of His Conversion to Conservatism*. New York: The Mentor Center, 2006.

Farris, Scott. *Kennedy and Reagan: Why Their Legacies Endure*. Guilford, CT: Lyons Press, 2013.

Freeman, Jo. *At Berkeley in the Sixties: The Education of an Activist, 1961–1965*. Bloomington, IN: Indiana University Press, 2004.

Gaddis, John Lewis. *The Cold War: A New History*. New York: Penguin, 2006.

Gibbs, Nancy and Michael Duffy. *The Presidents Club: Inside the World's Most Exclusive Fraternity*. New York: Simon & Schuster, 2012.

Hannaford, Peter. *Reagan's Roots: The People and Places That Shaped His Character*. Bennington, VT: Images From the Past, 2012.

Hannaford, Peter, ed. *Recollections of Reagan: A Portrait of Ronald Reagan*. New York: William Morrow, 1997.

Hannaford, Peter. *Presidential Retreats: Where the Presidents Went and Why They Went There*. New York: Threshold Editions, 2012.

Hannaford, Peter. *The Reagans: A Political Portrait*. New York: Coward-McCann, 1983.

Higginbotham, Don. *George Washington Reconsidered*. Charlottesville, VA: University of Virginia Press, 2001.

Holden, Kenneth. *Making of the Great Communicator: Ronald Reagan's Transformation from Actor to Governor*. Guilford, CT: Lyons Press, 2013.

Hufbauer, Benjamin. *Presidential Temples: How Memorials and Libraries Shape Public Memory*. Lawrence, KS: University Press of Kansas, 2005.

Jefferson, Thomas. *The Jefferson Papers 1770–1826*. Boston: Massachusetts Historical Society, 1900.

Kengor, Paul and Patricia Clark Doerner. *The Judge: William P. Clark, Ronald Reagan's Top Hand*. San Francisco: Ignatius Press, 2007.

Kengor, Paul. *God and Ronald Reagan: A Spiritual Life*. New York: Regan Books, 2004.

Kengor, Paul. *The Crusader: Ronald Reagan and the Fall of Communism*. New York: Regan Books, 2006.

Laxalt, Paul. *Nevada's Paul Laxalt: A Memoir*. Reno, NV: Jack Bacon & Co, 2000.

Lossing, Benson John and Rufus Wilmot Griswold. *Life of Washington: A Biography, Personal, Military, and Political*. London, UK: Virtue and Company, 1860.

McCaslin, John. *Inside the Beltway: Offbeat Stories, Scoops, and Shenanigans from around the Nation's Capital*. Nashville, TN: Thomas Nelson, 2004.

McKnight, John and Peter Block. *The Abundant Community: Awakening the Power of Families and Neighborhoods*. ReadHowYouWant.com, 2011.

Meese, Edwin, III. *With Reagan: The Inside Story*. Washington, DC: Regnery Gateway, 1992.

*Memorial Services in the Congress of the United States and Tributes in Eulogy of Ronald Reagan, Late a President of the United States*. Washington, DC: Government Printing Office, 2005.

Minutaglio, Bill and Steven L. Davis. *Dallas 1963*. New York: Twelve, 2013.

Morrell, Margot. *Reagan's Journey: Lessons from a Remarkable Career*. New York: Threshold Editions, 2011.

Morris, Edmund. *Dutch: A Memoir of Ronald Reagan*. New York: Random House, 1999.

Nofziger, Lyn. *Nofziger*. Washington, DC: Regnery Gateway, 1992.

Noonan, Peggy. *When Character Was King: A Story of Ronald Reagan*. New York: Penguin Books, 2001.

Novak, Robert D. *The Prince of Darkness: 50 Years Reporting in Washington*. New York: Crown Forum, 2007.

Nuland, Sherwin B. *How We Die: Reflections on Life's Final Chapter*. New York: Vintage Books, 1994.

O'Neill, Tip with William Novak. *Man of the House: The Life and Political Memoirs of Speaker Tip O'Neill*. New York: Random House, 1987.

O'Sullivan, John. *The President, the Pope, and the Prime Minister: Three Who Changed the World*. Washington, DC: Regnery, 2006.

Padover, Saul K. *Jefferson*. New York: Mentor Books, 1942.

Patrick, Curtis. *Reagan: What Was He Really Like? Vol 1*. New York: Book Surge, 2007.

Patrick, Curtis. *Reagan: What Was He Really Like? Vol 2*. New York: Morgan James Publishing, 2011.

Phillips, Kevin. *The Politics of Rich and Poor: Wealth and the American Electorate in the Reagan Aftermath*. New York: Harper Perennial, 1991.

Quiggle, Dan. *Lead Like Reagan: Strategies to Motivate, Communicate, and Inspire*. Hoboken, NJ: Wiley, 2014.

Randel, Don Michael, ed. *The Harvard Biographical Dictionary of Music*. Cambridge, MA: Harvard University Press, 1996.

Reagan, Maureen. *First Father, First Daughter: A Memoir*. Boston: Little, Brown and Co., 1989.

Reagan, Michael. *Making Waves: Bold Exposes from Talk Radio's Number One Nighttime Host*. New York: Thomas Nelson, 1996.

Reagan, Michael. *Michael Reagan: On the Outside Looking In*. New York: Zebra Books, 1988.

Reagan, Michael with Jim Denney. *The City on a Hill: Fulfilling Ronald Reagan's Vision for America*. Nashville, TN: Thomas Nelson, 1997.

Reagan, Michael with Jim Denney. *Twice Adopted: An Important Social Commentator Speaks to the Cultural Ailments Threatening America Today*. Nashville, TN: Broadman & Holman, 2004.

Reagan, Nancy with William Novak. *My Turn: The Memoirs of Nancy Reagan*. New York: Random House, 1989.

Reagan, Nancy. *I Love You, Ronnie: The Letters of Ronald Reagan to Nancy Reagan*. New York: Random House, 2000.

Reagan, Ron. *My Father at 100: A Memoir*. New York: Penguin, 2011.

Reagan, Ronald and Richard G. Hubler. *Where's the Rest of Me? The Autobiography of Ronald Reagan*. New York: Karz Publishers, 1981.

Reagan, Ronald. *An American Life: The Autobiography*. New York: Simon & Schuster, 1990.

Reagan, Ronald. *Speaking My Mind: Selected Speeches*. New York: Simon & Schuster, 1989.

Regnery, Alfred S. *Upstream: The Ascendance of American Conservatism*. New York: Threshold Editions, 2008.

Rollins, Ed with Tom DeFrank. *Bare Knuckles and Back Rooms: My Life in American Politics*. New York: Broadway Books, 1996.

Ronald Reagan Presidential Foundation. *Ronald Reagan: 100 Years: Official Centennial Edition*. New York: Harper Design, 2011.

Sabato, Larry J. *The Kennedy Half-Century: The Presidency, Assassination, and Lasting Legacy of John F. Kennedy*. New York: Bloomsbury, 2013.

Schlesinger, Arthur M., Jr. *Journals: 1952–2000*. New York: Penguin Books, 2007.

Schlesinger, Arthur M., Jr. *Robert Kennedy and His Times*. Boston: Houghton Mifflin Harcourt, 1978.

Schweizer, Peter. *Reagan's War: The Epic Story of His Forty-Year Struggle and Final Triumph Over Communism*. New York: Doubleday, 2002.

Schifando, Peter and Jonathan Joseph. *Entertaining at the White House with Nancy Reagan*. New York: Harper Collins, 2007.

Service, Robert W. *The Collected Verse of Robert Service*. Boston: Digireads, 1960.

Shakespeare, William and Isaac Reed. *The Plays of William Shakespeare*. Boston: Charles Williams, 1813.

Shepard, Tazewell Jr. *John F. Kennedy: Man of the Sea*. New York: W. Morrow, 1965.

Sherman, William. *Memoirs of General William T. Sherman*. Carlisle, MA: Applewood, 2008.

Shirley, Craig. *Reagan's Revolution: The Untold Story of the Campaign That Started It All*. Nashville, TN: Thomas Nelson, 2005.

Shirley, Craig. *Rendezvous with Destiny: Ronald Reagan and the Campaign That Changed America*. Wilmington, DE: Intercollegiate Studies Institute, 2011.

Singlaub, John. *Hazardous Duty*. New York: Simon and Schuster, 1991.

Skinner, Kiron K., Annelise Anderson, and Martin Anderson, eds. *Reagan, In His Own Hand: The Writings of Ronald Reagan That Reveal His Revolutionary Vision for America*. New York: Free Press, 2001.

Skinner, Kiron K., Annelise Anderson, and Martin Anderson, eds. *Reagan: A Life in Letters*. New York: Free Press, 2003.

Skinner, Kiron K., Annelise Anderson, and Martin Anderson, eds. *Reagan's Path to Victory: The Shaping of Ronald Reagan's Vision: Selected Writings*. New York: Free Press, 2004.

Smith, Gene. *When the Cheering Stopped: The Last Years of Woodrow Wilson*. New York: William Morrow, 1971.

Solzhenitsyn, Aleksandr I. *The Gulag Archipelago 1918–1956: An Experiment in Literary Investigation III-IV*. New York: Harper & Row, 1975.

Speakes, Larry. *Speaking Out: The Reagan Presidency from Inside the White House*. New York: Scribner, 1988.

Stockman, David A. *The Triumph of Politics: Why the Reagan Revolution Failed*. New York: Harper & Row, 1986.

Strock, James M. *Reagan on Leadership: Executive Lessons from the Great Communicator*. Rocklin, CA: Forum, 1998.

Viguerie, Richard A. *Takeover: The 100-Year War for the Soul of the GOP and How Conservatives Can Finally Win It*. New York: WND Books, 2014.

Walsh, Kenneth T. *From Mount Vernon to Crawford: A History of the Presidents and Their Retreats*. New York: Hyperion, 2005.

Weber, Ralph E., ed. *Dear Americans: Letters from the Desk of Ronald Reagan*. New York: Doubleday, 2003.

White, Theodore H. *America in Search of Itself: The Making of the President, 1956–1980*. New York: Harper & Row, 1982.

Wilber, Del Quentin. *Rawhide Down: The Near Assassination of Ronald Reagan*. New York: Macmillan, 2011.

Wirthlin, Dick and Wynton C. Hall. *The Greatest Communicator: What Ronald Reagan Taught Me about Politics, Leadership, and Life*. Hoboken, NJ: John Wiley and Sons, 2004.

Yager, Edward. *Ronald Reagan's Journey: Democrat to Republican*. New York: Rowman & Littlefield Publishers, 2006.

Zeiger, Hans. *Reagan's Children: Taking Back the City on the Hill*. Nashville, TN: Broadman & Holman Publishers, 2006.

## PERIODICALS

*Atlanta Journal-Constitution*
*Auxiliary*
*Blaze*
*Cato's Letter*
*Chicago Tribune*
*Daily News* (NY)
*Dallas Morning News*
*Denver Post*
*Edmonton Journal* (Alberta)
*Healthline*
*Human Events*
*Investor's Business Daily*
*Kansas City Star*
*Las Vegas Review-Journal*
*Libertas*
*Life*
*Los Angeles Times*
*Miami Herald*
*National Review*
*Neurology*
*New York Post*
*New York Times*
*Newsday* (NY)
*Newsweek*
*Oklahoman*
*Onion*
*Orange CountyRegister* (CA)

*Orlando Sentinel*
*Pasadena Star-News* (CA)
*People*
*Peoria Journal Star* (IL)
*Philadelphia Inquirer*
*Sacramento Bee*
*San Bernardino Sun* (CA)
*Santa Barbara News-Press* (CA)
*Spokesman Review* (WA)
*St. Louis Post-Dispatch*
*Texas Monthly*
*The Bulletin's Frontrunner*
*Time*
*Toledo Blade* (OH)
*Town & Country*
*Townhall*
*U.S. News & World Report*
*USA Today*
*Wall Street Journal*
*Washington Post*
*Washington Star*
*Washington Times*

## NEWS WIRES

Agence France-Presse
Associated Press
United Press International

## ELECTRONIC MEDIA

ABC
CBS
CNN
C-SPAN
FOX News
MSNBC
NBC
NPR
PBS

## VIDEO MATERIALS

Citizens United Productions, "Ronald Reagan: Rendezvous with Destiny"

College Republicans, "100th Anniversary of the College Republicans, Discussions with President Reagan"

Edmonds Associates Documentary, "Ronald Reagan: An American President"

Edmonds Associates Documentary, "Tribute to Ronald Reagan"

Enduring Freedom
Productions, "Ronald
Reagan: An American
Journey"
MPI Media Group, "Ronald
Reagan: The Great
Communicator"
NBC News, "Ronald Reagan"
Passport Video, "Ronald
Reagan His Life and
Times: The Hollywood
Years"
Passport Video, "Ronald
Reagan His Life and
Times: The Presidential
Years"
PBS Home Video, "Reagan,"
The Presidents Collection
Ronald Reagan Presidential
Foundation, "The Reagan
Years"
Ronald Reagan Presidential
Library, "November 7,
1988, President Reagan's
Speech at a Campaign
Rally at the Community
Concourse in Sand Diego
California"
The Blackwell Corporation,
"The Essential Ronald
Reagan"
Time Life Video, "Salute
to Reagan: A President's
Greatest Moments"
Young America's Foundation,
"Still Point In a Turning
World: Ronald Reagan and
His Ranch"
Young America's Foundation,
"50th Anniversary 'A Time
for Choosing'"
Young America's Foundation,
"CBS: Reagan: The '60
Minutes' Interviews,
1975–1989"

OTHER MATERIALS
Alzheimer's Association
Architect of the Capitol
Archives

Archived Collection Military
District of Washington
Archived Collection Reagan
Ranch and Ranch Center
Archived Collection
Strathearn Historical Park
& Museum, Simi Valley
Historical Society
Archived Collection,
Breitbart
Archived Collection,
Margaret Thatcher
Foundation
Archived Collection, National
Review
Archived Collection,
Newsmax
Archived Collection, Reagan
2020
Archived Collection, The
White House Office of the
Press Secretary
Archived Collection,
Townhall
Eureka College
General Electric Company,
A Legacy Of Progress
Collection
Life, "Remembering Reagan"
Massachusetts Institute of
Technology Archives
Monticello Archives
National Institutes of
Health, U.S. National
Library of Medicine
Archives
Presidential Records, Ronald
Reagan Presidential
Library
Private Archives Collection
of Cal Thomas
Private Archives Collection
of Attorney Sam Harrod
Ronald Reagan Presidential
Foundation and Library
The World Bank Group Data
U.S. Bureau of Labor
Statistics
U.S. Energy Information
Administration

United States Capitol Police
Archives
University of California,
Berkeley
University of California,
Santa Barbara, The
American Presidency
Project
University of North Carolina
at Chapel Hill Archives
University of Notre Dame
Archives
University of Texas at Austin
Archives
Washington National
Cathedral Records

INTERVIEWS
Ahearn, Rick. Interview by
Craig Shirley. March 25,
2014.
Barbour, Haley. Interview
by Craig Shirley. January
21, 2014.
Bond, Linda. Interview by
Craig Shirley. April 15,
2014.
Bufkin, David. Interview by
Craig Shirley. March 13,
2014.
Cannon, Carl. Interview by
Craig Shirley.
Cannon, Lou. Interview by
Craig Shirley. March 27,
2014.
Cannon, Lou. Interview by
Craig Shirley. November
28, 2014.
Colo, Steve. Interview by
Craig Shirley. June 3, 2014.
Dolan, Tony. Interview by
Craig Shirley. April 1,
2014.
Dole, Bob. Interview by Craig
Shirley.
Donatelli, Frank. Interview
by Craig Shirley. February
20, 2014.
Drake, Joanne. Interview by
Craig Shirley. February
20, 2014.

Drake, Joanne. Interview by Craig Shirley. January 17, 2014.

Drake, Joanne. Interview by Craig Shirley. January 29, 2014.

Drake, Joanne. Interview by Craig Shirley. March 19, 2014.

Duberstein, Ken. Interview by Craig Shirley. May 6, 2014.

Fisher, Marilyn. Interview by Craig Shirley. April 4, 2014.

Fisher, Marilyn. Interview by Craig Shirley. February 24, 2014.

Fisher, Marilyn. Interview by Craig Shirley. September 23, 2014.

Foster, Gary. Interview by Craig Shirley. April 28, 2014.

Foster, Gary. Interview by Craig Shirley. November 3, 2014.

Gaines, Gay. Interview by Craig Shirley.

Grande, Peggy. Interview by Craig Shirley. July 2, 2012.

Hannaford, Peter. Interview by Craig Shirley.

Higdon, Robert. Interview by Craig Shirley. May 30, 2014.

Hooley, Jim. Interview by Craig Shirley. August 1, 2013.

Hooley, Jim. Interview by Craig Shirley. December 5, 2014.

Hooley, Jim. Interview by Craig Shirley. March 7, 2014.

Hooley, Jim. Interview by Craig Shirley. October 30, 2014.

Jackman, Galen. Interview by Craig Shirley. May 14, 2014.

Judge, Clark. Interview by Craig Shirley. April 9, 2014.

Keene, David. Interview by Craig Shirley.

Kudlow, Larry. Interview by Craig Shirley. April 10, 2014.

Kuhn, James. Interview by Craig Shirley. September 3, 2014.

Lake, Jim. Interview by Craig Shirley. September 24, 2014.

LeBlanc, Dennis. Interview by Craig Shirley. May 31, 2012.

LeBlanc, Dennis. Interview by Craig Shirley. October 1, 2014.

Littlefair, Andrew. Interview by Craig Shirley. April 28, 2014.

Meacham, Jon. Interview by Craig Shirley. January 10, 2014.

Meese, Ed. Interview by Craig Shirley. March 19, 2014.

Morris, John. Interview by Craig Shirley.

Nofziger, Lyn. Interview by Craig Shirley.

Norquist, Grover. Interview by Craig Shirley.

Parvin, Landon. Interview by Craig Shirley. April 8, 2014.

Pearson, Ron. Interview by Craig Shirley. November 14, 2014.

Peele, Roger. Interview by Craig Shirley. May 9, 2014.

Rollins, Ed. Interview by Craig Shirley. May 2, 2014.

Rosebush, James. Interview by Craig Shirley. March 28, 2014.

Rosenker, Mark. Interview by Craig Shirley. February 26, 2014.

Ryan, Fred. Interview by Craig Shirley. January 17, 2014.

Ryan, Fred. Interview by Craig Shirley. July 31, 2013.

Ryan, Fred. Interview by Craig Shirley. March 5, 2014.

Schulz, Bill. Interview by Craig Shirley.

Short, Kristen. Interview by Craig Shirley. March 28, 2014.

Short, Marc. Interview by Craig Shirley. March 28, 2014.

Snyder, Dick. Interview by Craig Shirley. May, 2012.

Spencer, Stuart. Interview by Craig Shirley. February 4, 2014.

Wagner, Michael. Interview by Craig Shirley. March 24, 2014.

Weinberg, Mark. Interview by Craig Shirley. April 4, 2014.

Woodward, Michele. Interview by Craig Shirley. March 26, 2014.

# INDEX

# ABOUT THE AUTHOR

Craig Shirley is the author of two critically praised bestselling books on President Reagan, *Rendezvous with Destiny: Ronald Reagan and the Campaign That Changed America* and *Reagan's Revolution: The Untold Story of the Campaign That Started It All.*

His third book *December 1941: 31 Days That Changed America and Saved the World* appeared multiple times on the *New York Times* bestselling lists in December 2011 and January 2012.

Shirley is the chairman of Shirley & Banister Public Affairs, was chosen in 2005 by Springfield College as their Outstanding Alumnus, and has been named the Visiting Reagan Scholar at Eureka College, Ronald Reagan's alma mater, where he taught a course titled "Reagan 101." He is also a trustee of Eureka.

His books have been hailed as the definitive works on the Gipper's campaigns of 1976 and 1980 and the post-presidential years. He is a member of the Board of Governors of the Reagan Ranch and has lectured at the Reagan Library. He has spoken at the University of Virginia, Georgetown, Hillsdale College, Regent University, and many other colleges and universities.

Shirley, a widely sought after speaker and commentator, has written extensively for the *Washington Post*, the *Washington Examiner*, the *Washington Times*, the *Los Angeles Times*, Town Hall, the *Weekly Standard*, Newsmax, Breitbart, *National Review*, and many other publications. He also edited the book *Coaching Youth Lacrosse* for the Lacrosse Foundation.

Shirley and his wife, Zorine, reside at "Ben Lomond," a 1730 Georgian-style home in Tappahannock, Virginia, and at "Trickle Down Point" on the Rappahannock River in Lancaster, Virginia. They are parents of four children, Matthew, Andrew, Taylor, and Mitchell. Shirley's varied interests include writing, sailing, waterskiing, sport shooting, renovating buildings, and scuba diving. He was a decorated contract agent for the Central Intelligence Agency.

He is currently finishing work on *Citizen Newt*, a political biography of Newt Gingrich; a biography of Dr. Howard Snyder, the personal physician to Dwight Eisenhower; a fourth book on Reagan entitled *Wilderness*; and the life story of Mary Ball Washington.

*Last Act* is his third book on Ronald Reagan.